COROEBUS TRIUMPHS

Susan J. Bandy, Editor

COROEBUS
TRIUMPHS

THE ALLIANCE OF
SPORT AND THE ARTS

Edited by Susan J. Bandy

SAN DIEGO STATE UNIVERSITY PRESS

Library of Congress Cataloging-in-Publication Data

Sport Literature Association. Meeting (1st: 1984: San Diego, Calif.)
    Coroebus triumphs: the alliance of sport and the arts: proceedings of the First Annual Meeting of the Sport Literature Association, San Diego, California, July 1984 / edited by Susan J. Bandy.
        p. cm.
        Bibliography: p.

        ISBN 0-916304-76-0: $8.00
        1. Sports—Social aspects.   2. Arts and society.   I. Bandy, Susan J. II. Title.

        GV706.5.S735 1984   88-21655
        306'.483—dc19   CIP

Proceedings of the First Annual Meeting
of the Sport Literature Association
San Diego, California, July, 1984

Contents

PART
I

The Alliance of Sport and the Arts

1

The Alliance of Sport and the Arts

Susan J. Bandy

THE ANCIENT POETS TELL US that during the time of the full moon in the month of Appolonius in the year 776 B.C. a young cook from Elis won a great footrace in a meadow beside the river Alpheus at Olympia. That youth, Coroebus, was crowned with a wreath of wild olive from the twigs of a tree planted by Hercules in the sacred grove near the Temple of Zeus at Olympia. With this triumph, Coroebus became the first recorded victor in the ancient Olympic Games, thereby initiating the ancient Panhellenic festivals.

Through the arts we know of the great athletic triumphs of Coroebus and his successors in the ancient athletic festivals. They were immortalized by such well-known artists as Polycleitus and Phidias, Exekias, and Eupronius, and by Pindar and Euripides in sculpture, vase painting, and poetry respectively.

The relationship between sport and art was a reciprocal or symbiotic one in ancient Greece, particularly during its Golden Age of the fifth and fourth centuries B.C. Sport served as the subject for much of art to such an extent that it constituted a genre of art during this time. In turn, art compensated for the fleeting nature of sport, giving it enduring "life" as the artists captured its greatest moments, triumphs and heroes, which would otherwise have been lost with time.

This alliance of sport and the arts is a curious one, one that no culture or civilization prior to the Greeks or since has been able to achieve. The source of this alliance stems from the philosophy which matured and governed much of cultural life as the Greeks progressed toward the Golden Age. This philosophy placed humanity at its center as the principal source of all truth and the principal object of all truth. The importance placed upon the human being resulted in a philosophy and a cultural ideal which affected all aspects of Greek life. This philosophy developed from the time of Homer, requiring

3

men to strive to be good, noble, learned, and beautiful and later matured with the inclusion of *arete*, the striving for excellence, and *aidos*, honor, respect, and modesty.

The education of young Greek men was devoted to these ideals and consisted of gymnastics which trained the body and music which trained the mind. Together these comprised the whole of Greek education, which was devoted to the development of the harmoniously educated man, *kaloskathos*.

This philosophy of life and education granted sport a prominent place in Greek culture, for it was viewed, together with religion, art, and politics, as a manifestation of the harmoniously educated man. The athletic festivals demonstrated an intimate connection between sport and the arts. As part of a religious ceremony in honor of the gods, athletes at these festivals displayed their physical prowess and skill, striving always, as Homer suggests, to be first and to inspire others. There were also contests in music, poetry, and recitation to honor excellence in the other arts as other artists sought to display their excellence. With their unified view of humanity, the Greeks established a union of all forms of human expression, an alliance which granted sport a place among the other forms of art.

Although sport in contemporary American culture has not been associated with the arts in the way that it was in ancient Greece, their relationship has been debated widely among scholars interested in its basic nature, purpose, and status. During the summer of 1984 a collection of scholars, athletes, and artists from various disciplines convened in Coroebus' honor to celebrate the alliance of sport and the arts with the formation of the Sport Literature Association. The papers in this volume, the majority of which were presented at the Coroebus Conference, are in various ways devoted to furthering our understanding of the alliance of sport and the arts. In addition to the conference and the publication of this book, interest in sport and the arts is evidenced by the increase in the number of courses devoted to the aesthetic and literary dimensions of sport and by the inauguration of the Sport Literature Association's *Arete: The Journal of Sport Literature.*

This interest further represents a trend toward an interdisciplinary approach to the study of cultural phenomena in education in general as disciplines other than physical education (most notably history and sociology) have begun to examine sport; it represents as well a new perspective of sport within physical education in which the study of sport first began.

Only within the last two decades have the creative and artistic dimensions of sport been recognized by scholars in physical education. Prior to this time, sport was viewed primarily from biological, psychological, or sociological perspectives. With the interest in sport philosophy which began in the early 1960s and the more recent interest in sport literature, however, the creative and aesthetic dimensions of sport are being recognized.

As this relatively new subdiscipline of sport literature has developed, it has offered to the scholarly investigation of sport a more subjective view than had the other subdisciplines of exercise physiology, biomechanics, sport psychology, sport sociology and sport history. In so doing, it, along with sport philosophy, has revealed the perspective that only the arts can provide. This perspective returns us to our experiences in sport, reveals them to us once again and gives them an enduring "life." Moreover, as we are reminded by Huizinga, this perspective reveals the distinguishing feature of humankind— the basic human need and inclination to play; that is, to engage in and value things in-and-for themselves apart from their extrinsic and instrumental worth. From this, one can argue that this distinguishing feature of humankind is the basic source of art. If we accept this view, we recognize that Coroebus ran for the very same reasons that poets, vase painters, sculptors, and dramatists gathered at Olympia to celebrate and later capture through their various art forms human beings at play—thereby uniting sport and art.

It is hoped that the reader may be encouraged to play, to relive that one glorious and timeless moment in sport when all the beauty, simplicity, and unity of the universe is revealed; that the mind and heart are again "taken" with the captivating mystery of sport; that one is again encouraged to seek meaningful perfection through movement; or that one simply is at peace with the joyous pleasure given to us only by the arts.

1 February, 1986
Susan J. Bandy

PART II

Sport and the Hero

2

Introduction:
Sport and the Hero

Michael Oriard

IN HIS NOW-CLASSIC BASEBALL NOVEL *The Natural*, published in 1952, Bernard
Malamud imagined the contemporary descendant of Greek heroes and
Arthurian knights to be a simple country boy who could hit home runs more
often than anyone else in the game. In an age when an individual's physical
prowess was irrelevant to contemporary social needs, when individualism itself
seemed to be disappearing from a highly organized and bureaucratized society
(only two years before, David Riesman had announced that Americans had
become "other-directed," unlike their "inner-directed" forebears), Malamud
recognized that baseball dramatized an older style of heroism, that it served
spectators' psychic need to believe in larger-than-life saviors who controlled
their own destinies and redeemed others from mediocrity. It also recreated
America's own imagined heroic age, when "naturals" like Daniel Boone and
Kit Carson hewed a civilization out of a wilderness, depending entirely on
their own skill and courage. All this from a simple game played with bats
and balls.

Sports heroes are honored nearly everywhere in the world, but America
seems to have venerated its own with a distinctive intensity. One possible
explanation lies in America's youthfulness as a nation. Until the end of the
eighteenth century, "Americans" were simply Englishmen away from home,
their ancestral roots among the Germanic tribes that conquered the British
Isles in the fifth and sixth centuries, then the Normans who invaded in the
eleventh. Their great writers were Chaucer, Shakespeare, Milton; their scholars,
Bacon, Newton, and Boyle; their national leaders, a succession of Henrys
and Edwards, Jameses and Charleses, with an occasional Mary or Elizabeth.

9

But with their Revolution completed, Americans collectively had to pause and wonder, just what is an American, anyway? The major impulse behind American popular culture in the century that followed was the desire for self-definition. Actual men of exceptional accomplishment, from Ben Franklin and George Washington to Davy Crockett and Buffalo Bill, were transformed into mythic heroes by popular biographers fancifully reconstructing their subjects' lives. Defying the persistent belief that America could do no better in literature than to imitate England's great artists, novelists created a series of native woodsmen and Indian fighters whose exploits celebrated that American reality which distinguished it from more cultured Europe: a vast, terrifying, but rejuvenating landscape. Americans wanted heroes who proved America not equal to, but greater than any other people. Americans alone attempted to write a Great National Novel that defined their uniqueness. And Americans embraced the popular sports that became organized for the first time in the middle of the nineteenth century with the same myth-making fervor.

Sport served well America's need for heroes. Both the athletic contest and the season, with their distinct beginnings, middles, and ends building up to climactic ninth inning or end-of-season championship game, provided the familiar path for heroic triumph: the separation, initiation, and return which Joseph Campbell has found to be present in heroic tales everywhere. The games themselves were latent with heroic possibilities from the beginning. In the hands of publicists and promoters, this heroic potential came to full fruition. America knew no oral period when myth and legend emerged from spontaneous story-telling. Entirely a child of the print age, America's heroes have always owed as much to calculated promotion as to spontaneous creation.

The three papers in this section explore, from very different perspectives, that myth-making impulse in American sports culture. Joan Paul's essay on *The Brawnville Papers* focuses on a text that neatly encapsulates the efforts of a number of men and women in the middle of the nineteenth century to create one of sport's most enduring heroes: the athlete of sound mind in sound body. In the debates among the citizens of Brawnville one finds represented the major viewpoints of the years in which organized sports first gained a foothold in universities, religious organizations such as the YMCA and athletic clubs throughout the land. Given the religious objections to sport prevailing until mid-century, enthusiasts had to justify athletic games on moral as well as physical grounds; as a consequence, they bequeathed to future generations a belief in the amateur athlete's superior character created by sport. Anyone attentive to the latest controversy over sport's positive or negative impact on young athletes will find in Paul's discussion of *The Brawnville Papers* that little has changed in more than a century.

The muscular Christianity of Moses Coit Tyler, as well as Thomas Hughes and Henry Newbolt, lay behind the amateur ideal that Lyle Olsen contrasts to Ernest Hemingway's professional code. In Hemingway, Olsen focuses on the American novelist who most insistently made the sporting hero a model for the proper way of perceiving and living, but Hemingway's sportsman was a far cry, or a long throw, from Tyler's muscular Christian. From the clash between the two types, one frankly ideal, the other emphatically "real," emerges not just a contrast of sporting ideals but alternative visions of the world and its possibilities for joy and transcendence. "Amateur" and "professional" carry the connotations imposed on them by class and cultural biases of long standing. In his essay, however, Professor Olsen, himself a former professional baseball player, removes them from history to define opposing philosophies of human potential.

Finally, Tom Dodge shifts attention from the hero to the maker of heroes. During the National Football League Players' Association strike in the fall of 1982, in the midst of counter-claims by players and owners that *we* are the game, columnist Jim Murray, with tongue nestled comfortably in cheek, told both sides, no. *Sportswriters* are the game. He spoke a strange truth. Grantland Rice created the Four Horsemen of Notre Dame as surely as Ned Buntline created Buffalo Bill a half-century before. Babe Ruth's famous gesture in the 1932 World Series became legendary only after writers interpreted its significance. In sportswriters' metaphors and broadcasters' hyperbole, ordinary mortals ascend Olympus in the minds of readers and viewers. Dodge offers a portrait of one of baseball's most skillful myth-makers from the golden era of radio, before TV removed the diamond from listeners' imaginations to nineteen-inch screens. In Dodge's telling, Gordon McLendon becomes not just a victim of the corporate powers that manipulate the games we see, but himself a muse-inspiring defiant hero who failed to preserve the spirit of baseball from the unbelievers.

At the meeting of the Sport Literature Association in July 1984, Tom Dodge played a tape of McLendon calling an inning of a game—not just any inning of any game, but the ninth inning of the last game of the 1951 National League season when Bobby Thomson hit the homerun that Roy Hobbs failed to hit in Malamud's novel the following year. Heroes triumph and heroes fail, their victories and defeats emotionally satisfying to us in different ways: showing *us* how high we can go, reminding *them* they are merely mortal, too. Moses Coit Tyler created an ideal of the athlete who wins just by playing; Hemingway, an image of the sportsman who ironically "wins" only by knowing how to lose with dignity. Gordon McLendon, who immortalized Bobby Thomson for millions of Americans, knew that someone had to throw the pitch that Thomson hit over the left field wall, that for every Bobby Thomson there had to be a Ralph Branca. McLendon had this fact confirmed by his own experience. The hero of the sports page and sporting novel teaches many lessons: about success and failure, youth and aging, individualism and corporate leveling, transcendence and despair. About an entire culture's hopes, fears, and most cherished values. No three papers can exhaust the subject of sport and the hero, but Joan Paul, Lyle Olsen, and Tom Dodge explore a range of its possibilities.

.

3

The Brawnville Papers: Fact and Fiction

Joan Paul

THE GREEKS FIRST FORMULATED THE CONCEPTS of a "physical" education hundreds of years before the birth of Christ. However, with the growth of asceticism after the fall of the Roman Empire and the influence of the moralistic movement during the Renaissance, recreation and sport had become associated with many negative connotations, and these continued to be nurtured into the nineteenth century.

The Muscular Christianity movement spawned in England was introduced to the United States near mid-nineteenth century. Because of the remnants of puritanical thinking, which condemned the idea of play for the sake of pleasure, the early development of sport, gymnastics, and physical education often fell on infertile ground. However, this new movement portrayed the athlete as virtuous rather than sinful. It depicted the athlete as a man of high morals who avoided dissipation through his athletic endeavors—ideas directly contradictory to long standing values associated with taking time from work to indulge in sporting activities.

The introduction of physical education in America in the early 1800s was considered innovative yet controversial. The influx of immigrants who brought with them foreign systems of physical education and an increasing concern for health further enhanced the development of physical education in the 1850s and 1860s. However, opposition to the inclusion of physical education remained and provided much controversy in mid-nineteenth century American life.

With pungent and shrewd humor, Moses Coit Tyler, author of *The Brawnville Papers: Being Memorials of the Brawnville Athletic Club*,[1] recreates the conflicting attitudes toward physical education present in mid-nineteenth century America. Tyler, a graduate of Yale University and minister-turned-

---

[1] Moses Coit Tyler, *The Brawnville Papers: Being Memorials of the Brawnville Athletic Club* (Boston: Fields, Osgood, and Co., 1869). All unattributed quotes are from this source.

professor of English literature, was teaching at the University of Michigan in 1867 when he wrote of his "well-beloved Utopia of Gymnastics."[2] After having appeared first as a series of twelve articles in *The Herald of Health*, a physical culture periodical, the work was published by Tyler in book form in 1869.

Tyler weaves his fictitious tale around the significant but often conflicting influences derived from Victorian principles, sanitary reform, puritanical beliefs, and social biases of the era. Through his choice of characters who embody both favorable and unfavorable attitudes toward physical education, Tyler presents a fairly accurate portrayal of the conflicting attitudes permeating mid-nineteenth century New England.

The major actors in Brawnville, a fictitious New England town, are Judge Fairplay, a good albeit autocratic intellectual, who is the natural monarch of the town; Dr. Drugger, a kind-hearted physician with a tart disposition, who is independent, sarcastic and cold in manner, but benevolent and self-sacrificing; the school master, Thomas Richard Henry (usually affectionately referred to as "Tom, Dick, and Harry" behind his back by his students), who appears at first to be "frigid, expressionless, and repelling—in one word, a New Englander!" Henry is actually a warm but shy intellectual. Another major character is Reverend Samuel Bland, pastor of the second church in Brawnville, a genial, wholesome, liberal man with a "sunshiny" personality. Rev. Bland can "out-walk, out-run, out-jump, out-skate, out-swim, out-fish, out-hunt, and out-preach any other man for twenty miles around." Deacon Snipp of first church, Brawnville's herald of piousness, is the principal critic of the athletic movement and of Rev. Bland. Deacon Snipp and the other Brawnville Pharisees believe that Rev. Bland's major offense is that he is a Muscular Christian. Deacon Snipp thinks it unbecoming that Rev. Bland, a minister, skates, as there is no record of Jesus skating. He poses the question, "What can be more scandalous than for a minister of the meek and lowly Jesus Christ to be noted for being the best ball player in the county?"

Minor characters include Abdiel Standish, a Yankee farmer who lives just outside the village, and who often drolly chastises the Deacon Snipp for his conservative, puritanical ideas; Mr. Leonidas Climas, clerk of the village bank, whose main personal qualities are a thick head of hair and a thin crop of ideas, a small brain, a large mouth, and an enormous pair of lungs that nearly drive other members of the Brawnville Athletic Club to exasperation; Jerusky Snipp, spinster-daughter of the Deacon, who is enormously tall, lank, angular, sour-visaged, and shrouded in Victorian piety; and Rev. Job Fearful, pastor of first church, a modest and angelic dispenser of the gospel who is so humble he lacks the courage to express any opinion. These village characters created by Tyler are rooted in the diverse attitudes prevalent in and around the Boston area during the two decades of the 1850s and 1860s. Tyler's characters are

---

[2] Ronald A. Smith. "A Centennial: Moses Coit Tyler's *The Brawnville Papers*," *Journal of Health, Physical Education, and Recreation*, 41 (March 1970):71.

often depicted in polemic discussions that demonstrate his knowledge and understanding of the real gymnastic dilemma of that period. Because of the sordid reputations of gymnasiums of the era, to have his town consider building one was a liberal idea. Gymnasiums were often compared to the billiard parlors and saloons against which the moral reformers spoke harshly.

The interest in gymnastics and the ultimate idea of building a gymnasium in Brawnville grow out of a reading circle—actually a square, as the four men each sat at a table corner—made up of Judge Fairplay, Dr. Drugger, Rev. Bland, and Professor Henry, the schoolmaster. As they read Plato's thoughts on gymnastics, discussion ensues as to the desirability of such activity. These four main characters of Brawnville see Plato's "sound mind in a sound body" concept as supportive of gymnastics, although present-day students of philosophy blame Plato's idealism for creating the dualistic theory of man.[3]

The Judge proposes building a gymnasium in Brawnville and perhaps initiating a Sanitary Society or Athletic Club. The dialogue of the four characters embodies some of the major notions and actual movements then occurring in the Boston area and much of the northeastern United States. Judge Fairplay later reads Horace Mann's treatise that spoke of the ills of poor health being chased away through vigorous exercise. Health reformers, one class of mid-nineteenth century sanitary reformers, were adamant about exercise being a strong deterrent to illness. The most flamboyant and controversial of the health reformers were the strength seekers who often went about the country preaching "strength is health."[4] The voice in opposition to this actual exaggerated movement is Dr. Drugger's, who states that claims made in the name of gymnastics are extravagant, pretentious, and based on shallow and illogical clamour. He said gymnastics and strength development were usually soaked through with quackery.

In 1867, when Tyler wrote *The Brawnville Papers,* gymnasiums were being opened in Boston by strength seekers such as George Barker Windship, David P. Butler, and J. Fletcher Paul, who were making exaggerated claims for their gymnastics. These men who called themselves health reformers, claimed that through weight lifting they could cure diseases such as asthma, dyspepsia, pulmonary disease, chronic rheumatism, neuralgia, torpor of liver and bowels, deformities, displaced organs, diseases peculiar to women, and on and on.[5] Judge Fairplay agreed in part with Dr. Drugger that the claims for exercise were excessive, but said if the doctor favored the theory that mind and soul needed attending but the body could take care of itself, then perhaps there was no need for the medical profession.

---

[3] Dualism promotes the idea that mind and body work independently, and that mental activity is always superior to physical skill.

[4] Joan Paul "The Health Reformers: George Barker Windship and Boston's Strength Seekers," *The Journal of Sport History* 10 (Winter 1983): 41-57.

[5] See *Boston Directory,* Reels 3-9 (1867-1876); Lewis Janes. *Health Exercises: The Rationale and Practice of the Lifting Cure or Health Lift,* 7th ed. (New York: Lewis G. Janes, 1873).

George B. Windship

Rev. Bland expressed the views of the general public toward gymnastics when he stated that Brawnville was probably too small to support a gymnasium and too rural to need one. Rev. Bland said that their village had fresh air and easy access to the hills, rivers, and open fields that cities lacked. (The health reformers preached the need of fresh air for city dwellers.) Judge Fairplay viewed nature as the great cathedral of God. He argued that it was no more essential to build a church in the midst of such a natural setting than a gymnasium. As men can exercise in the woods, so can ministers preach their sermons there. The only necessity of either, Judge Fairplay proclaimed, was climate—rain, cold, heat. Rev. Bland then agreed with the Judge that a gymnasium would be good.

Professor Henry compares Plato's ideal commonwealth to Dio Lewis's marriage of music and gymnastics at the altar of education. Catharine Beecher was the first known native American to combine music with gymnastics. Being a strict Calvinist, she believed by playing music to gymnastics one could gain grace and poise while avoiding the immorality associated with dancing. Dio Lewis was actually an imitator more than an innovator, and more than likely copied Beecher in his application of music to his gymnastics. When Dr. Drugger explains that physicians think Dio Lewis is a quack, this illustrates that Tyler was either aware of the circumstances that shadowed some of Lewis's accomplishments in the field, or he was cognizant that many of the leading proponents of gymnastics were seen as charlatans by much of the medical profession. Dio Lewis's medical degree was only an honorary one from an obscure homeopathic hospital; Catharine Beecher openly accused him of pirating some of her gymnastic work, and Delphine Hanna of Oberlin College

Catherine Beecher   Dio Lewis

questioned the scientific principles of some of his exercises, to which Lewis reportedly replied that people did not mind being "humbugged."[6] However, in 1861, Lewis published his *New Gymnastics for Men, Women and Children*,[7] and is credited with having the greatest impact for at least a decade in the promotion of school gymnastics.[8]

To bring the villagers together to present his idea for establishing a gymnasium in Brawnville, Judge Fairplay receives permission from Rev. Fearful to hold a town meeting in First Church. However when Rev. Fearful tells his deacons, Snipp, with righteous indignation, threatens to burn the church first, plow the site, and sow it with salt before having it desecrated by so worldly and godless a purpose. He throws another dart at the muscular Christians by claiming that men were getting to care more for their bodies than their souls.[9]

This meeting to discuss the gymnasium is held in the schoolhouse so the people of Brawnville can be introduced to the "sanitary bearing of muscular

---

[6] Van Dalen, Deobold B. and Bruce L. Bennett, *A World History of Physical Education*, 2nd ed. (Englewood Cliffs, N.J.: Prentice Hall, Inc., 1971), pp. 379-380.

[7] Dio Lewis, *The New Gymnastics for Men, Women, and Children* (Boston: Ticknor and Fields, 1861).

[8] Geo. W. Tuxbury, Chairman, "Report of a Special Committee on the Subject of Physical Training," City Document No. 94 (City of Boston, December 10, 1860).

[9] Examples of the concern of these mid-nineteenth century Christians for their physical beings can be found in such articles as "Saints and Their Bodies," *The Atlantic Monthly*, 1 (1858), 582-595; see also "Mind and Body in Early American Thought," *The Journal of American History*, 54 (March 1968): 787-805.

exercise." Before the idea can be fully explained, Deacon Snipp objects saying that a gymnasium would encourage gaiety, frivolity, and dissipation. The crowd, disliking the Deacon and respecting the Judge's opinions, shows its displeasure by hissing and tapping heels. While waiting on the Judge to quiet the crowd so he can finish expressing his opinion, the miserable deacon would have made an admirable model, Tyler writes, for "Patience on a monument, smiling at Grief." Snipp then continues by warning that a gymnasium would open the door to dancing, card playing, billiards, and croquet.

Next, Dr. Drugger stands and gives his opposition to the idea as a man of science. He warns of health reformers failing to consider physiological facts by preaching strength as the road to health at the expense of considering the vital (cardio-vascular) system. He speaks against the concept that strength made a person healthy, and he tells of many athletes—acrobats, pugilists, and gymnasts—who were short-lived. Many writers warned that men who developed excessive strength died in the prime of life.[10] Dio Lewis was also an outspoken critic of the strength movement because he believed that the key to health was developing the cardiovascular system more than the muscular system.[11] It appears that Tyler was not completely knowledgeable of the exact roles Lewis and some of the other health reformers of the period were playing. He certainly was very familiar with Lewis's reputation, yet Tyler fails to distinguish between philosophical differences espoused by Lewis and his leading opponent in the health movement, George Barker Windship. Although Tyler wrote his book five years before Windship's death, it also was prophetic as it told of strong men dying early. George Windship, the best known of the health reformers preaching strength, died at forty-two even though at five feet, seven inches, and 148 pounds, he lifted 1250 pounds with his hands and 2,700 pounds with a yoke harness on his shoulders.[12]

Heartened by Dr. Drugger's support, Deacon Snipp again jumped to his feet and proclaimed that the money to be spent on the gymnasium could be better used if sent to convert the poor, perishing heathen in Africa. In spite of Dr. Drugger's and Deacon Snipp's opposition, the town voted overwhelmingly to form an executive committee of six men and six women to make plans for Brawnville's gymnasium.

Within three days the committee had raised the money to build the gymnasium. A four-story brick building housing a large room for gymnastics and lectures, a reading room, dressing room with laboratories, and a library with room for literary and social meetings was built. The people decided to call it the "Brawnville Athletic Club House" since gymnasiums too often

---

[10] William Gilbert Anderson, *Anderson's Physical Education* (Broadway, New York: A.D.Dana, 1897); Checkley, Edwin, *A Natural Method of Physical Training*, Revised. (Brooklyn, New York: William C. Bryant & Co., 1894).

[11] Dio Lewis, "Dumb Bell Exercises," May, 1862.

[12] *Boston Transcript* (September 14, 1876), in *Harvardiana*, compiled by William Abbot Everett, Vol. 6 (Cambridge, 1872-1892).

DUMB-BELLS

EXERCISES WITH BEAN BAGS
(From *The New Gymnastics*, by Dio Lewis, 1883)

Dumb Bell and Bean Bag Exercises (Dio Lewis)

had a reputation only for building muscles, being sites of dissipation, and at best places requiring no brains.[13] The people of Brawnville were concerned with the moral and intellectual as well as the physical. This dualistic theory was a nineteenth-century concept Tyler rejected in his *Brawnville Papers*.

A graduate of Dio Lewis's Normal School of Physical Education was hired to teach men, women, and children at the Brawnville Athletic Club.[14] A place in the middle of the gymnasium floor was left for the special work of Dio Lewis's Gymnastics, a combination of Catharine Beecher's and Swedish gymnastics, plus a few of his own ideas. His system used wooden dumbbells, wands, Indian clubs, bean bags, and massage. The great hall was further furnished with ladders, swings, horizontal and parallel bars, weights and pulleys, iron dumbbells, the wooden horse, and other German gymnastic equipment. All of the descriptions of the German gymnastics equipment are authentic, although the pulleys and weights and iron dumbbells are descriptions that came more from the strength seekers of that era.[15]

As speaker at the grand opening of the Club, Judge Fairplay invited Col. Thomas Wentworth Higginson, whom he described as a patriot, brave soldier, superb scholar, and "the most exquisite prose writer left to America after the death of Hawthorne."[16] Since Higginson was unable to attend, Judge Fairplay presided over the housewarming. Young people demonstrated the Dio Lewis gymnastics and the Judge and Rev. Bland gave short speeches, with the people in attendance shouting approval and wiping away tears of happiness. The

[13] See W. Sargent Ledyard, ed., *Dudley Allen Sargent: An Autobiography* (Philadelphia: Lea and Fehiger, 1927); Paul, "The Health Reformers."

[14] The first physical education teacher certification program in the United States actually was at Dio Lewis's school.

[15] One very interesting item in the description of the gymnasium which I cannot verify as fact or fiction is that Dio Lewis is credited with the invention of the folding chair. The great hall floor was described as being changed magically from a gymnasium room to a lecture hall at an instant's notice because of this chair, attributed to Dio Lewis, that could be folded and put on a rack at the side of the room.

[16] For an understanding of how Higginson's writing affected Tyler's ideas for *Brawnville*, see Thomas Wentworth Higginson, "Gymnastics," *Atlantic Monthly*, 7 (March 1861): 283 302.

Judge warned the people, however, that they must not become gymnastic bigots by developing athletic fanaticism.

Dr. Drugger compliments the boys and girls who performed in the Lewis gymnastic exhibitions, but feels compelled to state again his dislike for Dio Lewis and that he looked upon Lewis, the medical man, as a large-sized charlatan. He did admit, though, that he could find no fault in his gymnastic drills. The heavy German gymnastics were another matter however, and the doctor warned that they could lead to a variety of incurable diseases.

Then the deacon who "bores you to death in the august name of Godliness" asked to speak. Deacon Snipp called the opening of the Health Club the saddest day in Brawnville. He said he expected "to see the walls of Zion falling into decay, and the people going away with idols—ten pins, dancing, billiards, croquet, and other carnal pleasures." He stated that he would remain true to piety and conservatism if he had to stand alone.

Abdiel Standish responded to Deacon Snipp's remarks in his droll way. He said whether there was any merit in being conservative depended on what a person wanted to conserve. If one wanted to conserve things that were good, useful, or true, then conservatism was all right. Standish said he considered Brawnville's health club conservative because it was trying to conserve people's health. It stood for conserving youth, happiness, fresh air, pure water, wholesome food, and good customs. He said he had noticed that those who crowed loudest about good and bad and conservatism were usually those who didn't stop to consider good or bad, they just rejected any change. Abdiel Standish described some folks as so conservative that if God Almighty had consulted them about the creation of the world, they would have advised him to conserve chaos.

The two major obstacles to the early growth of Brawnville's Athletic Club were injuries and participation of women. The first near catastrophe occurred when Lionidas Climax fell off the horizontal bar just before the literary meeting was to begin one night. Word spread that he had been killed and the villagers became alarmed. Mothers said they would never allow their children to attend the Athletic Club again. After discovering that Climax, the indomitable orator had only broken his arm and would be all right, one man said it was a shame it wasn't his jaw. The Judge had to convince the people that all things held some dangers, and then Rev. Bland encouraged the group to immediately get back on the gymnastic apparatus so the ghost of fear could be killed.

The last obstacle was based on the Victorian premise that women could not be athletes. The topic at the Club meeting one night was to be: "Is it desirous that women should practice gymnastics?" Deacon Snipp had not been heard from since the inauguration of the Club, but this night he appeared in an infuriated state and flung a letter on the table in front of the Judge from his spinster daughter, Jerusky. After stating that this letter should convince the people of the scandalous and unscriptural nature of the Health Club activities, Snipp marched out.

Jerusky's letter chastised the Club members for being misguided mortals with a zeal for muscular and carnal grace. She called the Hall a temple to

Baal, an edifice erected to frivolity. Jerusky said her cup of grief was filled when she learned that the handmaidens of the village were also bowing to this pagan fashion. The letter quoted scripture in opposition to gymnastics, and told of the way in which Paul even made women cover their heads in public while women at the Athletic Club were willing to even show their ———, but she was too embarrassed to finish the sentence.

Jerusky further stated that woman was intended to be weak, was to stay at home and comfort her husband, and should bring children into the world by suffering. She said women were coming to the Hall and getting so strong that they were even bearing children without great pain, and were thus thwarting the righteous will of Heaven!

Rev. Bland, using Dr. Robinson's lexicon of the New Testament and the work of the American commentator, Albert Barnes, discussed the scripture Jerusky had quoted. "Bodily exercise," Bland explained, was thought to refer to the mortification of the body by abstinence and penance.

The Judge then took up the question of women and gymnastics.[17] The rights and privileges of women were being debated on every hand as mid-nineteenth century witnessed such women issues as the suffragette movement, the development of women's colleges, and the teaching of gymnastics to women. Public opinion leaned toward the exclusion of woman in practically every position that might have an adverse effect on her domesticity. Women were told by their parents, teachers, and fire and brimstone preachers that they would be jeopardizing their coveted roles as wives and mothers if they took up practices that were "unnatural" to women. Politics, professional careers, advanced education, and vigorous activity were all said to be anathema to womanhood and to the privileged pedestal on which ladies were placed.

As early as the late 1830s Catharine Beecher, daughter of the famous Calvinist, Lyman Beecher, introduced gymnastics at her female seminary in Hartfort, Connecticut. She was the first native American to develop a system of gymnastics, the first to coin the term "calisthenics," and the first to introduce the subject of physical education to women.[18] The only way the general public accepted such a thing was that it be done in the name of health. Also, in the 1860's women's dress was so restricting that the eighteen inch wasp-waist dress style caused fainting and the "vapors" to be an expected condition in women's behavior. It was not the vigorous, energetic, and strong willed woman that was seen as attractive, but the pale, languid woman who appeared helpless and fragile. Certainly the idea of gymnastics and sport for girls and women was met with opposition by the majority of the upperclass society, with only a very liberal minority offering support.

Tyler demonstrates his liberalism through Judge Fairplay when he has him take the supportive view on women. The Judge said that most talk of women involved either flattery or ridicule, but lately talk in the form of argument

---

[17] There is a plethora of works on women and society's expectations of her in the Victorian Age.

[18] Van Dalen and Bennett, *A World History*, pp. 378-79.

had been added. He felt this was hopeful. He said the pivotal question on every woman issue—the vote, a university education, entering a learned profession, practicing gymnastics—was whether woman was a human being or a goose. He said the goose theory was the most popular among men, and sadly, even women. Judge Fairplay said if a woman believed that women had no role to play outside the home, then you could accept her as a goose.

The Judge then elaborated on why it was necessary for women to develop greater strength—for health. He said Catharine Beecher had proclaimed that in all her acquaintances ("and you know the Beechers are acquainted with everybody"), there were not a dozen healthy women. Judge Fairplay told of the exercise given the Spartan women and how they were known for their great health and beauty.

The Athletic Club becomes a boon to Brawnville as people come from near and far to visit the Club and make inquiries of how to begin such a project. The end of Tyler's story of Brawnville parallels the growth of gymnastics and physical culture in New England at the end of the 1860s. The 1850s had marked the beginning of the growth spurt of school gymnastics. By the end of the 1860s, much of the New England population was probably aware of the first significant college physical education program that had begun at Amherst in 1861, was familiar with the first normal school begun by Dio Lewis in 1861 to train physical educators, and knew of the private gymnasia that were flourishing in the Boston area. Tyler's fantasy of Brawnville factually exposes the nineteenth-century attitudes and prejudices toward the growth and development of gymnastics and physical culture. It was due to the support of such advocates as Tyler that the growth of physical culture was possible in an era when many people associated evil and dissipation with the play spirit that was part of gymnastics and sport. The redemptive factor in gymnastics was its contribution to health—one of the basic arguments still used in support of physical education and sport today. As the reader reflects on Tyler's rationale for Brawnville's acceptance of gymnastics, it becomes evident to the discerning thinker that the lingering puritanical biases of our twentieth century society make physical education and sport easier to promote as a means to better health than as "play" activities that are essentially for pleasure.

4

Hemingway's Anti-Hero and the Olympic Ideal: It Breaks My Heart

Lyle I. Olsen

THIS IS ABOUT THE PURPOSE OF SPORT—specifically about the attitudes of professional and amateur athletes. Ernest Hemingway and Baron Pierre de Coubertin are cast as the central characters. My aim is to contrast the professional attitude displayed by Ernest Hemingway's sportsmen heroes with the amateur ideals of the protagonists in the popular nineteenth-century literary work of Sir Henry Newbolt and Thomas Hughes. In the process I will document the way in which Coubertin's amateur ideals were influenced by Thomas Hughes' novel, *Tom Brown's School Days*. My conclusions evolve from literary mythology rather than facts.[1]

According to my Hemingway instructor, Professor James Hinkle, the world's most impressive gathering of artistic talent occurred in 1924 on the Left Bank in Paris. The writers, musicians, and artists who made the twenties this century's greatest decade—Dos Passos, Picasso, James Joyce, the Fitzgeralds, Ezra Pound, Miro, Gertrude Stein and Ernest Hemingway—all were in Paris. All were friends

---

[1] Most arguments are based on personal perceptions and in an attempt to legitimize my endeavor, I will quote Northrop Frye: "Academics, like other people, start with a personality that is afflicted by ignorance and prejudice, and try to escape from that personality, in Eliot's phrase, through absorption in impersonal scholarship. One emerges on the other side of this realizing once again that all knowledge is personal knowledge, but with some hope that the person may have been, to whatever degree, transformed in the meantime." Frye at least gives one a feeling of hope.

   This work is not intended as literary scholarship: it expresses my personal apppraisal of the amateur/professional dilemma. These same ideas are used in my sport history classes; the intention (in the class and here) is to debate specific questions inherent in one's attitude toward amateurism. If successful, I would have each reader proposing his/her argument. Hughes, Hemingway, and Newbolt are used because they are the best examples I know of. To repeat, at no point do I speak with the authority of a scholarly consensus.

of Hemingway. Other major figures appeared: Dr. William Carlos Williams, Gide, Stravinsky . . . the list goes on. But the name of a crusading French intellectual who was campaigning to change French educational practice is missing from the list: Baron Pierre de Coubertin.

The Olympic Games were also contested in Paris in 1924. These same games were the loosely-followed model for the recent Academy Award film *Chariots of Fire*. Though not recognized by the film-makers, the aging *le Renovateur*, as Coubertin was labeled, was in attendance at the 1924 Games. Surprisingly the American sportsman Hemingway had departed for Spain— to fish and observe the running of the bulls in Pamplona—to record the impressions which led to *The Sun Also Rises*.

Literally and symbolically Hemingway and Coubertin were following different paths. Visualize the Cambridge athletes running for Britain in the *Chariots of Fire* representing Coubertin's amateur model while the emasculated Jake of *The Sun Also Rises* is a dramatic example of Hemingway's professional model, the anti-hero: a man with an "old pro's" attitude.

Many words have been written about the differences between an amateur versus a professional attitude in sports. The amateur attitude is distinguished by a joyful spirit of play which is evident regardless of the outcome of the contest. Of course, while the game is in progress nothing is more serious to the players (it appears to be a matter of life or death), but directly following the conclusion of the game all the contestants return rather quickly to the regular world. This spirited, serious approach to a game has nothing to do with money, rewards, or prizes. The players may receive direct financial rewards and still be amateur in spirit, for there exists a fundamental difference between amateur and professional sport that goes far beyond the technical distinction of whether an athlete makes money from his skill. Ideally, amateur games are defined as a hypothetical construct approximating an absurd world of play. Here the participants enter an *Alice in Wonderland* fantasy where all the players suspend their normal realistic and pragmatic habits of thinking. This play world is extremely fragile. It takes only one sneering scoffer or cheat to ruin the game. All the players must acquiesce or succumb to the magical world of play.

Professional sport, conversely, remains part of the real world, involving the entertainment of thousands of people and millions of dollars. Realistically, this environment usually entails corporate policies and a business-like assessment of each player's worth. Within this business-dominated arena professional players naturally assume a deadly serious attitude toward "working at" the sport—before, during, and after the contest. Frequently the business affairs of high-entertainment sport overpower the spirit of play which is the essence of a game, the *sine qua non* of amateur athletic competetion.

Let's take a closer look at the game itself. The game is the *source* of wonder, not something we artificially force on it. A. Barlett Giamatti, an ex-shortstop and, incidentally, the former president of Yale University, offers the following analysis of the "perfect" game—baseball:

It breaks your heart. It is designed to break your heart. The game begins in the spring, when everything else begins again, and it blossoms in the summer, filling the afternoons and evenings, and then as soon as the chill rains come, it stops and leaves you to face fall alone. You count on it, rely on it to buffer the passage of time, to keep the memory of sunshine and high skies alive, and then just when the days are all twilight, when you need it most, it stops. . . . It breaks my heart because it was meant to, because it was meant to foster in me again the illusion that there was something abiding, some pattern and some impulse that could come together to make a reality that would resist the corrosion; and because after it had fostered again that most hungered-for illusion, the game was meant to stop, and betray precisely what it promised. Of course, there are those who learn after the first few times. They grow out of sports. And there are others who were born with the wisdom to know that nothing lasts. These are the truly tough among us, the ones who can live without illusion, or without even the hope of illusion. I am not that grown-up or up-to-date. I am a simpler creature, tied to more primitive patterns and cycles. I need to think something lasts forever, and it might as well be that state of being that is a game; it might as well be that, in a green field, in the sun.[2]

Let's shift back to a nineteenth century code of manhood and the educational goals of Coubertin. Scholars such as John J. McAloon in *This Great Symbol: Pierre de Coubertin and the Origins of the Modern Olympic Games* and Patrick Howarth in *Play Up And Play The Game* report that Coubertin's ideas and educational theories were shaped significantly by his reading and subsequent worship of the most popular and influential schoolboy novel: *Tom Brown's Schooldays* by Thomas Hughes. This outwardly benign novel fostered obsessive notions of athleticism in Coubertin's mind.

He was susceptible to English public school athleticism because he had inherited a national shame with the defeat of French forces in the Franco-Prussian War. He really believed in the idea that the "battle of Waterloo had been won on the playing fields of Eton." It is significant in this appraisal of the mythology of amateurism that Coubertin's ultimate objective was to impose English public school athleticism on the curricula of elite French secondary schools.

Coubertin's devious strategy was to use the mythology of ancient Greek athletics (including the Olympic Games) as a shield to hide his true intentions. Thus, in theory, the French schools would accept a sports program which was inherited from the "golden days" of Athens. Coincidentally, of course, the activities would be almost identical with those found at Rugby (and similar English public schools). And all of these machinations were devised because French soldiers had proved inferior to the Prussians in their most recent war.

Coubertin's model, Tom Brown, portrayed by Hughes is a plucky, God-fearing young English gentleman, skilled at games, willing, almost eager, to sacrifice his body for his school or country in athletics or in war. The two activities (games and warfare) were almost interchangeable in the literature and mythology of the time.

---

[2] A. Bartlett Giamatti, "The Green Fields of the Mind," in Kevin Kerrane and Richard Grossinger, eds. *Baseball Diamonds* (Garden City, New York: Anchor Books, 1976), pp. 295-297.

In contrast to Hughes's typically Anglo-Saxon English warrior-hero, Ernest Hemingway's anti-hero—his sportsman—is a professional athlete, usually a boxer, big-game hunter, or bull-fighter. Hemingway's "Chapter XII" in *In Our Time* quickly and vividly dramatizes his professional's code of manhood:

> It happened right down close in front of you, you could see Villalta snarl at the bull and curse him, and when the bull charged he swung back firmly like an oak when the wind hits it, his legs tight together, the muleta trailing and the sword following the curve behind. Then he cursed the bull, flopped the muleta at him, and swung back from the charge, his feet firm, the muleta curving and at each swing the crowd roaring.

> When he started to kill it was all in the same rush. The bull looking at him straight in front, hating. He drew out the sword from the folds of the muleta and sighted with the same movement and called to the bull, Toro! Toro! and the bull charged and Villalta charged and just for a moment they became one. Villalta became one with the bull and then it was over. Villalta standing straight and the red hilt of the sword sticking out dully between the bull's shoulders. Villalta, his hand up at the crowd and the bull roaring blood, looking straight at Villalta and his legs caving.

Critics agree that Hemingway's sporting anti-hero is earnestly searching for a noble stance, constantly looking for a personal ritual which will permit him to confront death with grace and dignity. Thus it follows naturally that Hemingway's anti-heroes try to realize their manhood in the "blood sports" such as big-game hunting, boxing, and bullfighting. Further, Hemingway's protagonist is aliented from the normal social channels which offer assistance to someone acquiring a sense of self through family and society; he only finds values through intense personal experiences.[3] In this manner, Hemingway sets the stage for the inevitable tragedy.[4]

Tragic literature, from the ancient Greeks to the present, makes assertions of some kind, however equivocal, about the nature of man. These assertions emerge ambiguously, never explicitly, from the context of the writer's soul and art. Much of the serious literature written after World War I reflects this disillusionment with war, an impassioned rejection of all the old concepts of glory and honor. World War I marked the collapse of the nineteenth-century dream of progress and the perfectability of man. During the war, science and technology (the twin hopes of industrial capitalism's theology) created and manufactured the new machines and weapons which were used for

---

[3] Ernest Hemingway, *The Short Stories of Ernest Hemingway* (New York: Charles Scribner's Sons, 1953), p.181.

[4] My primary sources for Hemingway's work are Professor James C. Hinkle of San Diego State University and Philip Young's *Ernest Hemingway: A Reconsideration* (University Park: The Pennsylvania State University Press, 1966). Neither Hinkle nor Young, as the usual disclaimer reads, should be blamed for my misinterpretations. Those I willingly shoulder. The short pieces, Chapters XII and IX, were found in *The Short Stories of Ernest Hemingway.*

impersonal slaughter. Buried in the debris of this new kind of war was the warrior-hero, the hero whose distinctiveness depended on the force of his personal achievement, on the concepts of glory and honor, on noble sacrifice for God and Country.

Thus, it is not surprising that central to Hemingway's anti-hero is the loss—the awareness of the loss—of all the fixed ties that bind a man to his community, his attachments to a stable, meaningful order: work, family, country, and God. He not only lacks these ties, he scorns or fears them. Lieutenant Henry in *A Farewell to Arms* explains:

> I was always embarrassed by the words sacred, glorious, and sacrifice and the expression in vain. We heard them, sometimes standing in the rain almost out of earshot, so that only the shouted words came through, and had read them on proclamations that were slapped up by bill posters over other proclamations . . . and I had seen nothing sacred, and the things that were glorious had no glory and the sacrifices were like the stockyards of Chicago if nothing was done with the meat except to bury it. There were many words that you could not stand to hear and finally only the names of places had dignity. . . .[5]

Additionally and understandably, our democratic beliefs and scientific insight into human behavior eroded the aristocratic foundations of the heroes we inherited from the past. Further, belief in the power and insight of common people for self-government carried with it a passion for human equality which includes a suspicion or distrust of individual greatness.

Hemingway's emphasis on death, on dying well, which is so important in much of his writing, led him to an exploration of styles of living which would permit a man to die with dignity, even without any larger purpose to guide and comfort him. His emphasis on style defied the anarchy and barbarity of the world without. For instance:

> The first matador got the horn through his sword hand and the crowd hooted him. The second matador slipped and the bull caught him through the belly and he hung on to the horn with one hand and held the other tight against the place, and the bull rammed him wham against the wall and the horn came out, and he lay in the sand, and then got up like a crazy drunk and tried to slug the men carrying him away and yelled for his sword but he fainted. The kid came out and had to kill five bulls because you can't have more than three matadors, and the last bull he was so tired he couldn't get the sword in. He couldn't hardly lift his arm. He tried five times and the crowd was quiet because it was a good bull and it looked like him or the bull and then he finally made it. He sat down in the sand and puked and they held a cape over him while the crowd hollered and threw things down into the bull ring.[6]

---

[5] Ernest Hemingway, *A Farewell to Arms* (New York: Charles Scribner's Sons, 1928), p. 185.

[6] Ibid., p. 159.

Style is the buffer Hemingway kept between his profession and those he loved. It is the only prize remaining for his sportsman. In effect, style is the hero's protection against life itself. Hemingway's terse writing starkly complements the fatalistic attitude of his anti-hero.

Now let's return to examine the romantic English literature that influenced Coubertin, the popular literature with a warrior-hero protagonist. We come immediately to Sir Henry Newbolt, who glorified games-playing as the ideal training for warfare. Newbolt's first sight of his public school, Clifton, was one which he never forgot. As the setting for a story in one of his novels, Newbolt recollected his impressions of "a wide green sward, level as a lawn, flooded in low sunlight, and covered in every direction with a multitude of white figures, standing, running, walking, bowling, throwing, batting—in every attitude that can express the energy and expectancy of youth."[7] Patrick Howarth relates that Sir Arthur Quiller-Couch wrote to Sir Henry (in good humor) questioning Newbolt's right to that particular memory of Clifton: "Was it you or I, who heard the crack of bat on ball and caught his breath at first sight of the Close? It was, I, Sir, and here I catch you a-hugging one of my best memories."[8] Typically, Newbolt's poetry and prose were replete with cues and devices—which imprinted a manly athletic code of behavior on budding young English gentleman. The epitome of these warrior-hero poems dedicated to games-playing athletes begins innocently:

> There's a breathless hush in the Close tonight—
> Ten to make and the match to win—
> A bumping pitch and a blinding light,
> An hour to play and the last man in.
> And it's not for the sake of a ribboned coat,
> Or the selfish hope of a season's fame,
> But his Captain's hand on his shoulder smote—
> 'Play up! play up! and play the game!'
>
> The sand of the desert is sodden red,—
> Red with the wreck of a square that broke;—
> The Gatling's jammed and the Colonel dead,
> And the regiment blind with dust and smoke.
> The river of death has brimmed his banks,
> And England's far, and Honour a name,
> But the voice of a schoolboy rallies the ranks:
> 'Play up! play up! and play the game!'
>
> This the word that year by year,
> While in her place the School is set,

---

[7] Patrick Howarth, *Play Up and Play the Game: The Heroes of Popular Fiction* (London: Eyre Methuen, 1973), p. 6.

[8] Ibid.

Every one of her sons must hear,
And none that hears it dare forget.
This they all with a joyful mind
Bear through life like a torch in flame,
And falling fling to the host behind—
'Play up! play up! and play the game!'[9]

This warrior-hero, Hughes's Muscular Christian, was loyal—personally as well as institutionally loyal. Also truthful, dependable and predictable. Significantly, of all the component parts (the mental baggage) which English gentleman inherited from the nineteenth century, amateurism (a significant part of the baggage) came the nearest to slipping unscathed through the first half of the twentieth century. It is questionable, Howarth contends, whether the Olympic Games would have been revived in their modern form, particularly with the insistence on amateurism, if Coubertin had not encountered Hughes's work and succumbed to the English gentlemen's code of conduct.

True to their amateur ideals, English gentlemen served, we are told, not for profit or power or fame, though these were sometimes by-products of their actions, but for the deep inner satisfaction of service and the fulfillment of duty to family, country, and God. Ironically, it was only after World War II—when British industrial and technological expertise was being compared unfavorably with the emerging world powers, while at the same time English teams began to lose in the games which their forefathers had invented— that the moral ascendancy of the amateur was disputed seriously. It had been assumed always that gentlemen, when playing against their inferiors, would win at games in a just and sane world.[10]

That just and sane world was the remembered and revered world of *Tom Brown's School Days.* Howarth comments pointedly that the name of the author is omitted from the first editions. Credit was attributed to "an Old Boy." By this device Hughes asserted his amateur status as a writer. Reverend Charles Kingsley admired Hughes for both his ability as an athlete (he was excellent) and for his judgment and common sense. Kingsley attributed Hughes's ability

---

[9] Ibid., p. 1.

[10] My idea of matching a professional athlete's attitude with Hemingway's anti-hero came while attending a course taught by Professor James Hinkle. This attempt to write about the subject came about accidentally; I was trying to write a letter to Colin Veitch concerning an excellent paper he had written and presented about the novelist John Knowles. In his paper, Veitch analyzed games-playing as a preparation for war in the writing of John Knowles. My failure came in trying to make sense (in my own mind) about loyalty, team play, etc. in relation to the phrase "a separate peace." The more I wrote, the more tangled I became, in the subjects of warfare relating to school-boy athletics, loyalty, responsibility, pluck, and the right of an individual to stand up and be counted as going against the "team." I still haven't mailed the letter to Veitch as I still lack a clear grasp of the subtleties. But I am wrestling with the monster.

in practical matters to his pursuit of three of the four royal F's, namely fishing, fowling, and foxhunting.

In Hughes's story, Tom Brown is guided by Rugby's godlike headmaster . . . "the Doctor." Obviously the Doctor is Thomas Arnold and "the true sort of captain . . . for a boys' army, one who had misgivings, and gave no uncertain word of command, and, yet who would not yield or make truce with the forces of evil, would fight the fight out (so every boy felt) to the last gasp and the last drop of blood." "What," Tom's creator, Hughes, preaches, "would life be like without fighting? . . . Fighting, rightly understood, is the business, the real highest, honestest business of every son of man."[11],[12]

To review my argument, we have the fighting amateur arrayed opposite Ernest Hemingway's tough professional anti-hero. Hemingway's sportsman has the ability to retain his style and poise throughout the unequal contest. Thus their attitudes are sharply (if simplistically) contrasted. Hemingway's professional sportsman has the realistic approach. Because that is the way the world is. In the end we are all going to lose; if you love someone it is inevitable that you will lose that love or the loved one. Somehow fate will kill the object of your love. Hemingway's heroic attitude, then, is to fight with as much style as one can muster, knowing all the while that you are going to lose.

So I arrive at the crux of my contention that only an amateur's attitude distinguishes him from the professional. The professional plays to survive— to keep from losing. The "old pro's" creed is: don't do anything brash trying to win; wait and play the odds. Just keep from losing. Let the amateur play with all-out abandon. Let your opponent make the unforced amateur errors. A smart professional athlete survives with style, for he knows that games are lost through unforced errors. The "old pro" doesn't try for winners: winners are tough to make and lead to errors. The professional's objective is to survive long enough so his opponent will make enough errors and lose. The pro knows it pays to play by the book! Fate, fans, coaches, owners and especially sportswriters are heartless and cruel to the foolish player who gambles— and loses. There is no such thing as justice!!! Not in sports.[13]

---

[11] Howarth, *Play Up*, p. 16.

[12] The primary theme of this section was noted in *Play Up and Play the Game: The Heroes of Popular Fiction* by Patrick Howarth, London: Eyre Methuen, 1973. Throughout this section, my debt to Howarth will be evident, and all unattributed quotes are from his book. To repeat what I wrote earlier about the Young book: I am not a Newbolt scholar so I leaned heavily on Howarth. However, the mistakes of interpretation are mine.

[13] On the surface, the behavior of the Muscular Christian is so exemplary, one is hard pressed to see the vicious strait-jacket which this creed imposes. After all—who can stand up against patriotism, motherhood, and all that. My first glimpse into the insidious and slavish

Does my argument relate to reality? Let's examine the underlying premises: the pervasive characteristic of Hemingway's hero is his loss of purpose, his inability to find any meaningful direction to his life or to human existence. This loss of purpose is tied to the loss of God, (by whatever name you choose) heralded by Nietzche's cry of "God is dead." The anti-hero may be heroic—even noble—in behavior, but his heroism is quixotic or desperate. Hemingway's athlete is an outsider who lacks a god (even a tyrant) to rebel against. Left is an abstract fate that toys with men as they wriggle desperately, like ants on a burning log (Hemingway's image) to avoid their ultimate fate—death. "But they killed you in the end. You could count on that. Stay around and they would kill you" is the bitter thought of Lieutenant Henry, waiting for his Catherine to die in *A Farewell to Arms*. Henry's "they" is appropriately vague.

Is this the code one wishes to live by? Not for me. I will opt for the absurd life. A certain blindness is a blessing. An amateur plays to win. Nothing is going to deter his or her brash attempt at "grabbing the ring." I know it is silly to believe that the act of "standing up to the bully in the school-yard" (the willingness to fight for one's rights) will transfer into desired character traits. But that is not my argument. Also please forget about the debatable social values of games. In the end, as Roger Angell writes, "you always get back to this, back to the game itself."[14] Not that games satisfy everything. But as one lover of sports, Michael Novak believes, "the emotions [games] dramatize are deeper and more mystical than doubters will ever understand."[15], [16]

---

aspects of athleticism (all in the name of team spirit, etc.) was supplied by Professor Gerald Redmond at a sport history meeting at McMasters University in Ontario. Later J. A. Mangan's definitive study was brought to my attention: *Atheleticism in The Victorian and Edwardian Public School: The Emergence And Consolidation Of An Eucational Ideology* (Cambridge: University Press, 1981). Mangan's penetrating study should be banned from all coaches' reading lists. With the title banned, I know my coaching colleagues would move heaven and earth to read the book. And it definitely is a balanced scholarly work which they would enjoy and argue about.

[14] Roger Angell, "Baseball—The Perfect Game," *The New York Times*, Sunday, 1 April 1984, p. 8-E.

[15] Michael Novak, *The Joy of Sports* (New York: Basic Books, 1976), p. 43.

[16] My concluding contention came as a personal surprise. I had in mind a review of Hemingway's thoughts about war and the foolishness one hears about football being a substitute for war, etc. I intended to use some of Michael Oriard's throughts about football and war. But when I reached the summary, I could not stop. My emotions overruled what little good sense I had left. Just like any other "over-the-hill coach", I believe firmly my argument is "right." But I don't know how to sort out all the various ramifications. I will leave it as a "gut level" decision and attempt to write a rational argument in another place. if you think that is a weak rationalization, you are correct.

Following both Novak and Giamatti I will opt for an amateur attitude toward games even though

> I . . . know they will break my heart because games are meant to . . . because the game was meant . . . to betray precisely what it promised. [Of course] there are those who learn after the first few times. They grow out of sports. And there are others who were born with the wisdom to know that nothing lasts. These are the truly tough among us, the ones who can live without illusion, or without even the hope of illusion. I am not that grown-up or up-to-date. I am a simpler creature, tied to more primitive patterns and cycles. I need to think something lasts forever, and it might as well be that state of being that is a game; it might as well be that, in a green field, in the sun."[17]

---

[17] Giamatti, "The Green Fields," pp. 295-297.

5

The Old Scotchman and the Ghost of Baseball Past

Tom Dodge

Play ball with the Liberty Broadcasting System! Hello ever'body ever'where, this is The Old Scotchman, Gordon McLendon, bringing you the game today from Yankee Stadium, The House That Ruth Built, between the New York Yankees, the Ruppert Rifles, and the Bosox from Boston, Tom Yawkey's Boston Red Sox.

THAT INTENSE, APOCALYPTIC DELIVERY! Those rhythms! Those grandiloquent inflections! Those electric words, brittle rivets that break like curveballs through the afternoon air of thirty-five summers since, your potatoes dug, your corn shucked, your peas snapped, you were free to retreat to your room where the Old Scotchman described titanic combat between epic heroes like Ted Williams, Joe DiMaggio, Yogi Berra, Mel Parnell, Phil Rizzuto, and Hank Bauer. The very names carried eponymous magic of their own as they tumbled out of your Motorola speaker and, unknown to you at the time, out of radios in countless homes, stores, diners, soda fountains, and automobiles throughout the 31 states reached by 458 Liberty affiliates.

You had a choice between The Old Scotchman and Mutual's Game of the Day with Al Helfer, but Helfer's prosaic account of mere professional athletes working at their jobs compared with McLendon's as a suck-egg mule compared with Seabiscuit. "There's no question in my mind," says Wes Wise, one of McLendon's early proteges, "there's absolutely no doubt, that Gordon McLendon was the best baseball announcer there ever was and perhaps ever will be." In 1951, his fourth—and final—year, he was named America's Outstanding Sports Broadcaster and, other than Wise, his pressbox proteges included Lindsey Nelson, Jerry Doggett, Don Wells, and Dizzy Dean.

You may have been, say, an only child, living in a small town during those years. As a result, you naturally became preoccupied with the inside of yourself. Heroes from books, movies, and radio filled the world you made with adventure and might. Nightly, the voices of Brace Beamer as the Lone Ranger and William Conrad as Superman stirred you to commit marvelous deeds on behalf of justice. Those weren't weeds you were hoeing; you were lopping off the heads of evil-doers. Those weren't turkeys and chickens you were feeding, no sir. They were grateful townspeople. And that was no dog by your side. That was your faithful companion, Sancho.

Summer afternoons were reserved for The Old Scotchman and his thrilling broadcasts. He was a wizard of the radio waves. He knew the important role that imagination played in the success of radio. Transferred to television, The Lone Ranger was a joke, as was Superman. The producers of those shows could never have hoped to duplicate the pictures of these heroes that you carried in your mind. And television ruined baseball for you and millions of other Old Scotchman fans.

Before television, baseball was called "The National Pastime," and it had a great and glorious history. The Old Scotchman never let you forget that. Mays, Mize, Williams, Stanky, Dark, Robinson, DiMaggio, Mantle—they were the legatees of Cobb, Hornsby, Speaker, Mathewson, Grove, Ruth, Wagner, Dean, Ott, Van Lingle Mungo (how he loved to say that name!), and legions of other demi-gods in his limitless pantheon. Television reduced these titanic figures to tiny particulations of light on a twelve-inch screen.

Ron Powers has written a book about baseball, in the foreword of which he has supplied us with a wonderful metaphor. It is this: there is a single event that seems to carry the cosmic power to separate the first half of the century from the second half. It is Bobby Thomson's home run in the bottom of the ninth inning of the final play-off game between the Brooklyn Dodgers and the New York Giants at the Polo Grounds on October 3, 1951. That thunderous wallop won the pennant for New York but it signalled the end of an era, says Powers. Soon after, as if by design, the Boston Braves moved to Milwaukee, setting off a great expansion movement and leading to agents, to multi-million dollar contracts, to strikes, and to astro-turf (it looks better on television).

The Old Scotchman was there that day. Ironically, it was to be the last game he would ever broadcast. For you, it was the end of something so magical, that no one who has since been born could ever understand.

There are great hitters today, despite the lower averages (fielders wear leather baskets on their hands). Hank Aaron and Roger Maris have broken the Babe's home run records. But they ain't the Babe and there will never be another Babe because the great announcers like Ted Husing and Red Barber and Gordon McLendon are gone. They were mythmakers and they are gone and the myths are gone.

For McLendon, also a small-town boy (born in Paris, Texas, reared in Idabel, Oklahoma and Atlanta, Texas), radio was a source of relief from the hard realities of the Depression. Listening to the baseball games and reading, he stored up myths and metaphors like canned fruit, unknowingly preparing himself for the summer afternoons when he would sit behind his own microphone.

The metaphor goes on: Bobby Thomson knocked more than Ralph Branca's curveball into those short left-field stands of the Polo Grounds that day. He knocked America's myths out of the ball park too. After that, we peered through the Motorola screen and saw shifty-eyed politicians leering through mushroom clouds, quiz shows rigged to sell Revlon lips, assassinations, infanticide in Viet Nam and Kent State, student riots, race riots, police riots, cities in flames, Watergate, Abscam, all brought into your living room free of charge—all you had to do was hurry down to the mall and load up on the goods that sponsored these shows. The arc of Bobby Thomson's line drive separated the Age of Innocence from the Age of Obscenity.

Gordon McLendon helped build and preserve the Age of Innocence and knows more than he wants to know of the Age of Obscenity. He is 62 now and lives in semi-seclusion in a red sandstone building, which serves also as the headquarters of his labyrinthine empire, in the middle of a 100-acre estate he calls Cielo. From his office window you can see a movie set. He has never produced a hit movie, but each one has made money for him, including his most recent, *Victory,* which starred Michael Caine and Sylvester Stallone. From his lair at Cielo, he presides over an empire that includes substantial stocks in Columbia Studios, Subscription Television, and outright ownership of the Southwest's largest chain of drive-in theatres. His other extensive assets include real estate, broadcasting, oil, banking, strategic metals, mining and mineral interests, and Etruscan and pre-Pelasgian artifacts, much of which he donates to the Getty Museum. He is a genuine Dallas, Texas millionaire, each of his assets a boxcar on the long train he drives down the old Greenback Line.

Through his windows to the east lie the deep woods and, beyond that, the lake. Two other sandstone buildings serve as consultation and screening rooms, their bright blue leather furnishings resting on expansive Persian rugs of inestimable value. Every floor is covered with them, his study, his bedroom, banquet room, office, where a large German Shepherd-type dog sleeps, unimpressed by his expensive bed.

Imagine that the Old Scotchman had played such a formative role in your early life, had so stimulated your imagination, first taught you the difference between words that merely get the job done and those that shock you like smelling salts, between those that inform and those that incite. Thirty-five summers after you first tuned in his broadcasts, you are invited to spend an afternoon with him.

He greets you politely, casually, as if you came in every day at that time. He wears dark glasses inside an office that is itself unusually dark. Underneath are volcanic eyes with the underslung lids of the intellectual. He takes the glasses off as, deep in thought, he dictates a letter to his secretary. He has

about him the aspect of a nocturnal animal—canny, circumspect, wary—as
he squints against the sudden onrush of light.

He is a prodigious reader and lover of books; a dozen boxes of them
wait to be unpacked (he is re-modeling). Fitzgerald titles rest on the shelves,
among books by and about hard, pragmatic men, as well as numerous sports
titles. Artifacts from the ancient world hang on his walls. A replica of his
boyhood radio occupies a prominent place, as does the Liberty microphone
he used. His Yale diploma and his numerous awards are somewhere else,
perhaps stored next door with the 180 Persian rugs. The one in the office
is the largest these Johnson County eyes have ever seen. "I don't have them
here for vanity's sake. Like everything else you see around here, they have
practical value. When inflation returns, the value of tangibles will go through
the roof." But you are not interested in tangibles; you are interested in
intangibles. You have come here for "superior things." You have come to
discuss baseball.

And he is willing to oblige, maybe even eager. There are few people
nowadays who can engage him in a conversation about baseball history, and
those who try may be using it as a pretext for something. His attenuated
body has known the burden of pretexts. He looks twenty pounds lighter
than his photographs show him in his broadcasting days. His clothes are
well worn, chosen for comfort. His shoes are limp and collapsed oxfords,
as thin as potato skins. You can tell there is no female in his life—he has
a cowlick. He wears his eccentricity like a uniform. He is very like a general
now, behind the lines, moving great battalions of stocks around, in the constant
war against the dusty privation of his Oklahoma boyhood.

He does not smile gratuitously. He is a Texas millionaire, not a celebrity
or politician. He works too hard, seems not to eat right, and smokes too
much. But he brightens up when you let him know you remember when
he was the Old Scotchman, that you know baseball history, the greats, of
course, but also the near-greats and even the footnote guys, like Van Lingle
Mungo, Willie (The Knucks) Ramsdell, and Harry (The Cat) Brecheen.

"In those days," you say, "baseball was a big part of our lives, more
so than even football is today. I've heard it said that, in 1941, DiMaggio's
hitting streak captured the front page and was what everybody was talking
about, as well as Ted Williams's .406 season. And I remember vividly how
my high school would dismiss classes so we could watch the World Series."

"We don't have the announcers!" he says. "There is nobody today who
would be good enough for me to hire as a relief man. Vin Scully is one
of the best we have, but he would have been third string in my day. No,
they just don't see the drama that's unfolding out there on the field. That's
the main thing. And they have no sense of the history of the game. I heard
an announcer say not too long ago that he wonders who Hal Chase was.
Well, I can assure him that there were a lot of listeners who remembered
Hal Chase as a very fine but outlaw infielder from 1905 to 1920. It was a
terrible boner."

"I learned from Ted Husing and Red Barber. Ted was probably the greatest of his day, although he seemed to prefer football. It is said that I was better than anyone at baseball; if so I owe it to those two. Red (who's 80 now but still intellectually active) took me into the pressbox after the war and helped me get started. Ted was my boyhood idol, and I gave him a job with Liberty near the end of my life"—he actually said *life*—"near the end of my *career*," he went on, "when he was down on his luck."

Nothing could be gained by calling attention to this astounding subliminal revelation. Instead, you say, "How do you compare yourself to Husing as a broadcaster?" He reaches into a drawer containing hundreds of tapes, rattles them around like someone shuffling dominoes and, finding the one he wants, loads it into a small player.

"This is Ted," he says, "calling a football game." The voice is serious, authoritative—like the Voice of RKO Pathe News.

"It wasn't just his voice," he goes on, "he covered a game much like a good investigative reporter covers a story. He watched the teams practice, learned their basic strategies, even learned to identify the players by their gait. And he knew sports history. Again, most announcers today don't, and it goes without saying that the players don't. Read a book called *The Glory of Their Times* by Lawrence Ritter; it will show you that the old-time players knew baseball history. Baseball was their life in those days, but today—well, you know how it is today.

"You know," he goes on, "I had an odd but very definite advantage over Husing and Barber and Stern, and the rest, and that advantage was this: I had never, in those early days, ever seen a major league game, had never even met a major league ball player. I was just an East Texas boy with a big imagination, and that imagination enabled me to become the best there was at *re-creation.*. During those early years my father and I owned KLIF, which consisted of a small basement office in the Cliff Towers Building, and we had a guy stationed on top of a building across from the stadium where the game was being played. He would teletype the basic action to me, and I would re-create the game, play by play, as if I were there in the park. All I needed was 'grounded out to third, flied out to left, etc.,' and I filled everything else in. For crowd noise, we had a recording, and for hits, we whacked a baseball bat with a pencil. All I needed was that first cue and it triggered a motion picture in my head, and I could see everything that was happening on the field and in the stands. I only had to watch it unfold. It was a gift."

"And the way it was an advantage," he goes on, "was that since I had never seen a game or a player, I had built the players up in my mind as being larger than life, giants that no human being could ever live up to. So my romantic illusions came through in my broadcasts, embellished them, admittedly, but never inaccurately. Most of my listeners never knew the difference."

Willie Morris did. In his Pulitzer-Prize-winning book, *North Toward Home*, he includes an anecdote about a "short-wave prophet" in his home town of Yazoo, Mississippi. Listen to Willie:

> By two o'clock almost every radio in town was tuned in to the Old Scotchman. His
> rhetoric dominated the place. It hovered in the branches of the trees, bounced off
> the hills, and it came out of the darkened stores. . . . He had a deep, rich voice.
> His games were rare and remarkable entities; casual pop flies had the flow of history
> behind them, double plays resembled the stark clashes of old armies, and home runs
> deserved acknowledgement on earthen urns. Later, when I came across Thomas Wolfe,
> I felt I had heard him before, from Shibe Park, Crosley Field, or the Yankee Stadium.

Well, as Willie goes on to tell it, he was fiddling around one day with his new short-wave receiver when he came across the baseball game from New York. It was the eighth inning. Switching over to A.M., he tuned in the Old Scotchman. It was the same game, only he was describing the action in the fourth inning. Back to the live game—Carl Furillo pops out to short-stop, Hodges grounds out to second, and Campanella lines out to center to end the game. Back to the Old Scotchman and his account of the rest of the game. In the final inning, Willie is astonishd to hear Furillo pop out to short, Hodges ground out to second, and Campy line out to center to end the game! Although the action was the same, the Old Scotchman's account was livelier and more poetic, Willie says, and the crack of the bat and the roar of the crowd more pronounced. And the Old Scotchman reported things the other announcer "left out"—scuffles breaking out on the field, a kid licking an ice cream in the stands, the umpire's punitive glare. "When Robinson stole second base on short wave, he did it without sliding and without even drawing a throw," Willie says, "while for Mississippians, the feat was performed in a cloud of angry, petulant dust."

After the game he looked up "re-creation," a word the Old Scotchman had used at the end of his broadcast. His dictionary defined it as, "To invest with fresh vigor and strength."

Well, as the story goes on, Willie describes how he became a prophet in town, with his ability to predict the outcome of the ball games, even down to the exact plays. The Morris boy was the talk of Yazoo for awhile.

What about Mondays, when the teams were traveling and there were no games? Al Helfer's pressbox was "darker than the inside of a hog," to borrow a McLendonism.[1] Well, it didn't stop the Old Scotchman. He simply reached

---

[1] His colorful expressions were not only rural in origin but military and literary. Others include:
> "This game is tighter than seven sardines in a size six can."
> "Big siege gun in the arsenal"
> "Returning from the death agony"
> "The sacks are saturated with Chisox"
> "Back from the pale"
> "He's big enough to go bear-hunting with a buggy switch"
> "Serving the death warrant"
> "Fighting the final summons"

back into his stacks of old copies of the *Sporting News* and pulled out the play-by-play of the game of his choice from any in history. He brought you to the ball park where Gabby Hartnett hit his game-winning home run in the dark, or to the one where Johnny Vander Meer pitched his second no-hit game in a row, June 15, 1938, or to the double no-hit game between Fred Toney and Hippo Vaughn, May 2, 1917. You remember these and other special games of the past. The Old Scotchman, along with Wise, Wells, and Doggett, described the exploits of these great ghosts, down to the sag of their uniforms and the brand of tobacco they chewed. The way the fans dressed, the way the stadium looked, the weather that day, the umpire's histrionics, anecdotes about the players—all designed to provide a versimilitude that was based on equal parts of research and fancy. It was very realistic.

"On one occasion it worked too well," says McLendon with a chuckle. "Fred Toney had been out of baseball for years and hadn't kept up with the game since he retired. One day he was dialing the radio on his car and came across our game. He would ordinarily have switched it off but this time he heard his name mentioned. He was pitching! It scared him so badly that he thought he was going crazy, and he drove his car off into the ditch and wrecked it. We heard about it and felt the least we could do was to pay for his car to be repaired."

McLendon didn't originate re-creations, but he was the first to add sound effects and color. In addition to taped crowd noise and simulated hits, he hit a pillow with a drum stick to create the sound of a ball popping into the catcher's mitt. "Eventually, we got it down to a fine art," he says. "For example, when we did a game taking place in Brooklyn, what our audience heard in the background was actually Ebbets Field fans. We had sent a sound man around to all the ball parks to record the crowd noises. Even the hecklers at Fenway Park had Boston accents."

Often, nature and technology failed to cooperate, and it became necessary to extemporize and ad lib. When the Western Union service broke down, it would be a game delay due to "a dog running onto the field," or a "fight breaking out in the stands," or "the manager making a slow, interrupted stroll to the mound where a prolonged discussion occurred," or the batter fouling off dozens of pitches. (One former announcer named Dutch Reagan once said he had a batter fouling off forty pitches while the teletype was down—an intriguing analogy for his presidential technique.) But the all time champion for creative thinking has to be the late Bob Kelley, a re-creator from L.A.,

---

"Showing a heart of oak"

"Bearding the lion in his den"

"They're hopping around like floorwalkers in Macy's basement."

"They're mad as a flock of pelicans with lockjaw"

"It's the home half of the hello frame"

"He grabs, gobbles, guns." (An infielder catches a grounder and throws the batter out.)

who did big league re-creations in the afternoon and Angels games at night. He had a habit of going next door to the bar for a few quick beers before the game. Once, his sidekick was late getting to the studio and was listening on his car radio. He heard Kelley say, "Folks, it's starting to rain here in Portland," and instinctively knew he was in trouble. Hurriedly parking and racing into the studio, he saw the reason for the delay and the source of the sound of rain sprinkling on the pressbox roof: the bladder-embattled announcer was doing his Gulliver imitation into a metal wastebasket.

The Old Scotchman occasionally ran into such an anatomical problem also, but he eventually ran into a problem much more serious—a legal clash with the major club owners that ended his baseball career in 1951, just four short years after it began.

In *The Iliad,* Andromache, wife of Hector, the noble leader of the Trojan army, tells him: "Hector, your own great strength will be your undoing." And so it often is with the prerogatived. Their great gift lacks a tempering balance and it becomes the source of their downfall. Ironically, the Old Scotchman lacked age; such a gift and such success had proved to be too much, too soon, for a young man still in his twenties. He took on the club owners and all their might and money and they cleaned his plow. Like Icarus, that tragic boy of old, he fell from a great height; but unlike Icarus, he fell because he was *obedient* to his father:

> *Sing, Muse, of that honey-throated boy, the youth with Midas's tongue, whose every word he uttered turned to gold. Sing of the Empire of Words he built and how he fell, toppled by the sixteen Logophobes, rulers of the Empire of Diamonds. . . .*

> *And his father, seeing his son's great gift,*
> *Financed his flight to divers and myriad markets,*
> *Winging his way on words, bearing loads of dreams*
> *To luckless, toiling mortals Here, There,*
> *And Everywhere. Countless tales of wonder*
> *He wove of heroes of the Empire of Diamonds,*
> *How they struggled to capture bases.*
> *How with pluck and luck and bright bold power*
> *They fought their way from birth to death and back*
> *To life again, forever 'round the Cosmic Ring.*
> *To First, to Second, to Third, and finally*
> *Back to Home.*

> *How the rival Networks greatly feared him!*
> *How the Logophobes fought to stifle*
> *Gordon and his growing Empire of Words!*
> *They called a council of the Sixteen*
> *And decreed that Gordon must go.*
> *Like the great shortstop who dashes left and right*

Hauling in ground balls and hard line drives,
Dealing the foe a deadly blow
That sends them hunkering, fruitless,
Back to their bench, so did Golden Throat
Plunder with words rival Networks' sponsors
And loosen their ties with the Empire of Diamonds.

The Logophobes uncovered an unknown law,
A law forbidding him
To wing his words to divers and myriad markets
Of rival Networks without consent.
So Gordon to his father said, "What to do in '52?
You have practiced before the bar."
"Sue the Logophobes!" his father said.
"They violate the Clayton Anti-Trust Decree!"
And so it was that Golden Throat, un-Icarus-like
Obeyed his father's wish and filed the suit,
Fighting the forces of his fearsome foes.
The battle he won, for the law was on his side,
But his Empire of Words was rent and scattered
Asunder, his name forever after non grata.
Such was their burial of Gordon and his Empire of Words.

"I don't blame my father," he says, pensively. "Legally, it was good advice. The sixteen club-owners were a monopoly and were therefore in violation of anti-trust laws, but if I could do it over again, I would just disband the network and blast them verbally. We won a settlement of $250,000, but most of it went to the expense of dissembling the network. It was just nuisance money.

"I guess I would still be in the announcer's booth had it not been for that suit. It ruined my career. I was blackballed—and still am. There have been times when I would have enjoyed doing a guest spot, say when the Rangers were playing Minnesota. But don't you know that Clark Griffith's son, who now owns the Twins, remembers very well the law suit I brought against his father? No, my baseball career is over, and has been for these 33 years."

Perhaps most members of our materialistic society would be bewildered at his regrets, this powerful man whose real estate holdings are immense, this movie producer whose films always make him a profit, this overlord of tangible goods, this author of eight books, this Orson Welles of Radio, this wealthiest of men whose millions lie somewhere within the 200-600 range.

You suspect his accumulation of wealth has been motivated by these regrets for, in our culture, getting richer than one's adversaries is the ultimate revenge. But, he says he has enjoyed his second career and has plans to keep active. He has six or seven films in the hopper to shoot over the next four years—

a Fitzgerald short story, an adaptation of Ayn Rand's *Atlas Shrugged*, a re-make of a thirties romance, a couple of the matinee genre, and a Tom Sawyer adventure, which he wrote himself.

But then again, perhaps his place on the *Fortune 400* list was inevitable. The Depression left him with a profound sense of the random and uselessly cruel caprice of fate. "My father was a proud man," he says, "but I saw him so desperate in 1933, that he actually asked a man for gas money after he had given him a ride into town. You have read *The Grapes of Wrath*. That book was so true. Oh, the desperation of it. The desperation."

He is momentarily oppressed by the sudden tyranny of the palest abstraction of memory. He gazes distantly. What does the Old Scotchman see with those squinting, volcanic eyes, stinging with the flying dust of blown-away Oklahoma farm land? Does he see the ghost of baseball past, endless streams of all-star teams, flying by a Cliff Towers imaginary press box on 180 Depression-proof Persian rugs, driven by the magical power of Bobby Thomson's century-splitting line-drive home run?

Or is he simply surveying his bull pen and dugout, making sure they are loaded with big-siege guns for the final do-or-die showdown in the bottom of the ninth? "It's always two out in the bottom of the ninth," he might say, "and you can't ever have too many Thomsons in the dugout."

Not a bad idea. But, then again, when you consider that Don Larson ruined his life that day he had his ducks all in a row and pitched that perfect game in the World Series, when you consider that, when you consider that, then you might as well be Ralph Branca.

PART III

Knowing Sport —
Analysis or Experience?

6

Introduction: Knowing Sport— Analysis or Experience?

David Vanderwerken

WHILE PHILOSOPHERS CONTINUE TO DEBATE whether sport is a form of art, creative writers would seem to have settled the matter for themselves. Robert Wallace flat out calls a double play a poem. Richard Francis claims that a junkball pitcher is nothing less than a modernist poet. Marianne Moore argues that playing baseball and playing language are equivalent activities. Of course, American writers are notoriously unphilosophic, their imaginative energies intuitively heading for where the action is, where life is most intense, where human possiblility—in all its splendor and folly—is most open. No wonder, then, that so many language players are drawn to the stadium. It's a natural. Maybe this is what Norman Mailer meant when he said that American writers see themselves as athletes.

However, if poets tend to be untroubled by the question of sport as art, a considerable batch of philosophers are troubled, as the pages of *The Journal of the Philosophy of Sport* and *The Journal of Aesthetic Education* yearly attest. On one side stands David Best, who has remained consistent in his conviction that context determines definition, that a theater is just not a football field, and anyone who would link the two aesthetically is not thinking well. Sport has its intrinsic glories, Best argues, and needs no gilding from art. On the other side of this scrimmage line stands Spencer K. Wertz, who maintains that intention, not context, is the key to definition. For Wertz, intention and aesthetic control over one's medium—the body and the immediate environment—lead to artistic creativity, whether the context is a stage or an ice rink, whether the performer is Baryshnikov or Julius Erving. Even those thinkers who agree that sport is art are troubled by a further question: what is "knowing" in sport? In other words, how do we identify the qualities of the sport experience? Roughly speaking, philosophers break into two squads on this issue, those who look at the athlete's knowing externally, intellectually, analytically as opposed to those who go at the problem subjectively and phenomenologically. Paul Kuntz represents the analytic tradition while Drew

Hyland has written trenchantly about the athlete's experience from a phenomenological viewpoint.

Unlike philosophers, who write from disciplined "traditions," literary critics are a bit more eclectic and syncretic. Whatever illuminates texts is fair game. The pieces that follow reflect great variety in methodology, approach, underpinnings, and borrowings. While perhaps less rigorous than philosophical discourse, writing on literature—as the following essays testify—can be playful and a whole lot of fun. These critics understand that we are never more serious than when we are playing.

Seymour Kleinman's "The Athlete as Performing Artist: The Embodiment of Sport Literature and Philosophy" draws together the issues raised in the foregoing remarks by proposing that athletic performance be viewed as "operative art" and that a "phenomenology of the body" is an appropriate path to follow in discovering what constitutes athletic knowing. Kleinman supports his contentions with shrewd references to sport-centered texts. Certainly, gifted athletes who have become creative writers—Peter Gent, James Dickey, Tom Meschery—have revealed to us, as Kleinman notes, "dimensions of the athlete and activity which 'outsiders' find almost impossible to discover in any other way."

If the experience of Peter Gent's Phil Elliott in *North Dallas Forty* is tragic, may not the underlying mythos of football itself be tragedy? This is one of the provocative claims of "A Myth for All Seasons: Sport as Romance." Looking at our major team sports—basketball, football, baseball—as "texts," Stephen Mosher applies Northrop Frye's theory of myths and modes to them with penetrating results. The winter season and the game of basketball both reflect the mythos of irony. The ironic nature of basketball can be discerned through the clock, the court, and fouls. Similarly, the spring and summer game, baseball, offers the mythoi of romance and comedy. Finally, the "central unifying myth that brings all sport together" is a romantic one that celebrates life. Mosher has given us a helpful schema for fixing sport-centered literature against the backdrop of Frye's all-inclusive model.

Perhaps even more brilliantly useful in giving pattern to sport-centered literature is Christian Messenger's "A Structural Semantics for Sports Fiction," destined to become one of the seminal studies in the sub-discipline of sport literature. Using A. J. Greimas' "semiotic rectangle," Messenger positions the terms "Individual Heroism," "Collective Heroism," "Anti-Heroism," and "Play" on his quadrants and examines the dynamics and movements of a great number of fictional protagonists around, through, and across his rectangle. No brief digest can do justice to the complexity and care of Messenger's analysis.

George Leonard says that dance exists within the game. To extend Leonard, I submit that all three of the following pieces dance as well.

7

The Athlete as Performing Artist: The Embodiment of Sport Literature and Philosophy

Seymour Kleinman

"It is the law of my own voice I shall investigate."[1] This phrase is the title of an essay which appeared in a volume dealing with contemporary literature. The essay itself has nothing to do with the topic at hand, but this title struck me as an effective and powerful way of identifying the personal nature of experience, particularly the athletic experience. In fact, I find it even more appropriate to change the phrase to read: It is the law of my own *movement* I shall investigate.

As stated, it suggests a means of "getting at" the phenomenon of athletic performance. That is, it establishes, at the outset, the personal nature of experience and affirms and endorses the validity of seeking and adhering to the internal law residing in all of us. This law has been called "self expression," but I believe it goes deeper and implies more than this. It incorporates our desire to come to know and understand ourselves and our attempts to accomplish this through the variety of expressive activities in which we choose to become engaged. This "law of my own movement" implies the possibility of access to self-awareness and self-knowledge in and through the body. I contend that a phenomonology of the body is as appropriate a path to follow for exploring and penetrating the nature of our being as is a phenomenology of mind.

Phenomenology has been called a radical empiricism because it treats sensory experience in a new way. That is, it recognizes the subjective nature of experience and accepts it as a valid, relevant and essential ingredient of the "knowing" process. From this perspective, coming to know sport is much like coming to know ourselves. But this presents some serious difficulties

---

[1] Frank M. Magill, *Contemporary Literary Scene II* (Englewood Cliffs, New Jersey: Salem Press, 1979), p. 59.

for scholars and academics. The experiential and subjective nature of the process makes us rely on the descriptive, the intuitive and non-verbal devices and techniques which make intellectuals very uncomfortable because it calls into question the validity of public knowledge as the only path to truth.

However this private, subjective dimension cannot be ignored. Donald Westlake provides a wonderful illustration of the personal and subjective nature of knowledge in his novel *Kahawa.* The quote has little to do with sport but it has everything to do with *knowing.*

> In many African tribes, when a male child is born, he is not given his true name. This is done to confuse the spirits of death. Should the child survive his first years . . . he is given his permanent name. But even this is not his *real* name. That he selects for himself at puberty, and will probably never tell anyone. Thus, the African travels under an alias at all times, secure in the knowledge that *nobody knows who he really is*[2]

The law of my own movement necessitates a conception of the body-as-subject and a rejection of mind-body dichotomy not only in theory, but in practice. This constitutes a radical departure from traditional conceptions of the human being. For this we are indebted, not only to pragmatists, existential and phenomenological philosophers but to the practicing artists who, through the ages, have insisted on investigating the law of their own voices and movement.

For example, phenomenology and literature seem to come together when writers focus on sport and the body. Alan Guttmann's recent essay on sport in French literature of the 1920s provides an illustration. Guttmann says:

> Reacting against the French intellectual tradition which had for centuries elevated mind above body, writer after writer penned ecstatic descriptions of the "splendidly sculpted allure of . . . young bodies. . . . " Maurice Genevoix wrote a whole series of tributes to embodied perfection. (Andre Obey described a race as "intoxicating. intoxicating, intoxicating sensation of calling upon oneself and feeling oneself respond . . .!")[3]

This "law of my own movement" phrase also has prompted me to examine the relationship which exists between movement as it is expressed in and through sport, and the performing arts. I think most of us will agree that the body as a means of expression is involved in almost all of our acts. And when thought and intelligence impart intentional direction to events resulting in "meanings capable of immediate possession and enjoyment" this becomes what Dewey calls "operative art."[4]

---

[2] Donald E. Westlake, *Kahawa* (New York: The Viking Press. 1981), pp. 196-197.

[3] Alan Guttmann, "Le Plaisir du Sport," *Arete* 1:1 (Fall 1983): 115-116.

[4] John Dewey, *Experience and Nature* (New York: Dover Publications, Inc., 1958), p. 358.

I propose that athletic performance be viewed in this light, as a form of operative art. Also, I suggest that athletes play the game for subtle and more sophisticated reasons than heretofore supposed. And, it is this "law of my own voice and my own movement" which reveals to us this personal element of intention and expression. But it is a non-verbal law and therefore difficult to communicate. Yet graphic descriptions by writers and athletic performers themselves are becoming more commonplace as various segments of the academic and literary world begin to recognize the dimensions and sophistication of sport and athletic performance.

I think we have recognized for some time now that the arbitrary separation of the mind from the body, the artistic from the intellectual, has created more problems than it resolves. For the Greeks, the artist was an "artisan" and the artisan occupied an inferior position in their society. The enjoyment of art "did not stand upon the same level as enjoyment (and engagement) in rational thought and contemplative insight.[5]

The product of an artist was something that stemmed from and resulted in a thing of the body. The object of rational thought, however, was a result of the work of the mind and was regarded as having infinitely greater value. The use of rational powers was a function of mind and this was held to be the only path to truth and ultimate reality.

But the Greeks, at least, were consistent in their view. They espoused and practiced a dualism and they established an order, putting people and their pursuits in their "proper" places. Needless to say artists were not part of the upper strata of that society.

In our society today, although we claim, in theory, to reject a dualistic conception of the person (that is, we value ideas *and* objects, contemplation *and* creation), we continue the practice of treating minds and bodies as separate and distinct entities. This discrepancy between theory and practice has created a good deal of confusion. Although we don't know quite what to make of artists, we accept the work of art as valid and important. In fact intellectuals, for the most part, regard the arts as a means of providing access into the world every bit as much as the sciences.

Yet what falls within the realm of the arts can be a hotly debated subject. Also confusion and ambivalence arise, in part, because the arts admit of no parameters. Arbitrary limits cannot be placed upon them. As soon as rules are established an artist will break them.[6] Also, there's nothing special or sacred about the particular form art takes, although there *are* some who would establish a hierarchy. Countless forms of art have come into existence because of the intention and ability of people to express themselves in

---

[5] Ibid., p. 356.

[6] Currently there is controversy raging about the work of artists (or vandals—choose your side) who paint (vandalize) the subway cars in New York. See the movie "Beat Street" for a dramatization of this conflict.

particular and specialized ways. These forms of expression gain recognition and acceptance by the society at large in greater or lesser degrees. As a result, art forms continually come into and pass out of existence.

A good deal has been written about sport and art and perhaps it is appropriate, at this point, to state briefly my own position on sports' potential to become art. David Best who has written extensively on sport and aesthetics contends that sport is incapable of being an art form because it does not "allow for the possibility of the artist's comment through his art on life situations."[7] I disagree. Sport indeed has the possibility to become an art form, but it is dependent on the intention of the athlete to act as artist. Best's stipulation that an art form must have "the possibility of concern with life situations" is too closed a concept. Even if we were to agree with this stipulation, Best's judgment that "skating, diving, trampolining and gymnastics does not have the possibility of expressing (the athlete's) view of life situations"[8] is entirely erroneous. He says that "it is difficult to imagine a gymnast who included in his sequence movements (an expression of) his view of war, or of love, or of any other such issue".[9] To me, this reveals his unfamiliarity and lack of sensitivity to the experience of the athlete. I offer in response a quote from a gymnast writing on Dewey's view of art and its relationship to athletic performance:

> The gymnast squeezes the rings as he lowers towards an iron cross, feels those hands as individual beings part of the mind, the body, and yet related to his Will. In his mind the image of those hands grow as large as that of his own head. Then his arms become known as they fight to stop downward motion. This individual knows and loves his body feelings as learned through countless encounters with it. While on those rings his Will and body feelings are united in existence. . . . Since body feelings are meanings, encountering those feelings can be viewed as an artist views lines and colors in nature. The body itself can be perceived as an accumulation of meaning rather than a bulk of physical and physiological process.[10]

Surely a description of this kind offers, if not the actuality, "at least the possibility of a close involvement with life situations."[11] Rather than attempting to pass judgment on what is or is not involvement with life situations, it is more sensible to seek out the intent of the creator or participant. In this case, the description clearly reveals that the athlete wishes to be viewed

---

[7] David Best, "The Aesthetic in Sport." In E. Gerber and W. Morgan, eds., *Sport and the Body*, 2nd edition. Philadelphia: Lee and Febiger, 1979.

[8] Ibid, p. 354.

[9] Ibid, p. 353.

[10] R. Mitchell, "A Conceptual Analysis of Art as Experience and Its Implications for Sport and Physical Education." (Ph.D. diss., 1974), p. 6.

[11] Best, p. 353.

as an artist. And the merit of the work may then be based on whatever artistic principles the viewer believes in.

Best also admits to the difficulty of dealing with abstract works of art, because it is hard to say whether or not a comment is being made on a life situation. In admitting this, he reveals the fallacy in his own position. Who is to say what is or is not a comment on a life situation? And must sport be so closed a concept that it cannot and does not provide a possibility for making a statement about things such as risk, failure, success, flight, fear, courage and countless other aspects of the human condition? So I want to emphasize again that it makes more sense to attend to the question of intent.

The prime requisite is that the athlete must begin to view him/herself as artist. Until this happens, sport and art merge infrequently, at best, and only in an accidental manner. Some athletes seem to become vaguely aware that they are coming close to crossing an indefinable boundary line at times, taking sport into the artistic dimension. But this seems to be happening so infrequently and sporadically that it becomes noticed only by its peculiarity. What is probably necessary for the athlete to view him/herself as an artist is a transformation in the way one views one's self. But this is a radical step and one which is not easily taken.

The only example of this nature which comes readily to mind is that of John Curry. In my view, he is providing a model which other athletes may wish to follow. He has clearly and publicly stated his intention to be an artist. In addition, he insists that his performances be viewed in that light. He is drawing on other art forms, notably dance, in order to develop his own, and he is making demands that his audience view figure skating in another way. These objectives have not been easy to accomplish. Indeed, all of them have not yet been accomplished. But it is only through these measures that an art form comes into being.

American modern dance is a prime example of this. In its infancy, modern dance was looked upon as some sort of affectation and perversion of ballet, and thus, not worthy of being taken seriously. Over the years, however, through the insistence of modern dancers that they be regarded and treated as artists, this attitude has changed. It will take the same kind of dedication and commitment on the part of athletes if it is their intention to have sport come to be regarded as art. I see some signs of this, but not many. What must happen also, as a necessary condition for this transformation, is to effect a change in the expectation and vision of audiences.[12]

I suggest, at present, that sport is in a state of "becoming" and there is increasing evidence indicating that this society is beginning to accept the

---

[12] For a more comprehensive exposition of the argument see the author's essay "Art, Sport, and Intention," *Proceedings of the National Association for Physical Education in Higher Education* (NAPEHE), 1980. Also it's obvious that Spencer Wertz and I have been thinking along the same lines. See his essay, "Context and Intention in Sport," *Southwest Philosophical Studies* 8 (April 1984): 144-147.

possibility of athletic performance as an art form. I am convinced that a major reason for this is the growing interest and attention being given to sport by the intelligentsia. Within the last two decades academics have formed at least a dozen scholarly societies devoted to the study of sport through a variety of disciplines. These include history, philosophy, psychology, sociology, anthropology, physiology and medicine. And recently we've witnessed the creation of the Sport Literature Association. As further evidence of sports' movement towards academic respectability, a few years ago my own university awarded honorary *Doctor of Athletic Arts* degrees to Jack Nicklaus and Jesse Owens, two of our most illustrious athletic performers who matriculated but never graduated.

But it is the area of sport literature that I find particularly intriguing because it contributes material which stimulates us to consider sports' artistic possibilities. I wish to identify and comment on some things I have found in the literature which helped me gain some insight and support for this notion of athletic performance as art. First a short scholarly analysis:

In his essay, "Plays about Play," Kevin Kerrane notes the abstract similarity between sport and drama as two forms of play. He says sport and theater have in common:

1. live physical action,
2. a special ordering of space and time,
3. pageantry and spectacle,
4. a context of rules, rituals and performance conventions,
5. suspense and irony generated by conflict, crisis and reversal,
6. arrival at a clear outcome.

He cites some differences:

1. the athlete engages in no impersonation and,
2. sports events are unscripted and unrehearsed. [13]

Both of these are debatable. It may be argued that when anyone assumes a performing role they show a different dimension of themselves. That is, they play a part which is separate and distinct from the ordinary. In this sense the performing athlete does engage in a kind of "impersonation."

Perhaps the role of the athlete is more comparable to that of the dancer, a performer engaged in a choreographed event. Sporting events are indeed rehearsed and although the outcome may be unpredictable, there is most certainly a "script." An open-ended one to be sure, but one which is rehearsed to exhaustion. Athletic performance may be regarded as a combination of rigorously rehearsed activity with improvisation, and both of these are in evidence in almost every theatrical form.

---

[13] Kevin Kerrane, "Plays about Play" in Frank Magill, ed., *Contemporary Literary Scene* (Englewood Cliffs, N.J.: Salem Press, 1979) p. 137.

Kerrane goes on to point out that this dividing line between sport and drama is not always clear. "Sports dramatists have shown that fields and courts, rings and rinks are also stages for acting out our deepest conflicts and beliefs."[14] Serious writers and dramatists, as well as scholars, have demonstrated their interest in sport. Kerrane continues:

> Over the last ten years . . . a new kind of sports play has come of age substituting metaphor for melodrama and thoughtful comedy for vaudeville gags, using spectacle categorically and treating fantasy ironically. The contemporary play deals seriously with serious issues.[15]

I think this has come about because writers have come to recognize, at last, that the realm of sport and the world of the athlete incorporate all of the elements we look for and find in art. A more direct example from creative literature is when Donald Honig's major character Allie Branden in the *The Last Great Season* says:

> The theater is art. It's fine and beautiful and sometimes uplifting. But God-damn it, there's an animal quality out at the ball park. The unexpected. You can't afford one single God-damn mistake, otherwise you are in danger of having the whole thing come down around you. In the theater, there's only Opening Night; in baseball, there's every day. That makes it exciting.[16]

This "animal quality and excitement" of baseball doesn't remove it from the realm of art. In fact, Honig almost seems to be saying that it's a higher form of art. Later in the book, Honig seems to move even closer to viewing the athlete as artist. He has difficulty explaining this fascinating quality of sport but compares it once again to artistic performance. Todd McNeil, a sports writer in the novel, is trying to explain his obsession to his girlfriend.

> It's like when we're listening to Lilly Pons on your victrola and you're trying to explain the fine points of what she's doing. I appreciate all of her vocal qualities. But not the same way you do.
> Listening to Lilly Pons is a cultural experience, she said. I'm comparing reactions— yours to Lilly Pons and mine to Buddy Lockridge. Watch Buddy. Watch him go after the ball—he runs towards a concrete wall like its made of balsa wood. Watch him come around second and slide into third—the third baseman has to be careful of getting killed.
> But he's paid to do that, she said.
> Nancy . . . believe me, money has nothing to do with it. There's an intangible in there that's beyond explanation. I'll put it this way; if I could write as well as Buddy Lockridge plays ball, I'd be Shakespeare"[17]

---

[14] Ibid.

[15] Ibid.

[16] Donald Honig, *The Last Great Season* (New York: Simon and Shuster, 1979), p. 16.

[17] Ibid, p. 127.

While he doesn't explicitly state it, it is obvious that Honig regards the athlete as artist, and it is this capacity to do so which provides hope and justification for the proposition. The recognition of sport as art becomes simply an act of affirmation.

Let me offer one more example as an argument from analogy. Samuel Lipman in a recent article in *Commentary*, "Bartok At The Piano," draws the distinction between a composer and a performer. In doing so he defines the role of the performer. I leave it to you to draw the parallel between the musical artist Lipman describes and the athlete artist I am talking about:

> In its written state . . . a musical composition still requires decoding by a performer. When a performer accomplishes this decoding well, when he is able to select identifiable elements . . . and communicate them, he is said to have a *conception*, and to be an artist; if a performer takes these elements from his own gifts rather than from the work of art he is interpreting, he is said to have a *style*, and to be a star . . . In the case of the star (the performer has) managed to substitute himself for the work altogether.[18]

I think all of this indicates not only that the performing athlete and the performing artist may be one and the same, but that we are closer to accepting this fact than we realize. The following statements give an indication of this.

In the first issue of *Arete*, Michael Oriard remarks that "what [professional football players] do is physical, but it is surely as much art as it is labor."[19] From *USA Today*, July 23, 1984: "Ice skating will be elevated to a new artistic level when The John Curry Skating Company glides on to the ice at the Metropolitan Opera House Tuesday night." The headline of this story read: "Skating Dances Into Art Form Status."[20] Finally, the U.S. Olympic women's volleyball coach, Arie Selinger was quoted the other day as saying, "If we don't win the gold, at least they can be artists."[21]

Well, what's to be made of all this? First of all I think this exercise has served to confirm that a case can be made for the respectability of athletic performance as a legitimate field of endeavor. In spite of Eric Solomon's lament in a recent issue of *Arete* that nice Jewish boys don't become athletes, perhaps we can reassure their parents that they are really artists. (Although, "My son, the athletic artist", still doesn't ring as well as "My son, the doctor.")

---

[18] Samuel Lipman, "Bartok At The Piano," *Commentary* 77 (May 1984): 58.

[19] Michael Oriard, "On the Current Status of Sports Fiction," *Arete*, 1:1 (Fall 1983): 9.

[20] Enid Slack, "Skating Dances into Art Form," *USA Today*, 23 July, 1984 .

[21] Daily Camera (Boulder, Colo.), 24 July, 1984.

Secondly, it has reaffirmed my conviction that sport literature does indeed have a function. It serves to reveal dimensions of the athlete and activity which "outsiders" find almost impossible to discover in any other way. Good writers (artists) have insights about the nature of people and events and because of this we become the beneficiaries.

Finally, it has moved me to offer a proposal which I outlined in a letter to my university president recently. It's something which would have sounded bizarre just a few years ago, but the response I received was encouraging and I think its an idea whose "time has come." Here are some excerpts from that letter:

> What is necessary is a re-visioning of college athletics recognizing its study and practice as a performing art. Sport when performed at its highest level is as sophisticated, creative, and aesthetically redeeming as any of the other art forms. At present most colleges and universities have provided homes and programs for the student and teacher of music, drama, and dance. Degrees ranging from the Bachelor of Arts to the Ph.D. are granted to the aspiring musician, dancer and actor. No one questions the appropriateness or the legitimacy of ballet or modern dance technique, deemed essential to the development of the dancer. In fact it is *athletic ability* which constitutes the core of the performing arts.

The university and the gifted athlete have maintained, from the outset, a tenuous and uncomfortable relationship. Now it has reached a stage that promises to be destructive to both. What must be done to reverse this unhealthy state of affairs?

To begin with, the university should provide the athlete, who is so inclined, with the opportunity to pursue an academic course of study in Athletic Performance. In addition to the usual general education requirements in the arts and sciences, such a curriculum would include intensive work, on an increasingly sophisticated level, in theory and technique, much in the way a piano or violin student progresses.

The coaches, of course, would constitute the nucleus of the Athletic Performance faculty. The place of the coach in the university has been a source of discomfort amongst academics for a long time. In this plan the coach is recognized as a bona-fide faculty member with all the rights and responsibilities it entails. He or she would be subject to tenure review in accordance with the university's standards in the traditional categories of teaching, research and service.

In effect, the coach is both choreographer and conductor. As a professor of athletic arts he or she plays a role analogous to the conductor of the University Symphony or director of the University Dance Company.

The course of study which the Athletic Performance major would pursue is by no means an easy one. It is for the gifted student who is serious about studying to become best at what he or she is good at. It provides an avenue for the prospective performer rather than forcing a reluctant athlete into a contrived curriculum often designed to maintain eligibility.

I believe an approach like this may prove useful in resolving the problems plaguing big-time college sport. It is rather sad and a bit ironic to note that two of our former students are among the most illustrious in all of sport, yet they didn't graduate. I don't know whether or not they would have chosen to major in Athletic Performance but several years ago we did acknowledge them by awarding honorary *Doctor of Athletic Arts* degrees to Jack Nicklaus and Jesse Owens.

8

A Myth for All Seasons: Sport as Romance

Stephen David Mosher

IN THE WESTERN WORLD, the major contributing factor to the development of a "sport aesthetic" is not the active participation in sport, but passive consumption of sport as media. Our society forms its aesthetic ideas about sport through familiarity with theater and literature rather than with painting, sculpture, dance, music, architecture or other art forms. I believe this is because the "language" of theater and literature is composed of easily used and understood components—words and representative pictures—whereas the components of the "language" of other art forms are such abstract and difficult concepts as rhythm, color, depth, sound, and illusion. If sport may be called art, it is popular art that is "played" to the masses as *theater* and "speaks" to them through media as *literature*. I maintain that the aesthetic function of sport is the telling of a story. It is my aim in this essay to present a paradigm for sport criticism and offer evidence gathered from the sport experience itself to support and lead to an acceptance of it.

Recently, sport literature has become the subject of study for many scholars,[1] but none have devoted significant attention to what I believe is the most powerful and enticing theory of literature—that which is formulated by Northrop Frye in his classic work *Anatomy of Criticism*. Frye's system is based on the understanding that human existence depends on the dialectical yet cyclical nature of all existence. This synoptic view of human existence holds that all human activities change as nature changes. The most obvious changes of nature are its seasons; and Frye notices what seems to be an obvious

---

[1] See Wiley Lee Umphlett, *The Sporting Myth and the American Experience* (Lewisburg, Pennsylvania: Bucknell University Press, 1975); Neil David Berman, *Playful Fictions and Fictional Players* (Port Washington, New York: Kennikat Press, 1981); Robert J. Higgs, *Laurel and Thorn: The Athlete in American Literature* (Lexington, Kentucky: The University Press of Kentucky, 1981); Christian K. Messenger, *Sport and the Spirit of Play in American Fiction: Hawthorne to Faulkner* (New York: Columbia University Press, 1981); and Michael Oriard, *Dreaming of Heroes: American Sports Fiction, 1868-1980* (Chicago: Nelson Hall, 1982).

correlation between the seasons and the *mythoi* (plot structures) of literature. It is not important that there are four of each (a child notices that), but that each *mythos* of literature is suited to its own season; and that as the seasons change so do the modes of literature. Comedy is the *mythos* of spring, romance is the *mythos* of summer, tragedy is the *mythos* of autumn, and irony is the *mythos* of winter. As spring is considered the opposite of autumn, comedy is the other side of tragedy. As summer is considered the opposite of winter, romance is the other side of irony. As the seasons run into each other, comedy runs into romance, romance into tragedy, tragedy into irony, and irony back into comedy. In this manner the cycle begins and ends with the *mythos* of birth and the celebration of life.

Frye's paradigm, I feel, offers us an irresistible invitation to sport criticism. Contemporary American society has, without a doubt, the most highly developed array of spectator sports in the history of human civilization; yet there are only three spectator sports that exert any great influence on society's imagination. These sports—baseball, football, and basketball—are literally all that is necessary to complete the myth-telling function of sport. Just as the modes of literature are associated with specific seasons, so too are sports. Baseball is the game of spring and summer, football is the game of autumn, and basketball is the game of winter. No matter how much these sports run into each other's time, the influence of each sport's season and *mythos* remains powerful.

The appeal of sport as literature is its role as the drama for the masses—its popularity. Frye often associates archetypes and myths with popular literature: "In fact we could almost define popular literature, . . . as literature which affords an unobstructed view of archetypes."[2] The primary archetypal pattern is that of the seasons, and Frye maintains that the seasons are responsible for our myths, fairy tales, and legends. For Frye there are two distinct dimensions of archetypal imagery—*dianoia* (the static pattern or meaning) and *mythos* (the movement pattern or narrative).[3] It is in the *mythoi* of sport where its primary aesthetic appeal lies.

Frye offers the following summation of the themes of the four *mythoi*:

> The four *mythoi* that we are dealing with, comedy, romance, tragedy, and irony, may now be seen as four aspects of a central unifying myth. *Agon* or conflict is the basis or archetypal theme of romance, the radical or romance being a sequence of marvelous adventures. *Pathos* or catastrophe, whether in triumph or defeat, is the archetypal theme of tragedy. *Sparagmos*, or the sense that heroism and effective action are absent, disorganized or foredoomed to defeat, and that confusion and anarchy reign over the world, is the archetypal theme of irony and satire. *Anagnorisis*, or recognition of a newborn society rising in triumph around a still somewhat mysterious hero and his bride, is the archetypal theme of comedy.[4]

[2] Northrop Frye, *Anatomy of Criticism: Four Essays* (Princeton, New Jersey: Princeton University Press, 1957), p. 116.

[3] Ibid, p. 77.

[4] Ibid, p. 192.

Finally, it is the quest-myth that forms the central unifying theme of sport's narrative and, ultimately, its powerful grip on us. A closer examination of each archetypal category, using examples from the corresponding sport will build a critical house that offers a view that clarifies sport's function. As Frye says, "To use words, for any other purpose than straight description or command, is a form of *homo ludens.* But there are two forms of play, the contest and the construct."[5] Armed with the following diagram, I leave to others the *contest* and proceed to explore the *construct* of sport.

Adapted from Robert D. Denham, *Northrop Frye and Critical Method,* (University Park, The Pennsylvania State University Press, 1978) p. 68.

Basketball

A basketball game, like the White Rabbit in *Alice in Wonderland,* seems always to be late, always in a hurry to catch up with itself. Yet, most basketball observers endorse the posture that in order to see a basketball game all one has to do is catch the last two minutes. Basketball is truly a game of anarchy and confusion where heroism and effective action are doomed to defeat. Basketball is a game that is nothing less than an ironic exercise, and the theme of basketball, its essence, is *deception.* The combination of the facts that the actual skill required to score points is absurdly simple and that there is no substitute for height has made basketball a world populated by only three kinds of athletes—the exceptionally tall, the exceptionally deceptive,

---

[5] Northrop Frye, *The Stubborn Structure: Essays on Criticism and Society* (Ithaca, New York: Cornell University Press, 1972), p. 290.

and, most often, the exceptionally tall and deceptive. Basketball players seem, more often than not, to be caricatures. The normal person has no chance in this game. Also lending to the ironic mood of basketball is the fact that the rules of basketball were formalized less than a year after the game was invented, but hardly a season has passed without some radical change being required to keep the game from disintegrating into complete chaos. The chaos is avoided but the irony fostered by three basic elements—the clock, the court, and fouls.

The Clock.

People deeply involved with basketball are clock watchers who think not in terms of hours or minutes but seconds—three seconds, five seconds, ten seconds, twenty-four seconds, thirty seconds, forty-five seconds. Clocks are everywhere on the basketball court. The referee spends half his time slicing the air with his arm, measuring like a metronome the time left to the offense, for the clock in basketball forces teams to try to score.

Without a doubt the three-second and thirty-second (twenty-four seconds for professionals and forty-five seconds for male intercollegiates) rules are the major contributing factors to the mood of basketball. The three-second rule forbids an offensive player from loitering directly beneath the basket and using strength or force to score points. It encourages guile, cunning, and deception to the point of getting open under the basket for the easy lay-up. The thirty second rule requires the offense to attempt a shot at the basket within this brief time or give up possession of the ball. It encourages, indeed demands, that the game be played at a break-neck pace that renders meaningless individual goals. It is almost impossible to remember particulars about a basketball game. No matter how spectacular one shot is, there will be another one coming along in a few seconds. The clock sees to that.

The Court.

The lines that mark the floor of a basketball court would baffle the uninitiated with their complexity. There are straight lines, curved lines, circles, short lines, dotted lines, invisible lines, and, because basketball courts are often shared, irrelevant lines. While the jump circles have been enlarged and the three-second zone transformed from a "key" to a "lane" and the goal-tending cylinder and the three-point line introduced, the court has remained the standard fifty feet wide and ninety-four feet long and the basket has remained exactly ten feet above the floor and finally, the ball has remained the same size. The expansion of the three-second area and the introduction of the three-point line have both contributed greatly to alleviating the cramming underneath the basket but, rather than eliminating it, have served merely to relocate it (usually in the corners of the court). Failure is rewarded when an offense cannot penetrate and is forced to take the long three-point shot.

Luck is rewarded when the desperation shot at the buzzer goes in. All of this means, therefore, that the defense can play brilliantly and in the end give up three points rather than two. Only in basketball is an incompetent offense rewarded for its lack of skill. The forces of irony could not be more evident than in the game of basketball.

The fact that the limits of basketball space are barely out of the reach of normal people only serves to heighten the sense of irony. When the gymnasium is vacant, the players who can get above the rim but cannot palm the ball will find a volleyball and endeavor to "jam" it; and the player who cannot touch the rim or palm the ball will move to the eight-foot baskets at the elementary school court and pretend he is two feet taller. The world of irony creates such mad desires as these.

Fouls.

The free throw is unique in sports—an unmolested attempt at scoring points that can fail only as a result of poor marksmanship. It is fitting that the action which determines such a bizarre penalty as the free throw is an equally mystifying event. Fouls in basketball are unlike any other violations in other games. They not only occur with incredible frequency but, as often as not, are deliberately committed. There cannot be an act in sport more ironic than the "good foul" which is so lightly accepted by all involved with the game of basketball. In fact, if a basketball team uses its fouls wisely it can often force a poor free-throw shooter to the line and regain possession of the ball much more easily than by executing the difficult task of stealing the ball. Finally, a basketball team behind in the last few minutes of a game often will make no attempt to hide its purpose—foul to get the ball back— and quite often this task will work.[6]

Most basketball games, not just championship games, are determined at the foul line at the end of the game; and just one bad call (or non-call) by the referee can determine the outcome of the contest. The seemingly arbitrary and subjective pattern to the officials' actions stem from the fact that there are so many violations that could be called that the rhythm of the game would be destroyed if all of them were; and that the officials are reluctant to call all but the most egregious fouls in the last minutes of a game so as not to be accused of taking the game's destiny from the control of the players. The true problem facing the referee is that while the players are constantly faking each other out, the referee is expected to resist being deceived; in reality, the referee is even more susceptible to this deception because he must focus on five different player match-ups while, at the same

---

[6] In 1983, North Carolina State Univesity won the NCAA Basketball Championship by the "foul to get the ball back" method. The following year the so-called Valvano rule, which was intended to stop this practice, served only to increase deliberate fouling. The rule was abandoned mid-way through the 1983-84 season, the first time the author can recall such an occurrence.

time, watch for various other violations. Finally, even though everyone adheres to the adage that the fouls will even out during the course of the game, the truth is that they do not. In no other sport does the cry, "We wuz robbed," ring more true than in the ironic exercise called basketball. Basketball remains a sport all of us can practice (even alone) and develop adequate skills, but it is also a game more concerned with style than score. It is played best only by those very deceptive and very tall. It is fitting that basketball's final irony is that all of us want to play it *beautifully*, with style, and it drives us *crazy* that we can only sit and watch.

Football

If football is symbolic of modern American life, then we live lives that are tragic. Football players are, after all the armor has been stripped away, human; and their fate is, after all the games have been played, the same as ours. What makes the football player and his sport tragic is the grandeur and dignity with which the fate of *catastrophe* is faced. Football, therefore, does not represent modern life (real and ironic) but ideal life. Football actually is *heroic*; football actually does create *character*; and, most importantly, football actually provides a genuine *catharsis*, a violent catharsis that evokes the emotions of tragedy—fear and pity. It is also impossible to overlook the relationship football has with war. If the essence of contemporary life and basketball is deception, then the essence of war and football is *strategy*. Since strategy creates the mood of football, it can only be a tragic catastrophe when it turns out that the game is usually decided by something else. But what else can be expected? For, more than any other game, football is contested with an attitude of maintaining control at all costs. Football teams, rather than trying to win, most often try not to lose. Football's tragic atmosphere is created by the clock, the field, and *catharsis*.

If the clock in basketball is a metronome to dance to, and the clock in baseball stands still, then the clock in football can only be the enemy. The clock is always a force in football. It stops frequently, but not as often as the basketball clock; and yet, it attracts our attention most often when it is running—running out. We cannot help but watch the football clock because during most of the game nothing happens. A typical football game will produce no more than one hundred twenty plays and with the average play lasting five seconds, this means that for only ten minutes is anything really happening. The remaining fifty minutes are filled with unpiling players, marking the ball, huddling to call the plays, and (especially when the team ahead is protecting its lead) just plain dawdling. The clock may be the enemy but it produces the focus of the game. Football is not, as many would have it, a battle over territory, but a struggle over time. Nothing in sports can offer the same tension as the appropriately named "two minute warning." When the offense is behind and has the ball, the last two minutes of a football game can last a *real* fifteen or twenty minutes. Like any competent strategist, the team with the ball uses the clock, uses the enemy. The sidelines reveal themselves as temporal, rather than spatial dimensions, and are also manipulated. An offense that is ahead simply falls on the center snap and mocks the defense, which can only grasp for the phantom football and watch the clock tick towards their execution. The anxiety and cruelty of the last two minutes truly reveal football to be a game of catastrophe.

The Field.

The football field is, strictly speaking, for players only. As an heroic game, football strives not for a sharing with fans but a separation. Football goes to incredible lengths to establish distance from the crowd. Kicked scores are prevented from entering the crowd by nets, players fined if they throw balls into the stands, and dances of celebration in the end zones must not exceed prescribed limits, thus denying the fans even the slightest connection with the players on the field. Yet, in spite of all the attempts to assure the more-than-human qualities of its players, football is ultimately a game of failure, of disaster, of catastrophe. Even though there are more officials controlling this game than any other, even though incredible efforts are made and elaborate plans devised, the game is decided most often by the "tragic" shape of the ball. The football that can move so gracefully through the air is also the perpetrator of missed hand-offs, fumbles, dropped passes, and interceptions. It is indeed tragic that the players who strive so hard for control can be subject to the capricious bounce of the ball.

Catharsis.

The dimensions of violence and technology that are so apparent in football serve to set the stage for the catharsis necessary to tragedy. The ideas that football games are won in the "trenches" and by teams that can change the parts of their "machine" efficiently serve to elicit the Lombardism, "Winning isn't everything, it's the only thing." It is this adage that is truly a fatal flaw, a great error, the *hamartia* that is necessary for an event to be considered tragic. In his discussion of catharsis in football, Guttman clearly shows that watching or playing football will not decrease one's tendencies toward aggression: the release of destructive forces will not occur.[7] While Guttman is right in holding that football does not produce catharsis, his interpretation of catharsis is a didactic one. If we agree that the function of sport (or literature) is to entertain rather than instruct, catharsis takes on an altogether different meaning, a psychological meaning. The psychological interpretation of catharsis

---

[7] Allen Guttmann, *From Ritual to Record: The Nature of Modern Sports* (New York: Columbia University Press, 1978), pp. 130-36.

maintains, "that the spectator's emotional conflicts are temporarily resolved and his inner agitations stilled by having an opportunity vicariously to expend fear and pity."[8] With this understanding of catharsis we can see that football does indeed provide us this resolution, as Ross so brilliantly observes:

> . . . it makes us feel that something can be released and connected in all this chaos; out of accumulated pule (sic) of bodies something can emerge—a runner breaks into the clear or a pass finds its way to a receiver. To the spectator plays such as these are human and dazzling. They suggest to the audience what it has hoped for (and been told) all along, that technology is still a tool and not a master.[9]

The tragic hero is "a scapegoat, that is, a human figure upon whom we are able to load our emotions . . . through such a deep and complete emotional identification that he can carry them away with them . . . and so free us from the burden and the tension of keeping them from ourselves."[10]

Football attracts us and holds our attention because, as Ross says, "[it] metaphysically yokes heroic action and technology together by violence to suggest that they are mutually supportive."[11] The fact that this is a doubtful proposition seems to make little difference; and so it is appropriately tragic that, for all its attention to heroic excellence, this most masculine of games is usually decided not by those who personify the struggle, but by some midget foreigner who doesn't even have the decency to kick the ball with his toes.

Baseball

Baseball, to be quite direct, is the perfect game. If the nature of basketball is deception and football, strategy, then the essence of baseball is balance. A sport with more mathematical balance does not exist. Baseball is comedy and romance and its themes are recognition, triumph, and adventure. It is populated by happily-manufactured and dreamlike characters. Baseball is a shared experience. Anyone can do the same athletic feats the professional does, and anyone can experience the perfection of the game; for baseball is a game of perpetual childhood, a fountain of hopes and dreams, a world of myths and legends. The greatest legend in baseball surrounds its origins because, just like baseball, people can point to a specific moment and place of creation; only in this case it happens to be untrue. Nonetheless, the *idea* that Abner Doubleday invented baseball in Cooperstown is what is important.

---

[8] William Flint Thrall, Addison Hibbard and C. High Homan, *A Handbook to Literature* (New York: The Odyssey Press, 1960), p. 74.

[9] Murray Ross, "Football Red and Baseball Green: The Heroics and Bucolics of American Sport," *Chicago Review* (Jan.-Feb. 1971) : 38.

[10] Thrall, *A Handbook to Literature*, p. 74.

[11] Ross, "Football Red and Baseball Green," p. 39.

As Coffin notes:

> For there is no excitement in evolution, and even less in the idea that America's national game is rooted in English antecedents. Man seeks a dramatic moment when some doctor nails a peach basket to the running track above the gym floor, when some undisciplined player picks up the football and runs with it. Abner Doubleday will do. At least he is both definite and patriotic.[12]

The theme of baseball starts with ironic comedy which tells of the driving out of the *pharmakos* of society; and concludes with descriptions of adventures in the realm of contemplation. It is fitting that Northrop Frye's only serious discussion of sport in *Anatomy of Criticism* concerns baseball:

> There is certainly no evidence that baseball has descended from a ritual of human sacrifice, but the umpire is quite as much as a *pharmakos* as if it had: he is an abandoned scoundrel, a greater robber than Barabbas, he has the evil eye; the supporters of the losing team scream for his death. At play, mob emotions are boiled in an open pot, so to speak; . . .[13]

So much has been written about the comedy and romance of baseball that it would be redundant to continue most of these observations. Instead, I will focus simply on the temporal and spatial dimensions of baseball. Baseball is such a perfectly balanced game that even the most far-fetched speculations about the clock and the field carry with them the feeling of truth.

The Clock

Roger Angell, one of the most eloquent writers on baseball, speaks of an "interior stadium" in his book *The Summer Game*. Within this stadium baseball's unique relationship with time is analyzed:

> Within the ballpark, time moves differently marked by no clock, except the events of the game. This is the unique, unchangeable feature of baseball, and perhaps explains why this sport, . . . remains somehow rustic, unviolent, and introspective. Baseball's time is seamless and invisible, a bubble within which players move at exactly the same pace and rhythms as all their predecessors . . . Since baseball time is measured only in outs, all you have to do is succeed utterly, keep hitting, keep the rally alive, and you have defeated time. You remain forever young.[14]

Baseball time is indeed perfect. It is endless and it is also perfectly fair. Baseball goes on until one team wins. The game may be suspended for months at

---

[12] Tristam P. Coffin, *The Old Ball Game: Baseball in Folklore and Fiction* (New York: Herder and Herder, 1971), p. 6.

[13] Frye, *Anatomy of Criticism*, p. 46.

[14] Roger Angell, *The Summer Game* (New York: Popular Library, 1972), pp. 319-320.

a time and then resumed, making for some interesting situations. Players who are scheduled to bat when a suspended game resumes may be injured, traded, retired, demoted, even dead (as in the case of Thurman Munson); but the game is still waiting for them or their substitutes. Yet, while a game can go on forever, if the home team has scored more runs in eight innings than the visiting team manages in nine, the game is over—no sense rubbing it in.

The Field

In a very real sense, the space of baseball is as endless as its time. In baseball the foul lines are the only lines of great importance; and they serve to expand space rather than enclose it. The lines do not determine in or out, only fair and foul, and even the lines do not put the ball out of play:

> If the stands were removed from the football field, the game would still be conducted within its dreary box; if baseball's outfield bleachers were removed . . . the game could continue its space across the land, widening ever outward over the prairies and pastures of the Republic. The importance of baseball's potential for infinity cannot be ignored . . . baseball's space endows us with the opportunity for our imaginations to romp, untrammeled, with the gods.[15]

The space of baseball also creates a romance of numbers. In no other sport are numbers so important, so revealing. The path the batter travels around the square of the bases is exactly three hundred sixty feet—the number of degrees in a circle. When a runner passes through all three hundred sixty, he comes *home.* The theme of threes, sixes and nines comes from within the game—three hundred sixty feet, ninety feet, sixty feet six inches, three strikes, three outs, nine innings, three bases, three outfielders, nine players. Yet, no matter how geometrical baseball may seem it is not a mathematical formula, but a quest—a series of marvelous adventures around the three bases and the final arrival at home: "Think of it! The batter has come home. He has fulfilled his destiny, and by fulfilling it, transcended both the game and the idea of destiny itself. He has squared the circle."[16]

Finally, there is the baseball itself. As Coover says, it is hard and white and alive.[17] The ball has concrete substance (hard), but appears as a soul

---

[15] George Grella, "Baseball and the American Dream," *The Massachusetts Review* 16 (Summer 1975): 563.

[16] Robert Kelly, "A Pastoral Dialogue on the Game of the Quadrature," in *Baseball Diamonds: Tales, Traces, Visions, and Voodoo From a Native American Rite,* ed. by Kevin Kerrane and Richard Grossinger (New York: Anchor Press/Doubleday, 1980), p. xxvii.

[17] Robert Coover, *The Universal Baseball Association, Inc., J. Henry Waugh, Prop.* (New York: Random House, 1968), p. 242.

(white); and it reveals itself to be permanent (alive). All one has to do is take the ball apart. What keeps the hardness within, the cover, when laid out flat in front of us becomes two pieces of infinity. Stitched together again and the ball remains white forever—when the ball begins to soak up the brown of the earth it is discarded and a new one takes its place. From these most lyrical observations, one can easily conclude that baseball does indeed convey the *mythoi* of comedy (rebirth) and romance (adventure). Baseball is the sporting version of Frye's central unifying myth of literature as romance. There can be no doubt!

The End is the Beginning

It is true that a particular contest may have tragic elements just as it may have comic, romantic, or ironic elements; but if a paradigm for sport's dramatic appeal is to be developed, it must be synoptic rather than specific. Northrop Frye's system of criticism of literature offer us the synoptic paradigm that can adequately describe sport's aesthetic function. I have demonstrated the cyclical nature of sport and shown the way in which baseball, football, and basketball serve to narrate this cycle, but there is also the central unifying myth that brings all sport together—a romantic one that views sport as an eternal event that represents humankind's ideal vision and creates its own history.

The purpose of sport is not to determine a winner and a loser, but to engage in a series of marvelous struggles that serve to glorify and perpetuate themselves. Energy is expended and emotions are drained; yet, both the participants and the spectators can rest assured that for all their effort, care, and concern, there will be another game tomorrow. The true goal of sport is to *keep the game going!* Ultimately there can be only one reason to throw a ball—to get it back and throw it again. As long as there is a ball there will be someone to throw it. As long as the ball travels it will cover a course of never ending return. The very cyclical nature of contests, the struggles, rising and falling, and resolution only to repeat the contest is the best evidence for the romantic appeal of sport.

Sport is symbolic, therefore, not of death but life; and perhaps Nietzsche best describes the romantic impulse of life when he talks about death:

> Verily, Zarathustra had a goal; he threw his ball: now you, my friends, are the heirs to my goal; to you I throw my golden ball. More than anything I like to see you, my friend, throwing the golden ball. And so I still linger a little on the earth: forgive me for that.[18]

---

[18] Frederick Nietzche, *Thus Spoke Zarathustra: A Book for All and None*, trans. by Walter Kaufmann (New York: Viking Press, 1954), p. 74.

9

A Structural Semantics for Sports Fiction

Christian K. Messenger

MANY OF US IN THE PAST SEVERAL YEARS have been engaged in a project involving the very creation of a sports literature discipline. We have charted a literary history of sport in the United States. We have delineated the major symbologies of the sports material in fictional texts. We have found the sports subject in wilderness narratives, dime novels, children's literature, literary naturalism, high modernism, and in post-modern experiment. We have applied concepts from Huizinga, Derrida, and Victor Turner. We have learned from Henry Nash Smith, from Brian Sutton-Smith, and from Red Smith. We all know what Virginia Woolf said about Lardner, what Jacques Barzun said about baseball. Roy Hobbs and Henry Wiggen, Gary Harkness and Billy Clyde Puckett, Rabbit Angstrom and Biff Loman sometimes appear more real to us than the professional heroes on our VCR's and cable networks.

Yet with all our charting of play and ritual, of sport and the sacred, of sport and society, of the sporting hero, we have yet to formulate whether we really have a popular genre of sports fiction with certain defining characteristics—either formal, psychological or historical—such as the Detective genre or Science Fiction or the Thriller. This question and its possible answers must be left for another time. Towards defining the answer, however, I would like to propose a structural field description of sports fiction, a dynamic which might prove useful in charting a significantly large number of texts from many areas of sports fiction. I would hope to give us a way to speak of baseball, football, and basketball novels in the same breath with novels about man-in-nature and with self-reflexively playful texts.

To gain a wide perspective on the coding of sport in fictional texts, I propose a structural dynamic that is somewhat gerry-built in the best American tradition. I want to employ a semiotic rectangle of binary opposites, retrieve it for dialectical criticism, and then center on a few well-known fictional texts by application of some classical play theory. To add some late inning heroics, I will try to de-construct my model at the conclusion.

Mapping the Arena

The semiotics of A. J. Greimas appear most helpful in an initial formulation of a semantics for sports fiction. In his essay, "The Interaction of Semiotic Constraints," Greimas posits what has come to be known as the "semiotic rectangle," a four-term homology designed in quadrants to elicit "semes" of meaning. Greimas calls what is revealed the author's journey "punctuated with compelling choices that leads through a series of exclusions and options, manifesting personal and social phobias and euphorias to the constitution of an original and unique work."[1] Greimas's mechanism is intricately calibrated as far as the level of the individual *sentence*. While most critics have doubted the validity of any lexical set of categories to fully explain the imaginative work, they have cited the organizational tool that Greimas provides for the reduction of an inventory of characters, scenes, and plot to a constructed series of contraries and their generated negations.[2] Greimas's system is of binary opposites rather than dialectical opposites, but Fredric Jameson sees the procedure as retrievable for dialectical criticism "by designating it as the very locus and model of ideological closure." He flatly states that "it maps the limits of a specific ideological consciousness and marks the conceptual points beyond which that consciousness cannot go, and between which it is condemned to oscillate."[3]

Thus I want to suggest a grid to place over disparate texts, one that might map out the field of sports fiction and give us conceptual points among which individual authors *must* range, wherever they may choose to rest and concentrate any given cluster of characters and themes. Greimas's construct begins with a figure of four terms which defines the "conditions of existence for semiotic objects" and is labelled the "elementary structure of signification." An initial term S generates its contrary (S_1: S_2) and then the negation of the two terms ($\bar{S}_2$ and $\bar{S}_1$) produce the bottom of the rectangle.[4] Thus we have

---

[1] A. J. Greimas and F. Rastier, "The Interaction of Semiotic Constraints," *Yale French Studies* 41 (1968): 86. For a comprehensive look at Greimas's totally-developed system, see Greimas and J. Courtes, *Semiotics and Language: An Analytical Dictionary* [1979], trans. Larry Crist, et. al., (Bloomington: Indiana University Press, 1982).

[2] For critiques of Greimas's structure, see Jonathan Culler, *Structuralist Poetics* (Ithaca: Cornell University Press, 1975), pp. 92-95, 224-28; Fredric Jameson, *The Prison House of Language* (Princeton: Princeton University Press, 1972), pp. 163-68; Jameson, *The Political Unconscious* (Ithaca: Cornell University Press, 1981), pp. 46-49, 121-27, 166-68, 254-57; Robert Scholes, *Structuralism in Literature* (New Haven: Yale University Press, 1974), pp. 102-11.

[3] Jameson, *The Political Unconscious*, p. 47.

[4] Greimas and Rastier, "The Interaction of Semiotic Constraints,": 88.

the semiotic rectangle which I activate in the fiction about sport and play
by:

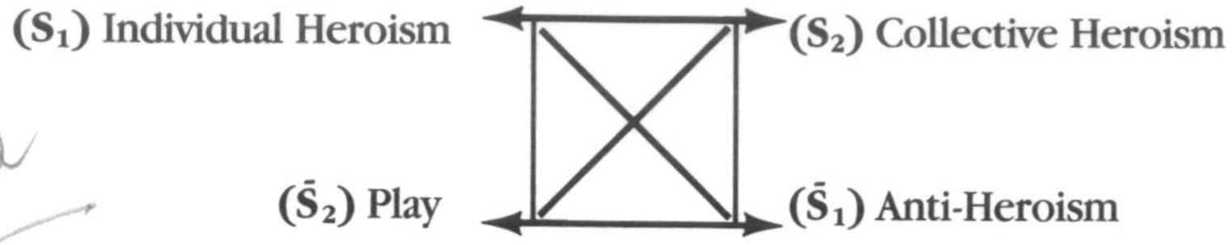

*novels usually a[?]
collective [?] →* (handwritten)

(S$_1$) Individual Heroism $\longleftrightarrow$ (S$_2$) Collective Heroism

*Greimas's
rectangle →* (handwritten)

(S̄$_2$) Play $\longleftrightarrow$ (S̄$_1$) Anti-Heroism

In essence, the sports hero begins in free Play, delighting in the freedom
and self-mastery of his body. Play informs the generating skill of the sports
hero, one converted into Individual Heroism as he wins some notable victory.
Individual heroes with a great skill are most often appropriated in American
sport by the larger society which in sports fiction is collectively represented
by the team. How the hero utilizes his great individual skill within strict patterns
of achievement and reward creates the tension between the individual and
the collective.

The sports hero's crisis is resolved in an Anti-Heroism in which he is
cast out of the team world, by the collective against his will or voluntarily
in an act of self-knowledge and/or martyrdom. Anti-Heroism as a conceptual
point leads either back to an ironic relation to Collective Heroism or returns
the hero to the freedom of Play from which he began. Play is the individual's
free point where he may reign with dominion over all signifiers but with
no positive relation to the collective.

The traversal of the above relations and the currents generated map out
the form of the individual's creative potential (Play), heroic identification
(Individual Heroism), seduction into the group (Collective Heroism), reversal
in Anti-Heroism, and return to Play. To project characters, scenes, and conflicts
into the oppositions is to begin the critical process of analyzing the sports
fiction.

Greimas's rectangle is an adaptation of the logical concepts of the contrary
and the contradictory and is a cornerstone of his major contribution to structural
semantics. In my adaptation, Collective Heroism is a *contrary* to Individual
Heroism. It has a positive value of its own, yet is antithetical to Individual
Heroism, while Anti-Heroism is the *contradiction* of Individual Heroism. This
system always depends on its initial critical programming. The first generated
term, in this case, Individual Heroism, will always include its antithesis. Thus
the one arbitrary critical decision is the choice of the first term's content.
The creation of the fourth term allows for the negation of the Collective
Heroism which is already antithetical to Individual Heroism. The fourth term
becomes the negation of the negation, the "not-not Individual Heroism," giving
the double negative a positive valence that may be expressed by Play. Play
is beneath and beyond the public assignments of heroism in the individual

and collective spheres and co-existent in subversive spirit with the negation inherent in Anti-Heroism. Thus the top two terms in antithetical relation comprise the public world of sports heroism and achievement while the bottom two terms are potentially in revolt. The generation of Play as the fourth term is a recuperation of the Individual and the Collective, and the revolt against the Individual and the Collective is a specific example of a text which as Jameson states "becomes the primary work which the [semiotic] mechanism is called upon to establish."[5]

Most all the critical texts on sport and fiction state that sport recapitulates the problems of the individual in society. If so, how can we deal with that major representation and include the generating power of play as well? Finally, how do we gauge the dramatic crises of affiliation and disaffiliation common to heroes in sports fiction? How can we keep the whole diagram cycling and still model closure and get something said while not prematurely privileging one set of facts or oppositions as *the* subject? How do we keep the center "open," a solid de-constructive technique, as well as one from Bobby Knight? For the next few pages, I will look for cutters and back door plays and try not to ignore the rebounds and fast breaks in the opposite direction.

Describing the Quadrants

I would like to move swiftly through two large subjects in order to get to the relation of Play as a mediating term. The two subjects are the relation of Individual Heroism to Collective Heroism and the relation of Collective Heroism to Anti-Heroism. In each opposition in the fiction, sport is textualized in fictional form. What must be remembered is that "sport in society" is already a textualization of the realities of individuals in relation to their societies. Thus the sports material is doubly worked-up, the game codifying relations in a society; the novel, the made-up novel, re-working the made-up game. To merely collapse the sport into just another novelistic subject is to perform a structural reduction whereby sport collapses into the "sports novel," never to be seen again as primary subject. However, to treat that sports novel as some inert given that merely reflects its social ground is also an error.[6] In this case, the sports material is all that matters in the fiction. "Sport in society" becomes the only focus as if it is not embedded in a novel at all. Either action produces ideology by privileging content or form. When we textualize a "made-up thing" we place it in a field of social contradictions where oppositions may be seen everywhere: Sport vs. Play, Individual vs. Society, Freedom vs. Authority. These oppositions may not be dispelled or mastered, not by the heroes in the texts, not by their authors, and certainly not by

---

[5] Jameson, *The Prison House of Language*, p. 176.

[6] Jameson, *The Political Unconscious*, p. 82.

their literary critics. Critics may re-present the field, supplementing and replacing terminology and texts. That is all but it is a major task in and of itself.

With such caveats in mind, the initial opposition of Individual Heroism to Collective Heroism is an impossible synthesis to achieve, and, of course, the subject of great commonality and scope throughout the history of American life and literature. As one of our strongest and most pervasive cultural experiences, team sport is a model of our American socialization into competitive groups for external reward. In our simplest sports fiction narratives, assimilation to the team after initial misgivings and strife is the commonest tale: reconciliation with the Collective without the denial of the Individual's identity. The new boy in town. The brash rookie. The individualist. The trouble maker. Growth. Maturation. Integration. The balance between the Individual and the Collective (in the guise of "team") is stressed.

Very seldom is such balance achieved in complex fiction about sport. The Collective is most often seen in opposition to the Individual who nonetheless must conform and work with others. The exception that proves the rule might be a novel such as Mark Harris's *Bang the Drum Slowly* in which the initial suspicion and adversary relationship of Henry Wiggen and the dying Bruce Pearson to the team is overturned. The team comes together in the face of Pearson's mortality. The players support and learn from one another and, not incidentally, win the pennant (the economic carrot, the victory for the team). *Bang the Drum Slowly* is decidedly in the minority. In the great majority of sports fiction, the team is owned and operated by a pack of low capitalist wolves; the coaches and managers are "characters" or have no character. The Individual Hero falls into a crisis vs. the authority of the Collective, his great skill consumed eagerly, his integrity threatened by his inability to get along or to go along. Bernard Malamud's *The Natural* (the novel—more about the movie shortly) documents Roy Hobbs's disaffection as he treads a minefield of sportswriters, evil owners, and temptresses in a world which devours heroes. *Bang the Drum Slowly* and *The Natural* are matched in their benign and malignant views of the Collective, respectively, by two football novels, Dan Jenkins's *Semi-Tough* and Peter Gent's *North Dallas Forty*. *Semi-Tough* is full of sly good ol' boys who slick New York-Texas-Hollywood—the new money/sport/media complex; *North Dallas Forty* is a naturalistic exposé of physical decay and moral emptiness in the professional sports establishment.

The fall into Anti-Heroism is the decline of the hero into crisis in an individual rebellion that is either forced or voluntary. The pressure comes from being benched, injured, scape-goated, traded, released, or cast out as a "loser" or "quitter." The Individual Hero is now isolated again as an Anti-Hero. The glare is solely on him, not for his achievements but for the lack of them now that he contradicts all that he has been in the public eye. There is an ironic centering on him as a problem where he once was the solution. Such a crisis may lead simply to a truism that Big Sport is a dirty business.

Or it may lead to a wiser, more wary and renewed relation to Collective Heroism. Or the hero may become fascinating to the society precisely because of his Anti-Heroic status in an overtly ironic relation. Or in an act of self-knowledge and martyrdom, the Anti-Hero's crisis may herald a return to the freedom of Play from which the Individual Hero began.

Sports novels of Anti-Heroism, most often those of football and boxing, have a strong emphasis on physical suffering and economic manipulation, the biological and environmental underpinnings of American Literary Naturalism. The novels most often conclude with the cry of "I am used up" or "I ain't marchin' anymore," as in the spirit's protest, especially in sports novels taking their ideological viewpoint from the 1960's Heroes deposit their uniforms in the laundry bin and limp away. Or they are carried out. Or they are cut by a surgeon or by the General Manager. Most football and boxing tales endlessly traverse the Collective Hero-Anti-Hero quadrant with no real resolution beyond pain and defeat.

Play as Mediation

As we move into the lower quadrant of what Greimas calls the "neutral relations," we have the opposition of Play to Anti-Heroism and Play's relation to Individual Heroism in the ascending quadrant. I want to stress Play as a fulcrum here between matter and form. Classical play theory has its origins in late eighteenth century German romantic philosophy. Friedrich Schiller derived from Immanuel Kant the concept of play as an interpretive device, a mediation between matter and form, between the sensuous and the ethical, between the material and the spiritual.[7] Thus we have, The Mediation of Play according to Schiller:

Stofftrieb ⟷	Spieltrieb ⟷	Formtrieb
"Sense Drive"	*"Play Drive"*	*"Form Drive"*
Sensuousness	Aesthetics	Reason
Matter	Beauty as Objective	Ethics
Content	Freedom as Goal	Spirit

By "playing" the relation between oppositions, we produce beauty (underscoring John Keats about truth/beauty). Thus Play is a third drive positioned between matter and form, the drive in which matter and form are neutralized and released from intolerable tension.[8] Play, then, is an

---

[7] Jameson has retrieved Schiller for a contemporary socio-political context in his *Marxism and Form* (Princeton: Princeton University Press, 1971), pp. 83-96.

[8] Jameson, *Marxism and Form*, p. 89.

intimation of freedom, the freedom to imagine a way beyond sensuality and ethics that partakes of them both.[9]

Now I want to take a single fictional work through its paces in terms of the posited structural dynamic and through play's relation of matter to form. I would like to look at *The Natural*, both in its novelistic and recent cinema presentations. In the novel, Malamud's Roy Hobbs keeps cycling through the binary oppositions, making two complete circuits in the film. He begins in Play, in the enormously nostalgic and suggestive pose of a farm boy having a catch with his father. The father-son relation is the relation most stressed in baseball fiction as a whole. Hobbs then moves to his first act of Individual Heroism as he vanquishes the Whammer on three pitched balls at the carnival, but he is immediately seduced and violated by the Dark Lady, Harriet Bird, avatar of the Collective Heroism's violent and wounding attention. She is the resentful witness to heroism. Hobbs is sent spiralling down into Anti-Heroism into a literal "wandering in the wilderness" before he returns at age thirty-four, a disciplined quester instead of a bright youth. When manager Pop Fisher finally consents to let Hobbs bat in a game, he tells him "to knock the cover off of it,"[10] which he does, *literally*, the ball unravelling as outfielders can find little to retrieve. Lightning flashes, thunder roars, rain pelts down, as the Knights and the arid wasteland team (managed by Pop, "the Fisher King"—a continual high-modernist cuteness by Malamud pervades the book) are regenerated. Hobbs has arrived as an Individual Hero through Malamud's play with literalizing the manager's command.

Here, the author's play is a point of coincidence which highlights both the hero's sport and the novelist's resources. To "knock the cover off the ball" is to perform an extra-physical feat which converts matter (the ball) into form (magical disappearance, extraordinary occurrence, deconstruction— call it what you will). Like all play, the scene re-works a mimetic moment and de-familiarizes it into an activity outside the everyday life, yet one which begins in the known sport. As play, Hobbs's feat is free, separate, uncertain (no one has seen anything like it), unproductive (anti-productive), and fictive (a fantasy).

Here is the clear mediation of Play that lifts Hobbs out of Anti-Heroism and into Individual Heroism once more. But Hobbs is not done with cycling through the diagram in Director Barry Levinson's film version. He now as Individual Hero falls into the Collective's hands once again as he duels the team's satanic owner, an evil sportswriter, and another temptress, Memo Paris.

---

[9] We should also add, perhaps, a fourth drive, the "Commodity Drive," of which Schiller at the dawn of western industrial capitalism could not have conceived. The "Commodity Drive" would be identified fundamentally by reification with production as objective and consumption as goal. Jameson attempts to construct a version of what I propose to call "Commodity Drive" by ingeniously wedding a twentieth century degraded reason (form) driving an equally degraded set of western appetites (content) with no further mediation of play. (Jameson, *Marxism and Form*, p. 96). I would position a "Commodity Drive" at the pole of Collective Heroism with the Individual Hero re-cast as the commodity.

[10] Bernard Malamud, *The Natural* [1952] (New York: Dell, 1970), p. 63.

He descends into another Anti-Heroism, the victim of indulgence and desire. Yet the film by dint of one burst of *Star Wars* technology—a pennant winning home run setting off a galactic ballpark light show—redeems Hobbs in director Levinson's "play." We last see Hobbs in Iris Lemon's field throwing the ball to their son; we are back at the tale's origins, having made two complete trips around the diamond/diagram.

The film alters completely Malamud's ending, which stops short of recuperation and redemption with Hobbs mired in an Anti-Heroism, having sold out and struck out, answering that most agonizing of baseball cries, "Say it ain't true, Roy"—"I'm afraid it is, kid." This is appropriately a bleak ending for a Camelot tale of Arthurian knights. However, to invent a sixteen-year-old son for Roy Hobbs and Iris Lemon, to invent a perforated stomach lining from the earlier shooting as the reason for his retirement from baseball, is to link the two complete heroic cycles and take the action away from Hobbs's will. It is a neat piece of Hollywood packaging as well as entirely consistent with fictional baseball narrative which stresses, as does the sport itself, journeying, "coming home," recurrence, and origins. Levinson and Robert Redford get closer to the appeal of baseball's satisfying closure than did Malamud. As another Hollywood athlete, Sylvester Stallone, says about *his* version of the pessimistic boxing tale in the *Rocky* series, "You wanted [Rocky] to win. And he does. . . . how many times can you stand to get involved with a character and then see him die or something?"[11] Stallone, obviously not a tragedian, would spare us mortality's starkness.

To play with and through the injunction "to knock the cover off the ball" is to use language immediately and playfully as an example of freedom for the character and author. Yet so much of sport's and play's experience is essentially physical and non-verbal and difficult to retrieve in narrative.

Another example of Play's mediating power, one in which language can be converted in and through action, occurs in John Updike's *Rabbit, Run,* in which Rabbit Angstrom hits a "perfect" golf shot. The scene finds Rabbit in a golf match with the Reverend Eccles who, in this contemporary version of a parish visit, wants to find out why Rabbit has left his pregnant wife and young son to live with another woman. Rabbit is a natural athlete and former high school basketball star who is imbued with a delicate touch and sensuous control. Yet as Eccles pursues him with shrill questions, it is clear that Rabbit is wallowing in an Anti-Heroism, hounded by the Collective's moral displeasure at his flight from society. He feels clumsy; the golf clubs will not respond to his touch. Their faces keep turning into those of his wife, his mother, and his lover. Finally,

> Very simply he brings the clubhead around his shoulder into it. The sound has a hollowness, a singleness he hasn't heard before. His arms force his head up and his ball is hung way out, lunarly pale against the beautiful black blue of storm clouds,

---

11 Sylvester Stallone quoted in Harriet Choice, "Life After Rocky," *Chicago Tribune Magazine,* 30 May 1982, p. 13.

his grandfather's color stretched dense across the east. It recedes along a line straight
as a ruler-edge. Stricken; sphere, star, speck. It hesitates, and Rabbit thinks it will
die, but he's fooled, for the ball makes this hesitation the ground of a final leap:
with a kind of visible sob takes a last bite of space before vanishing in falling. "That's
it!" he cries and, turning to Eccles with a smile of aggrandizement, repeats, "That's
it."[12]

Here, the moment of Play liberates Rabbit from Eccles's reasons and forms.
Nature had fled Rabbit's control. Now in the realm of plenitude, in response
to society, he converts club and ball to a transcendance, an orgasmic fullness,
both a re-conversion of matter to form (stricken; sphere, star, speck) and
a re-integration into fullness and weight. Rabbit's triumphant phrase, "That's
it!", truly signifies "That's me!; that's my physical skill and the only peace
I know in space."

This is the momentary dominance of "touch," the sports natural's grace,
but it is important to see it as a liberation from Anti-Heroism and a direct
rebuttal to the Collective. The scene is a breaking free of language in a physical
act, yet is described by the most beautiful language. It is the re-appropriation
of wordless grace *by* language. For an instant, the aestheticizing impulse has
given the golf club, the ball, the moment, and Rabbit's material predicament
a freedom, a liberation of sensuousness through Updike's artistic form which
is Rabbit's physical adeptness.

Nothing is resolved. Play does not resolve. Play mediates by playing
oppositions, here in the momentary perception of perfection and transcendance
which valorizes the base for Rabbit's Individual Heroism in sport and which
controls his status as sexual outlaw, as Anti-Hero. Malamud and Updike thus
provide telling examples of play momentarily mediating between matter and
form but always with reference to the constraints of Collective Heroism
represented by the team and society.

A third example of Play's power would be in the final scenes of Ken
Kesey's *One Flew Over the Cuckoo's Nest* when Chief Bromden kills the
lobotomized body of Randall Patrick McMurphy and escapes from the mental
ward.[13] The Chief's physical act is a freeing of McMurphy's spirit, a conversion
of matter to form. He does so even as the ward's inmates could deny the
living "dead" body was McMurphy's, for they had been taught the power
of Play *by* McMurphy, the con-man and illusionist. The smothering of
McMurphy, the master player, is an ethically complete act that will free
McMurphy and the Chief. The "act" is free, separate, and fictive in the sense
that the Chief has constructed a fiction that it is *not* McMurphy's body at
all, even as the men on the ward had been taught by McMurphy to see a
World Series forbidden to them by Nurse Ratched, on a dead, grey television

---

[12] John Updike, *Rabbit, Run* (New York: Knopf, 1959), pp. 133-34.

[13] I have discussed this novel at length in "The Dynamics of Ritual and Play: Kesey's *One Flew
Over the Cuckoo's Nest*," *Arete: the Journal of Sport Literature* 1,1 (Fall 1983) : 99-107.

screen; they had been taught to convert obdurate matter in Play. Likewise, the Chief's final action is to hurl the Combine's huge control panel through a plate-glass window. The material object soars into the moonlit night, its "absence" providing his path to freedom. This moment, too, has been prepared for by McMurphy's playful wagering as to whether the panel could be lifted at the novel's outset. By passing through the realm of Play, the degraded body of McMurphy has been reconverted through the Chief's Individual Heroism; the Chief has passed through psychic and physical barriers to freedom as well.

Malamud, Updike, and Kesey have all used Play to mediate between the pressures of matter and form. They satisfy our yearning to speak of matter and form together without being placed in bondage to sense or to reason. All three heroic actions have taken place against the intolerable terms posed by the Collective where ideology would control thought and lives.

Expanding the Structure

I do not wish to call Individual Heroism and Content or Anti-Heroism and Form as absolutely congruent in terminology. There appears to be a rough correspondence in my binary oppositions and their three individual terms to those of Schiller's mediated drives in a series controlled by Play. Individual Heroism is material, it is scoring, both in the sense of runs, points, and touchdowns but also in the sexual slang sense. Anti-Heroism does often involve an abstract ethical judgment on the Collective's means and goals, a rational decision to divest self from society. Just as often, that decision is made for the Collective Hero and is not a willed intellection but a victimization. Yet if I would take Play's role to a centering as Schiller does, it should be possible to do the same with the other terms in the binary oppositions.

To test the usefulness of the diagram's oppositions and the potential mediations, one can speculate as to the position of a number of sports fiction categories. I will do so briefly. Ritual sports stories of man-in-nature or in the deterministic arena work strongly in the Individual Heroism-Collective Heroism-Anti-Heroism quadrants with ritual as Collective act being underscored whereas Play is largely absent as a term. Ritual freezes and rigidifies into rule-dominated behavior where nothing is left free or uncertain. Such a sporting world was most congenial to Hemingway whose inheritors include Norman Mailer, James Dickey, and Thomas McGuane. The School Sports Hero traverses the Play-Individual Heroism-Collective Heroism quadrants with the emphasis on Individual Heroism. Tom Buchanan's "acute, limited excellence" in *The Great Gatsby*, and the bewilderment of Christian Darling after his one great moment in Irwin Shaw's "The Eighty-Yard Run" are primary examples of the Individual Heroism that cannot be converted to a complex life in society beyond the arena. The School Sports Hero's major defeat and frustration is

in his inability to convert matter to form, to convert his Individual Heroism
into any lasting victory for the spirit. That physical perfection in Individual
Heroism cannot locate the self-knowledge of Anti-Heroism is evident in John
Knowles's *A Separate Peace.*

Novels that deal with the fan or the witnessing sensibility of the Anti-
Hero traverse the bottom neutral quadrant of Play-Anti-Heroism-Collective
Heroism in comic renunciation where protagonists refuse to play for any "team."
Here the missing term is Individual Heroism. The witness will not or cannot
be a hero. He remains mired in form, in rational or irrational abstention
from heroics. He cannot "produce" for himself or the team. Heroes are both
self-deprecating and defiant in texts such as Philip Roth's *Goodbye, Columbus,*
Wright Morris's *The Field of Vision,* and Frederick Exley's *A Fan's Notes.* The
three major team sports—Baseball, Football, and Basketball—have definite
fictional patterns. Baseball narratives keep cycling, as I have discussed with
The Natural. The endless returning "home" (a serendipitous structural
congruity with the semiotic rectangle) moves through all quadrants; it is no
mistake, then, that baseball fiction has been the most supple and imaginative
of all sports fiction, allowing authors the greatest range of imaginative interplay. Football tales most often chart the deterministic fall through Collective
Heroism to an Anti-Heroism; the hero is a martyr-victim and ritual has turned
to spectacle. Basketball fiction is always concerned with transcendance and
upward space—and it is often simply spacy, comfortable in the Play-Anti-
Heroism negations where each player dances to his or her own moves.

The most brilliant sports fiction of self-reflexivity and language, that of
Robert Coover's *The Universal Baseball Association* and Don DeLillo's *End
Zone,* squarely confronts Play's relation to the Individual Hero of not only
the athlete but of the author-creator as well. Such fiction attempts to model
Play's mediation at the level of the text itself, which is what all fiction is
actually doing all the time. Thus self-reflexive fiction is consistent with Schiller's
mediation of Play. The Play of self-reflexive fiction counters the reification
of Collective Heroism, its direct contradictory, by refusing to become a
consumer product, by its willful difficulty and inventive form.

To re-emphasize, no novel or group of novels exists solely in one quadrant
or another. All partake of the system's dynamics. The question would be in
any synchronic analysis of a given scene, to find where the action under
scrutiny falls, and what the analysis through the diagram will yield toward
a knowledge of the novel's ideology and form. The diagram may not only
identify the locus of tension of the analyzed scenes but may in a series of
related paradigmatic and syntagmatic operations, locate the absent quadrant
or term. The operations may locate what is unconsciously the subject of the
text, even as that subject is absent.

Finally, I want to close with some related points that are a critique of
my own structure. They are offered in the spirit of Yeats in "Easter 1916"
who admonished us to "mock mockers after that," or of de-constructionists

who tell us to fold up any system, including our own, like a game board, or of Marxist critics who suspect premature closure—or even of Yogi Berra who tells us "it ain't over till it's over."

First, the diagram and its dynamic are expressly subject-centered and their persistence in the categories of the individual subject models my belief that American sports fiction is best explained through the passages of its individual heroes. However, I do believe that Collective Heroism, that team or public realm of the social and economic world, is by far the most dominant point in the structure. Nonetheless, I retain a commitment to the free individual as he battles the Collective, a commitment shared by the authors of American sports fiction. My description is more a conventionally hermeneutic one playing the politics of restoration and recovery, playing my trump card of Play at every promising opportunity, valorizing freedom through Play as a goal in the best liberal sense.[14]

I want to admit that Play, while what the Western liberal democratic system would begin with in monadic, individualistic freedom, is anathema to a Marxist hermeneutic that would describe freedom as achieved only at the Utopian moment of a Collective partial liberation from necessity. In other words, Play is under strong political attack as apolitical, private, and "humanizing" at the expense of political solidarity. At this time, American sports fiction models Western heroic individualism while the individual's Play models that individualism's rest points and origins, while suspiciously eyeing the Collective and its insistence on production and consumption. A properly revolutionary use of Play and illusion is beyond that fiction's conceptual points at present.[15]

In the best of our sports fiction, Play presides over the transformation of matter into grace and spirit, and spirit into matter and content—which is, after all, why we care about sport and Play at all in the articulation of our earth-bound mortal bodies against space and time. We value those authors who dramatize this struggle in all its complexity. They deserve our complex response in turn.

---

[14] To establish the three other possible mediated series in turn would be to valorize other "centers": commodity reification (Collective Heroism) with Play as an absent term; transcendental signification (Anti-Heroism) with Individual Heroism as an absent term; and sensuousness or matter (Individual Heroism) with form and reason (Anti-Heroism) as an absent term.

[15] Kesey's use of McMurphy and the Chief points to a collective revolutionary action through Play but is circumscribed by the strong messianic figure, a true individualizing force. The most suggestive revolutionary use of Play in American fiction is found in Herman Melville's novella "Benito Cereno."

PART
IV

The Use of Sport in Fiction

10

Introduction:
The Use of Sport in Fiction

Stephen David Mosher

JUST WHAT CONSTITUTES SPORT FICTION is a topic that has been the subject for much discussion. The hope that this issue will be resolved in one way or another is, perhaps, foolish. Whether or not the body of sport fiction constitutes a "genre" should not detract from its important function. Whether or not a particular piece of sport fiction qualifies as a representative of this "genre" may unnecessarily narrow the scope of those novels, short stories, and poems that seek to broaden our understanding of sport. Perhaps it is sufficient to observe that a particular work has particular implications for sport. In any case, the four essays in this chapter cover a tremendously wide territory and yet, in the final analysis, all have something unique and important to say about the sporting condition.

Kent Cartwright and Mary McElroy's "Dialectics and Sport in *A Separate Peace*" argues that John Knowles's prep school novel, although claiming to be about war, can be accurately described as a sports novel, since an overwhelming amount of its action and imagery is derived from sports; and that, in the intensely symbolic structure of the novel, sport is the single element which operates as a metaphor for peace as well as war. Cartwright and McElroy contend further that sports are the only vehicle which Knowles employs to suggest an ideal of unity, simplicity and the moral life. Through the sports metaphor, we can observe that sport not only gives us an explanation of our private world, but also becomes a moral tool that helps us develop our general knowledge.

Eric Solomon clearly demonstrates the powerful enculturation dimension of sport in "Varieties of American Work and Play Experience: The Example of a Popular Jewish Baseball Novelist." Through a close examination of Gerald Green's baseball novels, *To Brooklyn With Love* (1967) and *The Last Angry Man* (1956), Solomon argues that as the Jewish population became "Americanized" much of the tension that grew out of this process centered on the forces of work (used to represent the "old" ways) and play (employed to represent the "new"). Not surprisingly, baseball (and its many urban forms) becomes the primary metaphor for the spirit of play and the new society. As such, the National Pastime grows from mere play to a powerful social force that helps shape one of this country's sub-cultures.

If we were to claim that sport does contribute something of value to society, the concept of *Arete* (the pursuit of excellence as a process of striving toward a sense of fulfillment as an integrated human being) comes powerfully to mind. *Arete* is perhaps best typified in the modern world by the philosophy behind the Olympic Games; and it is to an understanding of this concept that Elizabeth Bressan writes in "Olympism and American Fiction." Through an examination of the use of sport in selected works of Thomas Wolfe and John Updike, Bressan demonstrates that, although Wolfe's characters are more heroic than Updike's and are actually capable of attaining great levels of achievement in sports, there is little evidence to support the claim that Olympism is a vital concept in contemporary society. Bressan concludes that a society that continues to espouse myths that are found false, may indeed by creating a fabrication. In other words, is Olympism a fiction?

Perhaps an affirmative answer to the preceding question is not as terrible as it first seems. Perhaps, if we relieve sport of the responsibility of being a "mirror of life," we would then find something of even more profound value. In his brief but brilliant essay, "Running to Disaster: Shaw's 'Eighty-Yard Run ,'" David Vanderwerken demonstrates quite clearly that the "high," the "peak experience," "the transcendent moment," in sport is of sport alone and cannot be duplicated in everyday life. Christian Darling's mistake, like that so many make, lay in believing that a great run in a football practice is an indication of his future success. The ironic fact that it was the greatest achievement of his life only intensifies his anguish many years later. Vanderwerken concludes that those who place too much importance on sport are doomed to miss its true and lasting rewards.

And the conclusion we can make about sport fiction is that those who try too hard to classify it are doomed to miss the breadth and flexibility of its meaning.

11

Dialectics and Sport in
A Separate Peace

Kent Cartwright and Mary McElroy

JOHN KNOWLES'S PREP SCHOOL NOVEL , *A Separate Peace*, was well received critically in the preppy early sixties: it was compared favorably to its precursor, *The Catcher in the Rye;* its personal yet "lyrical"[1] idiom, so reminiscent of *The Great Gatsby,* seemed to reveal a distinctly American style; and its dialectic, almost Manichean vision of the world made it born for the explicating genius of New Criticism. Yet in recent years, *A Separate Peace* has fallen on hard times. Since the early seventies, critical interest has flagged, and the novel is now sometimes consigned to the children's literature shelf of the library. As a standard bearer of New Critical approval, Knowles's tale seems today, despite its issues of life and death, rather too bloodless, too relentlessly organized, too modeled. For all of reality in *A Separate Peace* is divided into a system of opposites: war and peace; the intellectual and the athletic; joy and fear; reason and emotion; selfishness and generosity; innocence and experience; the past and the present; north and south; the winter and the summer; the First Academic Building and the Playing Fields; the Devon river and the Nagaumsett. And through all these runs the central, organizing opposition of Phineas, the star athlete, and Gene, the star scholar and narrator.

An additional structural interest in the novel is sport. Indeed, while *A Separate Peace* has often been called a novel of war, it might as easily be called a novel of sport, since sporting encounters are the principal moments which reveal the novel's values and since athletics seem to be the most synthetic of the novel's motifs, operating as a metaphor for both war and peace and their associated ethics. Sports are the killing field of this novel, the terrain on which real issues are played out, but they resist division into the novel's formulaic polarities. Indeed, they reinvigorate the novel with an unexpected complexity and mystery, and they may stand for a way out of the divided universe. An examination of sports, however, must lead us back to the opposing

---

[1] Jay L. Halio, "John Knowles's Short Novels," *Studies in Short Fiction* (Winter 1964): 107.

sensibilities of Phineas and Gene. What version of reality is ultimately the touchstone of truth in the novel: that of Phineas, whose life is ruled by inspiration, who views the world as harmonious, and who admits of only Olympian conflict, or that of Gene, who fears the rules, who maims Phineas, and who survives?

Gene, as the novel's narrator, frames the incidents he relates from his school days at Devon fifteen years earlier within an idealization of Phineas. Returning to Devon, a private and privileged boys school in New Hampshire, on a gloomy and rainy fall day, Gene, now in his early thirties, recognizes the "fear which surrounded and filled those days"—recognizes it because he has finally escaped it—and notes with approval the slow, harmonious change that has overcome his school: "So it was logical to hope that . . . I could achieve, perhaps unknowingly already had achieved, this growth and harmony myself" (p. 4).[2] Indeed, Gene speaks of his visit as a way of marking his own "convalescence" (p. 3), a word which we will come to associate with Phineas after his sacrificial crippling. Again, in the closing pages of the novel, when Gene reverts exclusively to the enlighted voice of maturity,[3] he holds up before us those norms of fearlessness, freedom from anger, and harmony which had been hallmarks of Phineas's life and the goals of his own moral hegira: "Only Phineas never was afraid, only Phineas never hated anyone" (p.196). While the "simplicity and unity" of others broke down under the war-induced discovery of the "overwhelmingly hostile thing in the world with them, . . . Phineas alone had escaped this. He possessed an extra vigor, a heightened confidence in himself, a capacity for affection which saved him. . . . nothing even about the war had broken his harmonious and natural unity" (pp. 194-195). Indeed, the final words of the novel not only commemorate Phineas's uniqueness but also validate his singular vision of the world:

> All of them, all except Phineas, constructed at infinite cost to themselves these Maginot Lines against this enemy they thought they saw across the frontier, this enemy who never attacked that way—if he ever attacked at all; if he was indeed the enemy.
>
> (p. 196)

Gene, moreover, makes it clear to us that what is best in him is what he has received from Phineas. After his crippling of Phineas, for example, Gene puts on his friend's clothes and feels immensely revived in spirit (p. 54); Phineas is a living presence for Gene even after his death (p. 194); at the end of the novel Gene identifies his moral progress with his nature becoming

---

2 John Knowles, *A Separate Peace* (Bantam Books: New York, 1969; first published 1960). All textual citations will be made from this edition.

3 For a discussion of the adolescent voice and the adult voice in this novel, see Ian Kennedy, "Dual Perspective Narrative and the Character of Phineas in 'A Separate Peace,' " *Studies in Short Fiction* (Winter 1970): 353-59.

"Phineas-filled" (p.196); and the "growth and harmony" which Gene hopes he has achieved at the outset of his fable are the culmination of his "doubleness" with Phineas.

But is Gene right? Is Phineas, that is, a standard of moral excellence which is the measure and proper goal for all others? Since Finny is a kind of Platonic *ne plus ultra* of athleticism, how we estimate his maturity, his fitness for the world, qualifies how we value the knowledge that can come through sports. Phineas has not been as equally loved by the critics as he has been by Gene. Early readers of *A Separate Peace* sentimentalized Phineas; some later ones have held him in suspicion. Even those who are awed by Finny's goodness describe him further as an archetypal "American innocent,"[4] an "American Adam"[5] who is incapable of the knowledge of good and evil which is the fruit of the Edenic tree from which he falls, and who thus represents the losing term in the "conflict between innocence and reality"[6] or in the "movement from innocence to adulthood,"[7] and who must also consequently become the "necessary sacrifice"[8] for Gene's passage to adulthood. For these writers, Finny's life in the novel is essentially static. For one critic, moreover, Phineas's innocence is "almost diabolical"; his "life is a continuous effort to control reality by creating comfortable myths about it"; and his "separate peace" is an unrealistic "ideal world of changelessness, irresponsibility, and illusion."[9] Is Phineas, the river sprite, the priest of sport, the godlike athlete apparently as perfect as a Phidean statue,[10] somehow fatally flawed for the world of emerging adulthood? Or, to ask the question differently, if becoming more like Phineas is the moral pilgrimage of Gene's life, then why must the athlete die young?

Finny's is a life taken from the boy scout manual: he lives in ever widening circles of loyalty, to friends, to class, to school, to mankind; he is fearless, even before the "irate, steely black steeple" of a tree which no Upper Middler had ever jumped from into the Devon river before (pp. 6-7); his body moves in an unbroken flow, a unique harmony of shifts, balances, and compensations; he is not only the school's best athlete but also its best sportsman and believes, idiosyncratically, that "you"—everyone—"always win at sports"; and of all the individuals in the novel, he is uniquely without malice or envy. To prevent such a characterization from descending into caricature, Knowles leavens this portrait with Phineas's indifference to studies and his relentless and carefree

[4] John K. Crabbe, "On the Playing Fields of Devon," *English Journal*, 52 (1963): 109.

[5] Paul Witherington, "*A Separate Peace*: A Study in Structural Ambiguity," *English Journal* 54 (1965): 795.

[6] Crabbe, 109.

[7] James Ellis, "*A Separate Peace*: The Fall from Innocence," *English Journal* 53 (1964): 313.

[8] Halio, 109.

[9] Witherington, 796-800.

[10] For a discussion of the connection between Phineas and Phideas see Peter Wolfe, "The Impact of Knowles's *A Separate Peace*," *The University of Kansas City Review* 36 (1970): 192.

breaking of "the rules." One of our first impressions of Finny is of his honesty, a theme which winds its way through the novel just as the Devon river bisects the campus and a theme which fundamentally separates Gene and Phineas. Indeed, one of the issues this novel explores is what it means to be honest— to oneself as well as to others. Finny's honesty is guileless, direct, and disconcerting. His forthrightness about his diminutive athletic stature Gene describes as "that simple, shocking self-acceptance of his"; his extraneous confession of having carelessly worn the school tie as a belt is what enables him "to get away with it" (pp. 20-21), to Gene's disappointment; and his directness in confessing his friendship for Gene has an audacious morality absolutely atypical of school boys: "It was a courageous thing to say. Exposing a sincere emotion nakedly like that at the Devon School was the next thing to suicide"(p. 40).

Gene, on the other hand, is less than honest: he either fails to recognize the truth, or avoids it, or lies. He lies at the beginning about his fear of the tree and his "tendency to back away from things," a lie which Phineas serenely dismisses, to Gene's chagrin (p. 10); he projects his own envy, his own sense of competition falsely onto Phineas (p. 45); on their first interview after the accident, he lies to Finny about having tried to save him (p. 57); he allows Finny to believe, falsely, that he has reserved his room for him (p. 75); he joshes away his guilt with Brinker (pp. 79-83); he lies to Phineas about his short-lived compact with Brinker to enlist (pp. 98-100); he refuses to face up to the reality of what has happened to Leper, even to acknowledge Leper's pain and brutal self-discovery (pp. 131-43); he rejects Leper's accusation over the crippling of Phineas (p. 137); he lies about the true nature of his southernness (p. 148); he lies repeatedly at the novel's climax about his guilt for the "accident" (pp. 162-66); and he misrepresents his earlier motives even at his moment of expiation (p. 183). Even his self-accusations over Phineas's death seem odd and only partly true (pp. 195-96).

But honesty is a complicated and elusive business in this novel, for Gene, on a visit to his convalescing friend, attempts a moment of fundamental honesty, telling Phineas of the accident that "I caused it . . . I jounced the limb. I caused it . . . I deliberately jounced the limb so you would fall off" (p. 62). Phineas, in a strange reversal of their roles, refuses to believe him. Phineas's honesty about himself aside, one wonders here if he is capable of being honest about the world outside of Olympian competition and brotherhood, capable of accepting a painful adult truth of hostility and betrayal by his closest friend. This moment of denial parallel's Finny's later apparent denial of the very existence of World War II in his elaborate fabrication that the war is a fake being foisted upon them by fat old men "who don't want us crowding them out of their jobs" (p. 107). In the depths of their hearts, then, is Phineas the prevaricator and Gene the nascent realist? At least one critic argues that Phineas fails to know his world and fails particularly in that Greek-prized, Socrates-inspired injunction to "know thyself."[11] By the end of the novel, however, Phineas does accept the truth of Gene's guilt: "I do, I think I can believe that," he says in response to Gene's confession, "I've gotten awfully mad sometimes and almost forgotten what I was doing. I think I believe you . . ." (p. 183). Indeed, Phineas has doubted Gene's innocence earlier, first shortly after the accident when Gene initially visits him in the infirmary: "I had this idea, this feeling that when you were standing there beside me, y—I don't know, I had a kind of feeling . . . It was a crazy idea, I must have been delirious" (p. 58). Later, after Phineas refuses to acknowledge Gene's confession, he calls Gene at school to confirm that the latter has saved his place in the room they share and thus protected and reaffirmed their friendship: "I knew that if you'd let them put anybody in my place, then you really were crazy. But you didn't, I knew you wouldn't. Well, I did have just a trace of doubt, that was because you talked so crazy here" (p. 75).

Finally, when Finny runs away from the inquisition that Brinker the "lawgiver" (p. 122) has convened to sort out the truth of the accident, it is not because he fails or refuses to recognize the progressive revelation of Gene's crime; rather, it is for another reason:

> "I don't care," he interrupted in an even voice so full of richness that it overrode all the others. "I don't care . . . You get the rest of the facts, Brinker!" he cried. "You get all your facts!" I had never seen Finny crying, "you collect every f—ing fact there is in the world!" He plunged out the doors.
>
> (pp. 168-169.)

Phineas somehow stands above these hard facts of betrayal, even as he irreversibly arrives at them. Indeed, the very way he arrives at them, sizing the world up with personal reservations, allowing the hard truths to sift gradually into his consciousness, perhaps affords him his special proof against corruption.

Gene, on the other hand, has a strange way of perpetuating the blind, crazy ignorance in the human heart which seems related to his dishonesty. Indeed, such are the words he uses or accepts to explain his crime: "It was just some kind of blind impulse you had in the tree there, you didn't know what you were doing. Was that it?," asks Phineas, as the two devise an understanding of Gene's motivation. "Yes, yes, that was it," says Gene. Phineas proceeds to explicate the act further: "Something just seized you. It wasn't anything you really felt against me, it wasn't some kind of hate you've felt all along. It wasn't anything personal." "No," confirms Gene, "It

---

[11] Franziska Lynne Greiling, "The Theme of Freedom in *A Separate Peace*," *English Journal* 56 (1967): 1270.

was just some ignorance inside me, some crazy thing inside me, something blind, that's all it was" (p. 183).

Gene later relates this explanation to the whole motive for human warfare: "it seemed clear that wars were . . . made . . . by something ignorant in the human heart" (p. 193). Most critics accept Gene's understanding of his crime, that it was "consciously" done and that it was yet also somehow "impersonal."[12] The controlling notion here is that Gene's confession of guilt to Finny early in the novel is only a "half-truth,"[13] that Gene's enmity suddenly and almost inexplicably touches off a much deeper savagery hidden and unrecognized until now beneath the garment of civilized behavior. In that sense, Finny's early denial of Gene's guilt has an element of unexpected accuracy. Reasoning along these lines, Peter Wolfe even calls Gene's cruelty "unconscious" and argues that "Gene obeys an urge deeper than reason or wounded vanity."[14]

The trouble with this idea of impersonal action, however, is that it does not square well with the way Gene actually behaves. Gene's crime, though sudden and unexpected, is not some kind of demonic, unpredictable, irresistible possession. Rather, his hatred is motivated in clearly marked stages of escalation in the evolving events of the story. Gene admits to envying Phineas because he "could get away with anything" (p.18), feels "a sudden stab of disappointment" when Phineas is not brought up short by Mr. Patch Withers (p. 21), and quietly resents Phineas's successful flaunting of the rules through his extraordinary charm (pp. 20-21). He is jealous of Finny for inventing and then excelling at Blitzball (p. 31). Later, Gene admits to hating Phineas for breaking the school swimming record, and he creates an enormous, unfounded delusion that Finny is bent upon destroying his studies and that the two are locked in a cold, hostile competition. Just before the fall, when Gene discovers that the rivalry is a wild delusion on his part and that there "never was and never could have been" any competition between them, he recognizes that "I was not of the same quality as he" and adds, as the final insult, "I couldn't stand this" (p. 51). Gene's maiming of Phineas is simply not motiveless malignancy.

Indeed, it is malignancy motivated in its classical form: it recalls the fundamental human inadequacy Iago feels before Cassio—"He hath a daily beauty in his life/That makes me ugly"—or Macbeth feels toward Banquo— "under him/My Genius is rebuk'd, as it is said/Mark Antony's was by Caesar."[15] Gene feels envious and personally diminished in Phineas's presence, and it is Finny's unselfconscious magnanimity—the princeliest of Renaissance virtues—which finally seals Gene's sense of inferiority and his hatred. Gene,

---

[12] Halio, 107-109; Ellis, 315,317; Ronald Weber, "Narrative Method in *A Separate Peace*," *Studies in Short Fiction* (Fall 1965): 70-71.

[13] Halio, 108.

[14] Wolfe, 193-94.

[15] William Shakespeare, *Othello* v.i.1920, Macbeth III.i.54-56, *The Riverside Shakespeare*, G. Blakemore Evans, ed. (Houghton Mifflin: Boston, 1974).

moreover, is aware of his own enmity. Despite Phineas's explanation, which Gene embraces, Gene's cruelty is absolutely and intensely "personal," it is exactly "something you really felt against me," a hatred for Phineas's goodness. That Gene's treachery is a "pointless waste of violence," as Wolfe observes, is not corroborating evidence that the act is "aboriginal madness."[16] As Dostoevsky's *Underground Man* shows us, people at their best can choose sanely and deliberately to engage in utterly irrational acts. In Gene's case, the madness of his jouncing the limb is not some blind beast of the dark corners of his psyche that momentarily overwhelms him. Rather, Gene's jealousy, competitiveness, and sense of fundamental insufficiency have turned him step by step into that beast. While Gene has grown enormously in the course of this novel, his intellectual self-knowledge, his honesty, still seems incomplete. Perhaps that is why he has come to us and to the old haunts of Devon as a Middle-Aged Mariner, a wanderer.

Why Gene commits his crime is the fundamental question in the novel. Upon its answer hinges the whole connection which Knowles makes between personal evil and social evil. But the novel denies us a satisfactory resolution. On the one hand, we feel sympathy with that view which says that human evil is somehow always immeasureably greater than its causes; indeed, all of *King Lear* is premised upon that insight. We feel that to some degree Knowles must share Gene's perceptions. On the other hand, it is difficult to imagine any reader who is completely comfortable with the view that Gene's crime is impersonal and unconnected with Phineas; indeed, the only motives of which we know argue otherwise. Ultimately, conscious yet impersonal are mutually negating descriptions of Gene's treachery, and the novel's opaqueness on this score is unsettling. Furthermore, not only are we uneasy with competing descriptions of the wellsprings of Gene's betrayal, we may be uneasy with the desire itself to make one or the other fit.

Possibly Knowles, or the novel, does not want us to be able to know, able to arrive at a conclusion based on "the facts" in the same way that Brinker would. Ultimately, the spirit of *A Separate Peace* is not realism or determinism but romance; to see the world steadily and to see it whole may be to invent it. Finny, after all, is a kind of unmoved mover; he simply exists. While Gene tells us that Finny is the most remarkable person he has ever known, the novel never offers us any understanding of the conditions that make him possible. Of their backgrounds we know far more about Gene, Brinker, and Leper than we do about Phineas; those three are all comprehendable within the world as we are made to know it. Phineas is not. But this sort of opacity is not necessarily a fatal jouncing of the meaning of the novel; rather, entrenchment in mystery might be one of its ultimate strengths. For this unmoved movement has its beneficial side, and it is no accident that Phineas comes to us as an Adonis, a priest, and a demi-god of waters.

---

[16] Wolfe, 194.

A precise intellectualization of Gene's motivation, a careful shaving of words into correlatives for emotion, then, may not be the goal of *A Separate Peace*. For one of the experiences that is most compelling for Gene is a sense of wonder, of inebriation, of intoxication that is utterly inexplicable. That unspeakable, oxygenic joy is connected, like the omnipresent yet elusive subject of honesty, with the even more omnipresent subject of athleticism, Phineas's defining quality. Indeed, honesty and joy are correlative terms of his existence. Blunt honesty, of course, is a virtue prized distinctly and sometimes exclusively by Americans, as readers of Henry James will recognize. It is the Lincolnesque genius of our country and the virtue of our guardian spirits, the Founding Fathers. And it is also a value which seems intrinsically part of the equipment, the very essence, of a great athlete. Jay Gatsby exposes this latter myth when, in *The Great Gatsby*, he says quite innocently (and wrongly) of Jordan Baker that she is incapable of an impropriety because she is a great sportswoman. Similarly, Finny's athleticism confirms our sense of his honesty. Like Natty Bumppo, like Hawthorne's prelapsarian Donatello, like the "natural" American sports figure, Phineas does not exactly make a moral choice to be honest; rather he simply does not know dishonesty. One of the great facts—and limitations—of *A Separate Peace* is that Phineas would have been less plausible if he were anything other than an athlete.

Sporting encounters are the central events for playing out the dialectics of honesty in the novel. Indeed, when Gene jostles Phineas out of the tree, they are engaged in a game and a rite of initiation, and they are just about to attempt a first "double" jump, like high divers showing a new form. The memorable and defining moments are frequently at sports: Finny's breaking of the school swimming record; Phineas's invention of Blitzball and his remarkable facility at it; Gene's fight with Quackenbush at the Nagaumsett boathouse; Leper's snow skiing and his fascination with the military ski troops; the Hitler Youth outing; Gene's run; the visit of Phineas and Gene to the gymnasium after the former's return to school; the Winter Carnival; Gene's final moments at Devon as he cleans out his locker and watches the soldiers on the Playing Fields. The list of such events marches across the landscape of the novel, and it is through these events that we come to know Gene and Phineas best.

We learn of Phineas, for example, that although he treads upon the school rules with a genial abandon, he lives himself by his own private set of maxims. About these rules, Gene tells us, "the one which had the most urgent influence in his life was, 'You always win at sports.' This you," Gene adds, with a note of sarcasm, "was collective. Everyone always won at sports . . . Finny never permitted himself to realize that when you won they lost. That would have destroyed the perfect beauty which was sport. Nothing bad ever happened in sports; they were the absolute good" (pp. 26-27). But, of course, Finny means something altogether different by winning at sports than does Gene. For Gene, winning is victory over another person; for Phineas the vigorous contesting itself is fulfilling. Indeed, if for Phineas conflict is Olympian and

Greek-inspired (p. 144), then the greatest moment of self-fulfillment, of athletic success, of the stretching of one's capacities to the absolute limit, is the moment of defeat. These values are why we know Phineas for his numerous awards for sportsmanship (p. 36) as much as by his triumphs, and why, too, we often see him enjoying himself most in defeat. On the way toward dinner early in the novel, for example, Gene and Phineas are bumping each other and rough-housing: "I threw my hip against his, catching him by surprise, and he was instantly down, definitely pleased" (p. 11). Much later at the Hitler Youth outing, "We ended the fight the only way possible; all of us turned on Phineas. Slowly, with a steadily widening grin, he was driven down beneath a blizzard of snowballs" (p. 146). Even Phineas's poker playing is emblematic of the particular fulfillment he seeks in games: "Phineas losing even in those games he invented, betting always for what *should* win, for what would have been the most brilliant successes of all, if only the cards hadn't betrayed him" (p. 73). For Phineas, the collective you always does win at sports; for Gene, the obverse of that notion—they always lose—reveals the competitiveness and estrangement that lead to his betrayal.

A comment by Gene midway through the novel provides a clue to Phineas as a sportsman and a human being together (for him, the two are inseparable). Reflecting bemusedly on Phineas's insistence that the war is a fake, Gene remarks, "This was my first but not my last lapse into Finny's vision of peace. For hours, and sometimes for days, I fell without realizing it into the private explanation of the world . . . What deceived me was my own happiness; for peace is indivisible, and the surrounding world confusion found no reflection inside me" (p. 115). Gene, with exactly this same notion, anchors our sense of Phineas's unity and harmony and absence of rancor at the end of the novel: Phineas had "a way of sizing up the world with erratic and entirely personal reservations, letting its rocklike facts sift through and be accepted only a little at a time . . . No one else I have ever met could do this" (p. 194). Phineas, like Gatsby, believes in this mediating "private explanation of the world," and the truest example of that vision is sports. Like art, sport selects from reality those aspects it is interested in, exaggerating some, dismissing others, to create its special conditions, its rules, its possibilities. As with art, that "private explanation" is both its artificiality and its truth. Sports, of course, generally involve a kind of collusion of many, a temporary and collectively private reconstruction of the world. Finny expresses his creative power through sports. His artistry sets him apart from Gene, who is basically a grind, as his contrasting of his mind to that of Chet Douglass suggests. Finny's virtuosity at Blitzball is a matter of reverses and deceptions and mass hypnotism. At the Hitler Youth outing he deliberately defects from his own side to create confusion. Early in the novel we see him tripping Gene unexpectedly and being delighted when Gene turns the tables. Like an artist, Finny's wizardry at sports involves breaking the rules, or, to put it differently, altering the strictures of a game so as to create a whole new set of rules. In this way, the old legalisms become the necessary evil against which good is achieved; anarchy yields to order as innovations turn into new rules. That is art.

Finny understands both the integrity and the gigantic hoax of sport, for which all one needs is a medicine ball and an arbitrary set of conditions: "When they discovered the circle they created sports" (p. 29). It is no coincidence that this imagery of the circle, so central to sports, is also the submerged metaphor that Gene uses for Phineas's harmony with the world and his loyalties: "Finny had tremendous loyalty to the class, as he did to any group he belonged to, beginning with him and me and radiating outward past the limits of humanity toward spirits and clouds and stars" (p. 34). John Knowles makes Phineas a great athlete in part because the secret to Phineas's harmony is his angular vision of reality, his "private explanation," that capacity which enables him to charm the faculty, mesmerize Gene as though he were under a spell, and reach out to others for genuine human contact across the wreckage of the "rules."

A second reason why Knowles makes Phineas a sports hero is because sports represent in the novel a special kind of knowledge, a benevolent pathway to the human heart which provides a countercurrent to the blind impulse for evil which Gene defines. Knowles points repeatedly toward a level of experience which is deeper and truer than the intellect. It is a perception, a belief, which echos through all of Gene's commentary: "In the deep, tacit way in which feeling becomes stronger than thought ..." (p. 1); or "Everyone has a moment in history which belongs particularly to him. It is the moment when his emotions achieve their most powerful sway over him . . . " (p. 32); or "But something held me back. Perhaps I was stopped by that level of feeling, deeper than thought, which contains the truth . . . " (p. 40); or finally, " . . . that deep layer of the mind where all is judged by the five senses and primitive expectation . . . " (p. 139). These formulations parallel exactly the "blind impulse" and the "crazy thing inside me" which Gene offers to us as explanation for his treachery toward Phineas. What is ominous in such statements is that primitive emotionalism suddenly looms not as a momentary aberration in behavior but as the steady bedrock of truth. If this prereflective layer of emotion and intuition dominates our lives, overwhelms our reason and our sense of civilization, yet is dangerous, even destructive, and uncontrollable, then what is the point of drawing moral distinctions at all? We are simply victims of the irrational.

That is not a comforting thought. But Knowles does not quite leave us in these dire straits. Rather surprisingly, sports provide a kind of counterbalance. Put in its simplest form, sports tap hidden powers, creative possibilities, that we never knew existed inside us before, and because sports provide a controlled environment of conditions and rules, a "private explanation" of the world, these discoveries can become achievements. (When Gene knocks Phineas from the tree, one recalls, it is because he had suddenly broken the rules of the game.) This exhilaration of sports becomes their *raison d'etre* in the novel. Phineas's triumphs at Blitzball are one example:

The odds were tremendously against the ball carrier, so that Phineas was driven to exceed himself practically every day when he carried the ball. To escape the wolf pack which all the other players became he created reverses and deceptions and acts of sheer mass hypnotism which were so extraordinary that they surprised even him; after some of these plays I would notice him chuckling quietly to himself, in a kind of happy disbelief.

(p.31)

Gene has a similar experience when he finds his wind during one of his training runs: "Then, for no reason at all, I felt magnificent . . . an accession of strength came flooding through me. Buoyed up, . . . I lost myself, oppressed mind along with body; all entanglements were shed, I broke into the clear" (p.112). It is a central moment for Gene, a discovery of freedom, mental as well as physical, a moment at which self-knowledge comes as a release from his old habits of body and mind, a release of his old demons. "You didn't even know anything about yourself," observes Phineas. "I don't guess I did, in a way," answers Gene, and it is no coincidence that Gene with this experience suddenly feels himself to have "grown bigger" inside the same body (pp. 112-113). This surpassing exhilaration is also the climax, the achievement, of the Winter Carnival and the hallmark of the "separate peace" in which Gene and Phineas exist. The Carnival recreates an Olympian otherworldliness of athletic and spiritual intoxication, a communal enlightenment of physical excitation. It was, says Gene, "our own exuberance which intoxicated us, sent restraint flying." This intoxication inspires Phineas

to create a droll dance among the prizes, springing and spinning from one bare space to another . . . Under the influence . . . of his own inner joy at life for a moment as it should be, as it was meant to be in his nature, Phineas recaptured that magic gift for existing primarily in space . . . It was his wildest demonstration of himself, of himself in the kind of world he loved; it was his choreography of peace.

(p. 128)

This same intoxication inspires Gene to ski jump with "a sensation of soaring flight, of hurtling high and far through space" and allows him to qualify in Phineas's contrived Olympian Decathlon trials, to "run as though I were an abstraction of speed, to walk the half-circle of statues on my hands, to balance on my head on top of the icebox on top of the Prize Table." For Gene, Phineas, and the others, this athletic and spiritual inebriation is "escape," "liberation," a "special and separate peace." The Carnival is deeply symbolic in the novel, for it represents for Gene—the grinding student and intellectual, the fearer and obeyer of all rules, the quietly hostile competitor against all others—a release, a reprieve from the entrapment of his own mind, from the crazy thing, the ignorance, the war inside him. Just as Gene is associated with falling in the novel and Phineas with flying, would it be an exaggeration to say that sports offer one kind of answer, one kind of redemption against the fall of man from the tree of his own evil?

Indeed, sports are the reconciliation of summer to winter. They are the ultimate art in the novel, because sports represent art brought into the world; they draw upon our most elemental, biological selves in order to recreate beneficiently the conditions of existence. The Carnival may mark, as Wolfe argues, Phineas's own maturation, his "acceptance of reality," "imperfection," and "life's harshness,"[17] But if Finny's separate peace is a coming to terms with the world as Gene knows it, it is also an act of joy. It is the fullest realization of the promise and exhilaration of summer, with all of summer's wildness (p. 17), summer's "inebriating" acts of athletic virtuosity (p. 37), its "intoxication" of sunshine and water and movement (p. 39), its "breath of widening life" and "oxygen intoxicant," a feeling so "hopelessly promising" even that Gene forgets "whom I hated and who hated me" (p. 47). That phrase, "a separate peace," derives, of course, from Hemingway's *A Farewell to Arms.* It marks Frederick Henry's realization that the values for which he has fought in the war are hollow, that the behavior of the men all around him is capricious, absurd, and without honor, that "they always get you in the end." Henry's separate peace is nihilism and withdrawal; Phineas's is integration, the creation of meaning through recreation.

But Gene himself calls this separate peace "momentary and illusory," a phrase which draws us back to the problem with which we began, the death of Phineas. For his destruction by the "hard facts," the "rocklike facts" of the world seems to prove his essential fragility, his unsuitability for life. Some critics argue that when Gene brings evil into the idyllic summer he "sets in motion a chain of events which lead with Hellenic inevitability to Phineas' death."[18] The elementary evil of the world, in this view, must always destroy its Phineases. The proximate reason for Phineas's death, however, is the lodging of a particle of his own bone marrow in his heart during Dr. Stanpole's setting of his broken leg, as if, Knowles might be saying, Phineas dies from an overplus of his own animal vigor. Phineas's death is pathetic but it need not be considered tragic, for it is fundamentally accidental in a way that little has been accidental in the novel heretofore. The fresh break in Phineas's leg is "simple" and "clean," according to Dr. Stanpole (p. 185). It is not a refracturing of the old crippling injury which, we are led to believe, is healing stronger than before. It is a fresh break, made possible, yes, by Phineas's unsteadiness on foot, but caused more directly by the hard "factness" of the marble steps, and precipitated more indirectly by Brinker's relentless pursuit of guilt and blame, of the rules, a pursuit with which Finny wishes

---

[17] Ibid.

[18] Crabbe, 110.

no part. Though Gene takes responsibility for Phineas's death—"I killed my enemy there" (p. 196), he says—he is wrong. When Phineas rushes headlong from Brinker's inquisition, he does so not because he wishes to deny the inescapable revelation of Gene's treachery in the tree; he does so because he despises Brinker's obsession with "collecting every f———ing fact there is in the world"; he does so because "I don't care . . . I just don't care" (pp. 168-69). Phineas lives on a plane that is beyond that sort of information and the recrimination which is its purpose. And indeed, collecting all of Brinker's facts would never save anyone, Brinker, Gene, or Phineas, from the elemental hardness of stones when chance or intention brings us into collision with them.

The circumstances of Phineas's death, then, are in some sense external to the circumstance of his life. Further evidence of that distinction is that "reality" does not defeat Phineas even though it destroys him, for Phineas lives on in Gene. When Phineas says that when you love something enough it loves you back in whatever way it can, he is more right than wrong. It is Gene, once his "opposite," who now becomes his surrogate and double. The excavation in Gene's heart, made by the expiation of his anger, is "filled" by Phineas's nature, which remains a living presence in him. Phineas, in an odd and unexpected sense, has indeed trained Gene for the Olympics, after all.

12

Olympism and American Fiction

Elizabeth S. Bressan

THE SPIRIT OF OLYMPISM conjures up images of ancient Greek athletes engaged in classic forms of competition, locked in a Herculean struggle which somehow epitomized the human ideals of beauty, fortitude and dignity. Olympism thus conceived takes on the status of a myth, not in the sense of a fabrication, but in a rich cultural sense in which a myth describes in part what people believe and in part what people want to believe. Olympism, as a cultural myth about participation in competitive sport, seems to run contrary to many documented aspects of the sport experience in the United States. While the subsequent contrast between myth and reality is evidenced in a number of direct confrontations, it is within more subtle formats that the pervasiveness of the conflict may be appreciated. The role of the sport experience in American fiction as a device for character development is one such format. Two authors have been selected as examples for this exploration because both provided sport experiences as an integral part of their development of main characters. One author, John Updike, uses sport as a dominant force in determining his character's behavior. The other, Thomas Wolfe, employs sport as an illustrative event to underscore qualities within his characters that had been introduced previously.

Olympism may be described as an idea embedded in a conception about the quality of an individual's life. The idea is about the value of the competitive experience and the definition of "quality of life" is rooted in a commitment to the significance of the human struggle toward that which is "best" within us. The origins of Olympism may be traced to the ancient Greek Olympics, contests in athletics, poetry and music held every four years. The sporting contests quickly became the glamour events of the games. Excellence in sport performance was regarded as a kind of tribute to the gods. The sport hero was accorded a revered status, bringing spiritual blessings and good fortune to the city state which he represented. Prior to the collapse of the games due to increased politicization and the problems brought with professionalization of the athletes, the notion of competition as the pursuit of excellence was reflected in the ideal of *arete.*

Arete is a term which identifies the glory in competition as the quality of the struggle to become excellent, the striving to overcome the obstacles of fate as well as mortal forces. Perhaps the admiration, even worship of the "true" amateur lies in part within man's capacity to endure all of the normal vicissitudes of life, yet still find the strength and courage to surpass all expectations, to exceed that which is supposed to be "humanly" possible. It is through *arete,* the glory found in the struggle, that the mythic value of Olympism begins to emerge.

James has suggested that the games served three mythic functions in ancient Greece.[1] First, they provided an escape from the mundane level of life by establishing the athletic arena as a separate place, a special place where the winner would be the man who deserved to win; the man who had trained properly and who had been judged to be worthy by the gods of fate. Athletes and spectators both could enter into this special world where the rules were followed and the outcomes matched the efforts. Second, the establishment of the games served to present achievement-oriented behavior and the glory found in dedication to goal accomplishment as desirable social behaviors. The third function was proposed as the recognition of sport as an opportunity to create meaning and to cultivate some of the more noble qualities of which man is capable. With the exception of exploits during wartime, sport offered man in a civilized society one of his few opportunities to be truly heroic in a publicly displayed context.

The revival of the modern Olympic Games in 1896 resurrected aspects of sport's mythic potential. Actually, the spirit of Olympism had survived through the writings of scholars during the Renaissance and had taken shape already in the nineteenth century phenomenon of Muscular Christianity and in English gentlemen's conception of sportsmanship and amateurism. Within all of these traditions, sport was elevated once again to that "special place" where a man could demonstrate his "manliness" in terms of such noble qualities as courage, honesty, perseverance and honor in the face of adversity.[2] With the modern Olympics as its showcase, the espoused principles of amateur athletics assumed mythic functions similar to those found in ancient Greek culture.

The promotion of sport as an escape from the mundane aspects of existence has been a primary thrust of various forms of media throughout the twentieth century. Through newspapers, radio and television coverage, spectatorship has become established as a socially approved escape mechanism. The bureaucracy which has organized and controlled amateur sport has gone to extreme lengths to establish an image of the amateur athlete as a pure, honest and hardworking individual who plays for the love of playing. Sport, it is

---

[1] Z. D. James, "Sport: A Myth About Consciousness," *Quest,* 30 (1978): 28-35.

[2] Such actions are labeled "masculine" in psychological terms, and athletics as the showcase of masculinity has been an enduring image since ancient times.

still suggested, is the place where young people learn achievement oriented
behaviors that will prove productive later in life. Industry, dedication and
discipline are the key ingredients in successful sport participation
. . . or at least that is how the myth goes. Sport is also suggested as a significant
opportunity to display one's courage and one's character. The tension and
temptation that surrounds participation has been conceived of as a kind of
moral test. In sport, the myth suggests, man can rise to his full glory, or
fall to his deepest level of failure.

The notion of Olympism has been wedded, then, to a modern extension
of the ancient Greek myth about sport participation. While sociological and
psychological studies have indicated that there is nothing *inherent* in the
doing or viewing of sport that cultivates either escapism, achievement
orientation or moral development and expression, Olympism yet lingers as
a promise of what sport "could" be. The potential of the sport experience
to fulfill its mythic promise may be related to the degree and intensity of
support and acceptance that a society in general feels for the spirit of Olympism.

One way to gauge the prevalence of positive feelings and belief in the
tenets of Olympism is to review the manner in which participation in sports
is used within literary works. Rather than examine novels in which sport serves
as the central focus (in which case the author's interpretation of sport would
have to carry the story), it might be more illustrative to regard the use of
sport in novels in which sport serves to create images or impact on the lives
of the characters without becoming the primary context for their behavior.
By selecting "non-sport" fiction for perusal, perhaps an indication can be
discerned about the common perception of sport as an integral part of the
American life experience.

An Example from Current American Fiction

John Updike's *Rabbit* trilogy has been selected as an example of the use
of sport as a crucial determinant in the development of the main character,
Harry Angstrom, although the reader never meets Harry during his "playing
days." In terms of the myth of escapism, Harry Angstrom presents the case
of the ex-jock. The first novel in the series, *Rabbit, Run,* begins with twenty-
six-year-old Harry Angstrom stopping for a pick-up game of basketball with
some skeptical neighborhood boys. All the old moves come back to him
as Updike reveals sport as a highly sensual, even aesthetic experience. As
the story continues, the reader realizes that Harry's past as a high school
basketball star has defined his character and has become a reference point
for his identity. Throughout the novel, he is introduced to others as a "former
basketball player." Indeed, Harry's recurring inability to deal with the present
and future appears to be an outcome of the exaggerated status he was accorded
during his playing days. As Harry states:

I once did something right. I played first-rate basketball. I really did. And after you're first rate at something, no matter what it is, it kinds of takes the kick out of being second-rate.[3]

Life is a second-rate experience for Harry, compared to his existence in basketball. This is not the escape from the mundane advocated in Olympism, but rather a permanent retreat into the past in an effort to avoid dealing with the present or future. As with many ex-jocks in American literature, sport is a kind of albatross around the neck of Harry Angstrom; a constant call to live in the past because the present and future will never measure up.

The deteriorating influence of Harry's sport participation is extended in the second novel, *Rabbit Redux.* Harry's disastrous efforts to "find himself" are summarized by his own admission to Jill, a girl with whom he is having an affair:

She asks him:
    "You don't think much of yourself, do you?"
He replies:
    "Once the basketball stopped, I suppose not."[4]

Harry's continued efforts to recover the sense of fulfillment he ostensibly found as a player could not be called properly a "search." He never lets go of his youthful images of success and appears to dedicate his actions to spreading his unhappiness and despair. It is as though life after sport is pointless and pale by comparison, with nothing more than death awaiting at its conclusion. The book closes with some hope for Harry as he seems to realize, finally, that the past in which he has been wallowing should be acknowledged as the past: " . . . it was an ice cream world he made his mark in,"[5] he admits, and his ice cream world is gone forever.

In the final novel in the trilogy, *Rabbit is Rich*, Harry's life has taken the form of middle class acceptability, as have his sport experiences. He and his wife, Janice, have joined the country club where he plays golf and she plays tennis, then they meet for cocktails at poolside. Sport scores from the professional teams become safe topics for conversation whenever Harry is uncomfortable. He is still introduced as a former basketball player, however, and at the settlement of his father's-in-law estate, he discovers that Fred Springer had kept a complete scrapbook of Harry's athletic career in anticipation of the day when Harry would join him in his used-car business.

Like any model middle class American, Harry has become overweight and taken up jogging. He finds references to sport in his everyday life

---

[3] John Updike, *Rabbit, Run* (New York: Alfred A. Knopf, 1960), p. 107.

[4] John Updike, *Rabbit Redux* (New York: Alfred A. Knopf, 1971), p. 200.

[5] Ibid., p. 393.

experiences, noting how his dislike for one of his long-time cronies was because he was " . . . one of those locker room show offs always soaping himself for everybody to see."[6] Sport provides Harry with a central analogy for life itself. In thinking about his golf swing, he notes:

> It is like life itself in that its performance cannot be forced and its underlying principle shies from being permanently named.[7]

The images of sport presented by Updike through Harry Angstrom's life are rooted in the notion that sport may be an opportunity for young men to achieve, but there is no reason to suspect that achievement orientation will be learned from it. Success in sport can be a useful calling card in a man's future and may provide him with a bevy of images with which to console himself as he stumbles through life. It is important to note that Harry stumbles, he does not struggle through life. No chance for *arete*. The reader cannot help but wonder if the sport world ruins a young man's future by offering him the fleeting role of hero, only to abandon him once his playing days are over. There appears to be no moral climate of growth surrounding Harry's sport experience, either. In fact, Harry's former high school coach was dismissed from his job for some association with gambling.

Sport within the Rabbit trilogy is a far cry from Olympism. While Harry says nothing to give the impression that he would have been better off without sport success, the reader is left with the suspicion that sport has had a negative influence on Harry's life. There appears to be nothing of the personal growth or expression through sport that is associated with the spirit of Olympism. Sport in America, as defined by Updike, is a social experience for young men which is potentially distorting. In fairness to Updike, however, he did need some agency to debilitate Harry, and sport was a convenient vehicle. Perhaps if novels were reviewed where sport is not forced into such an antagonistic role, a more "Olympic" image would be discovered.

An Earlier Example From American Fiction

Thomas Wolfe's novels are from a very different period in American literature, yet both Updike and Wolfe present main characters who are at odds with the world around them. Wolfe's characters, however, appear to be more immersed in a real struggle to come to terms with life. They make various efforts, they agonize over failures and reflect with great intensity upon the reasons behind their difficulties. This more heroic presentation of the efforts of the main characters in Wolfe's works may be a function of the strong autobiographical tone of his writings. In any case, he does not employ sport as a central or determining experience for his characters' development, but

---

[6] John Updike, *Rabbit is Rich* (New York: Alfred A. Knopf, 1981), p. 56.
[7] Ibid., p. 50.

rather allows sport to be an occasion where dimensions of characters are revealed or enriched. This disposition toward sport as a revealing experience is more in accord with the premises of Olympism.

In *Look Homeward, Angel*, Wolfe traces the life of Eugene Gant as he grows through childhood toward a career as a novelist and playwright. It is in Eugene's boyhood that sport is presented as an occasion where he confronts himself and his failure to relate to other boys his age. Eugene is described by Wolfe:

> He played games badly, although he took a violent interest in sports. Eugene tried vainly to imitate the precision and power of this movement which drove the ball in a smoking arc out of the lot, but he was never able . . . he never learned to play on a team, to become a limb of that single animal which united telepathically in a concerted movement. He became nervous, highly excited, and erratic in team-play, but he spent hours alone with another boy . . . passing a ball back and forth.
>
> But he was in no way able to submit himself to the discipline, the hard labor, the acceptance of defeat and failure that make a good athlete; he always wanted to win, he always wanted to be the general, the heroic spearhead of victory. And after that he wanted to be loved. Victory and love. In all his swarming fantasies Eugene saw himself like this —unbeaten and loved. But moments of clear vision returned to him when all the defeat and misery of his life was revealed . . . he remembered, with a drained sick heart, the countless humiliations, physical and verbal, he had endured . . . His eagle had flown; he was himself, in a moment of reason, as a madman playing Caesar.[8]

For Eugene, the aspiration to be a hero tantalizes him, for in a boy's world, sport (in this instance, baseball) provides the chance. That Eugene has tied victory to love and defeat to humiliation is not far from the Olympic idea of associating special, almost spiritual qualities with victors in sport. The worship of athletic heroes was commonplace in ancient Greece. Eugene is even sensitive to the hard work and discipline that could be an element of *arete*, the noble struggle that a true athlete endures. Wolfe uses sport again as an opportunity to define Eugene's basic insecurity. His driving desire to be loved is reflected in his efforts to gain the attention and approval of his mother:

> He shrank from the physical conflict of boy life, but knowing her eye was upon him, he plunged desperately into their games, his frail strength buffeted in the rush of strong legs, the heavy jar of strong bodies, picking himself up bruised and sore at heart to follow and join again the mill of the burly pack. Day after day to the ache of his body was added the ache and shame of his spirit, but he hung on with a pallid smile across his lips, and envy and fear of their strength in his heart. He parroted faithfully . . . about the spirit of fair play, sportsmanship, playing the game for the game's sake, accepting defeat with a smile, and so on, but he had no genuine belief or understanding.[9]

---

[8] Thomas Wolfe, *Look Homeward, Angel* (New York: Modern Library, 1929), p. 186.

[9] Ibid., p. 197.

Sport does not fail Eugene; Eugene fails sport. He is unable to join in what Wolfe pictured as a grand experience. Is it surprising that Wolfe's presentation of sport is compatible with the spirit of Olympism? His characters all led rather tragic lives and struggled throughout against the powers of a fate of gigantic proportion. Tragedy and Fate were familiar themes in Greek literature. Eugene cannot escape into sport, though he longs to. He cannot join the other boys effectively as they joyfully enter the achievement oriented world of sport. He envies them as he questions his own worth. He is distraught because he cannot embrace the moral code of the sportsman; though he yearns to believe, he is able only to put up a shallow pretense.

It is not surprising that even in this cursory examination of the novels of two American authors, one would seem to reject Olympism while the other seems to reinforce it. Updike is an author from this decade. His character, Harry Angstrom, is from the late 1950s, sixties, and seventies. In Updike's work, the corporate mentality has taken over everything, leaving it depersonalized. Sport was Harry's last personal experience in which he felt in control and effective. He was skillful; he was a star. The rules of the corporation never make sense to him, and he is left only with memories. Sport did not help Harry learn achievement oriented behaviors; it did not have a positive impact on his moral development, and his escape into sport is an escape into memories not an involvement in the sport world itself.

Wolfe wrote during the 1920s and thirties. His characters grew up in a different America. That sport in Wolfe's novels would assume an image which resembles Olympism should not be considered only a function of this "dated" aspect of the period in which he wrote. True, sport was more of a personal experience and less of a social institution prior to the explosion of big time sport that has marked the last half of this century. But also an attitude about the individual as an agent in his own destiny is more pronounced in Wolfe's work than in Updike's. Such a conceptualization of the individual as capable of striving, despite the odds, is close to the Olympic ideal.

What may be cause for consternation among sportsmen and sportwomen interested in recreating or perpetuating the spirit of Olympism is that Updike's depiction of the sport world as a social institution without attention to the development of the future behaviors of players, is not a radical one. In fact, when reading the *Rabbit* trilogy, there is nothing particularly upsetting or confronting about the state of the ex-jock who is lost now that his playing days are over. However, Wolfe's images make us feel the anguish of Eugene as he longs to enter into sport, although that anguish is just a portion of a greater tragedy that dominates the novel. Both authors present sport as a young man's pastime, though Wolfe leaves room for Olympism and Updike does not.

Summary

As with all myths, the influence of Olympism on sport in America is dependent upon a large base of popular sport. If popular American fiction is viewed as an indicator of the pervasiveness of broad social attitudes, then the resilience of the myth of Olympism may be explored by noting the impact of sport participation on characters in related works. While America prior to World War II may have held the sporting experience close to the myth of Olympism, there is reason to doubt that the proximity of sport to an "Olympic ideal" has been sustained through the postwar period to this day.

With Thomas Wolfe's *Look Homeward, Angel,* the sport experience is offered as an unique opportunity for an individual to reach the heights, as it were, of human splendor. The sport experience is coveted, revered . . . it is *Arete,* the struggle to achieve, and the glory is in the struggle. But the postwar fiction of John Updike's Rabbit Trilogy suggests no such noble role for sport. Achievement, not the struggle toward it, seems to be the hard currency with which contemporary characters deal.

Where in the mythic function of Olympism is American fiction? Where is the promise of sport as an escape from the mundane, or a fundamental respect for the process by which goals are achieved in sport? Where is the cultivation of sport as an opportunity to create personal meaning and display "the best that is within us?" Are these conceptions about sport all buried in the American past? If one listens to the rhetoric that typically surrounds the Olympic Games, one might get the feeling that indeed Olympism is alive and well. And yet the "real" impact of Olympism is difficult to discern with all the current challenges to the definition of amateurism and the obvious political overtones of the Games.

The mythic function of Olympism on sports in America may be evaluated in terms of its impact on the way Americans think, talk, play, and write about their sport. If a cursory comparison between Thomas Wolfe's and John Updike's conceptions of sport reveals anything, it reveals a possible change in the American view of sport over the past fifty years. That change may suggest that the myth of Olympism, while still espoused, is no longer seriously regarded. Once any cultural myth falls from a position of credibility, it is considered to be a fabrication. Noting the way American authors conceive of sport, a reader might ask, "Is there any real relationship between sport and Olympism? Is Olympism a fiction?"

13

Varieties of American Work and Play Experience: The Example of a Popular Jewish Baseball Novelist

Eric Solomon

I

CONSIDER THE CASES of two Jewish-American baseball players during the 1930s. Al Shacht (three years in the major leagues; 14-10 pitching record) loved baseball as his work despite his mother's desire to see him become a concert pianist. Moe Berg (fifteen years in the majors as a catcher; .243 batting average) loved baseball despite his Princeton-Columbia-Sorbonne education, his vast knowledge of languages, his advanced degrees in law and linguistics, his years as a master spy for the U. S. government. Both men were marginal, if competent, players of a game. Both men had other career opportunities, more appropriate to the traditions of their ethnic backgrounds, Shacht as an entertainer on the stage or in movies, Berg as an international lawyer or university professor. Yet neither could really break away from the fields of play. "I was nuts about the game from the first time I heard the crack of the batted balls as they echoed up from Harlem,"[1] said Shacht, and he hung on to baseball for his lifetime, first as a coach who did comic turns, then as a baseball comedian, "the clown prince of baseball." Despite the many professional and patriotic pressures—and familial—Moe stayed for years in the demeaning role of bullpen catcher for the Boston Red Sox because he

---

[1] Al Schacht, *Clowning Through Baseball* (New York: Bantam, 1949), p. 1.

loved baseball, the players, the special American male ambiance.[2] And yet, and yet. Shacht nervously mocked the play aspect by parodying baseball's characters, even the game's physical moves—since to be a comedian was an accepted work role for a second generation Jewish-American. And Berg insisted on his work role in a proper Jewish fashion by garnering degrees, becoming a master-intellectual.[3] This double vision, this tension, is, of course, quintessentially American. For the Jewish-American novelist as well as for the athlete, work was adult, play was childish. But work could be killing, and play could be vivifying.

In simplest terms, even if immigrants didn't expect to find American streets paved with gold, they were overwhelmed by the realities of pavements and pushcarts. Memoirs, histories, newspaper reports attest to the Jewish work ethic in particular. Whether slaving in a sweatshop or peddling fruit, housepainting or storekeeping, man or woman, adult or child, the first generation had only work to consider, not so much for success as for survival.[4] Some rose from rags to riches, some took solace for poverty in religious withdrawal. The pages of Michael Gold and Anzia Yezierska provide a plethora of examples.

As for the second generation, the children, what of play? While games were not forbidden by parental order they represented personal weakness and socio-economic doom. If, in Irving Howe's *World of Our Fathers*, one frantic parent is shown writing to Abraham Cahan's *Jewish Daily Forward* bemoaning a son's penchant for baseball—"What is the point of this crazy game?"—and Eddie Cantor can recall that "to the pious people of the ghetto a baseball player was the king of the loafers,"[5] Cahan himself realized just how strong the pull of play, of sports, particularly of baseball, was to the youth as a leisure activity and an acculturating force. He printed a diagram of the Polo Grounds with instructions, in Yiddish, as to how the game was played. The article, "Der iker fun di baseball game, erklert for mit keyn sports layt," the essentials of baseball explained to people unfamiliar with sports, appeared in the *Forward* on August 27, 1909.[6] Yet playing was just that: a threat because it was "not-work." Stickball games brought sons into the streets where lurked danger and foul language. More importantly, if one was playing

---

[2] In his sister's scrapbook now in the Baseball Hall of Fame Library, Berg's father, a Ukranian-Jewish immigrant, declares that he never accepted the ballplaying. "Moe could have been a brilliant barrister, but he gave it all up for baseball."

[3] He even appeared on the high-toned quiz show "Information Please," as did the great philosopher Morris Raphael Cohen who specialized in baseball questions.

[4] Milton Meltzer quotes a guidebook for immigrant Jews: "A bit of advice for you: Do not take a moment's rest. Run, do work and keep your own good in mind." (Milton Meltzer, *Taking Root* (New York: Dell, 1977), p. 135.

[5] Irving Howe, *World of Our Fathers* (New York: Harcourt Brace Jovanovich, 1976), p. 182.

[6] Gunther Barth, *City People* (New York: Oxford University Press, 1980), p. 191.

with a bat and ball, one was neither attending to the immediate business of life—minding the store, say—nor preparing properly for the future by going to school, Public or Hebrew, thus caring for the economic and spiritual business of life.[7]

Play was suspect. Many Jewish ballplayers took assumed names, not for fear of anti-semitism but to protect the innocent, their families who would be ashamed of a nice Jewish boy playing a game rather than using his brain or his artistry. There were, for example, at least seven Cohens who played major league ball, only one of whom, Andy, retained his name, while others became Kane, Cooney, or Bohne. Only those who were gangsters or boxers and literally fought their ways out of the slums were more willing publically to accept their culturally anti-typical roles. Ed Reulbach, a great Jewish pitcher, wondered in 1926 why this situation prevailed. "If I were a magnate . . . I would send scouts all over the United States and Canada in an effort to locate some hook-nosed youngster who could bat and field. . . . The Jewish people are great spenders and they could be made excellent fans."[8]

Thus, baseball was perceived as good or bad, depending on the generation doing the perceiving. Most often, fathers, rather than mothers, understood their sons' needs for the sport as an acculturation device. While both Irwin Shaw and Philip Roth have written extensively about the connections formed between male generations by a mutual love for baseball—indeed, building on an image first caught by Abraham Cahan in his novel *Yekl*—and Leslie Fiedler wished for spotless WASP parents who "continue to stir envy and emulation in children like me, who had neither dog nor cat, only Yiddish-speaking grandparents and a father who never joined me at playing baseball,[9] perhaps Max Apple stated the benign possibilities most movingly. His working class father

> . . . alone knew what I wanted and loved. My grandfather wanted me to be a rabbinic scholar, my grandmother thought I should own at least two stores, my sisters and my mother groomed me for a career as a lawyer or a "public speaker." My father knew that I wanted to play second base for the Tigers and have a level swing like Al Kaline. [The play motif]. I probably love and write about sports so much as a

---

[7] Worst of all (*pace* Schacht and Berg and nearly one hundred other professional baseball players from the first in America, one Lipman E. Pike, through Barney Pilty (the Yiddishe curver), Johnny Kling to Harry Danning, Hank Greenberg, Sid Gordan, Al Rosen, Sandy Koufax) would be actually to *become* an athlete, a professional player, rather than a doctor, a dentist, a lawyer, or, all else failing, a teacher.

[8] John McGraw, of course, did that, searching for a Jewish Babe Ruth but coming up with the likes of Moses Solomon, the "Rabbi of Swat," who could hit homers, alas, only in the minors, or Andy Cohen, once considered a rival to Rogers Hornsby, but who lasted only three years with the Giants, despite a .281 batting average, because of his slowness afoot. Sam Bohne, the Cincinnati infielder, responded to Reulbach by explaining that Jews simply would not apply themselves to a game, because their "keen and active" minds enabled them to become interested in real work: business. F.C. Lane, "Why Not More Jewish Ballplayers," *Baseball Magazine*, XXXVI (January 1926): 341.

[9] Leslie Fiedler, *What Was Literature?* (New York: Simon and Schuster, 1983), p. 8.

way of remembering him. [The writer's ploy, joining work and play.]. I carry a baseball with me the way he carried my mittens in the glove compartments of a half-dozen trucks to remind him of his little boy who grew up to study the secrets of literature but still does not forget to check the Tigers' box score every morning of the season.[10]

Mostly, however, the sons of immigrants had little fatherly support for baseball play. The anger of a father in Ludwig Lewisohn's *Upstream* demonstrates how even more assimilated German-Jewish fathers were appalled by the national game's attractions for an Americanized son: "He is a baseball 'fan' . . . [accepts] the naked vulgarity of the streets and of the baseball diamond. . .."[11] Far more disappointed were Eastern European Jewish fathers: "My father won't allow us to play ball on the lot. He says it's a waste of time and a disgrace to make such a lot of noise over nothing. He was raised in Poland."[12] And this tension remained, even though Roger Kahn could define the entire range of father-son love through the son teaching the father to love baseball— and substituting acceptance and tenderness for opposition or fragmentation; or Irwin Shaw could describe the reverse situation as a father teaches the meaning of America to his son by taking him to Yankee Stadium to see Joe DiMaggio as *his* father had taken him to see Babe Ruth; or, Philip Roth could find the source of his entire education in math, geography, history, or literature emanating from baseball lore. Charles Angoff had an assimilated uncle:

> When Kivve took his three boys to Boston Common to watch a baseball game, my father was so flabbergasted that words failed him. He merely looked at Kivve long and silently, as if to say, "May the good Lord have mercy on you for degrading yourself and your family so!" My father's attitude was rather complex. He knew I watched a baseball game once in a while but that didn't bother him. He apparently thought that I would outgrow it when I reached the age of, say, thirteen or fourteen. But he thought it was not right for a father to aid and abet his children in the baseball foolishness.[13]

Baseball foolishness, indeed. Playing the game with its seeming disorder, lack of social commitment, freedom from ethic or intellect, seemed to block the need for second generation Jews to work desperately to shift social class from poor to middle, labor from handwork in factory to brainwork in business or law office, residence from Brownsville to White Plains. Still, the middle range between work and play occupied by the formal *game* of baseball, with its ordered rules, its public performances in the clearly marked confines of

---

[10] Max Apple, "My Love Affair With English," *New York Times Book Review*, (22 November 1981), p. 9.

[11] Quoted in Abraham Chapman, ed., *Jewish-American Literature* (New York: Signet, 1974), pp. 206-7.

[12] Quoted in Meltzer, *Taking Root*, p. 18.

[13] Charles Angoff, "When I Was a Boy in Boston," Asriel Eisenberg, ed., *The Golden Land* (New York: Thomas Yoseloff, 1964), p. 251.

a green center in the city, was attractive to those who sought assimilation not only to American history, heroes, and records, to traditions, but also to the best American work habits. Steven Riess documents the utility of baseball's myths, symbols, realities, rituals, statistics as ways of teaching children familiar American values and assimilating new citizens into the dominant culture, showing "courage, honesty, patience, and temperance as well as ...teamwork."[14] A well-known Boston rabbi hailed the game for bringing the urban worker into the open air, mixing with masses of fellows; and, most interestingly, making men better qualified for the workplace by their observance of baseball's scientific complexity, which is similar to "the interplay of vast and complex machinery, but . . . incalculably more admirable because carried out by cooperating men, and as a rule, by superb specimens of physical manhood."[15] Baseball, more than any other sport, worked well in the 1920s and 1930s as a non-violent, "national" urban function. And it worked best for Jewish immigrants—who had come to America to stay and were eager to grasp the crucial center of American experience. To escape the disorientation brought about by the loss of the ordered existence of the *shtetl*, the attachment to the fortunes of a professional baseball team worked wonders of assimilation.

Gunther Barth brilliantly analyzes the work values set forth by baseball to the city dweller. First, baseball taught new city folk that "rules regulated the happiness of their world, too, and that beyond the fences of the ball park, restraints tempered the competition to get ahead in the world." Second, those immigrants who did not have enough English to read a book or watch non-Yiddish theater could learn from sports spectacles. Third, rooting for a city team "gave rootless people a sense of belonging" to the metropolis, to America. Additionally, games taught how to express dissent within limits (boo the umpire); to lose one day, win the next, to grasp a new and swiftly-changing history (records made and then broken); and to comprehend a statistical—Talmudic, almost—measure of success. "In the context of averages spanning several seasons, the achievements of players and teams created a shared historical experience among people without a common history."[16] Indeed, this aspect of play substituted for the myths left behind in Europe or lost in the work of Hebrew school. "Traditionally, Jewish youths found transformations of the immediate in the stories of the Bible and the legends of Jewish folklore. For some first and second generation Jewish-American youth this storehouse of myth has been supplemented if not entirely replaced by the myth and legends of baseball."[17] That the players themselves, except for the few Rosens and Arnovichs, Sherrys and Weintraubs, were not actually Jewish

---

[14] Steven Riess, *Touching Base* (Westport, Conn.: Greenwood Press, 1980), p. 14.

[15] Charles Fleischer, "A Bit of Baseball Biography," *Baseball Magazine*, I (June 1908): 34-35.

[16] Barth, *City People*, pp. 149.

[17] Walter Harrison, "Six-Pointed Diamond: Baseball and American Jews," *Journal of Popular Culture*, vol. 15, no. 3 (Winter 1981): 117.

role models, was unimportant. According to one reminiscence of Brooklyn in the 1920s, "I don't think my contemporaries and I believed that the figures who loomed largest in our imaginations—say . . . Babe Ruth . . . were actually Jewish, but we never clearly thought of them as anything else, in a period when most of New York's Jews were striving desperately to become Americanized. . . ."[18]

II

It is of interest to examine one Jewish-American novelist of the many who employed baseball either as subject or as controlling metaphor for their novels. Certainly, the name of Gerald Green appears in no previous accounts of what I classify as the Jewish-American baseball novel—a work of fiction that concentrates on baseball, written by a Jewish novelist who seeks to use the sports theme as a way of defining the American experience. After some tentative approaches, usually in stories by writers like Paul Goodman or Delmore Schwartz, baseball became a major theme in the 1950s and 1960s in fiction by such Jewish novelists as Irwin Shaw, Charles Einstein, Eliot Asinof, Mark Harris, Bernard Malamud, and Philip Roth and has developed into a minor genre in the last decade in the fiction of Jerome Charyn, Jay Neugeboren, Sylvia Tennenbaum, Roger Kahn, Gary Morgenstern, Donald Honig, Harry Stein, David Ritz, Michael Schiffer, David Garkeet, among others. For Gerald Green, I would submit, baseball as play became the necessary structural and thematic device to counter the fixed success-failure work motif that characterizes most urban ethnic novels.

In Green's marvelous novel of growing up absurdly Jewish and awkward in a Depression urban wilderness, *To Brooklyn With Love* (1967), baseball (play) saves, while medicine (work) does not. As in those many turn-of-the-century ironic novels of business success and personal failure entitled "The Rise of . . . ," *To Brooklyn With Love* establishes a clear conflict between career achievement and moral success gained through a game. The tension between work and play provides the novel's psychological and narrative strength and complexity as well as asserts its socio-political angle of vision.

Author of nearly twenty books, and screenplays, television shows (most recently the Holocaust series), Gerald Green is easily categorized as a popular, commercial writer. His books sell well, get widely reviewed, become book club choices, appear in paperback, become movies—yet rarely, if ever, reach a literary critic's notice. Nevertheless, for the student of American culture, Green's books are a rich resource. I would like to examine two of his novels, *The Last Angry Man* (1956), which is ultimately flawed, I think, because of its single-minded focus on the failure of work values in 1950s America that makes the novel too harsh and shrill, and the aforementioned *To Brooklyn With Love*, a 1930s memoir that becomes one of the most rewarding works

[18] William Poster, "'Twas a Dark Night in Brownsville," in Eliot Cohen, ed., *Commentary on the American Scene* (New York: Alfred A. Knopf, 1953), pp. 55.

in that long line of American fiction stretching back to Mark Twain's *Adventures of Huckleberry Finn*—a novel evoking lyrical childhood memories of escape into play from a dark world dominated by adults whose work ethic threatens the loss of youthful vitality, commitment, and freedom of spirit.

Basically, *The Last Angry Man* deals with two kinds of American work, both of which lead to a wasteland. The novel's hero, and he is just that, is Dr. Samuel Abelman, and is he a worker! Trapped in a slum practice, Dr. Abelman represents the best kind of working doctor in what should be one of America's most rewarding—financially and spiritually—professions: healing. And he is a fine doctor, intelligent, well-trained, persistent, careful, in every way an able man. He makes the American way up from an impoverished background as an immigrant with a tailor father and a tubercular brother who works in a shirt factory. Abelman works steadily, first as an eager office boy for a dreaming, failing wholesaler of paper bags, then as secretary to a gymnasium teacher. And here, for the only time, games—physical culture rather than free play—provide an alternative to sheer work. Sam Abelman, powerful and a fighter, becomes a playground instructor and, in a scene mentioned by Gerald Green in the later novel as well, defeats an anti-semite in a street fight. Next, medical school, Bellevue, incredible work loads: "He had midyear examinations all that week—clinical medicine, special pathology, surgery, obstetrics, and therapeutics. He enjoyed the challenge; he knew he would do well."[19] And he is one of the ghetto workers in the dawn. "The ghetto people were on their way to work—Brownsville auslanders making their sodden pilgrimages to the East Side, to lower Manhattan." He, indeed, is called "the poor but honest Horatio Alger" (216). Yet the American work dream goes awry.

His father dies, Abelman must work too hard, at too many jobs; he falls asleep over a dissecting table, has his moment of academic crisis because of excessive labor, and is saved by the advice of Harlow Brooks, a professor who describes an old woman's personally-invented therapy for pneumonia: calisthenics. So Samuel Abelman learns that he can never quit. "He might collapse from lack of sleep, his grades might plummet him into the bottom quartile of the class . . . but he knew he could not give up" (248). Of course, he survives medical school, marries, goes into general practice—but the story starts to move against the ideal American work ethic.

Green recounts Abelman's work record slowly, counterpointing it with a second American work tale, not of genuine work like medicine, but of false work, the most alienated work in the realms of American culture . . . and of its fiction: advertising and its spawn, television.

Much of the narrative viewpoint in *The Last Angry Man* comes through Woodrow Thrasher, an extremely successful account executive in a large agency, a winner in the boardroom, a creative whiz, a gifted adulterer, and in trouble

[19] Gerald Green, *The Last Angry Man* (New York: Berkeley, 1980), p. 216. All subsequent references to this edition will appear in the text.

because of the failure of his last campaign. Green tries to endow Thrasher with some work ideals—"did it ever occur to us that we're not just in business to sell?" (265). Supposedly a believer in culture, he gains a momentary stay in his job by creating a new program concept, "Americans, U.S.A." where the lives of real people will be depicted—the first, of course, drawn from a chance newspaper report, will be of the Brownsville doctor who has treated a battered black girl. That the story is overblown, written by Dr. Abelman's *schnorrer* nephew Myron, a nearly illiterate newspaper stringer eager for better work—fits Green's structure and theme. The good worker Abelman, puffed by an absurd false worker, Myron, will become the subject of a cynical worker's (Thrasher's) manipulated product, a television program. The novel's curvelinear structure is predictable. The cynic will recapture his ideals and reject his own false work once he comprehends the basic values of the idealistic physician's real work. What saves this novel from the banalities of the usual Carnegie-Alger success story is Gerald Green's own dark vision regarding the American workplace. *All* work turns out to be valueless or momentary, and all workers are either "crap artists," in Dr. Abelman's phrase, or condemned to large defeats and minor victories, as the course of the doctor's career makes clear.

While half the novel resembles *The Hucksters* as Green displays Woody Thrasher's twists and turns to keep his career alive and to deal with the frauds that make up the workplace of the mass media, the other half is similar to *The Citadel* as Green shows the work of medicine to be constantly compromised by ambitious, self-protecting, self-serving medical frauds. Only Samuel Abelman M.D. is honest and hard working, and his career is, at best, marginal. A brilliant diagnostician, Abelman is reduced to trying to save a drug-hooked black teenager from an undetected brain lesion. While the doctor's early practice seemed heroic, as he saved whole families from influenza, his healing efforts are always dogged by non-workers, false professionals, like the health officer who wants to stop Abelman from treating patients because he has not filed enough reports. Gruff, angry, solid, the doctor lacks all smooth bedside manners, does nothing for his patients but save their lives, fights them and their beliefs as well as their non-payments and ingratitudes. While some work rewards appear—a tree as gift from the rare grateful patient, some peer respect from colleagues who have taken more ruthless and cynical paths to financial success, while he makes a modest living—still, the negative aspects of his work are stressed. Rarely can he indulge his warm humor or use his strengths, as when he repairs a complex piece of medical equipment with his own hands and screwdriver. More often his career suffers through betrayals at the hands of ambitious friends who seek great sums of money to come from private practices and private hospitals. Abelman, believing in the dignity of an honest practice among the needy, loves "the work, the challenge, the mystery, the rude camaraderie of the hospitals and the dressing room . . . [but] . . . it was no secret that the big money, the easy, regular hours, the dignity of being a 'professor' lay in the magic of specialization" (361). He remains stuck with "the Goldman girl with the rash that wouldn't go away, Louie Gruber and his erratic vision and hearing . . . some malingerers and some honestly sick with whatever it was that made them skinny and neurotic. It was the entire sorry bunch, the thousands and thousands he had looked at in forty-three years, loving them and cursing them, making each one of them, the best and the worst, part of him" (339).

For Green, then, all work is problematic. If the best of doctors hangs on in near poverty, dealing with hostile, ignorant or non-paying patients, living in a decaying house that is an island in a sea of black faces, the best of advertising men succumbs equally to professional doubts while hanging on to his job, which is similar to "liquifying and mixing everyone's brains in one great electric blender" (324). His marriage and his house are equally at risk because genuine workers no longer exist: "Doesn't anyone *do* anything right anymore? The redwood table doesn't fit; the last grease job on the station wagon, they forgot the transmission . . . What happened to all the people who did things properly?" (328). Green's answer is manifest: they are dying in Brownsville. While Thrasher pulls together the program and the doctor tries to help his black patients, the two worlds, advertising and medicine, join. Both physician and hack writer are trapped; the phrase applied to Thrasher also fits Abelman—" 'You're so full of contradictions that I don't know where to start . . . If you're so darn critical of what you do, why don't you get out?' " (334). Both are bored, both are being closed out. "In a way, his mode of life was more difficult than Sam Abelman's: while he and his associates walked a tightrope over the gorge of despair and failure, perpetually balancing and counterbalancing, the doctor had plunged into the canyon a long time ago and had, in his own way, adjusted to the cold and cruel realities" (397). Both continue their work. The program takes shape, the doctor makes more calls. The price is higher, however. Abelman thinks of suicide, Thrasher of quitting. Abelman's trauma highlights Green's critique of American work experience. " 'It's not the work that gets me. I love it. It's—it's the *bastards*. The haggling, and the ingrates, and the cheats, and the inlaws who are always ready to steal the patients for their brother, the doctor. They eat me up; they won't give me a chance to enjoy my work' " (435).

No Marxist vision, this. Green's mordant novel is apolitical; it bewails the human working condition. All the good doctor gets after years of gifted, devoted service—in contrast to the rich rewards garnered by quacks and opportunists—is " 'An attached house in Brownsville and a lot of aggravation from a bunch of lice who don't appreciate anything I do for them' " (434). And Thrasher, in trouble because he refuses the producer's plan to compromise Abelman's dignity, reaches his nadir: " 'We create symbols, illusions, states of mind; above all, we substitute fiction for reality' " (452—surely a reflexive comment on the novelist's role in *his* work). Thrasher realizes they are " 'drowning in bad talk,' " living illusions, assaulting the public ear and eye with an " 'incessant, relentless avalanche of useless information.' " That this false work makes more jobs for others, is his employer's defense: " 'Think simply of the jobs we create' " (454). Thrasher can do genuine work, for he has been an able editor. "He could redo a complicated, slovenly paragraph with new clauses, reworked punctuation, lengthy excisions, and make it completely readable" (483). Therefore, if the doctor possesses his basic healing gifts, the advertising man has his editorial skills. And good work, hints Green, brings good marriages. Abelman's is stable, and once Thrasher commences to write his script, he returns to his wife, to "the simple, regular rhythms of life" (487).

As the novel reaches its climax, all work breaks down: the union hacks have trouble setting up cameras; the warm-hearted cop fails to protect the woman account executive from being attacked; television is defined as feeding the public crap. Only the doctor's reading of Thoreau and cultivation of his small backyard garden have kept him from a life of quiet desperation, but now he suffers a heart attack and dies before the program that might justify his labors and reclaim his work from obscurity can be aired. " 'What awful, awful luck,' " for the program—for false work, "their illusory world of formats, of concepts, of ratings and sponsor identification" (533). But not such bad luck for genuine work: "All his life Sam Abelman had dealt in the dull realities of the world: in birth, life, death, pain, anxiety, hatred, and love. He had been a congenital enemy of symbols and illusions, of the mythology and fancy tales of the new talkers; even in death he was going to make it tough for the people whose coin they were" (533).

The novel ends on a not quite cynical, not quite sentimental note. Because Abelman becomes a posthumous success, Thrasher's commitment seems once more plausible, and his job is saved—"Talker society worked in curious ways its wonders to perform" (550)—he continues his work, balanced on his tightrope. And he is a better man for having known Abelman who represented a dying breed, the "pure doers." He was the last angry man, " 'fighting bitchery and fraud' " (553). So Thrasher is saved by absorbing "some of this archaic, uncompromising morality—the morality that had forced Sam Abelman to pursue an ungrateful hoodlum, the least of men, through summer heat in city slums, vainly hopeful to the last that he might be saved" (553).

Others he could save, but himself? Gerald Green gives his doctor a fine funeral, "a surging mass of weepers" (556). And the author returns Abelman from the world of work, of medicine and advertising, of policemen and bureaucrats, to his ethnic roots, to an aged rabbi and an elder brother, a traditional Jewish garment worker with features "soft and blurred, worn away by the attrition of cramped sweatshops and jeering gentiles" (557). Moishe says the prayer for the dead, and the old words "properly pay final tribute to the dead healer" (557). As Thrasher accepts his own work because of a renewed faith in the multiform use of words, Gerald Green closes this dark, angry repudiation of the ethics of American work with the possibility that family roots, that ethnic solidarity can supply a counter to the crushing force of work. In his revisit to Dr. Abelman's life, career, and family in *To Brooklyn With Love*, Green will sustain family by play, by the national game, by baseball.

III

In *To Brooklyn With Love* Dr. Samuel Abelman has become Dr. Solomon Abrams, but he is the same figure, furious at his patients and his profession. " 'Ah, why not give up the whole damn thing, once and for all,' "[20] the novel opens; this time, however, Gerald Green focuses on a new character, Albert Abrams, twelve-years-old, a baseball worshipper. The beginning frame has the adult Albert returning with his suburban children to the old neighborhood, the Brownsville of his youth, to a world alien to them, which they found crummy: "He longed to tell them about the schoolyard where they had played solugi, punchball, stickball, boxball, Chinese handball, stoopball, association, but he could not" (2). So he tells us about his longest day, July 1934, when his father "surprised him with a new softball, a genuine Spalding 'indoor,' whiter than an angel's robe, intoxicating with its odor of bleached polished cowhide . . ." (6). Now the blacks are in possession of his playing fields, but his story encompasses them as well—blacks, Jews, other immigrant children, adults, family, all in the lost urban world dominated by the great game of baseball. It is the same Brownsville world recalled by Alfred Kazin in his heartfelt memoir *A Walker in the City*: "But on the Chester Street side of the house I make out the letters we carefully pasted there in tar sometime in the fall of either 1924 or 1925: 'Dazzy Vance/World's Greatest Pitcher/ 262 Strikeouts/Brooklyn National League/Giants Stink on Ice/Dazzy Dazzy Dazzy.' "[21]

To his father's complaining voice, young Albert counterpoints his baseball litany, fondling his new ball, throwing it to the ceiling, dreaming he is "Len Koenecke patroling the outer garden for the Brooklyn Dodgers" (5). His day is filled with youthful promise of play—heat, sun, sports, friends, the new ball. Play will provide both the novel's major metaphor and its dramatic center as well as an opposition to his father's alienating world of work. Yet his father is not alienated from his son's play; the father gives the ball, is happy that his son can play—of course, Green is sufficiently Freudian to have Albert resent his father's sudden joy—calls the boy Lou Gehrig, defends the value of baseball against the mother's fearful sense of intellectual waste. " 'Let the kid play ball. That's important too' " (8). Dr. Abrams can fight the fact that he doesn't earn enough from his work by encouraging his son's commitment to a better world. " 'He told me they couldn't get a game going because nobody in this *fekokteh* neighborhood could afford a ball' " (9). Thus, he funds his son's escape from the sheltering home and mother, into a world where he can't be a sissy, where he must fight as did his father, the muscular gymnast. Despite his anger, Albert loves baseball too much to feel used, for baseball is more than play, it is Talmudic argument. "Briefly, he glanced at

---

[20] Gerald Green, *To Brooklyn With Love* (New York: Pocket Books, 1969), p. 5. All subsequent references to this edition will appear in the text.

[21] Alfred Kazin, *A Walker in the City* (New York: Harcourt Brace, 1951), p. 78.

the sports page of last evening's *Journal.* It paid to be prepared. One never knew when an argument over a batting average would develop" (9).

In the world of tough street kids, of Big Artie, Bimbo, the manic Bushy, Polish Teddy, the Raiders—the bespectacled Albert is an outsider. He must explain where he got the new ball, and Bushy is quick to attack: " 'How else would der Alby-tross get picked to *play* unless he brang the ball?' " (18). Always the butt, he drops the first throw to him. "Invariably he was odd-man out—the loner left on the pavement, squinting behind the eyeglasses that mangled his weak eyes, unsteady on weak ankles . . ." (19), while the others like Bushy moved with the skills and natural coordination of great athletes. Green beautifully catches the *angst* of the outsider, of the last boy to be picked, of the victim of baseball's harshest code, from sandlot to major league: only the best get to play.[22]

In his study of growing up Jewish in New York, Ronald Sanders emphasizes that the only accomplishment that moved his contemporaries was baseball skill "In these games . . . I had developed what seemed like a permanent bent for dropping fly balls, throwing crookedly, and either striking out or popping up to the nearest infielder. My reputation was such that the preliminary 'choose-ups' to our games provided some of the most agonizing moments of my life."[23] But it *is* Albert's ball, and he gets to play rather than submit to his accustomed role of umpire, scorekeeper, lost-ball chaser, or spectator.

Before the game he must fight a different battle with Bushy, not with fists, for his mother's influence stands in the way—"His mother was not part of his street life of punchball and baseball, curses and taunts. No! She read English novels and played bridge and had good manners" (22). Still, baseball can respond to his mother's intellectual approach. Rather than engage in fisticuffs, Albert challenges Bushy to a game of Baseball Players, "an intellectual game. His memory was a fine instrument, honed through endless hours of homework, in cool libraries" (22). Each inning consists of a player presenting the first and last letters of a major league ballplayer's surname, between which the opponent must add the missing letters. Albert is unbeatable because of his Jewish intellect, his Talmudic skill; he is a "Relentless reader of box scores, a sponge who absorbed names endlessly . . ." (23). Haslin vs. Holland, Hoag vs. Porter, then Albert presents DK, Tigers. Bushy can't beat the boy who

---

[22] It is fascinating to note that when a Jewish writer, in this instance Syd Hoff, the cartoonist, creates a children's book about baseball, *The Littlest Leaguer* (1976), his protagonist is a *klutz.* From the jacket picture, which shows a small, bespectacled youth watching a strike sail by, to the opening page where, begloved, he awaits in terror an approaching fly ball, the story is one of wimpish awkwardness. The lad tries and fails, is a water boy and bench sitter, and he is tormented by the team's best hitter. Hoff's book is a gentle fantasy, and his Harold strikes a blow for all weak-eyed Jewish kids when he properly times a three-and-two slow ball and belts it for a home run with the bases loaded. Back in the real world, however . . .

[23] Ronald Sanders, *Reflections on a Teapot* (New York: Harper & Row, 1972), p. 96.

reads sports pages rather than hits a punchball, for Bushy never heard of Doljack, who pinch hit the previous day.[24]

Albert triumphs and heads home, secure in his intellectual strength, the doctor's son. Thus, Green establishes his novel's tension, the doctor's work against the son's play, the street kids' physical abilities against the son's imaginative play of mind, the mother's creative pretensions against the son's love for street play, the powerful father's admiration for physical battle against the son's fear of fights. This July day will hardly sustain the novelistic resonance of Leopold Bloom's June day, but Abramsday will be a baseball dream/ nightmare.

Albert is rarely free from the shadow of his compulsive working father; in his leisure time he with "biceps of steel" gardens while encouraging Albert who has his mother's "smooth unmolded arms and legs" to gain muscle by body-building exercises, for in baseball one merely stands around. Dr. Abrams doesn't really believe his condescending farewell to his son, " 'Hit a home run. Be another Ty Cobb,' " and his son doesn't believe in the medical practice that keeps his father in a constant state of anger. Despite his mother's pleas to protect his weak ankles, his father's preference for gymnastics, Albert Abrams, age twelve, arms himself for the joust; he finds his glove and bat and goes to play in the streets. The glove "was the best on the block—a genuine Chick Hafey, burnished mahogany brown with neats-foot oil. The bat was rather scarred and the base of the handle was chipped. But his father had wound adhesive tape around the haft and it was regarded by the Raiders as the *second* best bat on the block. Little Artie owned the best one—a Louisville slugger he had found in an empty lot—an ancient gray-yellow weapon, bearing the burned signature of Lefty O'Doul" (33). Employing the loving attention to remembered detail that is the hallmark of nostalgic sports fiction, Green moves from a Proustian to a Joycean tone: "Glove hooked around his belt, bat on shoulder, ball in hand, he left the bondage of his house, his father's fury and his mother's fears, to meet his friends again. Maybe he'd get a hit today. Or make a great catch. But at least he'd get to play" (34). In the smithy of baseball play, Albert Abrams would forge his soul in ways Dr. Solomon Abrams would find ever eluding him in his medical work.

The schoolyard game is an Homeric struggle, and it provides the vital center of *To Brooklyn With Love*. As in E. L. Doctorow's novel of boyhood trauma, *The Book of Daniel*, the schoolyard fascinates the Jewish boy who would trade all his brains to be able to fight or to hit a ball a great distance. In the sight of lurking, magnificently coordinated black youths who seem possessed of a special magic—"He wondered if anywhere in Brooklyn there were skinny, weak, scholarly colored boys who were rotten athletes" (36)—

---

[24] Neither, I must admit, had I; you have to look it up—Frank Doljack, six years with Detroit and Cleveland, .269 lifetime average. Albert's favorite player, by the way, was Len Koenecke who played three years for the Dodgers and compiled a .297 average before dying mysteriously in an airplane accident in 1935.

the Raiders go through their first ritual as the best athletes choose up teams. Because Albert brought the ball, he is rewarded by being chosen *second* to last by Teddy. With a pitcher, three infielders and two outfielders on each side, they play their serious parody of a baseball game. Because of his big glove, Albert patrols the outfield in the street. And as fate always prepares a doom for the fearful, a high fly ball is hit towards the quaking Albert. "High, high, rose the white ball, gleaming in morning sunlight. It was the center of the world, the only thing that mattered anywhere. It ascended into the hot blue sky, in a perfect arc (Albert wondering what equation would decide its trajectory), and then started a graceful descent, waxing bigger, approaching inexorable—*but beyond him, beyond his reach!*" (42). Responding to his heart's need, Albert runs into the gutter, regardless of his mother's fears, runs hopelessly, appalled that the runners on the bases had taken off, convinced that he could never make the catch. Triumph! "Desperately he threw out the Chick Hafey glove, heard the conclusive *splat*! and knew that the ball had stuck in the webbing" (42). And disaster! Play teaches as much reality as work does. Before Albert can throw the ball in, the black boys, led by his school acquaintance Lee Roy, swarm over Albert and steal from play the sacred softball—"A dollar twenty-nine cents' worth of his father's love"—the product of work—"from his old man who climbed four flights of stairs for two dollar fees" (43). Work and fathers, Marx and Freud, give way to the realities of urban social conditions. Teddy pursues Lee Roy, and in "the glory" of racial confrontation, Teddy soars "more Greek than Pole in the sunlight" (44), tips the ball to Albert, fights three blacks, and gains victory. Albert has caught a ball, has been loyal in combat, but he gets no accolades, only blame for having known Lee Roy.

Although Albert remains convinced of the world's injustice, he has sustained a great moment. He can *play*! Even his omnipresent father's warning remark when, on his way to visit an ancient Hebrew teacher, the sight of Albert in the gutter takes Dr. Abrams's mind from unrewarding work to parental fears, cannot reach Albert's new height of play-created strength. He gets set again in the outfield: "He could catch *anything*. He would run forever and catch them over his shoulder, off his shoelaces. He was Len Koenecke, Tris Speaker" (46). And, alas, his father's son. After Dr. Abrams ministers to the aged Jewish *melamud* who reminds the physician of his ethnic heritage, he once more sees "his only begotten son, his flesh and blood, playing baseball" (53). As in Irwin Shaw's brilliant baseball novel of fathers and sons, *Voices of a Summer Day*, here a "sense of continuity, of things going on, remembered, honored, buoyed him" (53). Dr. Abrams recognizes a thread joining the unpaid work of the Hebrew scholar to the badly paid, unrewarding work of the Jewish doctor to—and how American this recognition is!—the play of his baseball-obsessed son. "Maybe only a tradition, a mystique. What was it? Courage?" (53).

Similar to the rising and falling structure of Joyce's *A Portrait of the Artist as a Young Man*, Gerald Green's novel moves from youth's momentary triumph to its realistic aftermath. Similar also to the rhythm of the game itself, Albert's moment in the sun as a hero is followed by his time of despair as a goat. From fielding marvel to striking out-oaf—with two men on, Albert goes for the sucker pitch, and "disgrace was total" (54). A retreat home and a grim echo of news on the radio warning of Hitler and war give way to the imaginative balm of books, the long dreams of youth. He lives in a dream world of baseball: play as news—he reads of the batteries for the day's major league games; play as posture—as he goes to lunch with his cousin Ruthie, "He hitched his belt, and walked pigeon-toed, Joe Stripp coming in from the infield" (62); play as source for irony—Ruthie plans to become an actress, *"Like I am destined to play shortstop for the Dodgers"* (63); play as relief from endless family recitals about roots in the *shtetl*—"He knew all about Tony Cuccinello and Van Mungo, but nothing at all about these forebears" (64). His roots are not among Eastern European Jews but among midwestern American farmboy baseball stars.

Albert knows that there will be answers to life's imponderables because he has an organized mind, one that keeps a baseball scorecard accurate to every pitch, but he cannot yet deal with girls; he refuses to play catch with Ruthie and sublimates his first, faint sexual urges by wanting to hide. In the back yard. To oil his glove (ahem). When the world of Hitler and the Depression is too much with him, again, baseball supplies the appropriate anodyne. "Even the sports pages were a help. It was most reassuring not to be in the spiked shoes of Walter (Boom Boom) Beck, who, after pitching to eight men and allowing three runs in the first inning, threw the ball against the right-field wall. Poor Walter, that was *his* cross to bear" (77). When his father's fierce controversies with deadbeat patients resonate throughout the house, "It was also pleasant to assess oneself as better off than the Boston Braves, who were beaten twice by the Giants in front of 42,000 people. And shut out 15 to zip in the second game" (78). The ledger traps his father; the sports page relieves Albert. And he is capable of sparing his father ugly details of ball theft and strikeouts, and of repaying love with the heroic tale of his catch: " 'Teddy Ochab said he never saw a better one in the majors' " (83). For Dr. Abrams, however, Albert's world is still strange; baseball is not real play—that demands discipline, power, muscle. The ultimate connection between father and son remains blocked. "They sat in silence. The doctor knew nothing about baseball" (85). Albert grasps the reality of his father's work that is made up of unpaid two-dollar fees when the boy studies the doctor's ledger and calculates his meagre earnings. Moved by the disorder and sorrow of his father's work, Albert's play, his thoughts of the upcoming punchball game, even of Joe Stripp's batting average, fail completely to console.

So once more to the streets. Green gives a lavish, detailed, realistic narrative of an urban street event, a championship punchball game, that takes more than one-tenth of the novel—complete with a crowd of spectators made up of poolroom loiterers, gangsters, and gamblers. As "Talmudic" scorekeeper, Albert is but an observer. Depending on some mock-heroic effects—*"Doomed,*

*doomed to sit on a cindery tenement stoop keeping my detailed boxscore.
. . ."* (103)—Albert explains the game by inwardly lyrical streams of
consciousness and by careful narration to a dimwitted companion; by extension
he clarifies events for the reader by affecting an elegaic tone for a species
of urban play that is "a transitional game, a sport that must vanish someday"
(104). Its time will pass when the Depression ends, destroying the fields
of play by filling these streets with parked cars. A youth's game, but to Albert
the fundamental baseball thrill emerges: "It was just like the first man up
in a Dodger-Giant game" (109).

In imitation of a (Jewish) sportswriter, Albert describes the game in his
mind's eye by a parody of sports page inflated rhetoric. A circus catch, made
while tripping over a distant curb, becomes *"In all the annals of punchball,*
wrote Dan Daniel Abrams, *never have these orbs witnessed a more outstanding
display of patrolling the outer garden"* (111). A reflexive act, this, for Gerald
Green redeems the role of observer by turning him, as did Roth, Shaw, and
Mark Harris, into a writer. If Philip Roth in *The Great American Novel* calls
on the styles and spirits of classic and modernist novelists to enlarge his
baseball fiction, so Green has Albert dramatize his life as a scorekeeper by
comparing himself—in his search for an identity in a world of play in which
he is shunted off to the sidelines—as an outcast, a pariah, "a sinister figure
in a Joseph Conrad novel" (114).

While the punchball game takes up the main thread of the narrative,
the baseball theme is spoken also on a lower level. A black handyman delivers
within earshot of Albert a marvelous free-form monologue on major league
ball, setting forth the importance of this aspect of play in even the most
pressured of working-class lives. Baseball clearly has its uses as a social weapon.
"Next to religion Cowboy adored the New York Yankees" (116). His outsider's
paranoia is soothed by the sense that even winners must fight bigotry, for
the other seven teams in the American League are in a conspiracy against
the Yankees. Through his alcoholic musing comes a kind of Yankee blues.
" 'Cleveland a dirty ball club. Washington a dirty ball club. Red Sox an' White
Sox is dirty ball clubs, too. Dey al try to gang up on deh Yankees. Dey try
to hit deh ball past Crosetti and Lazzeri and ole Lou, but dey cain't. Deh
Yankees too smart and too good fo' all dem dirty ball clubs.' 'Das good.'
'Yeah, Detroit a dirty ball club. Dey most of dem dirty, 'cause dey all hates
de Yankees' " (116). Albert quickly grasps how similar these litanies are to
religious chants, "the Yankees are God or Jesus, and all the other teams are
the devil" (116).[25]

---

[25] Of course, most Jewish baseball writers, like Clive Miller or Roger Kahn, raise the Brooklyn
Dodgers to the pantheon; some hail the New York Giants; few praise the Yankees, the
fat winners who represent capitalism's excesses. Yet nearly all these novelists set their works
about baseball in New York, for, according to Alfred Kazin, "without New York, it would
no doubt all have been different, but without New York there would have been no immigrant
epic, no America. (Alfred Kazin, "The Jew as American Writer," in Chapman, ed. *Jewish-
American Literature*, p.589).

As the epic punchball game draws to a finish after the underdogs hang on by a series of marvelous catches and clever bunts, astounding the crowd of storekeepers and even the gangsters, Green sends the "formidable Ernie Cohen" (a seventeen-year-old ringer) to the plate, and Albert's narrative voice yokes popular boys' books to Jewish religion in his depiction of the scene. "The spectators edged forward. Old *bubbas* and *zaydes* on windowsills, understanding little of the savage encounter, confounded by the violence of their sons and grandsons, appeared caught up in the tension. What did the Talmud say about punchball? The clipboard dropped from Albert's trembling knees. Was ever man witness to a more thrilling climax? No! Not in all of Ralph Henry Barbour, not even in Jack London!" (118). Cohen gets a hit, the winning run scores, Albert the observer, the scorekeeper, falls into despair—but in a moment of victory for all bespectacled Jewish intellectual baseball fans (who have weak ankles), brains prevail. Albert the logician, the whiz with figures, realizes that " '*Ernie Cohen batted out of turn!* He's automatically out!' " (120). What is particularly splendid about this passage is Green's technique of evoking not only the Jewish motif of brains over brawn, but also the mystique of the game itself, for even in this corrupt street version of play, even with the umpire being Fleishacker the poolroom owner, even with Mutty Zetzkin who is *both* gambler and gangster and brother to one of the opposing players calling the shots, the rules, albeit belatedly, prevail. The acculturating effect of baseball is made manifest. Some events are not to be tampered with, since only in America, rules of the game are rules, even to the Mutty Zetzkins. " 'Now, ya hear what I'm saying?' Mutty began, 'The way I figure, a man bats outa turn, he's out . . . ' " (124). But Green is neither sentimental nor simplistic. Even in America, a gambler is a gambler, Arnold Rothstein and the Chicago Black Sox scandal were real, and Zetzkin finally rules that the run scores because Albert spoke up too late. And America is violence. Albert the Jewish scholar may have " 'it in black and white,' " (121), but for his truthful efforts he gets kneed in the groin and takes spit full in his eyes. The Jewish scapegoat, " 'little four-eyed *putz*' " (122), weeps with shame and pain. Even in his humiliation, Albert considers himself in terms of a Conradian outcast. He still tries logic on the killer, Zetzkin. With the combination of laughter and tears that distinguishes Jewish writing, Albert speaks. "*Mr. Zetzkin?* Who, ever in the history of Brownsville had addressed the killer as *Mr. Zetzkin?* Who but A. Abrams? Visions of Walter Camp All-American dotted his mind. What would they do with the Zetzkin brothers at Harvard? How would you fit a fiend like Zetz into a Crimson sweater? He would have to draw up a recommended reading list . . . and make a fair-minded, sporty, good-tempered athlete out of him" (124). The reality is a savage fight between two players, a furious Jewish father breaking up the fight by driving his loafer, *"Layzer,"* son home with blows of a broomstick, and, finally, Zetzkin declaring all bets off, a forfeit, interpreting the action of the vengeful father in removing his son from the lineup an act of God. And Albert? He "tucked his scoreboard under his arm. The evidence, the evidence. He had called it. He had the essential knowledge, the truth. And what had it gotten him? Pain, humiliation, not a word of thanks" (130). The truth is mighty, and it shall prevail, but the Jewish writer understands the lot of the just witness. This punchball game stands as one of the truly fine American fictional descriptions of play, and it gives *To Brooklyn With Love* a rich and evocative core as well as a genuinely Jewish subtext of crowd assimilation and intellectual alienation.

From the turbid violence of the street to the peaceful retreat of his bedroom, baseball remains Albert's chief resource. He stumbles up to his room to listen on the radio to the final innings of a Dodger-Phillies game. But in the wider world of major league baseball, defeat continues as the Dodgers blow a three run lead. "His heroes—Al Lopez, Joe Stripp—gave him no lift. He switched off the radio" (133). Still, Albert has a better resource, one familiar to many youngsters fascinated with baseball, one that would later provide the basic concepts for Robert Coover's superb novel *The Universal Baseball Association*. Chance seems to provide the given of this kind of play, a mental baseball game that depicts a diamond with players dressed in 1910 style and with a variety of possibilities from walks to double plays that are decided by a spinning drum so that two teams can compete. While chance is important, the player has more control over the game than ever happens in the real world of work *or* play. "If the real world failed to answer his needs there was always a fictional escape" (133). Albert Abrams's game is therefore like Gerald Green's novel.

This inner game is indeed creative, for Albert, like generations of American boys, embellishes it with his own inventions. He considers it unique, having never seen another like it, although his father had found it in a department store. The game is central, because as Albert plays, he is a god, a creator, an author. "It was not merely a game, it was a way of life. For what Albert had created was his own league. He invented teams. He set a schedule. He kept notebooks crammed with batting averages, team standings, pitching records. He kept box scores. He was league commissioner and president. And he was also owner and manager of one team, the unbeatable Panthers. They always won the pennant. He saw to that. But he did not really cheat. However, by clever manipulation of the game, he could always insure a Panther victory" (134). He keeps statistics, several years' worth, in dog-eared copy-books, exactly parallel to Coover's J. Henry Waugh. In this way, Albert uses play for control—"He wallowed in power" (135). His game allows him to efface the only too real agonies of the streets. Like a Stephen Dedalus, Albert Abrams is a god, above and beyond his creations. Beyond control, moreover, this game gives Albert an opportunity as writer, as creator of characters in a world, of ballplayers who have detailed histories similar to but more colorful, more archetypal than, most major leaguers. "His own, his very own players. He knew them better than he knew the Dodgers. Tony Vincenzo was the fastest man on the double-play pivot in organized baseball. But he had a trigger temper and he scrapped a lot, maybe too much for the team's good"

(135). Each player has his own colorful peculiarity: Abner Deems in center
field, a prematurely gray, red-faced dirt farmer from Tennessee; rookie Tut
Breckenridge, a too-cocky kid from Clinton, Iowa; cleanup hitter Joe Mulqueen,
a jolly Irishman from Haverhill, Mass., a veteran who could still hit, for "canny
skipper Al Abrams still had faith in the big guy" (135). And so on, down
the lineup of Frenchy Le Grange and Spider Matthews, all based on familiar
baseball character types, names, and nicknames—not unlike the lovingly
created rosters in the pages of Robert Coover, Mark Harris, and Philip Roth.
There is a real favorite, interestingly enough, a victim of the foul-mouthed
hillbilly Matthews, "the brilliant Sammy Schiffman. Sammy was one of the
league's few Jewish players," a great fielding shortstop, but nervous, erratic,
not aggressive, "a brooding young man who read serious novels. At times
he regretted his decision to play baseball, when he could have accepted an
athletic scholarship to Columbia and studied dentistry" (136). It is a marvelous
cameo, encapsulating in a paragraph the entire life and family situation of
what might be a stereotype of Jewish baseball players as indicated in the
work of Shaw and Roth—and in biography after biography of real Jewish
ballplayers as collected in the dusty files in the Cooperstown Baseball Hall
of Fame Library.

Despite Albert's attempts to let his cocoon of fantasy or control of destinies
serve as a counterforce to his actual wins and losses, the grim realities of
his father's ledger that recount actual losses from unpaid bills, disturb the
boy's peace. Baseball in his room is friendly to the Jews; even the notebook
in which he keeps his player roster is one discarded from Hebrew School,
opening from right to left. But the game's play fantasy Jew flying around
the bases is returned to a bureau drawer. Nevertheless, the son's play does
help to assuage his father's work troubles. Albert permits the doctor to think
that the discovery of a batter out of order is important. Where father and
son most agree, however, is in the lack of value Jewish religious tradition
has in their secular work and play places. The *shul* has only a vestigial appeal
for the Abrams men during most of the book. For Albert, the game of *Batter
Up!* is more soothing, more anxiety relieving than any direct religious
observance. The game gives him a sense of order, and he can will his first
uncompromised victory of the day: "He'd try to arrange for Mulqueen to
belt one over the right-field wall. That would be the ball game" (154).

Up to this point, 150 pages into a 270-page book, baseball as metaphor,
as fact, as fantasy has dominated the work motif with a play ethic. The remainder
of the novel shows a more serious rite of passage during the waning moments
of the day; play now supplies a more muted tone. His father's work woes
predominate, and Albert can only look forward to the night ahead where
it will be possible to reflect on the wild hours just past and to review the
baseball scores that have already become, in a comforting way, history. When
his mother tries to engage him in conversation about literature, about her
aborted career as a writer, his mind drifts off to *his* favorite literature, the
sports fiction of Barbour and William Heyliger, and "the deathless Lester

Chadwick, creator of the equally immortal *Baseball Joe*, Big Joe Matson himself" (168). In the streets, soapbox orators preach left-wing politics (the setting *is* the 1930s), but the boys rehearse the earlier struggle, the game that has now passed into "the unrecorded annals of Brownsville," having attained mythic status. For himself, Albert promises, this game will be his lead to the writing of immortal prose: "*In all the annals of organized punchball there have been fewer examples of raw unadulterated courage, of pure valor, than the hot afternoon of July 1934. . . .* " (174). His ultimate heroes are the sportswriters, men of the word, Dan Daniel, Bill Corum, who were genuine stars. "Now had anyone, anyone in the history of sports, ever said it better?" Albert romanticizes himself as the last somber witness of the death of ancient street games. And while the boys measure their day, the major leagues are the backdrop. An Italian boy is a Yankee fan, which makes sense because of their Italian players, but another boy likes Pittsburgh for no apparent reason, just as one might prefer one poet or artist. "It was puzzling but admirable to Albert that Teddy should stand so loyally by unimaginative ballplayers like the Waner brothers and Arkie Vaughan" (181).

Again reality intervenes. Albert barely evades a fight with a black boy— the stolen baseball is the cause. Wandering these mean streets, Albert realizes that he both loves and fears the gusto, the liveliness of pitchmen and goniffs. Finally, he must fight Bimbo, his morning's antagonist, and, wonder of wonders, Albert wins. Fighting bridges a gap between play and work, for it is hard and brings as its reward acceptance into the gang. All passion spent, baseball returns a kind of peaceful order to the boys' violent society. They play a mocking game of nipping at each other's fly; one scores a hit for each button opened. Like the scenes on Keats' Grecian Urn, their contests take place against a timeless, permanent backdrop: "Ahead of them Bushy leaped, spun . . . tossing his Spalding and catching it, tireless, unbeatable" (224). And Albert is purged of hate after his fight. "*We can look at pictures in my father's books. We can match baseball cards*" (225).

Reality, once more—his father has an angina attack, a terrible fire breaks out, excited crowds gather; only the black man is oblivious as he mutters his paranoid baseball blues: " 'Now look at dat Cleveland. . . . Dey a dirty ball club. Averill and Trosky and Kamm, dey dirty ball players, but only 'gainst deh Yankees' " (239). Albert runs to get his father, who revives at the news that his son has actually won a fight, and together they stride to the father's work, to the scene of the fire, to the suffocated old Hebrew teacher. As Albert's play day ends, he can admire his father's work in the evening. "*My father, my father. My old man. let them gossip about him and tell stories, and say he's crazy, and call him names, and run to the specialists, and the clinics and the chiropractors. He is my father and he can save somebody's life, or at least he can try*" (256). In Green's code, father and son observe the dead man's secret: a meticulous miniature reconstruction of the magic city— Jerusalem, a vision, Albert understands, that the scholar had derived from books. *His* work had no financial value; it was close to play. Green's point for father and son alike to grasp is that both efforts have their own rewards. The old teacher may have failed to reveal the secrets of the Talmud to children more interested in how Tony Cuccinello, the Dodgers second baseman, turns a double play, but the playful, scholarly creation saved the old man's spirit. Night falls on Brownsville; the radio reports of Hitler's rise in Germany fade into the background; Albert's father decides that if the old teacher can struggle and survive, so can a doctor; and Albert can dream of fielding his position as well as Travis Jackson, the Giants shortstop, does. *To Brooklyn With Love* is a fine nostalgic novel, one that employs baseball as form and content to establish both a code of conduct and a source for metaphor; and much of the book's strength comes from the tautly sustained tension between work and play.

Epilogue

In 1975 Gerald Green wrote a gloss on his earlier books, a narrative of his son's experience as a high school football star, on a losing team, and the father's own bemused admiration of the youth's strength, courage, and physical persistance. *My Son the Jock* also comments on Green's Brooklyn childhood, this time directly. "He's a way I never was, never will be." (27) The father ran from street fights, the son (half-Italian, on the mother's side) shows "no sign of the prayerful, cerebral, apologetic, introspective Semite— my contribution" (15). Green made Phi Beta Kappa at Columbia but hardly ever won a fist fight in Brownsville. Exactly like Albert Abrams, Green describes himself "cursed with weak ankles, slowness, poor eyesight from too many hours of reading, straight A's in school, and a saintly, intellectual mother who taught me to run from fights . . . " (18). He recalls his one victory over Sambo Schwartz, even though Green would rather have remained "squinting into Ralph Henry Barbour novels" (19). His "irascible, muscular, frustrated tower of outrage" of a father can't understand why his son cries after *winning* a fight, and Gerald Green reveals the autobiographical source of much of the novel's lyric beauty. "Was I sorry for Sambo? Possibly. Or perhaps I was sorry for all of us, in dubious battle, living out our lives in crumbling schoolyards playing box ball. . . ." (20)

Green gives himself Albert's heroes, great punchball players for the Prospect Place Pirates (ca. 1931-1937) and "baseball gods of my youth, Mungo, Stripp, Lopez" (24). Green recounts the real black thieves, the street heroics. He goes on to reveal himself to have grown up to become a passable intramural softball center fielder at Columbia (shades of Portnoy!), capable of memorable catches yet choking in the clutch as a hitter. His father was a remarkable gymnast, poorly coordinated for games but possessed of enormous strength. And the exploits of Green's son, a jock among tough American kids, enable the writer at 51 to become an American himself, assimilated, acculturated, with something in common with Bridgeport bowling club members. Green recalls his debate with Sholem Bernstein over whether Glenn Wright or Ossie Slade played more games at shortstop for the Dodgers, which was interrupted by a demand to fight a black boy. Mostly, the author reaffirms his sense of a more innocent past. "How innocent the world was! They played their nine innings and were gone" (134). Ultimately, his own softball experiences help to form a bond with his athletic son, and drawing on Eugene O'Neill—as Albert drew on Joseph Conrad—Gerald Green accepts our American need for "illusions, myths and fables to help us get from one day to the next" (190). And if a father didn't gain athletic victory in his 1930s youthful play, perhaps in the 1970s his son will earn the respect that eluded the parent in his boyhood.

14

Running to Disaster:
Shaw's "The Eighty-Yard Run"

David Vanderwerken

IN LIGHT OF THE RECENT SPATE of sports-centered fiction, it may be worthwhile to reconsider one of the first serious efforts in this direction—Irwin Shaw's "The Eighty-Yard Run," collected in *Mixed Company*.[1] *Esquire*'s reprinting of the story in its Fortieth Anniversary Issue[2] reminds us that, more than forty years ago, Shaw was formulating the questions about the significance of sports in American life that recent writers are exploring in abundance. Shaw, like Updike, Whitehead, DeLillo, Roth—all of whom have written penetratingly about sports—examines the shibboleth that sport prepares one for life by developing certain character traits assumed necessary for success in a competitive society. Shaw's analysis of that rationale for organized sports finds it an illusion built on a void. Indeed, by focusing on Christian Darling's "high point," his long run in practice, in contrast to his fifteen-year "decline,"[3] Shaw suggests that Darling's football experience is a central cause of his self-deception.

Football plays a major role in shaping Darling's expectations from life. He seems to have accepted that all too easy analogy—success on the field leads to success in the future. However, like Updike's Harry Angstrom in *Rabbit, Run*,[4] Darling discovers that everything following his athletic experience is "second-rate." Darling's later malaise possibly stems from two misconceptions he holds about his moment of glory. First, he overvalues the importance of his act. After all, his run happened in practice, not during a game. Yet, he feels this deed wins Louise: "He knew, for the first time, that he could do whatever he wanted with her."[5] And second, Darling assumes that his long run is merely the herald of a continuing series of brilliant successes,

---

[1] Irwin Shaw, "The Eighty-Yard Run," in Irwin Shaw, *Mixed Company* (New York: Random House, 1950), pp. 13-28.

[2] *Esquire*, 80 (October, 1973).

[3] Irwin Shaw, *Mixed Company*, p. 27.

[4] John Updike, *Rabbit, Run* (New York: Fawcett Crest, 1960). p. 90.

[5] Shaw, *Mixed Company*, p. 16.

that analogues of his achievement await in football and in his career: "he could do anything, knock over anybody, outrun whatever had to be outrun."[6] Of course, nothing ever does equal his supreme moment, and even his subsequent varsity career, although praiseworthy, "had never been as satisfactory as it should have been. He never had broken away, the longest run he'd ever made was thirty-five yards, and that in a game that was already won . . ."[7] Darling resentfully adjusts to being a second-fiddle "important figure"[8] and years later pettily gloats over Diederich's broken neck: "That, at least, had turned out well."[9]

Darling's post-college life begins promisingly enough, marrying his "Golden Girl," working for his father-in-law's ink company, enjoying the pleasures of New York City, as if suggesting a valid parallel between football proficiency and successful living. However, Shaw injects a bored tone into the two paragraphs telescoping Darling's years from 1925 to 1929. Darling is remininscent of Fitzgerald's Tom Buchanan in *The Great Gatsby*, discontentedly existing, looking for the "dramatic turbulence of some irrecoverable football game."[10]

With the coming of Black Tuesday, the loss of his business, Louise's assuming the role of principal breadwinner, and his subsequent series of dead-end jobs, Darling's discontent becomes depression, and soon, alienation. During these years, Darling notices his wife growing, changing, developing, "a stranger in a new hat, with a new expression in her eyes under the little brim, secret, confident, knowing," patronizing and placating Darling by calling him "Baby."[11] While Louise attempts to adapt or, at least, to understand the thirties—social and political upheaval, non-representational art, leftist literature—Darling remains emotionally and intellectually stunted. He hates the Braques and Picassos lining his walls, preferring "pictures with horses in them."[12] And "Who's Ernest Dowson?"[13] Darling wonders. Again, similar to Tom Buchanan, fearing the rise of the colored empires, Darling sees cultural collapse all around him: "Frenchmen who painted as though they used their elbows instead of brushes, composers who wrote whole symphonies without a single melody in them, writers who knew all about politics and women who knew all about writers, the movement of the proletariat, Marx, somehow mixed up with five-dollar dinners and the best-looking women in America and fairies who made them laugh . . ."[14] Shaw suggests, as does Fitzgerald

---

[6] Ibid., p. 16.

[7] Ibid., p. 17.

[8] Ibid., p. 18.

[9] Ibid., p. 26.

[10] F. Scott Fitzgerald, *The Great Gatsby* (New York: Scribners, 1925), p.6.

[11] Shaw, *Mixed Company*, p. 21.

[12] Ibid., p. 20.

[13] Ibid., p. 21.

[14] Ibid., p. 22.

concerning Buchanan, that Darling's football experience contributes to his inflexibility. And, if we will recall any number of pronouncements by coaches and players, Shaw's point that football fosters cultural conservatism is well taken. Just as Buchanan must place all human conflicts in a competitive context—the white race versus the colored empires, the old rich versus the new rich, he and Gatsby facing each other across the scrimmage line—so does Darling. He feels himself losing his wife to Cathal Flaherty, the "better man."[15] Yet it is less than that that Louise has opened herself to new possibilities and experiences, while Darling has retreated to liquor and his central memory. Both Buchanan and Darling are unable to deal with ambiguity and change; both yearn for that simple and clear and defined one-hundred yard world.

Sitting near the stadium, a "deserted ruin in the twilight,"[16] preparing to relive the most significant event of his life, Darling realizes that football inadequately prepared him for the vicissitudes, ironies, and complexities of life: "He had practiced the wrong thing, perhaps. He hadn't practiced for 1929 and New York City and a girl who would turn into a woman."[17] The coaches' truism proves false.

Although attacking the deceptive assumption that athletic success and success in life go hand in hand, Shaw's story does not deny the reality and validity of the transcendent moment possible in the sport experience. Shaw stresses that a nearly magical moment does occur during Darling's run, a moment of insight, of awareness of one's being, "all suddenly clear in his head, for the first time in his life not a meaningless confusion of men, sounds, speed."[18] Moreover, many of the more recent sports-centered works also affirm the moment of transcendent human excellence. Let two examples, among many possibilities, suffice. Gary Harkness, the narrator of Don DeLillo's novel *End Zone*,[19] describes one such moment during football practice: "The afternoon went by in theoretically measured stages, gliding, and I moved about not as myself but as some sequence from the idea of motion, a brief arrangement of schemes and physical laws abstracted from the whole. Everything was wonderfully automatic, in harmony, dreamed by genius." This passage is only a more abstractly articulated version of the order, proportion and clarity that Darling felt during his moment. And Phil Romano, a character in Jason Miller's drama, *That Championship Season*,[20] recalls the only time he was really alive—twenty-five years ago as a member of the state basketball champs: "Sometimes I think that's the only thing I can still feel, you know, still feel in my gut, still feel that championship season, feel the crowds

---

[15] Ibid., p. 27.

[16] Ibid., p. 17.

[17] Ibid., p. 27.

[18] Ibid., p. 18.

[19] Don DeLillo, *End Zone* (New York: Pocket Books, 1973), p. 49.

[20] Jason Miller, *That Championship Season* (New York: Penguin, 1983), p. 91.

. . . my best memory to date, yeah, nothing matched it, nothing." Again, the similarities between Phil Romano and Christian Darling are readily apparent.

Yet, as Shaw and others suggest, the transcendent moment possible in sport is of sport alone and cannot be approximated in everyday life. Sport is not a mirror of life nor a metaphor for life—it is better than life. What our current writers lament is a society that confuses sport and life, although the Tom Buchanans, the Christian Darlings, the Harry Angstroms, and the Phil Romanos are legion: "men who reach such an acute limited excellence at twenty-one that everything afterward savors of anticlimax."[21] Shaw's seminal story will continue to resonate as more and more American writers turn their creative attention to sports in America.

---

[21] Fitzgerald, *The Great Gatsby*, p.6.

PART
V

Play Up, Play Up, and Play the Game: Sport, Language, and War

15

Introduction:
Play Up, Play Up, and Play the
Game: Sport, Language, and War

Lyle I. Olsen

> Sport is an activity in which it is peculiarly difficult to get away
> from the condition of our language which enforces the identity
> of facts with values. . . .

Fred Inglis in *The Name of the Game*

IN THE YEAR THAT GEORGE ORWELL MADE FAMOUS with *Nineteen Eighty-four,* the Sport Literature Association held its first meeting. Of special interest during the course of that meeting were four papers which addressed the power of language, a power Orwell understood. Including the language of sport. And make no mistake the language of sport carries a peculiar and unique cultural power.

Orwell's power as a novelist is well documented, but in this introduction I refer to his journalistic thoughts about the supposed friendship engendered by competition between teams representing rival nations. Orwell argued convincingly that "Serious sport has nothing to do with fair play. It is bound up with hatred, jealousy, boastfulness, disregard of all rules and sadistic pleasure in witnessing violence: in other words it is war minus the shooting." In this seminal essay, "The Sporting Spirit," Orwell debunks the notion that modern international sport is waged as a constructive "war without weapons."

An apologist for sport could and probably would quibble. And the easiest point of controversy is the elusive definition of the notion of sport, since sports and games form an untidy category. I will immediately acknowledge that starting with its limited French origin, the English use of the word sport has enjoyed a bewildering and amazingly wide use. Sport touches life at so many points that it is difficult to define the concept or set limits to sporting activity. As an activity, sport ranges from mountaineering to making love, from motor-racing to playing practical jokes. As a noun it can refer to a man, a game, a pastime, a chase, a hunt, a fight, or even a botanical freak.

Sport also has military and political dimensions. In Western European literature it has been firmly tied to military and political activity since the time Pelops defeated Oenomaus in a chariot race in one of the myths about the founding of the Olympic Games. Sport as a military training method was certainly lauded when Sparta used victories in the Olympic Games as proof of her soldier's vitality and prestige. And one can argue easily that sport was "war without weapons" in ancient Greece. But Orwell's essay was directed at modern, post World War I sport in Britain.

Would Orwell have directed his attack at sport a half-century earlier? Or, in other words, what would Orwell have found wrong in a late nineteenth-century world in which young lads played rugby and cricket in white trousers? Where the action on playing fields on glorious autumn afternoons reminds us that undergraduate life is the best life, that sports and honor and "fair play" and *beaux gestes* should go on forever. Where the playing fields are bathed in a magic light; where carriages full of lovely ladies decorated with flowers, swathed in fur, are waiting to be escorted to the post-game ball.

In *Unquiet Souls*, a perceptive survey of the British aristocracy up to and during World War I, Angela Lambert gives us part of Orwell's answer as she blames the near demise of an entire social class on sporting attitudes learned on public school (actually "elite private schools") playing fields. Young English gentlemen who had played cricket for Rugby or Harrow would never deign to shirk in the trenches, she reminds us, and this inability to shirk, this dogged (slightly dense) insistence that war was just another kind of game, led thousands of young gentlemen and millions in the lower ranks to undignified and grisly deaths, wiping out almost an entire generation.

And, surprisingly, the game did continue for some; the intricate plays in the sky, the *beaux gestes* (the wordly effects of a downed American pilot are parachuted back into the American camp with a note in German saying he'll be given a hero's burial; captured German pilots are treated to long, comradely evenings before being driven off to a comfortable prison). In certain sectors, World War I was still a gentlemen's war, with white silk scarfs and plenty to drink, and the word *splendid* on everyone's lips.

From early on, these British public school products, who were schooled in Latin and read Greek, modeled themselves on earlier graduates of Cambridge and Oxford who had served their "empire" as gentlemen, amateurs in the best sense. But the classics in these elite schools were taught poorly, one reason being the state of near-anarchy in the classrooms early in the 1800s. This chaotic condition was finally changed midway in the nineteenth century by headmasters who coupled the existing fagging system with the institution of controlled team games.

Before 1850, public schoolboys were sportsmen without supervision. Headmasters were either uninterested or disapproving; assistant masters felt little responsibility for boys outside the classroom. Left to themselves, some boys chose to play cricket and football but others preferred to run wild over the countryside, killing birds and animals and alienating the locals. When Mathew Cotton went to Marlborough as its new headmaster in 1852 he found the standard behavior to be bullying, poaching, and general lawlessness. Many boys at Harrow kept dogs and cats, the former to kill the later, and fought pitched battles with the navvies building a nearby railway line.

In a circular to parents, Cotton unwittingly launched public school athleticism which has also been labeled "muscular Christianity." His motives were practical. Organized games meant less vandalism and disorder; masters involved in games meant better relations between boys and teachers, which in turn improved classroom discipline and improved learning. The machinery of athleticism was established over opposition, not least from the boys themselves, but the forces of athleticism prevailed.

One of the principal reasons that so much effort was devoted to promoting sports was, of course, the headmaster's belief that games provided for a boy's physical, ethical and moral well-being. Sport gave him courage and a tenacious loyalty to his house, the team, decency and the virtues of "playing it straight." There was, moreover, an easily seen straightforward relationship between physical courage on the playing field and moral worth.

Coexisting with the institution of athleticism one persistent, indeed dominant, theme circulated through contemporary essays and poetry was a connection between games and war. Newbolt's "Vitai Lampada" is perhaps the best known example, but the poem's message of "play up, play up, and play the game," whether the "game" be on the playing field or on the battle field, appeared constantly in school literature both before and after he wrote it. The inherent power residing in this type of sporting language is the subject of Anthony Mangan's paper. And the games cult of "fighting the good fight" was intimately linked to Britain's imperial expansion. Inevitably, as the imperial tide began to ebb, a correspondent in *The London Times* suggested that the catastrophes of the army in the Crimea were caused by defects in the cricket system at Eton. On the outbreak of the Boer War the *Lorettonian* printed a poem "To Loretto From Her Volunteers," which promised:

> For the bowling we are ready
> And will keep the right foot steady
> And try not to flinch as they hum past our
> head.

The analogy was in force at the start of the First World War, when Old Stoneyhurtians serving in the trenches with Kitchener's army were told by the editors of their school magazine that "the name of English sportsmen lies at stake."

The effect of such shallow, emotional non-thinking was captured by R. C. Sherriff in his play *Journey's End,* in which Stanhope, former head of house and captain of the rugby team, cracks up once he is actually in the trenches. War, he discovers, bears hardly any resemblance to a game of cricket or rugby. As Orwell once remarked, if it is true that the Battle of Waterloo was won on the playing fields of Eton, it is equally true that every battle since then has been lost there.

To refute the critics, supporters of athleticism went to even greater lengths to show the relevance of games not simply to war but to life as a whole. Anthony Mangan argues persuasively that such use of the language of games to transmit simple moral messages to the English public school boy was both wide-spread and insidious. The first two papers in this section, by Mangan and Colin Veitch, display a view of a corrupted use of school boy sport and sport-related literature as an adjunct of military thinking. Both Mangan and Veitch demonstrate the way in which the upper-middle-class British culture was reflected in its turn-of-the-century poetry. British journalists contributed significantly to this misguided mythology, a mythology which shaped the conduct of soldiers in World War I. This "games code of conduct" transferred to war led to millions of deaths as soldiers "played the game" while charging machine-gun nests with bayonets.

Sadly but typically, part of the sport/military mythology reflected reality in the British Empire, but these unquestioned ideas and attitudes were misleading when transferred away from *The Shooting Party* ambience which Isabel Colegate captures so grippingly. Colin Veitch begins his argument with factual examples from the London *Times.* In this way, he projects the accepted popular version of the myth as reported in an influential newspaper. "During the course of the First World War there were at least five documented occurrences of British troops going 'over the top' dribbling a football as they charged the enemy lines." But Veitch's paper goes past superficial reporting to re-evaluate those incidents, showing in particular that they were used to gloss over real disunities concerning the interrelationship of sport and war that arose during the first nine months of the conflict. "Sport, far from being a source of national unity in the country's hour of need," according to Veitch, "became embroiled in a bitter and often bigotted controversy as the Football Association declared its intention of continuing professional soccer league play in spite of the war in Europe."

II

While Douglas Anderson does not investigate a "code of conduct" he reports on his analysis of an equally significant factor: who decides what is to be printed. Thus one may surmise the way in which thoughts are planted by non-thinking editors of sporting ideas which are in effect matters of policy. Even though Anderson examines matters which are relegated to the newspapers' "department of toys and games," in a manner of speaking, his examination is more important than an analysis of editorial policy. For Anderson investigates the way in which decisions are made which affect how one values one of the most significant aspects of thousands of lives. Sport.

Policy decisions which affect individuals are unconscioulsy made by the words and phrases used. As one example, the decision as to whether or not girl's and women's sport is reported in the sports page may not be a matter of life or death, but it does have the power to change lives. Possibly just as important as the printed material is what is *not* read on the sports page. The topics selected reflect *status quo* "cult phrases" which are just as powerful as the unthinking assumptions implicit in the "code of conduct" which prescribes the conduct of English gentlemen.

Consider the power of sports language as reflected in the late nineteenth century, a period during which many words and phrases from sport found their way into general usage. Nearly all of them have subtle power with an ethical connotation. Hiding just below the surface, like brass knuckles inside boxing gloves, is a moral commitment to sportsmanship in the frequently heard admonitions to "play the game," "it's not cricket," "no fair hitting a man when he's down," "no holds barred," "fair play," "no hitting below the belt," and many others, all suggest an ethic which is easily understood.

In this electronic era of "Monday Night" football we do not have to belabor the idea of a communications revolution in sport. But it has to be addressed.

In 1905 with the advent of the sports page and one newspaper photo of a battered player, college football came under attack and was brought to the attention of the President of the nation. Later, following the success of the media barrage for the 1932 Olympics in Los Angeles, the Germans used radio (for the first time) to augment their propaganda barrage during the 1936 Nazi Olympics.

With the Nazi Olympics, a revolution in attempts at social control through indoctrination had reached formal levels. And with the advent of the electronic age it is interesting to note the way in which these shaping editorial decisions are reached; decisions reflected but not reported on the sports page. While Mangan and Veitch demonstrate the power of sport phrases which become part of the "code of conduct," Anderson describes the way in which newspaper editors muddle through their decisions about what is finally printed. And as English teachers contend, what is selected and the way it is written shapes the message. Incidental use of the power of sport is just as significant as its contrived use, especially today.

Reflecting the obverse side of the above argument, Nanda Fischer examines the fictional refusal of some anti-heroes to be seduced by their national sporting ethic. While examining sport we tend to overlook the young people who rebel against sport. And especially the dominant Apollonian sport culture. Fischer writes perceptively about German youth who use play and games to counter the prevailing sports code. She does this by examining Günter Grass's characters in *Cat and Mouse*. In this sensitive novel, Grass writes as an outsider trying to preserve his identity against the coercive power of the prevailing sports establishment mentality. And I believe the contrast between Grass's German anti-heroes and the earlier look at British gentlemen is a clear example of the far-reaching power of sport, its language, and ethos. Interestingly all are involved with war.

Many scholars, of course, view war as the negation of culture. Alas, this humanitarian assumption is not borne out by critical studies. In the past "limited" wars have stimulated the production of culture and, at the same time, expressed the existing culture of those same people. Thus the "game" mentality carries a double load as it goes to war. And Americans are not exempt. We are all victims of unthinking assumptions transferred from the playing fields. Both sides of this malady, of course, were what George Orwell addressed so forcefully. Germans, British, Americans—we are all susceptible to a peculiar form of nationalism that encourages us to think that our country has the right and duty to serve as a moral example to the remainder of the world. In America the idea is as old as the Puritans who were told by John Winthrop that they should be as "a City upon a Hill" and that the eyes of all the people would be upon them. We went to war (just as the British and the Germans) because we ascribed to ourselves a special moral mission to spread our way of life (including our games codes) to the rest of the world. These thoughts are expressed frequently and insidiously through common sporting phrases. Phrases which prescribe our conduct. And this use of language reminds us with eloquence, power, and passion that war, like sport, is a form of intercourse. And our game codes unveil the deepest assumptions that a nation makes above itself and its relationship to the outside world.

16

Moralists, Metaphysicians and Mythologists: The 'Signifiers' of a Victorian and Edwardian Sub-culture

J. A. Mangan

THE "SPEECH" OF A CULTURE orders the experiences of its members and shapes their reality.[1] Wright Mills once wrote of language in this sense, that "socially built and maintained, it embodies implicit exhortations and social evaluations. By acquiring the categories of a language, we acquire the structured 'ways' of a group, and along with the language, the value implates of those 'ways'." He continued, "Our behaviour and perception, our logic and thought, come within the control of a system of language. . . . A vocabulary is not merely a string of words: immanent within it are societal textures—institutional and political co-ordinates. Back of a vocabulary lie sets of collective action."[2] More simply, Whorf expressed the same belief in thought as an outcome of sub-cultural language in his discussion of the differences of perception reflected in the speech patterns of Standard American English and Hopi.[3] "The statement," he reminded his readers, "that thinking is a matter of 'language' is an incorrect generalisation of the more nearly correct idea that thinking is a matter of different tongues."[4] Both Mills and Whorf suggested that in large measure

---

[1] "Speech" in this context is a generic term for all forms of language including poetry, prose and song. See Dell Hymes, "Models of the Interaction of Language and Social Life" in J. Gumperez and Dell Hymes, (eds.), *Directions in Socio-Linguistics* (New York: Holt, Rinehart & Winston, 1972).

[2] C. Wright Mills, "Language, Logic and Culture," in I. L. Horowitz, (ed.), *Power, Politics and People: The Collected Papers of C. Wright Mills* (London: Oxford University Press, 1973) p. 43.

[3] Quoted in John B. Carroll, *Language, Thought and Reality: Selected Writings of Benjamin Lee Whorf* (New York: John Wiley, 1956), p. 134.

[4] Carroll, *Language, Thought and Reality,* pp. 134-59.

social identity is the result of language acting as a coding system controlling both in creation and organisation of specific meanings.[5] They emphasised that social reality is created through sub-cultural speech patterns. A common vocabulary is an inventory of the ideas, interests and preoccupations of a community. From this thesaurus it is possible to discern ideological fashion.

In literate societies, it has been further argued, it is literature that is assigned a major role in the task of creating and sustaining the communal symbolism necessary for the maintenance of ideologies: "How our society wants us to meet death, . . . to go to battle, or to found families—what could be called the 'styles' and 'forms' of living, dying, fighting and mating, is taught us in modern society through literary depictions."[6] Furthermore, literature has both intrinsic and extrinsic purposes. The metaphors and similies of the poet serve both the individual and his community. A work of literature is rooted in a particular social soil; at the same time it is the outcome of subjective experience. Literature is not simply the consequence of, nor is it a mere epiphenomenon of the social structure.[7] External factors influence internal creativity. To this extent the history of a literature is the history of a culture.

The power of words to mold as well as to express thought has been linked to educational communities and their ideologies by Bourdieu.[8] The organisation of symbolic expression into a system of linguistic tracts, he maintains, highlights certain aspects of reality while ignoring others; in this way products of a specific "school," usually designated by terms ending in "ism," are given prominence and the "ism" comes to determine reality. "Ism" here is a synonym for ideology. And the desired outcome of ideological fashion is security in the form of the ordering of reality. Creators and neophytes sustain their reality until new knowledge challenges old assumptions, or new needs or power groups arise, or simply boredom with familiar stimulates the search for new orders of meaning and fresh linguistic symbols. In essence, the vocabulary of an ideology is critical to its transmission and survival; it constitutes a symbolic code which articulates values, aids commitment, produces security, defines the boundaries of action and structures reality.

The public school system which catered to the British upper middle classes in the late nineteenth century was one of the most significant educational systems in the history of the world. Its impact has been worldwide. A central

---

[5] B. Bernstein, "A socio-linguistic approach to social learning," in *Class, Codes and Control* (Vol. 1,) (London: Routledge & Kegan Paul, 1971), p. 125.

[6] Hugh Dalziel Duncan, *Language and Literature in our Society* (London: Bedminster Press, 1961), p. 5. See also Monica Wilson, *Religion and the Transformation of a Society*, (London: Cambridge University Press, 1971), p. 54.

[7] Diane Laurenson and Alan Swingewood, *The Sociology of Literature* (London: MacGibbon, 1971), p. 59.

[8] Pierre Bourdieu, "Systems of Education and Systems of Thought" in Michael Young, (ed.), *Knowledge and Control* (London: Collier-MacMillan 1971), p. 195.

tenet of the system was a belief in the educational values of games.[9] To the initiated, and there were many, they had instrumental and expressive consequences: "physical and moral courage, loyalty and cooperation, the capacity to act fairly and take defeat well, the ability to both command and obey."[10] These constituted the "famous ingredients of character-training which the public schools considered their pride and their prerogative."[11]

The Victorian and Edwardian public schools produced composers of doggerel in profusion. E. C. Mack once commented "if there was a good deal of poetry about the schools, it can hardly be said that much of it was first or even second-rate." And he added: "it was . . . for the most part banal and uninspired."[12] Here I take issue with him. He argues out of context. In context, more than he allows, some was inspired, and it inspired. While for the most part it trapped experience within the most conventional of linguistic symbols and was mostly simple verse, it drew on common experiences, touched unsophisticated nerves and outlined acceptable moral practice. Its writers were men of their time and community. Mack failed to understand their fervor; he underestimated their appeal; he failed to comprehend their purpose. He dealt in absolutes when he should have dealt in relativities. These "public school poets" were the voices of a period sub-culture; the poetasters of an upper class Victorian community, they moved the men of their generation. They were parochial; they could be banal; they were not uninspiring. They had, to borrow Goldmann's expression, a "world vision" (in my view more appropriately called a communal vision). Their verse threw "an encompassing structure" around given events and activities containing, explaining and giving them significance.[13] Their task was teleological. They strove to achieve internal coherence and external validity in their *Weltanschauung.* They attempted to catch and transmit "the whole complex of ideas, aspirations and feelings which differentiated it from others.[14] Their "vision" was the narrow abstraction of a social class; and this abstraction found concrete form in their verse. Furthermore, it was more than an attempt to engender a "collective consciousness" serving to unify the group; it was an attempt to sustain order through the maintenance and extension of a moral superiority allegedly inherent in a class disposition, and while purpose received their close attention, it must not be overlooked that they were as much concerned with means as with functions.

---

[9] J. A. Mangan, *Athleticism in the Victorian and Edwardian Public School,* (Cambridge University Press: 1981), pp. 6-9.

[10] Mangan, *Athleticism,* p. 9.

[11] Ibid

[12] E.C. Mack, *Public Schools and British Opinion* 1780-1860 (New York: Columbia University Press, 1941), p. 146.

[13] F. Inglis, *Ideology and the Imagination* (London: Cambridge University Press, 1975), p. 74 and p. 62. See also F. Inglis, "Bourdieu, Habermas and the Condition of England," *Sociological Review,* vol. 27, no. 2: 353-69.

[14] Laurenson and Swingewood, *Sociology of Literature,* p. 67.

Here I want to consider four "public school" versifiers in an attempt to extrapolate from their writing their particular vision of the world as members of a specific sub-culture. These men were the troubadours of a once powerful and now ridiculed ethic. They recorded *and* shaped it. Their verse is heavy with pedantic propositions. They exuded the all-pervasive Victorian atmosphere of didacticism and moralism.[15] They carefully depicted archetypes, priorities and possibilities. They were the "guardians" of ideals, the expositors of principle and the repositories of tradition. They constituted a choric group acting as the conscience of the community, echoing its deepest convictions.[16] They employed a common stock of symbols and sustained a common view of life by means of their imagery. They shared and reflected a widespread adherence to a belief in the efficacy of team games in the development of character—the essence of Victorian and Edwardian education; an adherence summarised in puerile but accurate fashion, in this satirical Charterhouse verse:

> Hark to a story of England
> List to a lay of our land
> The seat of a world wide empire,
> Outstretching on endless land.
> Ye know how its strength was gained,
> Learn now of its way of teaching,
> How English youths are trained.
> We send them forth in their wildness
> With the rudest of nature's tools;
> We cast them adrift in cities,
> Which we call our public schools.
> Then, lost in a world of wonder,
> They stumble and blink and gape,
> And struggle along to manhood,
> Knocked, hammered and drilled to shape.
> And what do they learn to master!
> . . . They race for a flying ball,
> And flourish a costly willow
> In the greatest game of all.
> All hail to the men with colours!
> And woe to the fools who shirk!
> . . . Fives, Football, Racquets and Cricket
> And everything else—save work![17]

And even more bitterly in the *Ten Commandments* of the Public School System outlined by H. B. Grey in his *Public Schools and the Empire:*

---

[15] Reñe Wellek, *A History of Modern Criticism 1750-1950* (London: Oxford University Press, 1966), p. 141.

[16] Hugh Dalziel Duncan, *Symbols in Society* (New York: Oxford University Press 1968), p. 96.

[17] *Charterhouse School Magazine* vol. XI, no. 373, February 19, 1912: 16-17.

There is only one God; and the captain of
school is his prophet.
My school is the best in the world.
Without big muscles, strong will and proper collars,
there is no salvation.
I must wash much and in accordance with tradition.
I must speak the truth even to a master, if he
believes everything I tell him.
I must play games with all my heart, with all my
soul and with all my strength.
To work outside class hours is indecent
Enthusiasm, except for games, is in bad taste.
I must look up to the older fellows and pour
contempt on newcomers.
I must show no emotion and not kiss my mother in public.[18]

The four public school versifiers to be considered below are Sir Henry
Newbolt[19] (1862-1938), pupil at Clifton College and later Poet Laureate; John
Bain, assistant master at Marlborough College (1879-1913); Norman Gale,
assistant master of Oakland Preparatory School and Edward Bowen, assistant
master of Harrow School (1857-1901). They were all eager imperialists. And
to a lesser or greater extent they took their cue from Tennyson, who in common
with them glorified in the ever-reaching Empire of his age, and played his
small part in its advance. In the belief that "The song that serves a nation's
heart is in itself a deed."[20]

Tennyson dramatised in verse the splendid heroic gesture—at Lucknow
in the Mutiny, on the Revenge before Spaniards, at Balaclava among "the
Russian hordes."[21] Yet it was in a "disguised rhythmic form" according to
Vincent Kiernan, that he served the cause of imperialism best. In his *Idylls
of the King* he attempted to render the spirit of his times in the more acceptable
and compelling context of the past and created "an Arthur turned into a
Victorian gentleman, refined and rarified, but a muscular Christian." Fittingly
he was a type of hero not unlike General Gordon, who helped build the
empire while supposedly liberating it from the darkness of bondage and
superstition.[22] Throughout Tennyson's Arthurian tales, says Kiernan, an imperial
dimension is clearly visible: "Arthur's expanding Kingdom is in itself a small

---

[18] H.B. Gray, *Public Schools and the Empire* (London: Williams & Norgate, 1913), pp. 172-173.

[19] Sir Henry Newbolt (1862-1938): "His faith in Christianity and the influence of tradition, social,
historical, and literary, was in his mind and work."

[20] Vincent Kiernan, "Tennyson, King Arthur, and Imperialism," in R. Samuel and G.S. Jones, (eds.),
Culture, Ideology and Politics (London: Routledge & Kegan Paul, 1982), p. 131.

[21] Ibid., p. 130.

[22] Ibid, p. 137.

empire, subjugating and overawing less civilized areas and bringing them within the pale of Christian manners."[23]

Tennyson shared his imperial enthusiasm with other poets including W. E. Henley, Francis Doyle, A. Frewen Aylward, George Barlow, Alfred Austin, and Sir Henry Newbolt. All glorified in "the British mystique of splendour in misfortune" so vividly portrayed in the paintings of Lady Elizabeth Butler: *The Remnants of an Army, The Defence of Rorke's Drift, Steady the Drums and Fifes, The Survivor* and *Floreat Etona*,[24] but it was Newbolt who was the link between the parochial "poets" of the public schools and the chauvinistic songsters of "Greater Britain." He shared the period infatuation with military heroism and located one source in the educational system of the private schools of the upper classes.

Newbolt was obsessed with "a courage, a pride, a rapture sprung of the strength and splendour of England's war," with "the joy that spurs the warrior's heart," with the virility of the hawk-eyed knight-errant and the shadows of dead heroes:

> ENGLAND! where the sacred flame
>   Burns before the inmost shrine,
> Where the lips that love thy name
>   Consecrate their hopes and thine,
> Where the banners of thy dead
> Weave their shadows overhead,
> Watch beside thine arms to-night,
> Pray that God defend the Right.
> Think that when to-morrow comes
>   War shall claim command of all,
> Thou must hear the roll of drums,
>   Thou must hear the trumpet's call,
> Now before they silence ruth,
> Commune with the voice of truth;
> England! on thy knees to-night
> Pray that God defend the Right.[25]

In his verse, games of cricket and football were interwoven with the greater game of war: the garment was seamless. Nostalgic memories of the fierce moments of a keenly fought housematch provided the spiritual resource to face the tests of the morning's bloody conflict. So in *The School at War* the last moments before the battle are filled with inevitable memories of former playing-fields:

---

[23] Ibid, p. 139.

[24] James Morris, *Pax Brittanica* (Harmondsworth: Penguin, 1968), p. 337.

[25] Henry Newbolt, *Poems New and Old* (London: Murray, 1912), p. 80.

All night before the brink of death
   In fitful sleep the army lay,
For through the dream that stilled their breath
   Too gauntly glared the coming day.
We heard beyond the desert night
   The murmur of the fields we knew,
And our swift souls with one delight
   Like homing swallows Northward flew.
We played again the immortal games,
   And grappled with the fierce old friends,
And cheered the dead undying names,
   And sang the song that never ends.[26]

Newbolt gloried in this sacrificial vision of the schoolboy athlete on the battlefields of the empire:

Our game was his but yesteryear;
   We wished him back; we could not know
The selfsame hour we missed him here
   He led the line that broke the foe
Blood-red behind our guarded posts
   Sank as of old the dying day;
The battle ceased; the mingled hosts
   Weary and cheery went their way:
"To-morrow well may bring," we said,
   "As fair a fight, as clear a sun."
Dear lad, before the word was sped,
   For evermore thy goal was won.[27]

And the burden of glorious death was taken up by his fictional schoolboys with the stoic acceptance of a pre-ordained destiny. The progression was inexorable and the relationship secure. Bloodless strife led to bloody battle. The heroes of the XI and XV merely exchanged one kind of immortality for another:

"O Captains unforgot," they cried,
   "Come you again or come no more,
Across the world you keep the pride,
   Across the world we mark the score."[28]

---

[26] Ibid., p. 89.

[27] Ibid., p. 70.

[28] Ibid., p. 92.

Every upper class schoolboy had the responsibility of assisting at England's "Vigil"; all were cast in the same mold:

> Single-hearted, unafraid,
>   Hither all thy heroes came,
> On this altar's steps were laid
>   Gordon's life and Outram's fame.
> England! if thy will be yet
> By their great example set,
> Here beside thine arms to-night
> Pray that God defend the Right.[29]

The most famous of Newbolt's poems *Vitai Lampada* is the triumphal anthem of the Victorian and Edwardian public school system; games were the prologue to war.

> There's a breathless hush in the Close to-night —
>   Ten to make and the match to win —
> A bumping pitch and blinding light,
>   An hour to play and the last man in.
> And it's not for the sake of a ribboned coat,
>   Or the selfish hope of a season's fame,
> But his Captain's hand on his shoulder smote —
>   "Play up! play up! and play the game!"
> The sand of the desert is sodden red, —
>   Red with the wreck of a square that broke; —
> The Gatling's jammed and the Colonel dead,
>   And the regiment blind with dust and smoke.
> The river of death has brimmed his banks,
>   And England's far, and Honour a name,
>   But the voice of a schoolboy rallies the ranks:
>   "Play up! play up! and play the game!"
> This is the word that year by year,
>   While in her place the School is set,
> Every one of her sons must hear,
>   And none that hears it dare forget.
> This they all with a joyful mind
>   Bear through life like a torch in flame,
> And falling fling to the host behind —
>   "Play up! play up! and play the game!"[30]

---

[29] Ibid., p. 81.
[30] Ibid., pp. 78-79.

From father to son the pact was passed on. The School Chapel was the location of the traditional exchange:

> This is the Chapel: here, my son,
>   Your father thought the thoughts of youth,
> And heard the words that one by one
>   The touch of Life has turned to truth.
> Here is a day that is not far,
>   You too may speak with noble ghosts
> Of manhood and the vows of war
>   You made before the Lord of Hosts.[31]

These "vows of war" were brutal and explicit:

> To set the cause above renown,
>   To love the game beyond the prize,
> To honour, while you strike him down,
>   The foe that comes with fearless eyes;
> To count the life of battle good,
>   And dear the land that gave you birth,
> And dearer yet the brotherhood
>   That binds the brave of all the earth —[32]

And the destiny honorable, even desirable:

> God send you fortune; yet be sure,
> Among the lights that gleam and pass,
> You'll live to follow none more pure
> Than that which glows on yonder brass.
>
> "Qui procul hinc," the legend's writ, —
> The Frontier grave is far away
> "Qui ante diem periit:
> Sed miles, sed pro patria."[33]

It was precisely this destiny that produced the verse of the Marlborough schoolmaster, John Bain. After an education at Winchester and New College, Oxford, he taught at Marlborough from 1879 to 1883 and again from 1886

---

[31] Ibid., p. 76.

[32] Ibid., p. 76.

[33] Ibid., p. 77.

to 1913. During the Great War he contributed 118 poems to the school magazine, *The Marlburian*. These were mostly elegies for boys from Marlborough, whom he had known and whom he remembered with affection and sorrow. It is difficult to believe that those who read these outpourings of grief and love were not moved. The gentle, unsophisticated verses have a powerful intensity; but more than this they are a record of period values. They eulogize the fallen heroes of the games-field. They confirm a belief in the relationship between character and conditioned reflex. In memory of R. W. Lagden, brilliant games player, Oxford triple blue, international football player, Bain sang:

> A King was he of high degree,
> King of the boys who love
> The lads they know can tackle low,
> And the lusty lads who shove.
> King of them all, and King of the ball,
> Whatever the colour be;
> Red, white and brown, they owed his crown,
> And King of them all was he.
> Good was his name, he played the game,
> And he made the red ball hum,
> A king beloved as he stood and shoved,
> Or burst through the reeking scrum.
> Farewell, young King. Away you fling,
> All in the flush of youth,
> Playing the game, the grand last game,
> For England and for Truth.[34]

Of the less famous but high-spirited companion of the fives court he remembered:

> In the old days, a Voice would call,
> A cheery voice, just after Hall;
> To Cotton House, gloves, shoes and all,
> I'd run, young Leather,
> And there we'd knock a little ball
> About together.
> And now you've played a grimmer game;
> Old England called—you heard and came
> To shot and shell, to fire and flame,
> To death or glory,
> To fight and fall, and link your name

---

[34] See J. A. Mangan, "Athleticism: A Case Study of the Evolution of and Educational Ideology," in Brian Simon and Ian Bradley, eds., *The Victorian Public School* (Dublin: Gill & MacMillan, 1975), p. 165.

With England's story.
O cheery voice that once I knew!
O hand and eye so quick and true!
It's hard to think on death and you,
Old Friend, together.
Goodbye the old days when the fives-balls flew,
Goodbye, young Leather.[35]

A photograph in a London weekly inspired his tribute to Second Lieutenant H. J. Goodwin:

I saw your brave face in the *Sphere* —
I had not seen it since the days
When, term by term, and year by year,
You taught the ball to go your ways.
Cricket and Hockey, Rackets, Fives —
Aye, you were the master of them all;
I see your hand as it contrives
The old spin that made the wickets fall.
And now you've played your noblest game,
And now you've won your grandest Blue,
And Marlboro' lads shall read your name
Upon the wall and Honour you.[36]

While an obituary in *The Times* stirred memories of another old Marlburian:

I read — it all rushed back again —
The merry games we played together,
The old squash court, the shine, the rain,
The Boy who'd play in any weather,
The heart not pinned to Honours Lists —
That knew the joy of hard fought matches;
The steady eye; the supple wrists,
The sinewy hands that gripped the catches.
Aye, Marlborough knows you played the game,
Dying you set the gem upon her,
Giving her yet another name
To sparkle on her Roll of Honour.[37]

---

[35] Quoted in Mangan, "Athleticism," p. 263.

[36] Quoted in Mangan, "Athleticism," pp. 263-264.

[37] Quoted in Mangan, "Athleticism," pp. 262-263.

And the appalling loss of three Marlborough brothers, stimulated this verse:

> Three years! and every year has taken one,
> Each in its turn has reft away a son.
> O, Mother, mourning for your splendid dead,
> Let proud drops mingle with the tears you shed.
> Falling they leave behind them as they fall
> A nobler fame than that of bat and ball.
> On English fields' life's happiest years they spent,
> New dead for England, lo! they lie content.[38]

Bain wrote only of Marlburians but his verse exemplified the tragedy not simply of a school, but of a whole generation. It also illustrated educational purpose brought to terrible realization. The role of public schoolboy was honor through self-sacrifice. As we have seen, it was a concept older than the Great War. Bain was at the end of a line of naive romantics who urged the crown of martyrdom on willing and brave schoolboys long before Mons, The Somme and Passchendale, in the imperial skirmishes at Isandhlwana, Omdurman and the Kyber. The public school *beau idéal* in the New Imperialism of late Victorian Britain was the warrior "and the ultimate glory, sacrificial."[39] The admired symbol of duty done was Gordon of Khartoum. He was celebrated again and again in the pages of the public school magazines. The *Haileyburian* proclaimed of him:

> . . . who so reads
> Thy glorious history, let him keep thy name,
> Thy great unselfishness, thy matchless zeal,
> Thy dauntless gallantry in battlefield
> Fresh in his memory: and there the flame
> Of patriot valour still shall live to heal
> All civic strife, and lasting glory yield.[40]

While the *Cheltonian* lamented

> Gone from our sight, in our heart he still lingers,
> Crown of self-sacrifice — death — he has won;
> Martyr to duty, with pitiless finger,
> Beckoning onwards, our hero has gone.[41]

---

[38] Quoted in Mangan, "Athleticism," p. 264.

[39] See J. A. Mangan, *The Games-Ethic and Imperialism: Aspects of the Diffusion of an Ideal* (London: Penguin/Viking, 1985).

[40] *Haileyburian*, vol. XXXIV, no. 268, April, 1885, p. 40.

[41] *Cheltonian*, vol. XXVIII, no. 283, June, 1885, p. 16.

And John Bain himself resurrected him in the agony of the Great War as an inspiration and an ideal.

At first sight, the Oakfield school master Norman Gale stands in contrast to John Bain. Gale had a passion for cricket and wrote several books of verses indulging his enthusiasm: *Cricket Songs* (1894), *More Cricket Songs* (1905), and towards the end of his life, *Messrs. Bat & Ball* (1930) and *Close of Play* (1936). He composed a large number of unremarkable, well-mannered lyrics redolent with his quiet love of green squares, white flannels and blue skies. In Gale's domestic and idiomatic verse for fellow cricket-lovers, there was only one romance—in Spring a young man's fancy turned to bats and pads:

> Beside the pillar-box a girl
>   Sells daffodils in golden bunches,
> And with an apron full of Spring
>   Stays men a moment from their lunches:
> Some fill their hands for love of bloom,
>   To others Cupid hints a reason;
> But as for me, I buy because
>   The flowers suggest the Cricket season![42]

Gale was not merely the writer of self-indulgent lyrics. Many of his verses are parables symbolizing the civilization implicit in the regularity and regulations of the cricket field, a landscape free from sad human dilemmas. The cricket field epitomized security and serenity. And among the laconic, whimsical stanzas there was a quiet conviction of the wider role of his much loved game in the national and imperial scheme of things:

> O Statesmen who devise and plot
>   To keep the White above the Black
> Who tremble when your bolt is shot
>   Lest love and loyalty grow slack,
> There's not a deed of craftmanship,
>   There's not a thing Red Tape can do,
> Shall knit the Hindu with the Celt
>   As much as this the Cambridge Blue![43]

Pax Brittanica in Gale's sanguine view, was more likely to be achieved by sixes flying over the boundary than by six inch shells flying over the natives:

> This will be a perfect planet
>   Only when the Game shall enter

---

[42] Norman Gale, *More Cricket Songs* (London: Alston Rivers, 1905), p. 59.

[43] Norman Gale, "Dark Blue," in L. Frewin, *An Anthology of Cricket* (London: MacDonald, 1968), p. 26.

Every country, teaching millions
   How to ask for leg or Centre.
Closely heed a level-headed
   Sportsman far too grave to banter:
When the cricket bags are opened
   Doves of Peace fly north instanter![44]

The illegitimate passions of nationalism would be responsive only to "the Kingliest game on earth":

Would you have, in distant regions,
   Furioso change to largo,
Add the implements of Cricket
   Promptly to a steamer's cargo!
Let us ship evangelizing
   Umpire, Bowler, Batsman, Scorer
Far from home, to prove the friendship
   Active in the flying Fourer!

Paradoxically Gale embraced a dialectic which verged on a contradiction: the game was for simple pleasure *and* serious purpose. His first book of verse, *Cricket Songs,* was dedicated to "all Rugby boys in general, and to John and William Denton in particular"[45] and the Victorian homilist is exposed in several of the verses, naked and unabashed. He strongly favoured the epiplexis. His *Buzz Her In, Advice Gratis* and *Lay On* are heavy with well-meaning admonitions. And *Buzz Her In* demonstrates that, even for Gale, the honoured cliche that decent fellows were not too concerned with winning and played the game for the game's sake, was no more than that:

Don't trot by the the side of the ball like a dolt,
   Buzz her in!
But cram on the pace like a fine Derby colt,
   Buzz her in!
Pick her up, dash her in true and fast to the sticks,
And teach the best batsmen to look to their tricks!
The team that can field well the team is that licks —
   Buzz her in![46]

While *Lay On,* like Newbolt's *Vitae Lampada* but in a minor key, is filled with public school messages of the ethical lessons inherent in games:

---

[44] Norman Gale, "Pax Brittannica," in *Messrs. Bat & Ball* (Rugby: Norman Gale, 1930), p. 40.

[45] Ibid., p. 39.

[46] Gale, *Cricket Songs,* Introduction.

One wicket to fall, and the Telegraph's face
    Rather unkind!
No doubt we are caught in a very tight place,
    Thirty behind!
O Jones, be contained if you worship your school,
    Block her and snick;
But punch her to leg if she's handy; keep cool;
    Lay it on thick![47]

However understated his imagery, Gale was as wedded to the sacrificial view of the English public schoolboy as Newbolt and Bain. He fully understood the martial purpose of the hours spent on cricket squares:

See in bronzing sunshine
Thousands of good fellows,
Such as roll the world along,
Such as cricket mellows!
These shall keep the Motherland
Safe amid her quarrels:
Lucky lads, plucky lads,
Trained to snatch at laurels![48]

And in *Chuck Her Up*, a period cry of encouragement to the fielder, Gale reminded his Rugbians in no uncertain terms that the bruised hand from the stinging catch that earned the captain's compliment might well be a foretaste of a grimmer destiny:

You may purchase praise by a twinge of pain
In the midst of battle and giant blows!
And next, when the English Flag's on the hill —
Though many are never again to sup —
For the love of your land where the words were planned
Cry out to your men—'Chuck her up!'[49]

The most notable schoolmaster poet of the English public school games-cult was Edward Bowen, assistant master at Harrow School from 1859 to 1901. Bowen personified the schoolmaster ideal of the late nineteenth century—the athletic pedagogue. He was a philathlete extraordinary,[50] who

---

[47] Ibid., p. 4.

[48] Ibid., p. 22.

[49] Gale, *More Cricket Songs*, p. 51.

[50] Ibid., p. 55.

overshadowed both predecessor and successor in the heyday of athleticism in the English public school.

It was in his verses celebrating games and games' fields that his part as propagandist was most forcefully played: "He was the verse chronicler of the Golden Age of Athleticism." He sang sweetly of the "great days in the distance enchanted" and "days of fresh air, in the rain and the sun"; he described the great dramas of the Eton and Harrow Match played every July at Lord's; he wrote whimsical doggerel about footballs and cricket bats; he composed possibly the most beautiful and tender elegy in the poetry of the cricket field for a fellow lover of Harrow games, Robert Grimston."[51] It was in this elegy in particular, that he easily refutes Mack's accusation of uninspirational banality:

> Still the balls ring upon the sunlit grass,
> Still the big elms, deep shadowed, watch the play;
> And ordered game and loyal conflict pass
> The hours of May.
> But the game's guardian, mute, nor heeding more
> What suns may gladden, and what airs may blow,
> Friend, teacher, playmate, helper, counsellor,
> Lies resting now.
> 'Over' — they move, as bids their fieldsman's art;
> With shifted scene the strife begins anew;
> 'Over' — we seem to hear him, but his part
> Is over, too.[52]

However it is in his Harrovian song *Tom* that he is seen most clearly as the forceful advocate of the muscular morality of the era. Tom is the *beau ideal* of the public school system; the vital proof of its efficacy; the stuff of empire builders; the Darwinian Ideal the school sought to manufacture in large numbers in subscription to a distorted interpretation of the concept of "survival of the fittest:"

> Now that the matches are near,
> Struggle and terror, and bliss,
> Which is the House of the year?
> Who is the hero of this?
> Tom!
> Tom, who with valour and skill, too,
> Spite of the wind and the hill, too,
> Takes it along sudden and strong,
> Going where Tom has a will to;
> Tom, who is sorry and sad, too,

---

[51] See J. A. Mangan, "Philathlete Extraordinary: A Portrait of the Victorian Moralist, Edward Bowen," *Journal of Sports History* vol. 9, no. 3 (Winter, 1982): 23-40.

[52] Ibid., pp. 36-37.

When there are bruises to add to;
Why did he crush Jack with a rush?
Only because that he had to!
Base is the player who stops
Fight, till the fighting is o'er;
Who follows up till he drops,
Panting and limping and sore?
Tom!
Tom, who with scuffle and sprawl, too,
Knows where he carries to ball to;
Ankles and toes! look how he goes!
Through them and out of them all, too![53]

Myth, we are told, is an essential tool for exploring, mapping and delimiting the world of experience. "Man constructs the myths, the social institutions, virtually the whole world," maintains Terence Hawke in his *Structuralism and Semiotics*, "and in so doing he constructs himself."[54] Myth is a semiotic system. Tom was a mythical hero of Victorian upper-class pedagogy. He had the most serious purpose. He was a model for his peers: "an inimitable and approved symbol, an abstraction in concrete for an unsophisticated audience with a restricted frame of reference."[55] His role was to channel emotion, mobilize the will, direct energies and determine action. Bowen cut through the essentials of the public school's pedagogue's "world vision" to achieve these ends. In keeping with all mythologists, he carefully abolished the complexity of human action, giving it an elemental simplicity.[56]

Elsewhere Bowen pressed home the message of the essential morality of the manly:

Jog, jog, tramp, tramp, down the hill we scud;
In the dull December, splashing in the mud;
Legs, as their manner is, turn to black and blue;
Mud spatters head to foot — well, and it if do?
Legs yet will carry us through another day;
Mud is only water modifying clay.
  Down the hill, down the hill, after dinner drop,
  Sulky boys, sulky boys, stay upon the top![57]

[53] W.E. Bowen, *Edward Bowen A Memoir* (London: Longmans, Green & Co., 1902), pp. 404-405.

[54] Terence Hawke, *Structuralism and Semiotics* (London: Methuen, 1977), p. 14.

[55] Mangan, "Philathlete Extraordinary," p. 34.

[56] Hawke, *Structuralism and Semiotics*, p. 15.

[57] Bowen, *Edward Bowen*, p. 399.

and

> Work, with her sister, Play, came by —
>   Awake boys, awake!
> Plenty to learn from both, they cry,
>   Awake boys, awake!
> There's pleasure in toil no doubt, no doubt;
> There's also pleasure, perhaps, without;
> There's books that pray to be read today,
> There's balls that long to be kicked about;
>   But none who roost on the Drowsy tree
>   Can ever be friends with me, or me![58]

True to his social class, Gale in his poem *The Female Boy* was equally unequivocal:

> If cursed by a son who declined to play cricket,
>   (Supposing him sound and sufficient in thews,)
> I'd larrup him well with the third of a wicket,
> Selecting safe parts of his body to bruise.
> In his mind such an urchin king Solomon had
> When he said, Spare the stump, and you bungle the lad!
> The feminine boy who declines upon croquet,
> Or halma, or spillikins (horrible sport!),
> Or any amusement that's female and pokey,
> And flatly objects to behave as he ought!
> I know him of old. He is lazy and fat,
> And sadly in need of the thick of a bat![59]

Idlers were the damned; athletes were the chosen—for the qualitites they epitomised: "I offer it as my deliberate opinion," wrote Bowen, "that as the best boys are, on the whole, the players of games, I had rather regenerate England with the football elevens than with average members of Parliament . . . When I reflect on the vices to which games are a permanent corrective—laziness, foppery, man-of-the-worldness—I am not surprised at being led to the verdict which I have just delivered."[60] In this and other essentials Bowen was as one with his contemporaries. He saw the closest relationship between

---

[58] Ibid., 400.

[59] Gale, *More Cricket Songs*, p. 15.

[60] Quoted in Mangan, *Athleticism*, p. 158.

playing-field and battlefield. Harrovians were part of an ancient military tradition:

> When Raleigh rose to fight the foes,
>   We sprang to work and will;
> When Glory gave to Drake the wave,
>   She gave to us the hill.
> The ages drift in rolling tide,
>   But high shall float the morn
> Adown the stream of England's pride,
>   When Drake and we were born!
>   For we began when he began.
>   Our times are one;
>   His glory thus shall circle us
>   Till time be done.[61]

and in *An Episode of Balaclava*, a Harrovian hero, who took part in the famous charge of the Light Brigade, is set up to inspire the future guardians of Empire:

> O soldiers of a bloodless strife,
>   O friends in work and play,
> Bear we not all a coward life
>   Some moment in the day?
> So, lest a deed of gallant faith
>   Forgotten fade from view,
> I take the tale of Lockwood's death,
>   And write it down for you.[62]

"In their attempt to classify mankind into different types," remarks C. M. Bowra, "the early Greek philosphers gave a special place to those men who live for action and the honour which comes from it. . . . They held that the life of action is superior to the pursuit of profit of the gratification of the senses, that the man who seeks honour is himself an honourable figure."[63] This was also true of the Victorian upper-class schoolmaster. And as among the early philosophers of Homeric Greece so it was among the upper-class pedagogues of Victorian England: the greatest heroes were men of action. For this reason: "battle provides the most searching tests not merely of strength and courage but of resource and decision."[64] In the absence of war, Bowra has observed, the Grecian lust for honour was pursued in their "games."

---

[61] Bowen, *Edward Bowen*, p. 378.

[62] Ibid., p. 413.

[63] C. M. Bowra, *Heroic Poetry*, p. 97.

[64] Ibid., p. 97.

The "mimic strife" of Olympia was a serious substitute. This was equally true of the Victorian.

The verses of Newbolt, Gale and Bowen served both mimetic and pragmatic purposes.[65] The mimetic role of literature as suggested long ago by Plato, and then Aristotle, is to complete and fulfill nature rather than simply imitate it. Literature has an effective purpose—the excitation and catharsis of the emotions. The reader lives vicariously through the experience portrayed in the work of art, associates with the drama, assimilates the essential nature of the passion. In the sacrificial verse of Newbolt and Bain the mimetic intention is abundantly clear but it is also evident in the ingenuous hedonism of Gale and Bowen. They were the troubadours of the cricketing romance, who constructed idylls of summer in celebration of the sweetness of the experience. But for all the simple sensuality of much of their verse these men were pragmatists—in the literary tradition of Sir Phillip Sidney. The purpose of their verse was not merely to satisfy the emotions "but rather to instruct the mind, or if to please at all, then merely in order finally to persuade."[66] It served moral ends. It was essentially didactic. It met the spiritual and moral requirements of a particular audience.[67] Their verse constituted the world of the ideal, rather than the world of reality. They sought to transform. While their verse is a record of experience, it is also a statement of aspiration. It was meant as a source of redemption for some, elevation for others and fulfillment for all. It was an attempt through linguistic symbol to give meaning to the world of the English schoolboy. It was as full of earnest didacticism as it was of jocular hedonism. In a very real sense, they wrote, in the words of I.A. Richards, "in the service of the most integral purposes of life."[68]

These Victorians shared many of the literary ambitions of Matthew Arnold. Through their verse they sought to master the world and provide an adequate interpretation of it; they had a view of poetry that was almost hieratic; they saw spiritual discipline coming from its ennobling effects; they had an idea of poetry as utterance as much as form.[69] If Arnold was, as Nieman suggests, a model Victorian in his earnestness, in his esteem for the plain virtues of strength and honesty, in his personal reticence, in his admiration for "backbone, nervous energy, and power of honest work" so were they.[70] His statement that poetry was "morality with emotion" admirably describes their philosophy

---

[65] I have drawn freely on the ideas in the stimulating Introduction to Giles B. Gunn, *Literature and Religion* (London: SCM Press, 1971).

[66] Quoted in Gunn, *Literature and Religion*, p. 16.

[67] See Vincent Buckley, *Poetry and Morality* (London: Chatto and Windus, 1959), pp. 30 and 70.

[68] Gunn, *Literature and Religion*, p. 17.

[69] Buckley, *Poetry and Morality*, p. 34.

[70] Fraser Neiman, *Matthew Arnold* (Cambridge: Harvard University Press, 1960), p. 163. See also W. Stacey Johnson, *The Voices of Matthew Arnold* (New Haven: Yale University Press, 1961) for an interesting discussion of Arnold and the Victorian concept of morality.

and purpose. The suggestion is not simply that they wrote to establish the practices of a particular generation but this was assuredly a clear intention. They interpreted the everyday actions of the schoolboy on his playing field largely in terms of a selective and limited context—moralistic, and sacrificial.

It was an interpretation summarised well in these words from *The Hill*, Horace Vachell's novel of Harrow School before the Boer War, which were eventually to possess an ironic and terrible poignancy:

> To die young, clean, ardent; to die swiftly, in
> perfect health; to die saving others from death,
> or worse disgrace; to die scaling heights, to
> die and carry with you into the fuller ampler
> life beyond, untainted hopes and aspirations,
> unembittered memories, all the freshness and
> gladness of May—is not that cause for joy
> rather than sorrow.[71]

Self-sacrifice was the presiding principle of their verse and gives it coherence and purpose. They saw poetry as the "magister vitae." They enunciated moral laws and interpreted the moral world for their charges. In their verse they were concerned with the problem of how to live and die correctly.

Of course, they were men of common sense and perception. They recognized that plain didacticism was deadly and wrapped up their messages in light comedy or heavy drama and made them palatable. They created a reality shrewdly by turning the instruments of schoolboy pleasure into the means of moral realization. They took the schoolboy's frame of reference— the playing field—and transformed it into an arena for moral training. The romanticism of Wordsworth or Coleridge meant little to them. The concept of the poet and his creative imagination was too grandiose, too egocentric, too awesome for the plain purposes of these uncomplicated and well-meaning men. Literature for them was not a personal surrogate for theology but an extension of it. Profane acts on playing fields were transformed into hierophanies.[72]

At one level, their celebration of games was hieratic in the sense that Novak describes it. It offered momentary salvation from "the obsessive seriousness and confusions of everyday life." [73] It permitted transcendence of the routine and the tedious. At another level, it offered a means of ultimate salvation through duty unto death. The progression from anticipation to fulfillment was in the most complete sense, from playing field to battle-field.

---

[71] H.A. Vachell, *The Hill*, (London: Murray, 1905), p. 236.

[72] For a valuable discussion of this concept, see Vincent Buckley, *Poetry And the Sacred*, (London: Chatto and Windus, 1968), pp. 12-13.

[73] See Richard S. Gruneau, "Freedom and Constraint: The Paradoxes of Play, Games and Sports," *Journal of Sports History*, vol. 7, no. 3(Winter 1980): 71.

In this respect, as we have seen, the men cannot be viewed separately from the cultural matrix from which their writing emerged, nor can they be dismissed cursorily by the disillusioned heirs of Owen, Sassoon and Bridges as naive, banal and uninspiring. They wrote for their era and their audience. They were the metaphysicians of a sub-culture. They preached the metaphorical character of the games-field. They issued mimetic statements about ultimate possibilities. They were transcendentalists—muscular moralists who *made* muscular moralists. They reflected, created and dramatized their community for their own ends. They now serve to exemplify it to a larger community bored with their idealism, irritated by their naivety and amused by their nobility. To the weary agonists of Eliot's *Wasteland,* they have nothing to offer except as period curiosities. They are the foolish and sentimental voices of a defunct and arcane community, but to the social historian who uses literature wisely, they provide evidence of both a "world vision" and a presiding principle which jointly constituted an attempt to order the daily existence of the Victorian and Edwardian schoolboy in one of the most influential education systems the world has witnessed.

17

Team Games, Trench Warfare and the London"Times": British Football, the Nation and the First World War, 1914-1915*

Colin R. Veitch

AN EXAMINATION OF SPORTS AND GAMES in the British literature of the First World War period is a curious and often contradictory undertaking. Many are familiar with the oft-recited examples of British bravado displayed in the face of certain death as platoons of soldiers dribbled footballs towards the German lines during murderous assaults across no-man's land.[1] Few are aware however, that the British popular press adopted and exploited sport in its propaganda process, nor are they conscious that an identifiable genre of "athletic war poetry" emerged during these years.[2] These are but two of many unplumbed depths in the literature of the era.

Though educational, social, military and sports historians have, to a varying degree, made references to sports, games or physical education during the First World War, their comments in the majority of cases are cosmetic, and in some cases, misleading. Certain statements regarding the role of sport in the British response to the War are undoubtedly perpetuating what soldier-writer Sydney Rogerson had called "the grim-smiling-faces-of-undaunted-boys' war of the early correspondents with attacking battalions dribbling footballs

---

*A version of this paper appeared in the *Journal of Contemporary History* 20 (1985): 363-378.

[1] There were in fact, at least five such recorded incidents. See C. R. Veitch, "Sport and War in the British Literature of the First World War, 1914-1918" MA thesis, University of Alberta, 1984), pp. 9-17.

[2] See C. R. Veitch, "Play Up! Play Up! And Win the War! The Propaganda of Athleticism in Britain, 1914-1918," a paper presented at the Olympic Scientific Congress, Eugene, Oregon, U.S.A., July 1984, and Ibid.

across a sporting no-man's land."[3] Just as he and Terraine urge the military
historian to escape this view of the First World War—"to blow away the smoke
and get at the fire,"[4] so this paper will attempt to make a more critical
examination of the role of sport in the opening months of the war. Building
upon the excellent studies of both Walvin and Mason,[5] it will attempt to
show that the opening nine months of the war saw the British popular press
vigorously endorsing the pervasive maxim that good sportsmen naturally made
first-class soldiers. In particular, it will focus on the bitter and often bigoted
outpourings from privileged supporters of the traditional *amateur* game of
soccer which greeted the decision of the *professional* soccer teams not to
curtail their games despite the onset of hostilities in Europe. In many ways,
the diatribe which greeted this course of action was emblematic of the
dissatisfaction felt by many of the amateurs over the changes wrought in the
social fabric of the game of soccer over the previous twenty years. That British
sportsmen were not in the front line wielding rifles against the German armies
was of serious concern; that these self-same footballers were *professionals*
was insufferable. As will become more clear, this increasingly vocal dispute
crystallised as much around notions of the relative values of amateurism versus
professionalism in sport as it did around a genuine concern for the welfare
of the nation at war. "The Times" newspaper, with its traditional privileged
contributors, was well to the fore as the debate raged on for the first nine
months of the war.

     Great Britain declared war against Germany at 11:00 p.m.on 4 August,
1914. Four divisions of the British Expeditionary Force were mobilized and
landed in France between 9 and 17 August under the command of Sir John
French. At home the recruiting offices were packed with young men wanting
to sign up with Kitchener's new armies, eager not to miss the war. Amid
the patriotic euphoria, an American, Herbert Kaufman, wrote with prophetic
insight to *The Times* on 19 August:

> Personal heroism, the heroism of individual brawn and boldness will achieve little
> opportunity. The range of weapons and modern tactics have set the struggle on the
> basis of mathematics. . . . This is to be a war in which Death will keep tally on
> automatic adding machines. Past military experiences will furnish slight guidance. It
> demands new rules and new tools.[6]

     Despite this sombre warning, it was those very qualitites of "individual
brawn and boldness" inherent in the nation's sportsmen that became the

---

[3] Quoted in John Terraine, *The Smoke and the Fire: Myths and Anti-Myths of War 1861-1945*
     (London: Sidgwick and Jackson, 1980), p. 137.

[4] Ibid., p. 14.

[5] James Walvin, *The People's Game: A Social History of British Football*, (London: Allen Lane,
     1975); Tony Mason, *Association Football and English Society 1863-1915* (Sussex, England:
     The Harvester Press, 1980).

[6] Herbert Kaufman, "The Silent Briton—An American Tribute," *The Times*, 19 August 1914, p.
     8.

focal point of the army's recruiting drive. *The Times* was undoubtedly the staunchest ally of this drive and, in a remarkable display of ambiguity, published the following poem with its sporting exhortations to military excellence on the very same day as the previous letter:

> Lad, with the merry smile and the eyes
> Quick as hawk's and clear as the day,
> You, who have counted the game the prize,
> Here is the game of games to play.
> Never a goal—the captains say—
> Matches the one that's needed now:
> Put the old blazer and cap away
> England's colours await your brow.[7]

The sentiments and language of this poem, with its references to blazer, caps and colours, were calculated to appeal to the high-spirited, games-playing ex-public schoolboys who had been reared on the military expectations embodied in the code of athleticism.[8] Such young men were in immediate demand by the army, who offered all public school and university men an immediate officer's commission for the duration of the war.[9] "The Times" encouraged these young men to come forward, appealing to its own readership: "All Varsity men, Old Public School Boys—men who are hardened to the soldiers' life by strenuous pursuit of sport should enlist at once,"[10] and continued to keep its readers informed regarding the progress of such sportsmen-soldiers following their enlistment. The public school and university men responded to the nation's plight with alacrity. Some 37,000 students or Old Boys were swiftly commissioned in the opening weeks of the war.[11] Of these, more than 20,500 had previous Officer Corp experience and were characterised by one of their commanding officers thus:

> They are the figures of British youth with the principles of honour, manhood, justice and courage instilled into them, and with a very real idea of what sacrifices of ease and luxury and possibly of life are demanded today.[12]

---

[7] R. E. Vernede, "The Call," *The Times*, 19 August, 1914, p. 7.

[8] Athleticism was the educational ideology prevalent in many of the British public schools of the late nineteenth and early twentieth century which held that beneficial character development would accrue from participation in team games. Sports and games were believed to mold the boy for later life, fostering patriotism and preparing for any moral or military battles he may have to face. A fuller definition may be sought in J. A. Mangan's *Athleticism in the Victorian and Edwardian Public School. The Emergence and Consolidation of an Educational Ideology* (Cambridge: CUP, 1981).

[9] *T.P.'s Weekly* vol. 24, no. 614 (15 August 1914) p. 227.

[10] Walvin, p. 89.

[11] Reginald Pound, *The Lost Generation* (London: Constable, 1964), p. 29.

[12] Alan R. Haig-Brown, *The OTC and the Great War* (New York: C. Scribner and Sons, 1915), p. 83.

The formation of these essential characteristics was naturally attributed, if only in part, to the football field, as the author conceded: "even today there are amongst us those who really imagine that Wellington trained his officers between the goalposts."[13] The contribution of the public school men, however, did not extend solely into the officer corps. As early as 18 August one "Old Haileyburian" suggested that collecting old public schoolboys together into units would circumvent valuable training time being wasted in the inculcation of qualitites already present among their numbers: "Such companies would from the first possess that cohesion and spirit of mutual confidence and pride in their corp which it is one of the main purposes of military training to instill."[14] A. A. David of Rugby School encouraged fellow public school men to enlist in the ranks rather than wait for a commission, reasoning there was a "splendid opportunity of giving a lead to young men of all classes. Here also, is a supreme test of school spirit and character." With the sanctioning of "Pals Battalions" for integration into Kitchener's armies, whereby groups of friends, relatives, workmates or fellow team players could all enlist and serve together, the way lay open for the formation of a Public Schools Battalion. Within days of its being announced, 1,950 ex-public school and university men had enlisted—enough to form not one, but two battalions— in order to serve alongside their peers. A reporter pointed out: "They are all of the well-to-do-class, and are paying their own expenses," and noted that many wore their old school caps and colours as they paraded from Hyde Park to Victoria Station, enroute to Epsom Downs for training.[15] Their dutiful and enthusiastic patriotism was celebrated in "The Recruits" by I. Gregory Smith:

> O! Hearts ever youthful, like schoolboys at play
> So be it with you in the thick of the fray;
> In the crash and the smoke and the roar of the fight
> Be it yours, if it need be, to die for the Right![16]

The "Sportsman's Battalion" of the Royal Fusiliers actually advertised for recruits to its ranks, specifying that they should be between nineteen and thirty-five years old and from "Upper and middle classes only." An entrance fee of three guineas was charged to each successful applicant.[17]

The patriotic zeal exhibited by the public school fraternity was matched by many of the nation's amateur sporting organisations, who curtailed their seasons in order to encourage enlistment among their members. Early in

---

[13] Ibid, p. 93.

[14] The Times, 18 August 1914, p. 4.

[15] Ibid., 11 September 1914, p. 5.

[16] Ibid., 15 September 1914, p. 5.

[17] Pound, p. 114.

September, Mr. Philip Collins, vice-president of the Hockey Association and chairman of the England Selection Committee, suggested that all coming matches should be abandoned as this would release some forty thousand able-bodied men for military service.[18] Two days later, all rugby clubs in Kent were asked by their association to scratch all games and encourage players to join.[19] The following day, the Rugby Football Union announced its intention of forming a unit of rugby players to fight in France, and in a column headed "Patriotism Before Sport" invited volunteers who wished to carry arms with associates from the rugby fraternity to send an application to Twickenham, the traditional home of English international rugby football.[20] Their Irish national team counterparts joined up with the 7th Battalion, Dublin Fusiliers amid a similar flurry of enthusiastic press coverage.[21] Many amateur football associations decided to cancel all matches during the war on the grounds that it "would be desecrating their playing fields to use them for sport at such a time."[22] Such demonstrations of patriotic intent, deemed entirely in accord with the traditional response of the English sporting gentlemen, were celebrated as essential sacrifices necessary for the successful defense of the realm. A suitably vociferous expression of outrage occured, therefore, when the Football Association announced that their program of professional league games would not be curtailed in spite of the national emergency.[23] In the often bitter debate that followed this revelation, decades of controversy surrounding the growth and development of the game of football were brought to light and aired in the convenient cause of national unity.

The game of football had diffused liberally through the social strata of British society following the formation of the Football Association in 1863, and had been swiftly adopted by the working classes of the industrial heartlands of England. This social diffusion brought with it ethical and ideological turmoil for those players and administrators who had been reared on the game in the closeted environments of the nation's public schools. Under the tenets of athleticism, they had been taught to value, in Vernede's words, "the game the prize" rather than the result. Football, like other team games, was to be played in a spirit of sportsmanlike good conduct, where rivalry was good-natured and the quality of the match surpassed the final score in importance. The vast intrusion into the game of the lower classes, bringing with them unwelcome novelties such as partisan supporters, lack of sportsmanship and the ultimate bane of the amateur gentleman ethos—the professional

---

[18] *The Times*, 2 September 1914, p. 3.

[19] Ibid., 4 September 1914, p. 10.

[20] Ibid., 5 September 1914, p. 12.

[21] Ibid., 18 September 1914.

[22] H. W. Wilson and J. A. Hammerton, eds., *The Great War. The Standard History of the All-Europe Conflict*, vol. 2 (1915), p. 118.

[23] An identical controversy in Australia is the subject of Michael McKearnan's "Sport, War and Society: Australia 1914-1918," in *Sport in Australia: Selected Readings in Physical Activity*, (Sydney: McGraw-Hill, 1976).

footballer—was held to be detrimental to the progress and practice of football.[24] It was from those sympathetic with this line of argument that the wartime criticisms largely stemmed, for they represented a section of the population who felt that their values and their game were being undermined by a challenge from the new working men's brand of soccer.[25] The decision taken by the F. A. to continue professional league soccer was thus swiftly branded as an almost treasonable offense, quite against the grain of national unity.

The first shot in the exchange was fired by the *Evening News*, which announced the curtailment of its sports paper section in a column headed "Duty Before Sport":

> This is no time for football. This nation, this Empire has got to occupy itself with more serious business. The young men who play football and the young men who look on have better work to do. The trumpet calls them, their country calls them, the heroes in the trenches call them. They are summoned to leave their sport, and to take part in the great game. That game is war, for life or death.[26]

Renouncing football and enlisting to "play the greater game" for King and Country shot to disproportionate prominence in the early months of the war. Recruitment for Kitchener's "New Armies" was based exclusively on a voluntary basis. Consequently, a vocal minority saw it as expedient to the national effort that the Football Association should be forced to abandon its programme of games, and encourage players and spectators alike to sign up. The responses from the amateur clubs and associations only served to emphasise the "unpatriotic" stance of the professional footballers. Perhaps the most notable contribution on this topic was penned by none other than the redoubtable cricketer, Dr. W. G. Grace, who noted that professional cricket too, should give way to more serious matters:

> The fighting on the Continent is very severe and will probably be prolonged. I think the time has arrived when the county cricket season should be closed, for it is not fitting at a time like the present that able-bodied men should play day after day, and pleasure seekers look on.[27]

Conscious of its somewhat delicate position in the limelight of the nation's press, the Football Association put its complete administrative structure at the disposal of the War Office, and offered the use of all league club grounds

---

[24] These were the roots of the controversy which split the F. A. into rival factions during the Edwardian years, and the organization only recovered its unity in the year prior to the outbreak of the war. It is also interesting to note that equally antagonistic claims were made against the "professional gladiators" of the US Olympic team in Stockholm, 1912. John Lucas, *The Modern Olympic Games*, (New York: A. S. Barnes & Co., 1980) pp. 91-95.

[25] Mason, p. 222.

[26] *The Times*, 3 September 1914, p. 6.

[27] *TP's Weekly*, vol. 24, no. 618 (12 Sept. 1914), p. 316.

for the purpose of recruitment and training. It was announced that Glasgow would form a battalion of football players and followers, and that recruiting rallies would be held at soccer grounds during the half-time interval on match days. One poster displayed at a London ground encouraged fans with the words:

> Do you want to be a
> Chelsea Die-Hard?
> If so
> Join the 17th Battalion
> Middlesex Regiment
> "The Old Die-Hards"
> And follow the lead given
> by your favourite Football Players[28]

These acts, however, were insufficient to quell the protests which reached a sensational peak on 8 September when one F. N. Charrington, an East End temperance worker, sent a telegram to the king, asking for the playing of football to be banned during the war. Earlier that year, George V had been the first reigning monarch to attend a Cup Final, and had also become the honorary patron of the Football Association. In a diplomatically worded reply, the king's personal secretary told Charrington: " . . . the doings of the Association will be carefully followed having regard to the King's position as its patron."[29] Undeterred, and convinced of the validity of his cause, Charrington attended the Fulham club's next home game, and in attempting to cause a disturbance was set upon by two over-zealous club officials at half-time.[30] Undoubtedly he was not alone in his condemnation of the continuation of league soccer, as is revealed by an entry for 16 December in the diary of a young journalist that year:

> Going to football matches in the old days we used to be confronted with evangelical posters greatly concerned for our eternal welfare, asking us, among other questions, "Are you prepared to meet your God?" and bidding us "Repent, for the time is at hand." In these days the posters carried by a line of sandwich-men, walking up and down before the gates of the Chelsea ground, ask the crowds such questions as "Are you forgetting that there's a war on?," "Your Country Needs You," "Be Ready to Defend Your Home and Women from the German Huns." So far as I could notice, little attention was given to these skeletons at the feast. Inside the ground there was excitement and uproar.[31]

---

[28] Walvin, p. 89.

[29] *The Times*, 8 September 1914, p. 4. Both telegrams are reproduced in full in *The Great War*, vol. 2 (1915), p. 145.

[30] *The Times*, 8 September 1914, p. 4.

[31] Michael MacDonagh, *In London During the Great War: The Diary of a Journalist* (London: Eyre and Spottiswoode, 1935), p. 44.

Incidents such as these appear to have toughened the resolve of the Management Committee of the league, who stated: "The Committee are even more decidedly of the opinion that in the interests of the people of this country, football ought to be continued."[32] The defiant stance of the F.A. was a source of considerable disappointment to the army's recruiting officers:

> It has a moral effect. . . . These professional footballers of England are the pick of the country for fitness. Nobody has a right to say that any body of men are not doing their duty, and there may be excellent domestic reasons why every one of these thousands of players does not enlist. But when the young men week after week see the finest physical manhood of the country expending its efforts kicking a ball about, they can't possibly realise there is a call for every fit man at the front.[33]

And the controversy was fueled by the publication in the same issue of the following poem. The first stanza in particular reveals the poet's bias:

> Come, leave the lure of the football field
> With its fame so lightly won,
> And take your place in a greater game
> Where worthier deeds are done.
> No game is this where thousands watch
> The play of a chosen few;
> But rally all! if you're men at all,
> There's room in the team for you.
>
> You may find your place in the battle-front
> If you'd play the forward game,
> To carry the trench and man the gun
> With dash and deadly aim.
> O, the field is wide, and the foe is strong,
> And it's far from wing to wing,
> But we'll carry through, and it's there that you
> May shoot for your flag and King.
> Then leave for a while the football field
> And the lure of the flying ball
> Lest it dull your ear to the voice you hear
> When your King and country call.
> Come join the ranks of our hero sons
> In the wider field of fame,
> Where the God of Right will watch the fight
> And referee the game.[34]

---

[32] *The Times*, 8 September 1914, p. 4.

[33] Ibid., 24 November 1914, p. 5.

[34] "The Game" by A. Lockhead, *The Times*, 24 November 1914, p. 9.

A shorter, and openly sardonic, poem of the same sentiments had appeared earlier that week, complete with explanatory heading:

"Professionalism as Usual"

(The Football Cup Competitions are to proceed as usual—Daily Paper)
Two-and-twenty fighting men
Fit as fit can be
Kick the football, though the war
Is fought on land and sea.
"Play as usual," run and kick,
Though the foemen land,
Goals must be defended still
If Britain is to stand.[35]

The Times reported in a bitter tone that recruitment drives at football league matches were having dismal results, despite large crowds. On Saturday, 21 November, only six volunteers came forward from the crowd at the game between Cardiff and Bristol Rovers, while at the Arsenal ground in London, a call for recruits yielded only one man.[36] It was noted that there was a "growing feeling that professional and spectacular football is incompatible with successful recruiting."[37] These observations ignored the fact that the month of November had been a highly successful one for the nation in recruiting terms. More than 160,000 men had come forward, a substantial increase over the months of September and October.[38] This would tend to suggest that the youth of the nation were quite willing to come forward and serve the nation in its hour of need, but chose not to enlist at the football grounds, where they went for recreation and a brief respite from the war. Such a line of reasoning was quite overlooked by the opponents of war-time football.

While this thinly-veiled struggle between the values and expectations of two polarized social classes was continuing to gain attention, there were more conciliatory attempts being made to persuade the youth of the nation that their footballing skills were an advantageous preparation for war. Sir Robert Baden-Powell, in his enormously influential unoffical training manual for the war, wrote that new recruits must be taught:

. . . from the first that they are like . . . players in a football team: each has to be perfect and efficient, each has to adhere patiently to the rules and to play in his

---

[35] *TP's Weekly*, vol. 24, no. 628, 21 November 1914, p. 561.

[36] *The Times*, 23 November 1914, p. 6.

[37] Ibid., 30 November 1914, p. 5.

[38] John Osborne, *The Voluntary Recruiting Movement in Britain 1914-1916* (Palo Alto: Stanford University Press, 1979), Appendix I.

place and play the game—not for his own advancement or glorification, but simply and solely that at all costs his side may win.[39]

Admiral Lord Charles Beresford, too, chose to remain aloof from what had become a dispute of distinctly acidic rhetoric, and in his appeal adopted reason in preference to rancour:

> I cast no stones. The men who play football, cricket and other games are our finest specimens of British manhood. I put it to them to consider—they are fit, strong, healthy and as sportsmen they are cheery; health makes vigour, cheeriness makes pluck— I put it to them that we must now all be prepared to stand by our country and to suffer for our country.[40]

While this situation remained unresolved, the troops in France prepared to spend their first Christmas in the trenches with little sign of the hostilities easing in deference to the occasion. However, on Christmas Eve along several stretches of the Flanders front, curious festive scenes began to take place. German soldiers were observed setting up a Christmas tree complete with lights on their parapet, and were soon heard singing and joking in their trenches.[41] Even more remarkable was the scene on Christmas morning when German soldiers clambered out into no-man's-land unarmed and encouraged the British soldiers to join them in a jubilant, spontaneous and totally unoffical truce. As the soldiers from both armies fraternized, exchanging food, souvenirs, cap badges and buttons, some of the most incredible sporting scenes in the war took place—in at least two places along the front, footballs were produced and impromptu matches started up between the German and British soldiers. A soldier in the Bedfordshire Regiment initiated one game in which teams of about fifty a side played until the ball snagged and punctured on the barbed wired that had been designated as one of the goal lines.[42] In the sector of the London Rifle Brigade another game was observed in the vicinity of Hill 60, where one member of the British forces is reputed to have found among the German ranks his former hairdresser, who played on the same local soccer team in Liverpool before the war.[43] All was not exactly quiet on the Western Front that day, however, and a proposed soccer game between the 2nd Argyll and Sutherland Highlanders and their German opponents was cancelled due to shells falling in their sector.[44]

---

[39] Sir R. Baden-Powell, *Quick Training for War: A Few Practical Suggestions Illustrated by Diagrams*, (London: Herbert Jenkins Ltd., 1914), p. 102. In September 1914 alone, this book sold over 50,000 copies in three impressions.

[40] *The Great War*, vol. 2 (1915), p. 117.

[41] John Terraine, "Christmas 1914 and After,," *History Today*, vol. 29 (Dec. 1979), p. 784.

[42] Ibid, p. 785 and D. Winter "Time Off from Conflict: Christmas 1914," *Royal United Services Institute Journal*, vol. 115, no. 660, (1970), p. 43.

[43] Terraine, p. 785.

[44] Ibid.

Such scenes were not to re-occur during the remaining years of the war and were certainly frowned upon by the military authorities on both sides of no-man's-land. Stern memos forbidding such incident were issued and severe punishments threatened for any offenders.[45] In the light of the prominence of football in the national eye at this stage of the war, it is interesting to note that not only did the press fail to make any political capital out of these incidents, but that the national press surveyed in this study failed to mention the Christmas frivolity at all. It would appear that there was a total news blackout on the affair, perhaps to protect the senior staff of the Army from a searching enquiry, or possibly to protect the treasured image of "Tommy Atkins" as the stalwart enemy of the Teuton foe. Certainly, the coverage of the "inter-enemy" football games would have been something of a knell of doom for those who had been so vociferous in their condemnation of professional soccer, and those who advocated football as an essential ingredient in the training of the Briton to overcome the Germans on the battlefield.

Professional football finally fell into line on 24 April, 1915. The "Khaki Cup Final" was played at the Old Trafford ground in Manchester between Chelsea and Sheffield United, the latter club winning by the only goal of the game. As he presented the cup and medals to the teams, Lord Derby effectively closed the debate on wartime professional soccer with the words "You have played with one another and against one another for the Cup; play with one another for England now."[46] Thus ended eight months consternation for the patriotic British reading public.[47] As Mason suggests, it must have been with some considerable relief that the news was broadcast later that year that the men of the First Battalion of the 18th London Regiment had gone into action at Loos, led by men kicking a football.[48] At last Britain's national game could claim total concord with the war effort, without the skeleton of active professional soccer at home in the cupboard. This was a far more desirable image—the British sportsman-soldier leading the fight against the Hun—and it undoubtedly quietened the former critics. It also set the tone for the future British war-reporting, which embraced the national sporting stereotype with renewed vigor. Nevertheless, the furor over the continuation of the game during the early months of the was had highlighted the Victorian legacy of intense social differentiation within the nation, particularly in regard to attitudes towards and valuation of team games and their contribution to the formation of national character. In particular, it reveals the extent to which the most vocal of the critics—especially those who raised their objections

---

[45] Winter, p. 43.

[46] Quoted in several sources, including W. J. Baker, *Sports in the Western World* (Totowa, N.J.: Rowman and Littlefield, 1982), p. 207.

[47] Although *The War Illustrated* published Sir Owen Seaman's poem "To a False Patriot" as late as 25 December 1915, which opened with the following lines:
He came obedient to the call/He might have shirked like half his mates/Who, while their comrades fight and fall/Still go to swell the football gates.

[48] Mason, p. 255. The incident was commemorated with an artist's impression of the event in *The War Illustrated*, 30 October 1915, p. 264.

within the columns of *The Times*—distorted the situation to give credence
to their assault on what was essentially an attack on their comprehension
of the working class ethos of sport. Their tirades ignored the fact that the
vast majority of working class soccer was amateur, and that many of the more
than 300,000 players registered with amateur teams had already enlisted in
the forces.[49] They paid scant attention to claims by the Football Association
that they were employing only five thousand professionals, of whom two
thousand were already with the forces, and only a further six hundred were
unmarried, amd thereby eligible for enlistment.[50] In their blind indignation,
they also ignored a plea from the men in the trenches—whom they were
ostensibly supporting by their protests—for football to be continued, as it
provided a welcome respite from the drudgery of war.[51] Although the Football
Association's claim that their organization had recruited 500,000 men by the
end of 1914 remains unsubstantiated, there is little doubt that their
administrative machinery was of invaluable assistance to the War Office in
the early months of the war.[52] Once again, this received little acknowledgement
from the self-appointed patriotic protesters who saw the continuation of the
game as the ultimate national evil. Quite evidently, those who had raised
their voices in protest made it extremely clear that, in time of war, football
was to be elevated to the distinctly amateur status of "the greater game,"
or simply not played at all.

---

[49] Walvin, p. 86.

[50] Mason, p. 253.

[51] Sapper, October 1914, p. 54.

[52] Walvin, p. 89.

18

Changing Thrusts in Daily Newspaper Sports Reporting*

Douglas A. Anderson

David Shaw, media critic for the *Los Angeles Times*, wrote a comprehensive article in the middle 1970s about the changing daily newspaper sports page. Shaw noted that many newspapers were getting away from the "meat and potatoes" approach (an emphasis on scores and statistics) and were moving toward more sociologically probing reporting. Shaw said that many sports page readers were "sophisticated and literate;" these readers wanted "to know more than *what* happened on the field." They wanted "to know *how* it happened and *why* (or why not), as well as what may have happened before (or after) the event, in the locker room, the courtroom, the boardroom and the bedroom."[1]

Shaw credited the quality writing of *Sports Illustrated* and the increasingly comprehensive coverage of sports by the electronic media as having a significant effect on the evolution of daily newspaper reporting.[2]

Michael Novak, author of *The Joy of Sports: End Zones, Bases, Baskets, Balls, and the Consecration of American Spirits*, however, noted what he regarded as the negative impact of television on sports reporting. He wrote in the *Columbia Journalism Review*:

> The most damaging effect of television has been its enervation of newspaper writers and their editors. On occasion, one cannot see the televised game. Then it is almost impossible to find out in the papers the drama of the game itself. The writers take for granted that their readers have seen the game; they write about everything else. They have lost faith in the power of the written word.[3]

---

*Portions of this paper are adapted from material presented more completely in the author's book, *Contemporary Sports* (Chicago: Nelson-Hall, 1985). Reprinted with permission of Nelson-Hall.

[1] David Shaw, "Sports Page: Look, Ma, No Decimal Point," *Los Angeles Times*, Feb. 7, 1975, p.1.

[2] Ibid, p. 3.

[3] Michael Novak, "THE GAME'S THE THING: a defense of sports as ritual, *Columbia Journalism Review* (May/June 1976) : 35.

While many critics contend that contemporary sports pages should delve more deeply into the away-from-the-field aspects of sport, Novak would temper this philosophy. He wrote:

> It is important to our kind of civilization to keep sports as insulated as we can from business, entertainment, politics, and even gossip. Naturally, sports involve all these elements. But none of them should be permitted to obscure the struggle of body and spirit that is their center. The athletic contest has too much meaning for the human spirit to be treated with contempt. Our civilization needs sports, and it needs as well the skillful exercise of the sportswriter's craft. The narrative forms that recount athletic struggle supply millions with a sense of form.[4]

Shaw pointed out that "even the most *avant garde* sportswriters admit that in their zeal to eschew the old scores-and-statistics approach, they often have overreacted and provided a surfeit of offbeat, interpretive, sociological stories at the sacrifice of solid news and analysis of daily happenings in the sports world."[5]

Daily newspaper sports reporters and editors seem to be groping to find their right place in journalism, to find a writing and coverage formula that is most effective. There is nothing new in this. Stanley Woodward, longtime sports editor of the old New York *Herald Tribune*, wrote in a book published in 1949:

> We have made great strides [in the coverage of sports] since the First World War. Jargon has been partially eliminated. The better sportswriters are now writing literately enough so that an aficionado of book reviews or the theater will not be too rudely shocked if inept thumbing lands him in the sports section.[6]

Woodward said sportswriting by mid-twentieth century had evolved into the "On-the-Button" school—a style that left "the hooray-hooray business to the radio announcers and yet refuses to make a career of sneering."[7] Woodward continued:

> The giants of our crafts, such as [Grantland] Rice, [W.O.] McGeehan and [Westbrook] Pegler, were the founders of this school. In its establishment something was taken from each of them. Rice contributed rhythm and euphony; Pegler a grumpy and grudging curiosity for fact, and McGeehan a certain twist, in the likeness of Anatole France, which could make an ordinary sentence interesting.[8]

Woodward said Rice, McGeehan, and Pegler "and others of their caliber were the pioneers of modern sportswriting."[9]

---

[4] Ibid., p. 38.

[5] "*Sports Page*," p. 1.

[6] Stanley Woodward, *Sports Page* (New York: Simon and Schuster, 1949), p. 45.

[7] Ibid., p. 60.

[8] Ibid., p. 61.

[9] Ibid.

The 1920s, a decade often described as the "Golden Era of Sport," saw some of the most flowery, romantic prose ever. Woodward wrote that reporters of this period "wallowed in jargon, florid phraseology and mixed figures. Even the best of them fell into line. It was the day of Jack Dempsey, Babe Ruth, Earl Sande, Red Grange, the Four Horsemen and such."[10]

Rice, one of America's sportswriting greats, possibly is best remembered for his lead paragraph that described the 1924 Notre Dame-Army football game:

> Outlined against a blue-gray October sky, the Four Horsemen rode again. In dramatic lore they are known as Famine, Pestilence, Destruction and Death. These are only aliases. Their real names are Stuhldreher, Miller, Crowley and Layden. They formed the crest of the South Bend cyclone before which another fighting Army football team was swept over the precipice at the Polo Grounds yesterday afternoon as 55,000 spectators peered down on the bewildering panorama spread on the green plain below.[11]

Rice also is remembered for the verse he used so often in his writing, but he once said he could not explain how he came to use so much of it: "How or why I ever fell into the habit of breaking up my columns with verse I don't know, but rhythm and rhyme seemed to come naturally, perhaps as a reflection of the meter I had enjoyed scanning in Latin poets."[12]

Not all of Rice's writing contained verse, however. His lead paragraph on the Jack Dempsey-Luis Firpo fight of 1923 was to the point, much in the manner of the inverted-pyramid style (where the most important information is placed in the first paragraph and other facts follow in order of descending importance in subsequent paragraphs) that has been and is so popular in journalism today:

> In four minutes of the most sensational fighting ever seen in any ring back through all the ages of the ancient game, Jack Dempsey, the champion, knocked out Luis Angel Firpo, the challenger, just after the second round got under way last night at the Polo Grounds.[13]

Certainly, there are examples of the straightforward inverted-pyramid formula on the sports pages of the "Golden Age," but much of the writing was overblown and flowery. A recent study, for example, examined baseball coverage of the New York Yankees of 1927 and of 1977. Alan J. Matecko hypothesized that the 1927 game stories would stress actions of players during the contests more than the 1977 stories would, but the 1977 stories would

---

[10] Ibid., p. 49.

[11] Grantland Rice, *The Tumult and the Shouting* (New York: A.S. Barnes & Co., 1954), p. 177.

[12] Ibid., p. 9. Rice majored in Greek and Latin at Vanderbilt University; he was graduated Phi Beta Kappa in 1901. Ibid., p. 7. Just before his death in 1954, he estimated that he had written more than 22,000 columns, 7,000 sets of verse, and more than 1,000 magazine articles during his half-century newspaper career. Ibid., p. xv.

[13] Ibid., p. 121.

emphasize non-action elements (such as business, medical, psychological, and so forth) more than the 1927 stories. For instance, Matecko cited a 1927 story published in the *New York Times*. It included this excerpt: "[The Philadelphia Athletics] were drawn, quartered, cooked in boiling oil, massacred and otherwise slaughtered by the champions [the Yankees] before 25,000 chagrined fans." The story was packed with cliches and flowery language. Reference was made to the Yankees romping "through to a giddy victory." The Yankee hitters were active. According to the story: "Crash, zam, and zowie went the New York bats." The story focused extensively on game action and used heroic prose to describe it. Matecko found that stories published in the *Times* in 1977 also focused on game action, but description was not as detailed or as flowery; these stories were supported more fully with information from interviews and documentary sources.[14]

Walter (Red) Smith, who many consider to be the best sportswriter ever, recalled in an interview in the early 1970s with Jerome Holtzman:

> I won't deny that the heavy majority of sportswriters, myself included, have been and still are guilty of puffing up the people they write about. . . . I've tried not to exaggerate the glory of athletes. I'd rather, if I could, preserve a sense of proportion, to write about them as excellent ball players, first-rate players. But I'm sure I have contributed to false values—as Stanley Woodward [sports editor of the New York *Herald Tribune* who hired Smith in 1945 from the *Philadelphia Record*] said, "Godding up those ball players."[15]

Smith might indeed have done his share of "Godding up those ball players," but Holtzman, like others, labeled Smith "most likely, the best sports columnist-reporter in the history of American journalism."[16]

By the early 1950s, the use of verse in sports stories had run its course. Still, many sports reporters were piling statistics on top of cliches and adjectives. Smith, however, in graceful, literary style, was conjuring up vivid word pictures. The first paragraph from one of his columns about the 1952 Olympics illustrates this:

> A full week of clean, refined amusement was concluded in Olympic Stadium today with a skinny little chemical engineer from the vestpocket duchy of Luxembourg weeping like a nervous bride on the breastbone of Bob McMillen, a comely tract of meat from Los Angeles. Joseph Barthel, Luxembourg's first Olympic champion since the foot-racers crawled out of their caves and learned to stand upright, had won the classic 1,500 meters, the "metric mile of the eons." Witnesses couldn't believe it. Barthel couldn't bear it. He bawled.[17]

---

[14] Alan J. Matecko, "Newspaper Coverage of the National Pastime: The New York Yankees of 1927 and 1977," Unpublished paper, University of Nebraska at Omaha, 1984.

[15] Jerome Holtzman, ed., *No Cheering in the Press Box* (New York: Holt, Rinehart and Winston, 1973), p. 259.

[16] Ibid., p. 243.

[17] Red Smith, *Views of Sport* (New York: Alfred A. Knopf, 1954), p. 148.

A cursory examination of newspaper sports stories from the 1920s through the post-World War II period certainly shows that writing styles constantly are evolving. No clear lines of demarcation exist, but the flowery, gushy prose of the 1920s and 1930s started to give way to a more spartan, streamlined style in the post-war years. Woodward wrote that the war made sportswriters temper their "regard for the nobility and intrepidity of individuals who were operating only as athletes."[18] Today, writing approaches (with *Sports Illustrated* taking the lead) are more balanced. In general, contemporary sportswriting is more literary than it was in the 1950s and 1960s—there certainly is less emphasis on play-by-play reporting and on nuts and bolts statistics. But the prose is not as flowery as during the early decades of the century—when writing was more romantic than realistic. At many newspapers today, reporters strive for a blend: a writing approach that goes beyond bare-boned statistics but, at the same time, steers clear of overblown prose and overuse of staccato statistics.

Wick Temple, Associated Press general sports editor, told the AP Sports Editors on the eve of the 1980s: "Sportswriters were cheerleaders for so long that coaches and players have come to expect newspapers to be a source of scrapbook material for them. . . . It is going to take another decade for sports reporters to gain acceptance as journalists and put an end to the conception that they are publicity men and women."[19]

Some of the nation's coaches think sports reporters and editors are moving too quickly in their efforts to report off-the-field developments aggressively. At a meeting of the AP Sports Editors in 1980, three coaches commented that "distrust and negative bickering" hampered dealings between coaches and writers. *Editor & Publisher* quoted Penn State coach Joe Paterno:

> I've gotten uptight over whether anything I say will be twisted to embarrass me. There's an anti-hero attitude today. Sports reporters are always trying to find chinks in the coach's armor politically, financially, any way they think they can make a story. I recall telling a reporter once that he ought to write more about the positive things that happen, and all he did was look at me and say, "But that's not the way it's done any more."[20]

The emphasis on probing reporting indeed is more apparent on the sports pages of many of the country's daily newspapers. But there are other trends— trends that are built around what David L. Smith of the *Dallas Morning News* said is the mission of today's sports editors: "to make sports sections easier and faster to read and provide more information for the reader."[21]

---

[18] "*Sports Page,*" p. 152.

[19] Celeste Huenergard, "No more cheerleading on the sports pages," *Editor & Publisher,* June 16, 1979, p. 11. See also John Consoli, "Have sportswriters ended the era of heroes?" *Editor & Publisher,* June 5, 1982, p. 44.

[20] I. William Hill, "Negative sports reporting irks top team coaches," *Editor & Publisher,* June 14, 1980, p. 17.

[21] David L. Smith, "A half dozen steps to the sports section of tomorrow," *ASNE Bulletin* (April 1983): 8.

Smith, an assistant managing editor and executive sports editor of his newspaper, said the following must be provided to accomplish the mission: (1) larger doses of opinion and analysis (Smith thinks knowledgeable sportswriters should cover a "game in the same manner [a] theater critic reviews a play or movie"); (2) a blend of shorter and longer stories, with an emphasis on the former (Smith looks for a combination of in-depth stories and *USA Today*-type shorter stories); (3) more graphics and charts, with a corresponding movement from the all-agate page (Smith finds it confusing for the reader to have to comprehend the game story on one page and then jump to the agate page for the box score); (4) more packaging of short tidbits (Smith says these articles are "light and breezy yet full of information") and (5) more extensive pre-event coverage.[22]

Clearly, progressive sports editors constantly are reevaluating the quality of their product. Possibly at no other time has there been such a concerted effort to upgrade their pages. Of course, not everyone agrees on which steps are most needed.

The purposes of my study are to explore trends in daily newspaper sports page coverage and to determine what the nation's daily newspaper sports editors think needs to be done to improve their product. The focus will be on the open-ended responses from a mail questionnaire survey of the nation's daily newspaper sports editors.

The quantitative aspects of the study, which were published in *Journalism Quarterly*, showed, among other things: Sports editing remains male dominated (less than 2 percent of the survey respondents were female); 63 percent of the sports editors had more than five years of experience in sports journalism and at least one year of non-sports newspaper work; 33 percent said their staffs followed written codes of ethics; 63 percent said their papers selected and published high school ratings; 78 percent said their papers selected and published all-state or all-area teams; 90 percent agreed (52 percent strongly) that sportswriting is better in their papers than three years ago; 69 percent agreed that it is better in general; and 71 percent agreed (36 percent strongly) that their newspapers had devoted more space to art (photos, charts, graphs) during the past three years.[23]

Method

A mail questionnaire was sent to 175 sports editors or executive sports editors of American daily newspapers (approximately 10 percent of the population). The survey, conducted in 1982, drew 106 responses (61 percent). Names of the editors were randomly selected from the *Editor & Publisher Year Book*.

---

[22] Ibid., pp.8-9.
[23] Douglas A. Anderson, "Sports Coverage in Daily Newspapers," *Journalism Quarterly* 60 (1983): 497-500.

Findings

A synthesis of responses that focused on trends in sports coverage and/or areas in which coverage can be improved resulted in the following list: (1) There is a continued movement from cheerleading and cliches; (2) More emphasis is being placed on soft writing styles—even morning newspapers are moving from a strong dependence on summary leads and play-by-play reporting; (3) There is more human-interest, people-oriented coverage; (4) There is a need for more thoughtful analysis; (5) More newspapers are using precision (social science) techniques to gather information for stories; (6) There is a push toward attractive layout and the use of more graphics and photos; (7) Local coverage is receiving more attention, particularly at smaller-circulation dailies; (8) There is a continued awareness of women's and minor sports—though it is clear that men's competitive sports still get and will continue to get the most attention and space; (9) There is a need to hire sportswriters who are well versed in minor sports or who are at least willing to develop expertise in them; and (10) Sports editors need to be more flexible in their coverage philosophies.

There is a continued movement from cheerleading and cliches. Don Duncan recently assembled a glossary of the most common sports cliches. He wrote in *APME News:* "There is a new breed of boys in the press box—college-educated, anti-hero, weaned on 'just the facts, ma'am.' " Duncan noted, however, that cliches continue to be found. He divided his glossary into sections: cliches for the all-purpose athlete (for example: "Star—The lowest athlete, amateur or professional, entitled to say 'ya know' and 'what I mean' in an interview"); cliches for all-purpose coaches and managers (for example: "We play them one game at a time—You'll never find us in two stadiums on the same day"); and cliches for all-purpose sports (for example: "Character—We got creamed, but we didn't walk off the field because we need the gate receipts for our 'program' "). Duncan vividly made his point: He listed dozens of cliches and made them appear all the more ridiculous by blending some of them together into narration.[24]

Tim Flowers, sports editor of the *Arkansas City* (Kan.) *Traveler*, responded to the survey: "Too many sportswriters write in jargon. That's fine if you are writing for the *Sporting News*, but not all readers of newspapers understand all the 'inside lingo.' A mother is more interested in what the coach thought of how her son played than in how many times he came down with a cross block. Write for the general public and use your column to talk shop if you feel you must."

Indeed, sportswriters likely are more conscious than ever before about choking readers on cliches. True, we still read about "frosh phenoms" and "sophomore sensations"; occasionally we find a reference to a bone-crunching

---

[24] Don Duncan, "Sports cliches—the 'real' story from a report that came to play," *APME News* (May 1978): 1, 4, 5.

block that opened a hole the entire student body could have run through; sometimes we read about ball carriers streaking into the promised land; and, if we look hard enough, we probably can find references to diminutive, sparkplug point guards. But cliches are not found with the frequency they once were.

Some sports editors have noticed a tendency to overreact to the war on cliches and cheerleading, however. Don McDermott, sports editor of the *Daily News* in Washington, N.C., said, "Reporters do less cheerleading than they did years ago, but now they have a tendency to be ultra-critical, simply for the sake of being critical."

It is important for sportswriters to remember, though, that cheerleading and cliches do not necessarily go hand-in-hand. Often they do, but writers can cheerlead without overusing cliches and write critical stories while using cliches. The best sportswriters find ways to be descriptive—without using cliches and without cheerleading.

More emphasis is being placed on soft writing styles—even morning newspapers are moving from a strong dependence on summary leads and play-by-play reporting. Indeed, during recent years there has been an increase in soft news approaches to what traditionally have been treated as hard news stories. For example, when Rick Cleveland, a sportswriter for the *Clarion-Ledger* in Jackson, Miss., investigated rumors that the University of Mississippi was looking to change head coaches, he saw that the story merited more than a terse summary lead.

So Cleveland put together a three-part series that focused on Bob Tyler, a former Mississippi State and North Texas State football coach who, while temporarily out of work, was living and writing in Oxford, Miss. Tyler was being mentioned as a possible successor to Steve Sloan, who was entering the final year of his contract at Ole Miss. Cleveland's narrative lead pulled readers into the lengthy first installment of his series:

> It was January 1981. North Texas State University desperately needed a proven football coach. Bob Tyler, who many felt proved himself at Mississippi State, desperately wanted a football job.
>
> After a hasty courtship, the two were wed. Less than a year and a half later, they were divorced. It was a short, stormy marriage, devoid of honeymoon, much less love. As in so many marriages, finances were a huge problem. Personality conflicts and differences in philosophy also played roles, perhaps even bigger roles than the dollars.
>
> In the end, both parties wanted out. It was a divorce by mutual consent. Simply put, Bob Tyler and North Texas State were not meant for each other.[25]

In another story, Mike Littwin, sportswriter for the *Los Angeles Times*, took readers back in time to an era when college basketball's stars scored at a furious pace. He could have led with a summary lead that spat out statistics,

---

[25] Rick Cleveland, "A most unhappy marriage," *The Clarion-Ledger,* 1 August 1982, p. D-1.

but he chose a careful blend of nostalgia, analysis, and statistics. Littwin's lead was compelling:

> He called his girl Slick, and she called him Johnny Cool, and they were the Bonnie and Clyde of their day. In another time, when their kind rode into town, you hid the women and children and put a double guard on the bank. Johnny Cool was the fastest, the smoothest, the coolest.
> But, alas, those days are gone, as sure as Butch and Sundance are gone.
> Who were those guys?
> Johnny Cool was Johnny Neumann. Pistol Pete was Pete Maravich. The Bird was William Averitt. Bo was Dwight Lamar. Free was Freeman Williams. On and on went the list. Until now.
> College basketball's great guns are an endangered species, maybe extinct. Yet another victim of progress.[26]

Like Littwin, Dennis Brown, a sportswriter for the *Phoenix Gazette*, could have used a straightforward lead on a story about a volleyball player at Arizona State University. But, like Littwin, he chose not to. Brown's lead quickly lured readers into the story. It began:

> Pure power: It fascinates us.
> Finesse is fine, but the power people of sports make us shudder.
> Lisa Stuck is pure power.
> Stuck, a junior at Arizona State, hits a volleyball as hard as or harder than any woman in college today. She doesn't just spike the ball, she crushes it.[27]

This style of vivid writing has existed for a long time on the country's daily newspaper sports pages. But, overall, today's general approach is more literary than in recent decades. Also, this readable, flowing style is not limited to the country's largest dailies.

There is more human-interest, people-oriented coverage. Bill R. Cox, sports editor of the *Jackson* (Tenn.) *Sun*, urged reporters to "write about people, their goals, disappointments, accomplishments, etc., rather than always on events and numbers. People like to read about people, whether it's on the obituary page, living section or sports."

An emerging sports feature form is the first-person account. *Sports Illustrated*, for example, occasionally publishes first-person articles from athletes in "as told to" format. Sometimes, though, athlete and writer are one. Cassandra Lander, a star woman's basketball player at Arizona State University, combined her skills to write a story that was published in the *Phoenix Gazette*. It began:

> Tomorrow is the first day of class at Arizona State. More than 39,000 students are going to be frustrated in finding parking places, locating classrooms, and standing in long lines at the bookstore.

---

26 Mike Littwin, "Shot down: College basketball goes great guns at killing scorers," *Arizona Republic* (from *Los Angeles Times* Syndicate), 5 December 1982, p. F-5.

27 Dennis Brown, "Pure power: Lisa Stuck puts dents in a volleyball," *Phoenix* (Ariz.) *Gazette*, 21 October 1982, p. F-1.

> I, too, will face those frustrations, but I am preoccupied with one thing today:
> The start of pre-season basketball training.
> Frankly, I'm a little frightened. Coach [Juliene Simpson] made clear to me last
> May what she expected: I was to practice every day all summer and hit the weight
> room religiously.

Lander's first-person story was pulled from her diary. The story began with her apprehension about the start of school and pre-season practice and concluded when the ball was thrown up for the first game of the season. Lander was candid as she told her story. She described the pain—and boredom—she sometimes felt during practice sessions. She described the chilly, spartan locker rooms she sometimes found herself in; and she confessed she longed for the simpler days of high school:

> Why can't it be like high school? I never worried about preparing for the season.
> When basketball came, there was excitement. We practiced, we played—it was over.
> In college, it's a year-round thing. Coaches expect it and I guess you have to
> do it if you want to be the best. For some reason, I never have adjusted to playing
> basketball all 12 months.[28]

Lander's style of writing is what Louis Stout, sports editor of the *News-Dispatch* in Michigan City, Indiana, must have had in mind when he wrote: "More human interest stories offering a broader spectrum of sports are needed. They should be written so the non-sports page reader can feel comfortable reading sports pages. Sports pages need to be humanized."

Leonard Parent, sports editor of the *St. Albans Messenger* in Vermont, however, cautioned that "impartial, straightforward reporting is needed." He said many sportswriters "treat their subjects like pieces of meat, instead of human beings."

Mike Sturm, sports editor of the *Bay City Times* in Michigan, said sportswriters should "strive for personality stories—family, ethnic, geographical backgrounds—personal stuff that TV-radio can't afford in time budgets."

There is a need for more thoughtful analysis. Sports pages are carrying more articles labeled "analysis" or "opinion" than ever before. Readers are interested in what the local sports editor or sportswriter has to say.

"Readers of sports pages are an opinionated lot; for this reason, I believe editorials, columns, and analyses are more important than on any other page but the opinion section," said John Akers, sports editor of the *Ames* (Iowa) *Daily Tribune.*

Jim Porter, sports editor of the *Macomb Daily* in Michigan also called for "more analysis on personalities and controversies in sports."

Analysis pieces are particularly effective in pre-contest coverage. Whether they agree or not, readers want to know the writer's opinion on such things as the effects of injuries, the effects of trades involving professional teams, the quality of new recruits to a college program, the likelihood that certain

---

[28] Cassandra Lander, "Dear Diary . . . One woman's record of what makes a college athlete tick," *Phoenix* (Ariz.) *Gazette,* 9 December 1982, p. E-1.

athletes will make the final cuts for their professional teams, and on the quality of managment of professional franchises. In all instances, however, it should be clear to the reader that the story contains analysis or opinion.

More newspapers are using precision (social science) techniques to gather information for stories. Which institution has the best college football team in America? For decades, this has been determined by sportswriters and coaches from around the country who vote in The Associated Press or United Press International polls each week. Naturally, biases can enter the voting.

During the late 1970s, the *New York Times* started to explore ways to apply social science methods (quantitative approaches in which numbers, aided by computer analysis, are used to measure and evaluate) to all aspects of reporting. The *Times* decided to enlist the aid of a computer to rate college football teams. There are those, of course, who would argue that sportswriters and college coaches have a better "feel" for the top-twenty ratings than a computer that merely is fed raw data. Nevertheless, the *Times's* ratings have generated much interest.

Not every newspaper in the country has the resources—the manpower and money—to conduct such sweeping precision journalism projects. But reporters at any newspaper can use statistical information as a basis for stories— statistical information that is used to contrast, compare, and analyze. This information, if efficiently gathered, can provide readers with insight that goes beyond team and individual statistics. Indeed, there is a difference between regurgitating mounds of numbers and actually using the numbers as a basis to draw conclusions or encourage discussion.

The sports staff of the *Omaha* (Nebraska) *World-Herald*, in the winter of 1982, decided to look back at twenty years of Nebraska Cornhusker football excellence. The staff decided to publish articles about the nation's top twenty teams in the period between 1962 (when Bob Devaney arrived as head coach at Nebraska) and 1981. This era was labeled A.D.—after Devaney.

"We started with no preconceptions," Sports Editor Mike Kelly wrote. "We didn't try to create a system that was either favorable or unfavorable to Nebraska. Once we decided on our methodology, we let the rankings fall where they may."[29]

Kelly hit on the key essential: the methodology. When tackling projects that require precision statistical techniques, sports staffs must think through their projects before leaping too quickly toward quantification.

The *World-Herald* staffers did not enlist the aid of a computer, but they did carefully create a numerical system in an effort to arrive at an "all era" rating. The formula for determining its two-decade top twenty was carefully spelled out in the *World-Herald*:

—20 points for first place in the composite Top Twenty ratings, based on Final Top Ten AP ratings from 1962 through 1981, 19 points for second, 18 for third, etc.

---

[29] Michael Kelly, "NU Still Rolling in Year 20 A.D.," *Omaha* (Neb.) *World-Herald*, 7 February 1982.

—One point for wins over losses. For example, Nebraska had a record of 186-43-4 over the period. That would be worth 143. (186 minus 43)
—Five points for each AP national title.
—Two points for each Heisman, Outland or Lombardi trophy winner.
—One point for each consensus (UPI, AP, Writers and Coaches Association) All-American.
—One point for each time team is in Final Top Ten.[30]

To accompany the main story, the *World-Herald* published a "20-year Top 20" that included the rating, school, conference, and total points using the newspaper's formula. The top five:

1. Alabama (Southeastern Conference) 261
2. Southern Cal (Pacific 10 Conference) 256 1/2
3. Nebraska (Big 8) 255
4. Oklahoma (Big 8) 232 1/2
5. Texas (Southwest Conference) 227

Howard Brantz's 45-column-inch story accompanied the easy-to-read charts. The story was an excellent blend of statistics, analysis, and direct quotations from athletic directors, coaches, and conference officials.[31]

The *World-Herald's* Top Twenty ratings made a big hit with readers. Undoubtedly, there were those who agreed with the methodology and the findings; there were others who likely did not.

Still, the sports staffers at the Omaha newspaper developed a workable methodology, conducted research, and put together an excellent package that included not only a main story, but mounds of statistics that were presented in charts.

Daily newspapers can compile stories such as those used in the *World-Herald's* Top Twenty project. Information abounds on every sport. But newspaper staffers should be certain that a sound, rational methodological approach is devised before a project is embarked upon. And, if a computer can help the project, a computer expert can be consulted. Care always must be taken, however, to interpret and analyze the statistics—numbers do not always speak for themselves.

There is a push toward attractive layout and the use of more graphics and photos. For the most part, the sports pages of daily newspapers are bolder than ever before. Newspapers, in general, have received a facelift during the last fifteen years, but sports pages usually rank among the most readable sections of the newspaper.

It is no wonder. Note the words of the authors of *Electronic Age News Editing:*

Sports pages are tailor-made for bright, brisk design. Sports editors need not feel inhibited by the stoic overtones of historical political events or world crises. Sports elements literally beg for innovative treatment. In no other section of the paper is

[30] "The Formula," *Omaha* (Neb.) *World-Herald,* 7 February 1982, p. C-11.

[31] Howard Brantz, "Alabama No. 1, NU 3rd in 20-Year Top 20," *Omaha* (Neb.) *World-Herald,* 7 February 1982, p. C-1.

there such a consistent flow of dramatic photos: pole vaulters stretching and straining eighteen feet in the air; distance runners struggling through the final yards of an exhausting race; sinewy basketball players driving the lane through a forest of arms, legs, and torsos; 255-pound linebackers crushing back-pedaling quarterbacks; gymnasts gracefully performing their poetic routines; and sleek hurdlers gliding over barriers. In addition, game stories, league roundups, analyses pieces, feature stories, ratings, predictions, columns, and statistics compete for space on sports pages.[32]

Bob Durkee, sports editor of the *Lake County Telegraph* in Ohio called for "an increased emphasis on color photos and the use of color in general." Indeed, today's sports pages are brighter than ever.

Still, not everyone is caught up in the push toward more attractive, colorful pages. Jerry Soifer, sports editor of the *Corona-Norco Independent* in California, said: "I think the use of graphics is way overdone. I think editors overdo the use of graphics to illustrate stories. The most pressing problems sports editors face is too much news, too little space and not enough staffers. More staff and space should be devoted to news and less to art and graphics."

The key, of course, is that attractive pages and strong news content are not mutually exclusive. A well-planned page can be both attractive and informative.

Local coverage is receiving more attention, particularly at small circulation dailies. Several sports editors of the under 20,000-circulation newspapers articulated views similar to those of Bill Wellborn, sports editor of the *Helena* (Arkansas) *World,* who said sports editors should "concentrate more on high school and recreational sports." He advised them to "depend less on strict game accounts and more on what the players and coaches have to say about specific events."

The sports editor of the *Lufkin* (Texas) *Daily News,* Gary Willmon, said "more emphasis needs to be placed on local sports coverage—too many hometown athletes are overlooked and/or overshadowed by the mass of stories concerning pro athletes."

There is a continued awareness of women's and minor sports—though it is clear that men's competitive sports still get and will continue to get the most attention and space. Larry Edsall, sports editor of the *Citizen-Patriot* in Jackson, Michigan, said "too many sports editors still are interested only in baseball, basketball and football, ignoring other sports and women and youths in sports."

Patrick Rini, sports editor of the *Meadville* (Pennsylvania) *Tribune,* agreed. He wrote: "Women's sports coverage and coverage of non-revenue sports is lacking. We must reduce play-by-play of professional sports, especially in papers where box scores are used. This would open some space for other material. With the amount of attention other media give big-time sports, and with the amount of TV watched, newspapers must respond to coverage wants of non-revenue sports."

---

[32] Harry W. Stonecipher, Edward C. Nicholls, and Douglas A. Anderson, *Electronic Age News Editing* (Chicago: Nelson-Hall, 1981), pp. 180, 183.

The sports editor of the *Daily Hampshire Gazette*, in Northampton, Massachusetts, Milton Cole, said there should be "greater emphasis on local sports and on girls' or women's sports in particular." Martin A. Renzhofer, sports editor of the *Morning News*, Blackfoot, Idaho, also said women's sports should receive more attention. "The major sports receive plenty of space but unless the minor sports are national championship caliber, they are ignored," he wrote.

At this point, it seems that the rhetoric about the need for increased coverage of women's and non-revenue sports exceeds the reality. Certainly, many newspapers have made an effort to cover women's athletics—particularly at the high-school level—and to cover minor sports. Still, in a space crunch, coverage of these sports generally is sacrificed.

Sports editors often are bombarded with complaints by parents and coaches of women athletes and minor sports competitors who seek more coverage. Many sports editors, however, rationalize their dilemma much like Bob Snider of the *Scottsdale* (Arizona) *Progress*: "When deciding how much space to devote to a topic and when to staff an event, editors need to look more closely at how many readers really want to know. Unfortunately, this means even less coverage for minor and women's sports."

Bob Davidson, sports editor of the *Hays* (Kan.) *Daily News*, wrote: "Long, boring stories on sports that draw no fan interest deserve the same amount of space and time in the paper. If people don't attend it, they sure as hell won't read about it."

There is a need to hire sportswriters who are well versed in minor sports or who are at least willing to develop expertise in them. One of the reasons— aside from space limitations—that coverage of minor sports might be lacking at some newspapers is that no one on the staff has a particular interest or expertise in them. Bill Griffin, sports editor of the *Daily Sentinel* in Nacogdoches, Texas, said: "Daily newspapers need to hire persons who are most experienced in the individual sports. I have found that it is extremely hard to write objectively about something which I have never competed in or played."

Blaine Johnson, sports editor of the *Seattle* (Washington) *Post-Intelligencer*, said there is a need for "more thorough reporting by reporters who possess the knowledge of the games they are reviewing and who know how to express complicated issues in concise form."

Sports editors need to be more flexible in their coverage philosophies. Dale Bye, executive sports editor of the *Star* and *Times* in Kansas City, vividly articulated the need for sports pages to grow with the times. He wrote:

> Historically, sports coverage has been defined in terms of baseball, basketball, football and golf (because all sports editors, of course, play golf). The sports boom—tennis, running, soccer, women in sports—caught most papers napping and most sports sections still have not come up with a formulaic method of handling all the information. Most obviously, sports coverage can be improved by a systematic method of giving all

sports adequate coverage—coverge without ignoring any sport. Complicating the whole problem is the overall reader-interest level. You can't ignore major-league baseball on Thursday just to give rock climbing its place in the sports section. On the other hand, you can't ignore rock climbing continually by hiding behind the traditional facade of major-league baseball.

The sports editor of the *Oklahoma City Times*, Bob Colon, also noted the need for coverage flexibility. He said: "Events should be evaluated and more attention given to the areas of the greatest attention. For instance, in our area, newspapers probably give far too much space to college baseball. It's baseball and everybody likes baseball. And it's a big college and everybody likes OU and OSU. So you get college baseball and the papers go overboard. There is some interest in this area, but not nearly as much as the coverage might indicate. The same is true for things like minor league hockey and baseball."

Discussion

Few surprises leap from the sports editors' comments. Without doubt, editors are cognizant of the need to continue to improve their pages. They recognize shortcomings. Editors, however, face two major obstacles: limited space and limited staffs. The burgeoning interest in recreational sports and the explosion of women's and girls' athletics are primary carpenters of these formidable barriers.

When these sports emerged, their participants and spectators clamored for attention. Almost overnight, potential coverage areas nearly doubled for the sports staffs of daily newspapers. However, additional space was not immediately forthcoming at most newspapers. The dilemma was real; it was tantamount to the problem the news side would face should there suddenly be two mayors, two city councils, and two state legislatures to cover instead of just one of each.

Very simply, sports editors often are not given sufficient column inches to adequately cover deserving events and issues. Even when they are given additional space, their staffs sometimes cannot keep pace. Staffs that were able to handle the traditional male football-basketball-baseball beats find themselves swamped as they try to report also on the expanding areas of reader interest.

Sports editors need to be courageous and innovative; in many instances, they need to rethink their coverage philosophies. If space cannot be increased significantly, the slices devoted to various sports should be resized to accommodate the deserving.

Two reactions would be easy, but not satisfactory: Editors could (1) continue to cover only those sports that were reported two decades ago, virtually ignoring new events of interest or (2) initiate across-the-board cuts of space for all events previously covered to give nearly equal treatment to emerging sports that, in most instances, still do not have the fan following enjoyed by some of the established sports.

Kansas City's Bye and Oklahoma City's Colon were on target when they talked of the need to redefine coverage philosophies. Each editor should scrutinize the interests of his readers. There is no magic formula, but an awareness of changing interests is a good beginning. Simply because a minor league baseball team received fifteen-inch pre-game stories twenty years ago (and the owners thus expect it to continue) does not mean it still is warranted. Instead, girls' prep basketball, which was not played twenty years ago in some states, might be deserving of a 15-inch pre-game story today.

In addition to rethinking coverage philosophies and space allotments, sports editors can take greater care to package and tightly edit wire stories to open more space for local coverage. Reporters then should meet the challenge by seeing that every story they write is worthy of the premium space. Sportswriters should take heed of Michael Novak's words: "Our civilization needs sports, and it needs as well the skillful exercise of the sportswriter's craft. The narrative forms that recount athletic struggle supply millions with a sense of form." Indeed, most readers appreciate strong, descriptive writing—devoid of jargon and cliches—that vividly recreates sports events and makes reading the sports pages a joyful experience.

19

The Role of Sports and Physical Education in Günter Grass's *Cat and Mouse*

Nanda Fischer

ALTHOUGH GÜNTER GRASS'S *Cat and Mouse* would certainly not be listed in an anthology of German sports literature, it fits into the context of sports and literature for several reasons. It extensively treats physical activity inside and outside of the schools in Nazi Germany. In fact, one third of the book deals with sports. It shows the hollow attempt to gain a positive personal and social identity through sports and physical activity during the Nazi period and the outcome of that attempt. And it demonstrates, in a highly artistic manner, the figurative and metaphoric use of sports. This makes it a rare and outstanding example of contemporary German literature of the 1950s and 1960s when sports was a rather exotic subject in top level serious literature. This is due, in part, to the association of sports with Nazi Germany and to a tradition of anti-sports spirit of many intellectuals.

In the following, I will reconstruct the story of the life of Joachim Mahlke and provide an analysis of the story. This will be followed by the metaphoric and figurative use of sport in Grass's novella and the essay will be concluded with an evaluation of Grass's statement of sports' closeness to war and violence through a discussion of the historic position and ideology of Günter Grass.

I

Cat and Mouse describes a period from the end of 1939 to the end of 1944, during which a group of high school age youngsters spend the first summers of World War II, before they are drawn into the war, with various kinds of physical activity.

In the opening scene Mahlke, the main character, falls victim to a violent game with his peers. One of them causes a cat to leap at Mahlke's overly large adam's apple, his mouse. This event is highly significant: cat and mouse become correlates of persecuter and persecuted, assailant and victim. In the novella Mahlke is doomed to be the victim because he is different. He represents the could-be-intellectual in a world that is oriented toward the idealization of the physical and its power. The cat, as a beast, becomes a symbol of the barbarian elements of the time. For example, the title picture, designed by Grass himself, shows an overly fed cat with the "Ritterkreuz" around its neck. If one understands this basic configuration of cat and mouse, one can analyze its elements. It is striking that the group's interests are almost entirely of a physical nature. The group members concentrate on gymnastics, team handball, the game of Schlagball (a traditional German game similar to baseball), and above all on swimming and diving, the latter obviously due to the geographic location of Danzig.

At first glance, it appears that intellectual pursuits are not of interest to the boys. They do not even seem to have an ideology. However, they are influenced by an ideology as they are students in an educational institution where the traditional spirit is distorted by the school principal and party officer, Klohse, in order to strengthen the trust in the German weapons and turn the students into brave soldiers and party sympathizers.

Even though Mahlke has absorbed the group's interest in sports, he is an outsider. In the opening scene he already has learned to swim and is a member of the intra-mural Schlagball team. Unlike the hero, Oscar, in *Tin Drum*, Mahlke very early recognizes his singularity and the threat it means to his existence. He foresees the attack of society which, during his high school years, is symbolized by his peer group, and he takes steps to meet it. Although he is gifted in the humanities, the group's interest in sports almost forces Mahlke to become an athlete. Once he realizes his "mouse-victim" role he tries to escape it. His intellectual talents do not earn him the desired position among his peers; therefore, he rather hides them. His sudden striving for excellence in sports is all the more striking since Mahlke had avoided physical activity whenever possible as a boy. He had always presented certificates from his doctor showing him to be sick, thus being freed from physical education classes. This suggests that his efforts directed toward achievement in sports are, in truth, of a compensatory nature.

Mahlke first attempts to bicycle and swim. During the winter he begins to learn how to swim in an indoor pool. His lack of athletic ability prohibits his progress and when spring arrives, Mahlke is still unable to swim. However, when his peers swim daily to a Polish mine sweeper, a tremendous ambition overtakes Mahlke. He then learns to swim within two weeks. He subsequently practices endurance swimming and diving alone and soon becomes the fastest swimmer and best diver of the group.

His ability to swim and dive changes his position within the group as evidenced by two verbal interactions. In the beginning Mahlke has to beg: "Please take me with you. I'll make it, I'm positive."[1] After two summers

---

[1] Günter Grass,*Katz und Maus* (Neuwied: Luchterhand, 1964), p. 10.

in which Mahlke has proven his outstanding achievements as a swimmer and diver, the other boys have to pester him: "Aw, come along. It's no fun without you."[2] Mahlke's position in the group has changed. He has moved up in the group hierarchy from last to first.

Between these two interactions, the Schlagball game that is reported in the opening scene takes place. The reference to time " . . . and one day, after Mahlke had learned to swim,"[3] reveals its true and important meaning. Even though Mahlke seems to belong to the group and even more: to be its leader, he remains an outsider. The other members of the peer group admire his performance, but at the same time find him disgusting.

If one more closely examines Mahlke's athletic performance, one understands why the group refuses to accept and follow him. Mahlke verbally communicates very little; his gestures and mimicry communicate much more. He swims and bikes stiffly and awkwardly. He performs the most difficult routines in gymnastics with unskilled form; thus he unwillingly communicates that he is no athlete by nature. He has not internalized sports. Despite his strong efforts sports never become a part of his identity, even though the level of achievement he gains is in complete compliance with the ideological norms of Nazi Germany. Automatization of motor skills which belongs to top level performance, and which the observer perceives as aesthetic or beautiful, during the NS time officially was not promoted; instead performance was praised when it showed the discipline, the effort, and the courage it was required to do. The peer group evidently received a more subtle perception of the classification of Mahlke's achievements. Such was also the case when Mahlke set a record during the highly controversial masturbation "olympiad" scene on the mine sweeper. Like his performance in sports, this record is not accepted by the peer group. They perceive it instead as a violation of the rules of sports and as an expression of a fanatic striving for achievement which violates the principles of sports as play.[4]

The formal climax of the novella and the turning point of the life story of Mahlke is reached when a Ritterkreuz recipient visits the school and presents a talk. During another such presentation by a Ritterkreuz recipient before, Mahlke already had been highly attentive and deeply excited, shown through trembling knees and sweating. In this case such reactions become much stronger. In the physical education class which follows the talk, the lieutenant and war hero participates and supervises part of it. Of course he is a top level gymnast. In a flawless motion he executes the exercises, completely different from Mahlke, who is one of the two students able to perform the same skills. However, looking at Mahlke is so objectionable that nobody wants to watch him.

---

[2] Ibid., p. 50.

[3] Ibid., p. 7.

[4] Ibid., p. 32. The German text is much clearer here: "Wir trieben sport und achteten die Regel" (p. 38).

Mahlke, who thus proves to be a loser in the gymnastics competition, takes pride in stealing the Ritterkreuz afterwards, and successfully smuggles it out of the locker room, even though everyone is checked very closely. This "heroic" deed of his is recognized by his peers because they regard it as an act of play. However, the adults do not regard it as an act of play and throw him out of the school, even though he returns the Ritterkreuz on his own will.

From then on Mahlke tries to fulfill the norms of the adult world. His ambition turns to one single objective: the Ritterkreuz or, in other words, to becoming a war hero. The course he follows is one rather common in the Nazi time: it leads from "Arbeitsdienst" to voluntarily, joining the army, even though some years prior he had commented that classmates who planned to do so were crazy. Thus Grass equates striving for athletic achievement and striving for military achievement. This becomes obvious when he has one of the Ritterkreuz recipients compare actions in war to actions on the playing field—shooting goals in team handball to shooting down planes: "It was pretty much the same as in the old days when we played handball . . . either I did not shoot a single goal or I'd shoot nine in a row."[5]

Mahlke stays on the path of record setting; now he sets records in war. Still a sergeant and a junior, he is awarded the Ritterkreuz.

Grass demonstrates through the case of Mahlke that in a society that perverts all values, effort for integration in that society degrades the person in his very attempt to become integrated. Mahlke, who was once an outstanding diver, has now become a specialist in killing.

But in spite of his proven heroism, society, represented by the principal, refuses to give him the right kind of recognition by preventing him from giving a talk in the Conradinum, his old high school, because of the theft of the Ritterkreuz. Mahlke thus finally recognizes that his attempts were in vain, his striving for a social identity failed. He reacts by refusing to serve society any further; he deserts.

A verbal interaction concerning physical activity clearly shows that he does not belong any more. Mahlke who originally had planned to swim to the mine sweeper and to hide in its cabin until there would be an opportunity to leave on a Swedish boat, suddenly declares: "I can't swim."[6] He argues that his stomach hurts, but his companion does not believe him, nor does the reader, since it is known that he never got sick, regardless of what he ate. In the context of the novella this statement finds its explanation; after freeing himself from the military element of society he then gives up the athletic element as well. His downfall in that society must be a final. Symbolically, *he who cannot swim, cannot dive.*

In *Cat and Mouse* Grass puts sports (and the church as well) in a fatal connection which lead to war and destruction; a fanatic drive for achievement

---

[5] Ibid., p. 46.
[6] Ibid., p. 120.

is the driving force behind both of them. Mahlke chooses this path originally because he wants to be loved and accepted by his peer group, later because he wants to be accepted by society. Leaving the Nazi society is an act of freedom. In saying: "I don't want anymore,"[7] he succeeds in giving up the role of the cat, which he wrongfully was striving for, and thus he is a moral victor in the end; but in his life situation this decision *means* the end.

Mahlke's intellectual existence enables him to take this step towards freedom, once he realizes he will never be the "cat." His quite extensive readings of Kierkegaard and also of Dostoevsky at the end of the novella suggest that, as in the case of his "pre-swimming" days, he has turned once more towards his intellectual existence. However, within a totalitarian system that controls all elements, objects and persons alike, an individual has to follow the general movement of the system—like his peers thus being enslaved, or step aside and be destroyed. Mahlke realizes very well this fact, thus his fear before he finally dives away.

II

Since Günter Grass began as a sculptor and graphic artist, one would expect the literary images in his work to be rather plastic and at home in the world of objects. Moreover, Grass wants his writings to be free of ideology and believes, if he presents the objects in a way that one can perceive them without interpreting and distorting ideological references, reality comes to existence.[8]

An analysis of the literary presentation of the development of key situations in this novella shows that meaning originates from object-like phenomena, the relations of which develop in a dynamic process infusing the phenomena more and more with metaphoric meaning. Physical activity can be understood as such a phenomenon in which an objective presentation is possible and might lead to an objective presentation of the reality dealt with in the novella— the Nazi period.

The following brief analysis of three decisive scenes may serve as an example of such a presentation. The opening scene of the novella has the effect of a picture that all of a sudden comes to life. In the foreground the boys are resting in the grass between their turns in an intramural Schlagball meet, a seemingly peaceful scene of sports in a sport's environment. Track and field athletes practice nearby and some noises from the team handball match in the stadium are heard whenever a goal is shot. This peace, however, immediately proves deceptive when the background becomes alive: "A trimotored plane crept across the sky, slow and loud"[9]; and due to the wind from the east one becomes aware that "the crematorium is working between

---

[7] Ibid., p. 161.

[8] V. Neuhaus, *Günter Grass* (Stuttgart: Metzher, 1979), p. 17.

[9] Grass, *Katz und Maus*, p. 7.

the United Cemetaries and the School of Engineering.[10] The crematorium and airplane are objects which suggest war and death to the alert reader. The foreground scene then changes to violence, when the cat is made to leap at Mahlke's adam's apple. It's just a game of cat and mouse now. Consequently Mahlke only suffers "minor scratches" for the time being, but this is the starting point of a dynamic process that turns play to deadly seriousness. The relation between the airplane and the team handball game is just a physical one that can be perceived at the same time through noises. Later in the story their relation changes, the attitude in shooting goals and shooting down planes is presented as one and the same. The sport field thus is identified as being a practice ground for the battlefield.

Another important scene that has similar effects is found in the seventh chapter, the climax of the novella. The Ritterkreutz recipient participates in the physical education class. Here again Grass describes the object in a manner that suggests the identity of the spirit of the "Turnstunde" and the spirit of war, as well as the spirit of church and religion.[11]

First Grass again just describes the objects and their relation. From earlier statements we know that the chapel of the Virgin Mary is a former gymnasium which still smells and looks like it. It is located in the midst of sport facilities; in the sacristy the progressive pastor plays table tennis with his altar boys, while they quote details of war technology during the service. The students call the locker room of the gymnasium the sacristy; for the gymnasium has neogothic windows. And while the bright "gymnast light" is shining into the chapel, the students do their gymnastics in the mystic light of the ogival windows. From the structure of the objects an effect is created "while in the mystical light of our gymnasium the simple act of choosing the two basketball teams . . . seemed solemnly moving like an ordination or confirmation ceremony. And when the chosen ones stepped aside into the dim background, it was with the humility of those performing a sacred rite."[12] This mystic unification of religion and sport reaches its climax when the hero of war, the Ritterkreuz recipient, joins in: "If I concentrate, I can still see the squat little lieutenant commander in altar-boy-red gym pants, executing airy, fluid movements on the flying trapeze. I can see his flawlessly pointed feet . .

diving into a golden sunbeam, and I can see his hands . . . reach our for a shaft of agitated golden dust."[13] However, the heroic spirit of all three phenomena proves to be a false one, for the gold towards which the hero is reaching is just dust.

In "Dog Years" Grass once again takes up the combination of sports,

---

[10] Ibid.

[11] Religion has been excluded from the discussion thusfar even though it has important meaning to the hero.

[12] Grass, *Katz und Maus*, p. 64.

[13] Ibid., p. 65.

religion, and war and identifies them as originating from the same root and therefore as interchangeable. All them show a fanatic drive for a false heroism:

> . . . the cardinal emotions weeping, laughter, and the grinding of teeth provide the deep seated foundation on which athletic scarecrows at split pea racing, and newly recruited scarecrows at close combat. How scarecrow outdoes scarecrow by a scarecrow head, how scarecrows keep battering their time at elevating scarecrow crosses, how they overcome barbed wire entanglement, . . . deserves to be recording on charts, and recorded it is. Employees of Brauxel & Co. measure and enter: Scarecrow records and rosary lengths. Three stalls that were blasted on potash mining days until they attained gymnasium length, church height, and the width of broad shouldered antiaircraft dugouts provide over four hundred team spirited scarecrows, halleluja scarecrows, hold out the last gasp scarecrows per shift with room in which to develop their electronically guided energies . . . indoor sport festivals, pontifical offices, and autumn maneuver or the other way around, athletic events for recruits, divine services in the front line, and the blessing of scrap-iron scarecrow weapons fill schedules in order that later on, when, as they say, an emergency arises, every record can be broken, every heretic unmasked, and every hero find his victory.[14]

In a third important scene at the very end of the novella the foreground again is made up from the world of sports: red gym pants. Mahlke is wearing this object of clothing before he dives away, never to be seen again. This simple object has been infused by the events with metaphoric meaning during the course of the novella. So at this moment all the phenomena responsible for Mahlke's failure are present and are represented by this object: the spirit of the high school, for red is one of the school colors; Mahlke's striving for achievement in sports in his high school days, for those are his school gym pants; his striving for religious achievement, for Grass describes the pants as being altar-boy-red; and his striving for achievement in war, for the pants are also referred to as flag-red (by way of another adjective metaphor).

The phenomena of sports, religion, and war become interchangeable, and the languages for each does also. Sports language can be used in a religious context. The altar boy Mahlke is referred to as a left winger. Even events that are not sporty at all, but show the record setting attitude, can be described with sport language, as in the case of the masturbation "olympiad" on the mine sweeper. Indeed the whole of life can be categorized under the aspects of win or lose or, using the sports terminology that dominates in the novella in a metaphoric meaning, of being able to swim or being not able to swim.

Swimming and diving and its compounds become metaphors characterizing Mahlke's position in relation to society. Therefore, from this point of view, it almost seems logical, that the book starts with a reference to swimming: " . . . und einmal als Mahlke schon schwimmen konnte," presents his downfall in swimming terminology: "ich kann nicht schwimmen" and ends with a phrase from the swimming context: "aber du wolltest nicht auftauchen."

---

[14] Günter Grass, *Dog Years* (New York: Fawcett Crest, 1969), p. 554.

III

If one tries to evaluate Grass's ideological position in connection with sports several questions can be raised: Is it the position of the author as a historian, as an intellectual hostile towards sports, or is he a critic of society?

Grass experiences sports in Nazi Germany as a twelve-year-old boy at the beginning of Nazi Germany and as a young soldier of seventeen at its end. It is not difficult to prove the connection between fiction and reality in the case of *Cat and Mouse.* Grass himself is just a little younger than his characters. He also was a student at the well-known Conradinum in Danzig. Many details, beginning with the phonetics of names of teachers to many geographical details up to the visit and talk of Ritterkreuz recipients, are identical in reality and fiction. This can lead to the conclusion of Brode: "Even though it is a highly artistic literary work, one can study this novella as one would study a historical source in respect to condition of life and youthful perception in the 'Dritte Reich.' "[15]

Grass's attitude towards war and sports seem to have been very similar to that of the peer group in his novella: "Braveness which was measured exclusively through military performance became to my generation a term for happiness. . . . It depended on how many thousands of gross tons were sunk, how many planes were shot down, how many tanks were shattered."[16] After the war it was a shock to young Grass to discover what all of this had meant. The seemingly innocent sporting spirit had been part of the deadly machinery. But I think Grass intends more; his criticism of sports does not only focus on its function in a historic system but also on its role in the present society. Grass discusses the close relation between sports and society and criticizes elite sports as well as backyard sports in his essay.[17] He already in 1971 recommends that peace research deal with the "competitive build up of arms" in elite sports which, in Grass's opinion, no longer originates in an individual ambition but rather stems from collective achievement principles. But also in sports-for-all Grass finds the danger of pressure for achievement—be it only to keep yourself fit to achieve more in your job. He therefore demands that sports adapt a principle which is opposite to the achievement motive: "sports without a stopwatch." In his opinion this can be accomplished only if society also changes.

In summary, Grass's critical approach towards sports is based upon its close connection with achievement on the way to heroism, which leads, once it becomes socially significant, to violence and war; but Grass does not harbor a general hostility towards physical activity if it is executed in a non-competetive spirit, and everyone is given a fair chance to participate.

---

[15] H. Brode, *Günter Grass* (Munchen: Beck, 1979), p. 88.

[16] Günter Grass, Rede von der Wut über den vevlorenen Milchpfennig. In: Über das Selbstvevständliche. Reden, Aufsätze, Offene Briefe, Kommentare (Neuwied: Luchterhand, 1968), p. 183.

[17] Günter Grass, "Sport ohne Stoppuhr," *Olympische Jugend* 11 (1971): 8-10.

PART VI

Everybody's a Hero:
Sport in the Cinema

20

Introduction:
Everybody's a Hero:
Sport in the Cinema

Stephen David Mosher

IN THE LONG AND INGLORIOUS HISTORY of sport in the cinema, there have been so many bad movies that even the mediocre ones stand out. Who could ever forget William Bendix's portrayal of the home run king in the *Babe Ruth Story* (1948)? Were your heart strings tugged as William Holden confronted the ultimate career decision—Classical Violin or Professional Prize Fighting—in *Golden Boy* (1939)? Did you really believe the fate of the big game in *Pigskin Parade* (1936) lay in the powerful voice of a fourteen year old, unknown singer named Judy Garland? More recently, have you noticed that any financially successful sport film causes a mad rush by Hollywood to exploit the situation and consequently tarnish the critical acclaim of the original? Sequels to *The Bad News Bears* (1976) [as in *The Bad News Bears in Breaking Training* (1977) and *The Bad News Bears Go To Japan* (1978)] and *Rocky* (1976) [as in *Rocky II* (1979), *Rocky III* (1982), *Rocky etc.*] serve more to offend our intelligence than continue the legend. Spin-offs of *Brian's Song* (1972) have featured athletes in different sports suffering catastrophic injuries or tragically early deaths. *Maurie (1973), Babe* (1974), *The Other Side of the Mountain* (1974), *Erick* (1975), and *Something for Joey* (1977) are only a few of the long list of sentimental tear-jerkers.

In spite of the huge number of truly bad movies, there have been enough serious sport films to warrant close critical examination. These films clearly show that, while the drama of sport centers on the contest, the sport film's narrative explores the *idea* of sport, its mythology. These films help explain why we care so much about sport and what we believe it to be. These narratives, therefore, impart knowledge, not values. The archetypes that emerge from them are not tied to any particular history or society. The following essays demonstrate that the contemporary sport film can not only achieve individual financial and critical success, but also contribute in a meaningful way to the understanding of sport itself and to the development of a group of films nearing the classification of a *genre.*

In "The Uncertain Glories of Competition in *Chariots of Fire* and *Personal Best,*" Walter Harrison explores the paradox that makes competition in sport such a vital area of concern. This paradox—that competition between individuals is supposed to bring out the best in human character and performance, yet these individuals are expected to battle not only for their own personal goals, but also for the common good of the team—is analyzed with respect to its treatment in these two highly successful and imaginative films about the Olympic Games. Harrison maintains that each film questions the implied values of competition and its consequential effect on the re-lationships between the protagonists as they struggle to discover their own places in sport and society. He concludes that, after raising important issues concerning competition, both films retreat to conventional conclusions: that, with all its faults, competition does bring out good qualities in human character; that the Olympics, for all their drawbacks, are worth the effort. Clearly, Harrison has demonstrated that analyses of individual sport films and comparative criticism of the issues they raise is a valuable tool to understanding the way in which our society comes to perceive sport.

In a larger sense, the body of sport films constitutes a *genre* that, according to Stephen Mosher in "The 'Close' Western: Contemporary Sport Films," has successfully supplanted the Western as the conveyor of the uniquely American fable that the frontier is the arena in which the hero develops his rugged individualism. As the American Western has become an anachronism, Mosher contends, it has been replaced by both space and sport films that offer new, different, and socially relevant wilderness. The space film is the "far" Western because it emphasizes the vast distance and great potential for mobility that exists in outer space, while the sport film is the "close" Western because it allows for a greater intimacy between the audience and the hero by locating the narrative in a clean, crisp frontier encircled by urban sprawl. The sport hero, armed only with a strict moral code, wanders through this wilderness searching for an identity and a place in a hostile society that will eventually defeat and ostracize him. These sport films and sport heroes, Mosher concludes, help modern viewers to develop their own moral codes as their society becomes increasingly more ambiguous.

The old saying about Hollywood is that, "If one strips away the tinsel and false glitter, one will discover that underneath lies the real tinsel and glitter." Of course, the same can be said for sport films, and I suggest that if one is willing to endure the frequent bombs like *Fast Break* (1979) and *The Slugger's Wife* (1985), the rare jewels like *Chariots of Fire* (1981) and *Bang the Drum Slowly* (1973) which make powerful and important statements about the sporting condition are well worth the wait.

21

The Uncertain Glories
of Competition in
Chariots of Fire and
Personal Best

Walter Harrison

EARLY IN *Chariots of Fire*, the 1981 film directed by Hugh Hudson, we find a scene that functions as a paradigm for the problems of the Olympic Games. Harold Abrahams, an English Jew just arrived at Gonville and Caius College at Cambridge, challenges for the College Dash, a feat that no one has accomplished in seven hundred years. The goal of the dash is to run around the parameter of the college courtyard in the time it takes the courtyard clock to strike twelve noon.

Abrahams, a determined runner who has never lost a race, appears in the courtyard at the appointed time, where he is surrounded by an excited group of college men, who are amused by Abrahams's ambitions but who seem to be genuinely behind his effort to make history at Caius. Just before the race is to begin, he is joined by Lord Andrew Lindsay, a fellow Caius student, who reports that he has heard about Abrahams's attempt and has decided to try it himself, just "to push you along a bit." He discards his flowing scarf and champagne bottle, and declares with a final bit of English public school bravado: "We challenge in the name of Repson, Eton, and Caius."

The suspense of that scene is built up splendidly; the race is exciting, beautifully photographed (a quality which is enhanced in Dolby Sound so that the racers actually sound like they are running around the theater). We exult with Abrahams when he finishes just prior to the final chime, thus becoming the first man ever to accomplish the feat, and we are happy for Lindsay, who has just missed but who has run a fine race.

But the entire event is marred by the comments of two Cambridge dons, masters of Caius and Trinity Colleges, who are watching the race from the

Caius master's rooms overlooking the courtyard. When asked by his friend
before the race about Abrahams, the Caius master responds that he is Jewish,
the son of a London financier who is "academically sound, determined, and
arrogant." ("As they invariably are," responds the Trinity don). When the race
is over, the Trinity don remarks, "Perhaps they really are God's chosen people."

That discordant note of anti-semitism contaminates the entire event,
undermines the joy of the scene, and serves as an example of the problems
of the 1924 Paris Olympics and of the Los Angeles Olympics sixty years later.
The challenges of sport, then as well as now, can not be separated from
the forces of the world surrounding sport—politics, patriotism, and prejudice.

Chariots of Fire and *Personal Best*, a film by Robert Towne released about
six months later, both explore the dilemma of the Olympic Games by
concentrating on the competition between two athletes from the same country
(Great Britain in *Chariots*, the United States in *Best*). The tension between
these characters ("rivals under the same flag," as a character in *Chariots* remarks)
becomes a central tension in each film and the emotional center of each
work. Both films explore the tension between the characters and their
motivations, and both cast this exploration of athletic competition within the
framework of the political pressures surrounding world-class athletes.

Johann Huizinga, whose work *Homo Ludens* has become central to any
study of sport and the play element in modern civilization, defines play as

> an activity occuring within certain limits of space, time, and meaning, according to
> fixed rules . . . A game is timebound . . . it has no contact with any reality outside
> itself, and its performance is its own end . . . Further, it is sustained by the consciousness
> of being a pleasurable, even mirthful, relaxation from the strain of everyday life.[1]

The College Dash fits Huizinga's definition perfectly. Although it is a
tradition carried over seven centuries, it has no meaning in everyday life.
The courtyard, normally a gathering place and a thoroughfare for the college's
students, becomes significant space for the event. The time it takes for the
clock to strike, normally a matter of a few seconds in a busy day, becomes
a significant challenge. And the task of running around this special space
in this special time becomes an event with importance backwards and forwards
through history. Finally, as the joyous spectators make clear, it is an event
of great joy and triumph. In the truest sense, it is victory for the human
spirit.

That is precisely why the comments of the dons are so devastating. Their
anti-semitic remarks violate not only the triumphal joy but also Huizinga's
dictum that play "has no contact with any reality outside itself." Even the
College Dash, an insignificant event outside the gates of Caius, is not separate
from the pressures of the outside society.

---

[1] Johann Huizinga, *Homo Ludens: A Study of the Play Element in Culture* (Boston: Beacon
Press, 1950), p. 28.

Anti-semitism affects the joy of sport in other, more subtle ways in *Chariots of Fire*. It provides a significant part of Harold Abrahams's motivation as a runner. He tells his friend Aubrey Montague, "It's an ache . . . and a helplessness . . . and an anger. One feels humiliated. Sometimes I say to myself, hey, steady on, you're imagining all this, and then I catch that look again, catch it on the edge of a remark, feel it in the cold reluctance of a handshake." He goes on, "My old man (a Lithuanian Jew who wanted to make Englishmen of his sons) forgot one thing: this England of his is Christian, and Anglo-Saxon, and so are her corridors of power, and those who stalk them guard them with jealousy and venom."

When Aubrey asks, "So, what now, grin and bear it?" Harold replies, "No, Aubrey, I'm going to take them on, all of them, one by one, and run them off their feet." And, as if to underscore Harold's dilemma, the collage of Harold's training and self-promotion that follows is accompanied by Gilbert and Sullivan's "He Remains an Englishman." The final scene of the collage shows Harold singing lead in the song in a Cambridge production of *H.M.S. Pinafore*.

As an English Jew, Harold finds himself in the painful predicament of many Jews in the Diaspora: he is proud to be an Englishman, he wants fiercely to identify with English tradition and patriotism, but he feels keenly apart, the classic outsider. Through his running, through being the nation's best runner, he believes he can at the same time cement his status as an Englishman and defeat his anti-semitic adversaries, both real and perceived. As he later tells Sybil Gordon, his running is a "weapon . . . against being Jewish."

Of course, Harold Abrahams is only one of two focal points in the film, the other being Eric Liddell, his chief opponent in Great Britain, who runs for somewhat different reasons. Liddell, the son of a minister in the Evangelical missionary wing of the Church of Scotland and a former national rugby player, must continually justify running to his sister Jennie, who disapproves because as a frivolous activity athletics diverts Eric from God's purpose for him.

Eric's answer to Jennie is straightforward, and in its way anticipates the modern Evangelical Christian sports movement, the Fellowship of Christian Athletes. "I believe that God made me for a purpose . . . but he also made me *fast*, and when I run, I feel his pleasure. To give it up would be to hold him in contempt. You were right. It's not just fun. To win is to honor Him." Eric Liddell's words to his sister betray his motivation as clearly as Harold Abrahams's words to Aubrey Montague. And both speeches are troubling. The motivation of athletes, beyond a rather elementary level of competition, is distinctly influenced by forces outside athletics. At the Olympic level, at least in this film, there is rarely a positive sporting spirit.

That is an important point, a forceful challenge to Huizinga's dictum that sport "has no contact with any reality outside itself, and its performance is its own end." The sanctity of sport at the Olympic level is challenged, according to *Chariots of Fire*, not only by the forces in the world outside of sport but

also by athletes' internalizing those forces in order to find a will to win.
In doing so, the film questions the entire concept of competition.

The other important Olympic film of the past five years, *Personal Best,*
also challenges the concept of competition, although in *Personal Best* the
athletes are American women preparing for the 1980 Olympics. Tory Skinner
and Chris Cahill are pentathletes who first meet at the Olympic trials in 1976
in Eugene, Oregon. Skinner, the older woman, qualifies for the Olympic Games
and Cahill, competing in the hurdles, fails dismally. Skinner takes her under
her wing, convinces her to train with her demanding coach, Terry Tingloff,
and convinces Tingloff to coach Cahill.

In many ways *Personal Best* is a more honest film than *Chariots of Fire.*
It depicts the complete devotion, the hard work, and the sacrifices of Olympic-
level athletes. The opening shot in the film, of sweat dripping from Cahill's
nose onto the track while a loudspeaker intones in the background, "Will
non-competitors . . . please leave the track?", is symbolic of the film's message:
one must compete to succeed, and one must sacrifice to compete.

The film is significantly complicated by Cahill and Skinner's relationship,
which blossoms early on into a love affair. The film poses the question quite
simply: can lovers compete against each other?

It is a difficult question. Things go well as long as Skinner is the dominant
athlete. She nurtures Cahill, trains her, protects her. But once Cahill emerges
as an equal of Skinner's on the track, the relationship changes. In a crucial
scene, Skinner advises Cahill to lengthen her stride in the high jump but
accidentally moves the starting mark with her spikes. Cahill, attempting the
ridiculously long stride, injures her knee. Unsure whether Skinner intentionally
moved the mark (as indeed most of us in the audience are), Cahill allows
herself to be influenced by Tingloff during rehabilitation and moves away
from Skinner, even taking a man for a lover.

The two finally reconcile at the 1980 Olympic trials, again in Eugene.
The two athletes learn that they can cooperate *and* compete, particularly in
an Olympic year when the American team is boycotting the Moscow games
and making the team (finishing in the top three) is as far as one can go.
Cahill sacrifices herself in the final event of pentathalon, the 800 meters, so
that Skinner can qualify. Cahill herself finishes second in the pentathalon
rather than first. Skinner finishes third.

Similarly, in *Chariots of Fire* the climactic duel between Abrahams and
Liddell never materializes. Liddell refuses to compromise his religious dictum
against running on Sunday and withdraws from the 100-meter dash. Given
a spot in the 400 meters by Lindsay, he wins that race, while Abrahams wins
his dash. Like Skinner and Cahill, they can both be winners.

Both films, then, avoid the questions that they raise. In doing so, they
both radically alter the formula of the adventure story they have followed.
John G. Cawelti has defined that story as follows:

The central fantasy of the adventure story is that of the hero—individual or group—overcoming obstacles and dangers and accomplishing some important and moral mission. The true focus of interest in the adventure story is the character of the hero and the nature of the obstacles he has to overcome.[2]

With that definition in mind, we can identify three stages in a sports adventure film:

1. an early focus on the hero, whose character is revealed in a series of conflicts or confrontations (in *Chariots of Fire*, the College Dash; in *Personal Best*, the first Olympic trials and the scenes that follow);

2. a series of tests, wherein the hero readies himself or herself for a final confrontation and is often romantically entangled (in both films the Olympic training);

3. the final confrontation.

In avoiding the final confrontation, both films sidestep the difficult question: To what extent does competition depend on victory as the goal? Is that goal to be achieved at the price of friendship?

As if to underscore its inability to make a final statement, Director Hugh Hudson steps back at the conclusion of *Chariots of Fire* and reinforces the patriotism that he has questioned throughout the film. The British team (with the exception of Abrahams) is united in victory on a wagon amidst cheering throngs. Even Abrahams, whose exclusion might label him finally as an outsider, is united with Sybil, and a subtitle at the film's conclusion tells us that he became "the elder statesman of British athletics."

Perhaps we shouldn't criticize these films too harshly. The questions they raise but fail to settle are those that the Olympic movement generally has not come to grips with. Can the Olympic Games, increasingly competitive and increasingly political, survive as sport? We who are involved with the Olympics and with athletics generally must find answers to these questions, even if these two popular films cannot.

---

[2] John G. Cawelti, *Adventure, Mystery, and Romance: Formula Stories as Art and Popular Culture* (Chicago: University of Chicago Press, 1976), pp. 39-40.

22

The "Close" Western: Contemporary Sport Films

Stephen David Mosher

IN 1976, THE YEAR *ROCKY* made such an impressive turnaround for the reputation of sport movies, Stanley J. Solomon wrote:

> In recent years the Western has gone into a decline, . . . This decline is probably temporary, however, since the Western embodies certain key myths of our culture and so is not likely to remain out of fashion for long. Still, even if no serious Western is made for a decade, . . . the impressive number of quality Westerns will insure that the genre's artistic heritage continues to be critically appreciated.[1]

Today, with the decade nearly complete and sport films such as *The Natural* (1984), *The Karate Kid* (1984) and *Vision Quest* (1984) attracting large and appreciative audiences, Stephen Harvey claims that, in spite of critical and financial disasters, *The Missouri Breaks* (1976), *Comes a Horseman* (1978), and *Heaven's Gate* (1980), Home Box Office's *Draw* (1984) are evidence that the Western is still alive and kicking. Harvey makes this claim even while explaining the way in which the Western has been supplanted by the Steven Spielberg-John Lucas space fables. He goes so far as to equate *Star Wars* with *The Searchers*, *Outland* with *High Noon* and *Blade Runner* with any standard bounty hunter film.[2]

While Harvey's argument is convincing, I believe it is incomplete with regard to the transformation of the Western and overly optimistic with regard to its return. In this paper I hope to show that the Western genre has, in its transformation, spawned two sub-species: the sport film, which I call the "close" Western; and the space film, which I call the "far" Western. Together, the new Westerns adequately narrate the fable, but the sport film conveys its *intimacy*, while the space film more readily captures its *movement*. I contend,

---

[1] Stanley J. Solomon, *Beyond Formula: American Film Genres* (New York: Harcourt Brace Jovanovich, Inc., 1976), p. 12.

[2] Stephen Harvey, "Is the Western Really Dead, or Simply in Disguise?" *The New York Times* 15 July 1984, Section 2, p. 16.

moreover, that as long as sport-space films continue to complete this fable and as long as the average age of movie-goers continues to decrease, the traditional Western will never make an effective return. As long as the West (whether Arizona, Fenway Park or a galaxy far, far away) remains unequivocally the wilderness, the Western will remain a parable. As Jack Folsom says, "As a fable the western is not necessarily an anachronism, for it makes little difference whether the Last Frontier is the Great Plains or the moon."[3]

Who were the ancestors of the Lone Ranger and Tonto? Who were the forefathers of Henry Wiggen and Roy Hobbs? Is it merely a coincidence that the archetypal figures of Natty Bumppo and Chingachgook created by James Fenimore Cooper in his *Leatherstocking Tales* serve as the models and inspiration for both the Western and the sport (space) hero? Were Cooper's heroes the first Westerners as Folsom, Robert Warshow or perhaps Frederick Jackson Turner would contend?[4] Or were they the first American sportsmen as Wiley Lee Umphlett has argued?[5] It matters little in the final analysis because both the Western and the sport (space) heroes find themselves in identical situations — located in a particular *landscape* and possessing the same moral *code*. Thus equipped, they must necessarily *move* to identical resolutions, the same fate.

To be brief, the landscape is the wilderness: the code is "hardboileddom": or; the movement is that of the quest. Locked into a vast openness, the old/ new Western hero relies only on his code: his quest to find himself turns on the degree to which he understands its meaning. As Umphlett shows, Saul Bellow's *Dangling Man* understands the code:

> . . . this is the era of hardboileddom. Today the code of the athlete, of the toughboy . . . is stronger than ever. Do you have feelings? There are correct and incorrect ways of indicating them. Do you have an inner life? It's nobody's business but your own. Do you have emotions? Strangle them. To a degree everybody obeys this code.[6]

Warshow demonstrates that the Western hero is "the last gentleman." This vague epithet is made clear through his action; "(the Westerner) fights not for advantage and not for right, but to state *what he is*, and he must live in a world which permits that statement."[7] What he is, of course, is a "killer of men." His destiny is to arrive at a point "where one moral absolute conflicts with another and the choice of either must leave a moral stain."[8] The Westerner

[3] James K. Folsom, *The American Western Novel* (New Haven: College & University Press, Publishers, 1966), p. 32.

[4] See especially Jack Nachbar, ed., *Focus on the Western* (Englewood Cliffs, N.J.: Prentice-Hall, Inc., 1974).

[5] Wiley Lee Umphlett, *The Sporting Myth and the American Experience* (Lewisburg, Pennsylvania: Bucknell University Press, 1975).

[6] Umphlett, p. 26.

[7] Robert Warshow, "What is a Western?" in Jack Nachbar, ed., *Focus on the Western* (Englewood Cliffs, N.J.: Prentice-Hall, Inc., 1974), p. 48.

[8] Ibid.

maintains a rigid posture that places himself above society. As the rugged individualist, he defines the self in opposition to the standard rule of society.

In truth, both the Western and sport hero become interesting only when their moral codes, "without ceasing to be compelling, (are) seen also to be imperfect."[9] So it is not outrageous to suggest that the Virginian and Henry Wiggen must arrive at similar "moments of truth." His individualistic moral code demands that the Virginian sacrifice his friend in a lynching: to save him would violate the image of self that the Virginian has made essential to his existence. The same code demands that Henry Wiggen keep Bruce Pearson's fate a secret: to tell the world will show that he has an inner life, feelings and emotions. In both cases, the rigid personal codes put everyone in jeopardy. In the end both heroes grow as human beings. Although the Virginian has avenged his friend's death and Henry has celebrated Bruce with his resolution ("From here on in I rag nobody!"), both have been forced to confront the ultimate limitations of their moral ideas, and their connection to a society they can never join.

The landscape against which the code is placed in both Westerns and sport films reveals itself in moral terms. In fact, the wide open spaces of the wilderness are merely options of the *showdown*. As Umphlett says, "[The hero's] fictional pattern is the *encounter*, wherein the hero, upon facing the demands of either nature of society, is confronted with a moral decision between a self-effacing code or private interests."[10] It is important to note that the result of the encounter is most often a happy ending, always qualified and dominated by melancholy. The hero's gifts have set him apart. He is a model and he knows he is different and better than other men. yet, he must recognize both his connection to the society and the limitations of his gifts. He will continue to exist—connected but alien—as society prevails in its everyday life. It can be no other way, moreover, because, as Folsom argues, "the right of the soil implies the right of the empire, for the way the land is used depends on the way of life of its possessors."[11] Cooper makes clear repeatedly that the right to hunt and the right to farm are mutually incompatible, and the stronger side—the farmers—will inevitably prevail. Consequently, history favors the strong over the just, and the law is an expression, not of morality, but force. Even if the hero wins a battle, civilization will always win the war; and hero's victories can only be individual and private. In the battle between *civilization* and the *individual* it is always civilization that forces the showdown and it is always the individual who, because of his code, cannot back down. Han Solo must face Darth Vader, and Rocky Balboa must confront Apollo Creed, just as Will Kane must draw with Frank Miller in *High Noon*. It is clear, however, that while Vader, Creed and Miller serve as occasions for the moral battle, and good will triumph over evil, the heroes'

---

[9] Ibid.

[10] Wiley Lee Umphlett, "The Dynamics of Fiction on the Aesthetics of the Sport Film," *Arete: The Journal of Sport Literature*, vol. 1, no. 2 (Spring 1984): 113.

[11] Folsom *The American Western Novel*, p. 50

victories merely lead to their separation from the society they have been called to defend. The constrictive pressure that society places on the individual narrows his choices and finally demands that the hero either conform (and be included) or suffer the consequences of isolation.

It is apparent, therefore, that when the society loses control when the balance is disturbed, the relationship of opposition is set in force and the hero is required. Once the hero fulfills his role, in terms of the fable, the narrative certainly becomes simpler, but it also becomes more intense. The hero struggles to find his place in society because he recognizes his connection to it, but he is unwilling to compromise himself. Thus the question the hero must always strive to answer: "How do I fit in?" More often than not, he doesn't: he remains locked in perpetual exile—living in society, but not of it.

Within the larger quest fable, cultural forces serve to locate the Western. America, circa 1870, no longer captures the comtemporary imagination and so new frontiers must be located. As noted previously, space films narrate this fable well because the potential for ever-increasing expansion of the frontier is always present. Today a chase through time warps and solar system is more appealing than along dusty trails.[12] Similarly, the sport film can focus on the confrontation in more intimate terms: the urban sprawl has by now completely encircled the wilderness, going so far as to, in many cases, change the ground from grass to plastic. Whether he is alone in the void of outer space or standing on the pitcher's mound, the contemporary Westerner is still in exile, still awaiting confrontation with the villainy that threatens society and still in possession of the *code* as his only fighting weapon. In sport films the wilderness has by not become fully enclosed and assumes an aura of intimacy and introspection wherein the villain is quite often the hero himself.

In 1961, when Alan Sheppard became the first American to soar into space, Fast Eddie Felson strode into the pool hall (saloon) armed only with his pool cue (six-shooter) and his cockiness to duel with Minnesota Fats. If *The Hustler* (1961) were an old-time formula Western, Eddie would die because he loses the game. On this green-felt frontier Eddie merely slinks away in defeat to question his imperfections. Sarah (representing justice and humanity) and Bert (representing greed and villainy) engage in a battle for Eddie's soul and Eddie fights everyone. In the end, Eddie defeats Fats and rejects both Sarah and Bert. He has remained *hardboiled*, but he is alone in the world, wiser but sadder, his back to the wall waiting for the next young punk to challenge him to draw.

In *Bang the Drum Slowly* (1973), Henry Wiggen struggles to teach Bruce Pearson how to play *tegwar*. If this were a traditional Western, the game would be poker, but in both cases the game represents life— T he E xciting

---

[12] The *Dirty Harry* films and their counterparts fail to qualify as modern Westerns because both antagonists are simply renegades of society. The battle they wage may take place on the streets of the city, but it is neither condoned nor appreciated; and the "hero" fails to acquire a moral sense of his actions.

G ame W ithout A ny R ules. The irony, of course, is that while Henry teaches Bruce how to play cards, Bruce (*a person*) teaches Henry how to play at life. Thus, by living the life of a pure natural, the good ol' boy from Georgia, Bruce Pearson, gave Henry his code by which to live. Henry finds himself, therefore, not at an end but a new beginning. It is, however, a painful one because Henry now has become a hero: "From here on in I rag nobody!" This rule by which he must measure his movement through life serves to isolate him from society.

Rollerball (1975) combines both science fiction and sport to yield a futuristic *Gunfight at the OK Corral.* Jonathan E is consumed with the struggle to discover for himself why he has become a "killer of men." He is forced to face the reality that the game is not a game and never was. In his search for himself he exposes the Corporation's insidious strangle hold on the populace. Further, once he realizes the game has never been his, he is able to challenge the Corporation and rise above the game to victory. Jonathan E's pyrrhic triumph, as in so many Westerns, assures his permanent exile from society.

Breaking Away (1979) shows the way in which a young bicycle rider's fantasy of joining the fraternity of the best professionals is shattered by his recognition of their deception and commercialism. His own life begins to take shape with his return to a completely individual (and consequently isolating) triumph. *Raging Bull* (1980) concludes with the washed-up Jake LaMotta confronting himself in the mirror. LaMotta's victory, no matter how small, is that he recognizes not that he could have been but *is* a contender. Even the real-life heroes of *Chariots of Fire* (1981) have their codes by which to race. Eric Liddell has Isaiah 40: "So who does the power come from to see the race to its end?" Knowing the source of his power, Liddell can conclude, "When I run I feel *His* pleasure!" Harold Abrahams, when faced with those, "ten lonely seconds to justify my own existence," succeeds because he has come to understand that "he can't win if he doesn't run." In the end, Liddell is with his God but not heroic because he is accepted by and conforms to society. Abrahams, however, finds himself a conqueror of runners ("He ran them off their feet!") but still the outsider and unaccepted by society.

In the final analysis *distance* separates the space hero from the sport hero. The other-worldliness of the space hero is so clearly understood that we can identify with him only in our wildest fantasies. The intimacy we feel for the sport hero is more genuine because we know that real people actually achieve this lofty status. The "closeness" of the sport film is actually felt and may serve to develop our own moral codes. It is not surprising, then, that the seemingly anachronistic image of Chuck Yeager climbing off his horse and into the cockpit as he dares his test plane to *literally* fly into outer space makes as much sense to us as Roy Hobbs's "wonderboy" *literally* knocking the cover off the baseball. Both these "naturals" have indeed got the "right stuff." They merely play in different arenas.

PART VII

Ancient Sport in Art and Literature

23

Introduction:
Ancient Sport in Art
and Literature

Thomas F. Scanlon

ANCIENT CULTURES, LIKE MODERN ONES, express their identities through their sports and seek to supercede the ephemeral nature of athletic glory by creating lasting monuments of art or literature. If sport can transmit the legacy of a people's glory, the expression of it in verbal or visual creations is a fitting vessel whereby the legacy is preserved. If sport is a reminder of a human urge to compete, it is also a legitimate escape from the world of serious competition which can, in the extreme, end in death. If, for the ancients, sport was inextricably bound to their military ideals and practices, it was, at least for the Greeks, also bound to peaceful worship of the gods, to the cults of heroic athletes, and to a sacred truce which has, perhaps misleadingly, inspired moderns to seek their own "Pax Olympica."

The following four essays have in common the theme of the power of art, both literary and visual, to create and perpetuate the cultural ideals of sport among ancient and modern peoples. The first two by Boe and Scanlon show the way in which monumental works like the Bible, the Homeric epics, and certain Greek classics have molded and reinforced a national consciousness. For the Semitic people of the Old Testament, sports was a foreign element to be associated with the pagans and therefore an aspect of culture to be disparaged. According to Boe the Jews prided themselves in their separateness from other races and nations and so distinguished themselves by adherence to certain laws (e.g. dietary) and their aversion to certain other customs among other peoples (e.g. the institution of kingship, excessive devotion to temple ritual, and indulgence in the visual arts). Sports may thus be grouped with certain arts considered to be "un-Jewish" in the Old Testament view. But, as Boe points out, there may have been much more widespread practice of sports in ancient Israel than Biblical authors imply since the filter of Jewish orthodoxy was a very fine ideological screen against pagan custom.

For the Greeks sports were, of course, an essential part of their "agonal" culture which extended the competitive ethic to all spheres of public life. Scanlon's essay thus shows the way in which athletic competition not only supported actual Greek military training and ideals but also helped to form Greek thinking about military combat by the use of agonistic metaphors in literature concerned with warfare.

Lattimore's analysis of early Greek victor statues similarly shows the perpetuation of the athletic ideals carried on by votive and honorific dedications. The custom of setting up athletic statues has a natural parallel in the monuments established by successful military victors in the same periods. The public display of statues for successful athletes and soldiers encouraged the *arete* or "heroic excellence" which was the *ne plus ultra* of civic life.

Young's essay illustrates the way in which the modern Olympic movement has mistakenly created a mythical link to the Greek legacy with the symbol of the five rings. Both Coubertin's desire to establish a universal peace, a "Pax Olimpica" (*sic*), under this sign, and Hitler's desire to identify the 1936 Games with the Greeks by the use of the same symbol have resulted in the currently widespread and unhistorical identification of the rings with ancient Greek symbolism and spirit. Young thus puts the symbol of modern Olympism at a distance from ancient Greek reality with his historical exposé of careless folly and deliberate fraud since 1913. Like the Jews of the Old Testament we may thus become more aware of our own cultural identity by its contrast to Greek athletic ideals, and like the Jews we can begin to shape our own honorable ethos through an independent attitude toward sports and through ideologies appropriate to our society.

The themes of war, politics, and religion are as prominent in the essays as is that of cultural identity through athletics. Boe shows that the clearest reports of sport-like activities in the Old Testament are associated with quasi-military or -political events: the tournament of soldiers in a mock battle in *2 Samuel,* Samson's making sport which ends with Philistine deaths in *Judges,* and Jacob's wrestling match which elevates him to political power in *Genesis.* Scanlon's essay shows the pervasiveness of athletic-military associations in Greek thought and practice. The victor statues described by Lattimore stood in the sacred Altis at Olympia alongside military memorials. The very custom of honorific statues for athletes may have been popularized in the newly democratized Athens of 509 B.C. when the tyrannicides were commemorated with a statue; Athenian athletes were frequently so honored thereafter. And Young shows that Coubertin's ring symbol was inspired by anti-war, pro-unification sentiment prior to the First World War. The ancient *sacred truce,* in contrast, could not stop war universally, but only exclude it from the territory of Elis around Olympia and protect pilgrims from hostilities. If the Greeks had a corresponding symbol, we may add, it was not the five rings of peace and unity, but the olive wreath of individual honor.

With regard to religious themes, we find in Boe's essay that Jacob's wrestling match with God (or His angel) confirms his worthiness as a leader of Israel and sport becomes a tool of sacred selection. The *terpsis* or "delight" mentioned by Scanlon as an essential element of Greek sport which distinguishes it from their warfare also associates sport with their religious festivals. Not only were certain victor statues, as described by Lattimore, set up as thank offerings to the gods, but these statues at times became associated with legends of the semi-divine athletic heroes. Thus the visual art becomes bound with the oral or literal in the elevation of men to a higher plane. Religion for the ancient Jews and Greeks thus set certain athletic contests or the athletes themselves apart from everyday activity; in Scanlon's terms, religion became a "disassociative aspect" of sports. Religion is, of course, absent in any real sense from modern sport, but Young reminds us that the five-ring symbol had been carved on a pseudo-Greek altar by the Nazis in 1936 in order to give the symbol the legitimacy or authority of an ancient religious monument.

Literature and art strive to make man's transitory efforts into eternal truths. Ancient sport as portrayed in the arts is both a relic of tradition and an inspiration for continued or renewed idealism. But the mere preservation of relics does not assure our correct understanding of them. Each of the following essays examines the evidence pertaining to sports from a distant past and by judicious interpretation suggests a new understanding of cultural identity through sport and the arts.

24

Sports in the Bible*

Alfred F. Boe

It is like sport to a fool to do wrong,
but wise conduct is pleasure to a man of understanding.

Proverbs 10:23[1]

It is doubtful that the kind of game, determined by anthropologists,
matters as much as the cultural perception of the game on the
part of the players themselves. We can learn a great deal from careful
attention to the games a society emphasizes. . . .

Allen Guttmann, *From Ritual to Record*

I

BUT WHAT OF ANCIENT ISRAEL, a society that seems to have had no games?

For a book as encyclopedic as it is, the Bible contains surprisingly little
reference to sport. The Bible tells us about almost every area of human
experience, many in great detail—politics, sex, agriculture, economics, music,
ethics, religion, of course; family structure and kinship systems, law and order—
and disorder: crime and warfare—but very little about sport.

The purpose of this essay is to examine what little there is about sport
in the Bible, to see what it may tell us about the place of sport in the life
of ancient Israel, and to speculate briefly on why there is not more about
sport in the Bible. The most basic reason for such a study, other than the
purely literary interest of understanding the biblical text better, is that there

---

*A portion of an earlier version of this paper was presented at the Olympic Scientific Congress,
    Eugene, Oregon, July 21, 1984, and an additional portion at the Coroebus Convention
    of the Sport Literature Association, La Jolla, California, July 26, 1984.

[1] Unless otherwise noted, all Biblical quotations are from the Revised Standard Version.

is very little other evidence available to us about life in ancient Israel (before 300 B.C.E.). No other written records survive from Israel itself. Documents from other neighboring cultures are silent on this aspect of Israelite culture, and even archaeology has not as yet cast any light on the subject of sport in ancient Israel. Social historians of Jewish culture have often indulged in speculation and wishful thinking regarding this matter, but, as Prof. Manfred Lämmer of the *Deutsche Sporthochschule Köln: Institut für Sportgeschicte* has so ably argued,[2] most of their speculations are indeed wishful thinking, based on essentially no evidence at all. Since the Bible is virtually our only source of knowledge for the customs and institutions of ancient Israel, a detailed examination of its references to sport seems called for.

We examine here only the Old Testament; the New Testament represents an entirely different time period and cultural milieu from the Old, reflecting Greek and Roman influences with the obvious elements of sport that those influences brought. The effect of Greek athletics on late ancient Jewish culture (3rd, 2nd, and 1st centuries B.C.E.), as shown in the apocryphal 1st Book of Maccabees, is substantial and well known.[3]

There is considerable difference of opinion about what the term sport means. Without getting into a debate with Huizinga, Caillois, and other theoreticians of sport, without sinking into a morass of semantics and hair-splitting definitions, I define sport, for the purpose of this paper, as any freely chosen physical activity that is done in-and-for-itself, that is, for the sake of the joy of the activity itself, and not for some extrinsic end.

As his title indicates, George Eisen cast his net somewhat wider in his pioneering article on our subject, "Physical Activity, Physical Education and Sport in the Old Testament."[4] His definition of sport and physical activity is very broad, including on the one hand, dance, and on the other, military training activities and other job-related physical activities, such as running great distances to deliver messages.

I would argue that job-related activities are by definition not sport (with one exception—professional sports themselves). Walking behind a horse or mule sixteen hours a day plowing a field may be excellent exercise, but it is certainly not sport. And which marathon run was the only one that was not sport? The very first one, of course. Archery practice designed to enable you to hunt your dinner successfuly or to kill your enemy in battle before he kills you is not sport. I am not denying that sports—some, at least—may have had their origin in the hunt and in military activities and other

---

[2]Most thoroughly in *"Ideological Tendencies in the Historiography of Sport in Jewish Culture," Physical Education and Sports in the Jewish History and Culture: Proceedings of an International Seminar at Wingate Institute, July, 1973*, ed. Uriel Simri (Netanya, Israel: Wingate Institute, 1973), pp. 54-72.

[3]See, for example, Harold Arthur Harris, *Greek Athletics and the Jews* (Cardiff: University of Wales Press, 1976).

[4]"Physical Activity, Physical Education and Sport in the Old Testament," *Canadian Journal of History of Sport and Physical Education*, 6:2 (Dec. 1975): 44-65.

utilitarian pursuits. I am only saying that there is a line there somewhere
that we all draw—not necessarily all in exactly the same place—between
hunting for survival and hunting for sport, between military training and
sports—between job and fun, between necessity and freedom, in other words.
In this paper I will stick to the side of the line that is clearly sport.

II

First, the Bible contains only three scenes that actually depict what might
be sporting events: Jacob's wrestling with God, or with God's angel, Genesis
32:24-32; Samson's "making sport" for the Philistines, Judges 16:23-31; and
a tournament-like "playing" of young men, II Samuel 2:12-17. Let us examine
them in reverse order.

The context of II Sam. 2 is one of civil war in Israel as David tries to
establish his reign in the face of the heirs of Saul, the previous King who
had died in battle. The opposing armies meet, apparently by accident, at
the pool of the town of Gibeon, and sit down, "the one on the one side
of the pool, and the other on the other side of the pool." Abner, the general
of the forces of Saul's son Ishbosheth, suggests to David's general, Joab, "Let
the young men arise and play before us." Joab agrees, and twelve young
men are picked from each army. The entire account of their "playing" consists
of one verse: "And each caught his opponent by the head, and thrust his
sword in his opponent's side; so they fell down together. Therefore that place
was called Helkath-hazzurim, which is at Gibeon." (The name means "the
field of the sword-edges.") The next verse says, "And the battle was very
fierce that day; and Abner and the men of Israel were beaten before the
servants of David." The story of the battle goes on, but it is of no concern
to us, as none of it is helpful in understanding exactly what is going on
in the "playing."

Now, were it not for that word "play" we would not even be looking
at this passage. One translation, in fact, gets around the problem by translating,
"Let the young men fight before us." This certainly makes good sense of
the passage—better sense, in fact, than the standard translation—but it
overlooks one problem: the Hebrew word in question does in fact mean
play, not fight.[5] It is the same word translated "make sport" in the passage
in Judges about Samson: "Call Samson, that he may make sport for us," and
could equally well be translated "that he may play for us." The word has
its root in "laughter," and it is the word for child's play, for playful activity
as opposed to serious activity, and for "make sport of" as in the modern
sense of "make fun of, deride."

So what is the nature of the young men's "playing"? Unfortunately the
Biblical text here, as it very often is, is so austere, not to say elliptical, that
we cannot really tell. The best conjecture, it seems, is that the young men

---

[5]Definitions and etymologies of Hebrew words are drawn from *Strong's Exhaustive Concordance.*

are fighting what we might call a duel, similar to the duel between Paris and Menelaus in Book III of the *Iliad*—and with similarly bad results! That is, apparently whoever "won" the "play" would win the town. But, either because the "play" got too serious, or because it was a "tie" and thus produced no result, or because of some combination of such factors, the "play", the duel, quickly degenerated into a full-fledged battle.

Whatever the case, it seems clear that we do not have a real sporting event here. But I think the passage is crucial because it suggests a transition from all-out military activity to a kind of symbolic, selective, stylized activity that is a real step towards "pure" sport. That such transitions are gradual and difficult is indicated by an anecdote Allen Guttmann repeats from Jusserand's historical study of sport in France: "The line between the medieval tournament and the medieval battle was not very finely drawn. At the Battle of Bremule in 1119, three men were killed; at the tournament at Neuss in 1240, sixty died."[6] The line between tournament and battle was not very finely drawn in II Samuel either.

A much clearer case of a sporting event being depicted is the story of the end of Samson's career, as mentioned above. Here the legendary strongman is brought captive before the crowd of Philistines at a religious and national festival to perform—make sport, play—and thus to be ridiculed for their entertainment. The context is quite clearly one of a public performance on a grand scale: "Now the house was full of men and women; all the lords of the Philistines were there, and on the roof there were about three thousand men and women, who looked on while Samson made sport" (Judges 16:27). But once again, unfortunately, the characteristic baldness of Biblical narrative frustrates our purpose: the text does not tell us what exactly he *did* to "make sport." We can safely infer, I think, one of two things: feats of strength, such as weightlifting, or some sort of gladiatorial combat. The latter is Yigael Yadin's assumption, in arguing that the Hebrew word *sachaq*, "play," used here and in II Sam. 2:14 refers to "a way of fighting which outwardly resembles a sport or amusement inasmuch as a few people are involved and the rest act as spectators."[7]

Three problems make me skeptical about Yadin's suggestion, though: (1) the word does not have this connotation anywhere else in the Bible; (2) the text contains nothing to suggest any opponent of Samson, either animal or human, despite its account of his several encounters with both kinds earlier; (3) the two situations are really not that analogous. By this last I mean that,

[6]Allen Guttman, *From Ritual to Record: The Nature of Modern Sports* (New York: Columbia University Press, 1978), p. 7.

[7]Yigael Yadin, "Let the Young Men Arise,. . . ." *Journal of Palestine Oriental Studies,* 21 (1948), pp. 110-116, quoted by Eisen, p. 51. For a brief survey of the apperances of the word *sachaq* (alternatively transliterated *sakhek*) in the Bible, see Shalom Hermon, "The Word Sakhek (Play) in the Bible (The Old Testament)," *Play in Physical Education and Sport: Proceedings of an International Seminar,* ed. Uriel Simri (Netanya, Israel: Wingate Institute, 1975), pp. 7-14.

although (if Samson is indeed performing as a gladiator) in each case selected fighters are watched by a larger group, the relationships between the fighters on the one hand and the groups on the other are entirely different. One case is an actual military encounter, even if in microcosm, while the other is intended strictly as an entertainment event, a spectacle of sport. I say "intended as," because it, too, ends up in a disaster, for the Philistines, at least, as Samson uses his strength to break down the pillars of the "arena" and kill everyone in it, himself included, "So the dead whom he slew at his death were more than those whom he had slain during his life." And we think *our* sports are violent!

At any rate, whether the sport in question was weight-lifting or something like boxing, it seems indisputable to me that we have here the clearest— and perhaps only real—portrayal of a sporting event in the Bible. Of course, the last thing particularly notable about it is that it occurs in Philistia, not in Israel. Nowhere do we find the Israelites honoring their God and celebrating their victories with sporting events. But that will be discussed later.

The third overt depiction of sporting activity in the Bible is, like the other two, tantalizingly skeletal. Jacob is on his way home to Canaan after laboring for several years in Aram or Syria, the land of his family's relatives, to acquire wives, children, and wealth in the form of flocks of animals. Fearing how he will be greeted by his previously hostile brother Esau, he sends his family and flocks on ahead. "And Jacob was left alone; and a man wrestled with him until the breaking of the day. When the man saw that he did not prevail against Jacob, he touched the hollow of his thigh; and Jacob's thigh was put out of joint as he wrestled with him. Then he said, 'Let me go, for the day is breaking.' But Jacob said, 'I will not let you go, unless you bless me.' " (Gen. 32:24-26) That is all there is of the description of the physical contest itself. After some brief discussion about their respective names, the "man," who it turns out is God—or, we might better say, an angel— blesses Jacob and leaves.

The crux here, it seems to me, is do we have a serious, life-threatening fight, or a more stylized, perhaps even rule-bound contest, a true sporting event? The very symbolic nature of the encounter suggests the latter: no reason is given for the contest, and no anger is mentioned. The atmosphere seems more that of a sportsmanlike competition. The angel's renaming of Jacob further underlines this: "Your name shall no more be called Jacob, but Israel, for you have striven with God and with men, and have prevailed." The wrestling match symbolizes, then, the struggles and victories Jacob has experienced on the way to becoming a champion of God, a Patriarch of Israel, the land and people named after him. It also fits nicely into the classic folk motif of a physical combat establishing mutual respect which blossoms into best friendship, as in well-known cases from Gilgamesh and Enkidu—a story possibly known to the writers of Genesis—to Robin Hood and Little John.

Since the encounter occurs at night and parallels a dream Jacob had when he went from Canaan to Syria many years earlier, one might argue that the encounter did not actually happen at all, that is was just a dream. But for our purposes that does not make any difference, since even if the author meant it as a dream, the dream itself takes the form of the wrestling match. What we want to do is determine the nature of the event the author had in mind and its purpose, which I think we have done as far as we can. We would also like to determine what it tells us about sports in ancient Israel. That is a bit more difficult, but at least, I think, we can conclude that the idea of athletic, as opposed to military or other life-and-death competition, is shown here. (Jacob does, of course, fear death as a result of the encounter, not from the wrestling itself, but rather from the simple fact that his opponent is "God," and one doesn't expect to see God face to face and live.)

A final thing we can say about this wrestling match is that, although it may be less explicitly a full-fledged sporting event than Samson's performance, it is the only one of our three depictions that can be called unambiguously positive. The first degenerated into bloody warfare, and the second was a pagan spectacle, although it did at least end up in a Hebrew victory. This third one, though, is a symbolic moral and spiritual victory as well as a literal athletic one, resulting as it does in Jacob's being blessed by God and being given a new name, the name of God's chosen people.

III

Besides direct depictions, what other evidence does the Bible offer about sport? It offers several metaphors, in situations where sport is not involved at all directly, but where an image drawn from sports is used to characterize something. Such usages in works of literature are often more revealing than direct depictions. Is this true of the Bible and sport? Unfortunately these more indirect references to sport are also very infrequent in the Bible. But let us see what they have to tell us.

Probably the most spectacular—and certainly the most positive—sports metaphor in the Bible occurs in Psalm 19, "The heavens declare the glory of God." In those heavens, the Psalmist says in the King James Version, God

> hath set a tabernacle for the sun,
> which is as a bridegroom coming out of his chamber,
> and rejoiceth as a strong man to run a race.

Let us pause over the first of the sun metaphors[8] only long enough to note how positively its sexual element characterizes the sun—and how it sets up the second metaphor, the one we are interested in.

The sun rises like a bridegroom—young, lusty, vigorous—and proceeds to run its course across the sky. Now although the King James translators

---

[8]Technically these are similes, not metaphors, but for our purposes we can ignore that distinction.

may have loaded the dice here by their use of the word "race"—after all, the sun has no opponent in its daily journey—they seem to me to have captured the tone of the image just right—the sheer, glorious exultation of strong running. This is not conveyed so successfully by the Revised Standard Version's "and like a strong man runs its course with joy," though the New Oxford Annotated Bible's editors give us this helpful gloss: "The skies provide a track along which the sun, like an athlete, runs his daily course." The word in question means a well-trodden road or path, and thence track, course, or race, so the King James translation is legitimate, and it is certainly better poetry.

Another very explicit race image, though one considerably less exultant, occurs in Ecclesiastes 9:11—probably the best known sports reference in the Bible: "Again I say that under the sun the race is not to the swift, nor the battle to the strong, nor bread to the wise, nor riches to the intelligent, nor favor to the men of skill; but time and chance happen to them all." The image does not tell us much beyond the simple fact that Qoheleth (the "Preacher," the speaker of the book) knew about racing, but that fact at least demonstrates the existence of competitive, sport running in his time— unfortunately uncertain; guesses range from 10th to 3rd century B.C.E.

Finally, Jeremiah 12:5 gives us a very clear racing image: "If you have raced with men on foot, and they have wearied you, how will you compete with horses?" The significance, then, of these three passages is that, unlike the dozens of other Biblical references to running, including the "Jewish Marathon," the Aphek-to-Shiloh run of I Sam. 4:12, they refer not to military or postal or other utilitarian running, but to competitive, sport running.

Two other running images, one a casual metaphor and one an actual depiction, are more ambiguous: they may refer to sport running or to utilitarian running. The metaphor is at Job 9:25: "My days are swifter than a runner; they flee away, they see no good." One would like to see this as an athletic image, but King James is probably closer to the mark in giving "swifter than a post," (i.e., a messenger). The other case is definitely a utilitarian one of message-carrying, but one detail suggests something beyond merely that. In II Sam. 18:19-27 a young man, Ahimaaz, volunteers to take back to David the news of his army's victory over his rebellious son Absalom. Joab chooses another messenger instead, but Ahimaaz takes off anyway, overtakes Joab's choice, and is spotted in the lead by David's watchman, who announces one and then the other runner approaching: "I think the running of the foremost is like the running of Ahimaaz the son of Zadok." Now this emphasis on the individual style of the runner may not prove anything, but it does seem to me characteristic of the way one discusses a runner rather than a postman. I must admit, however, that the Bible's only other reference to the style— or I should say ability—of an individual runner—"Now Asahel was as swift of foot as a wild gazelle" (II Sam. 2:18)—is in a specifically military context.

Some other sports more or less clearly indicated by casual metaphors include archery, hunting (with its siblings trapping and fishing), swimming, and there is even one reference to throwing a ball.

Most of the archery images are in the context of war, but a few seem to suggest target-shooting as a sport. Lamentations 3:12 and Job 16:12-13, for instance, emphasize shooting at a target, and I Sam. 20 gives an undoubtable picture of King Saul's son Jonathan practicing his archery. But is this really sport? II Sam. 22:35 (identical with Ps. 18:34) gives an image of "training" that suggests not:

> He [God] trains my hands for war,
> so that my arms can bend a bow of bronze.

This raises an interesting question, though: at what point does practicing a skill of war begin to become an interesting and pleasurable activity in and of itself? Wherever that point is, that is the point at which sport begins—the transition mentioned earlier in connection with tournaments.[9]

The same tricky question of where necessity ends and pleasure begins to predominate applies to hunting. Most of the hunting references in the Bible are to self-defense, i.e., killing an animal before it kills you (or your flocks), or to acquiring food. The one reference that seems to me to be to hunting as a sport is Job 39:18, and that is because it refers to hunting ostriches from horseback, an activity that seems so impractical it must be sport.

The one clear swimming image, Isaiah 25:11, does give a bit of detail about technique—"he will spread out his hands . . . as a swimmer spreads his hands to swim"—but the context is one of swimming for survival, not for sport.

And finally, the one ball image in the Bible, Isaiah 22:17-18: "Behold, the Lord will hurl you away violently, O you strong man. He will seize firm hold on you, and whirl you round and round, and throw you like a ball into a wide land. . . ." However suggestive this image may seem to us moderns whose greatest interest is in sports that use balls, it really does not tell us much more than that Isaiah was familiar with the throwing of round objects. And we must note, further, that the tone of the image is negative, even though the ballplayer is the Lord, for the thrust of the image is the Lord's rejection of those who aren't faithful to him.

---

[9]Although presented in a military context, a description of certain warriors in Judges 20:16 suggests that target practice with the sling may also have developed into a sport: *Among all these were seven hundred picked men who were left-handed; every one could sling a stone at a hair, and not miss.*

IV

From these few cases—three overt depictions, and about a dozen casual metaphors—and from the many additional instances I have ruled out because they are so clearly utilitarian, we learn that the ancient Hebrews were definitely not indifferent to physical qualities such as beauty, strength, swiftness, accuracy, etc. Biblical heroes as varied as Jacob, Saul, David and Samson, as well as many lesser lights, are favorably characterized as having such qualitites. And yet we still find that these qualities are vastly more likely to be seen in utilitarian contexts than in sporting ones. So once again we come to our initial question, why so few references to sport in the Bible?

My suggestion—and not a daringly new one at all, but one I am trying to argue a bit more carefully and thoroughly than has been done before— is that the Bible writers so thoroughly and totally associated sport with the ritual religious practices of the neighboring "pagan" peoples that they could not consider sport as a phenomenon separate from those practices.

Now, while I agree with Allen Guttmann that it is risky to argue a univocal theory of the origins of sport, it seems clear that *some* sporting activity has ritual origin. But what is less speculative is that sport, even those forms of it which seem clearly *not* to have had ritual origin—military-originated sports, for instance—frequently becomes very tightly associated with religion. We need only cast a quick glance at the literary and historical evidence from ancient Greece to confirm this association—the funeral games in the *Iliad,* for instance; the religious elements of the Olympian and other festival games, with their mythic origins, their ritual ceremonialism, sacrifices, etc., and their mythic celebration in the poems of Pindar.

I mention the Greeks not to argue any direct Greek influence, either positive or negative, over the ancient Hebrews—though tantalizing hints that the Philistines themselves were a Mycenaean people might incline us toward such an argument—but only as an example from a well-documented society of the close association of sport with religious ritual. Less clear and thorough, but almost equally certain evidence exists for this same kind of association among the Egyptians, Sumerians, Hittites, Minoans, etc.

And the one example that is immediately contiguous to the Hebrews *and* that is in the Bible itself is the Philistines and Samson's performing— "making sport"—for them; what I mentioned earlier as the only clear and certain depiction of a sporting event in the Bible. Let us go back and reexamine the episode.

Having revealed the secret of his strength to the wiles of Delilah, Samson has been shorn of same, blinded, and put to work at a mill in the prison— where, nobody seems to notice, his hair begins to grow again. But let the Bible itself tell the story:

> Now the lords of the Philistines gathered to offer a great sacrifice to Dagon their god, and to rejoice; for they said, "Our god has given Samson our enemy into our hand." And when the people saw him, they praised their god; for they said, "Our

god has given our enemy into our hand, the ravager of our country, who has slain many of us." And when their hearts were merry, they said, "Call Samson, that he may make sport for us." So they called Samson out of the prison, and he made sport before them. They made him stand between the pillars; and Samson said to the lad who held him by the hand, "Let me feel the pillars on which the house rests, that I may lean against them." Now the house was full of men and women; all the lords of the Philistines were there, and on the roof there were about three thousand men and women, who looked on while Samson made sport.

Our previous examination of this scene has established with relative certainty that we have here the depiction of some sort of sporting activity, performed as a public spectacle, and as part of a "pagan" religious festival.

Although in their usual reticent style the Bible writers do not editorialize here, their view is clear. *This* sporting event, at least, is an abomination. Even the fact that there are "men and women" there may be part of the writers' negative presentation of the scene—note how they repeat the phrase "men and women"—an unusual phrase itself in Biblical writing; and such repetition is usually significant in some way. The presence of women—might we imagine Samson the athlete as nude?—makes the event even more disgraceful.

Lest I be charged with basing too much of my argument on one isolated case, let me now turn to a more general way of looking at this issue. We know that the ancient Hebrews—their leaders, at least, and their scripture writers—tried to emphasize their differences from other people, both by rejecting (or trying to reject) certain customs and practices of those other people, and by creating unique customs of their own. The famous dietary laws are an obvious example. Another is I Samuel's treating the institution of kingship negatively. Against the good advice of Samuel (speaking for God) that they do not need a king because they already have one in God himself, the people say, "No, but we will have a king over us, that we also may be like all the nations, and that our king may govern us and go out before us and fight our battles" (8:19-20). "That we also may be like all the nations"— a big mistake—the chosen people are not supposed to be like other nations. In choosing to be like the nations by having an earthly king, the people are rejecting God, as he himself specifically says in 8:7. And in their dismal history of the kings, with very few exceptions such as David, the Bible writers show us how God punished the people for their decision.

Even more to the point for our issue, perhaps, is the Hebrews' rejection of the visual arts. Of course it was the association of the visual arts with pagan religion that caused their rejection—of that there is no doubt. Is it too farfetched to see a parallel between the arts and sport, and thus a parallel rejection of sport for the same reason?

And despite the *official* rejection of the visual arts, both the Bible itself and archeological evidence show us that the ancient Hebrews did have *some* visual art, however negatively the Bible writers themselves viewed it. Might not the same have been true of sport?

Furthermore, we come to the fact that ritual itself—even appropriate ritual devoted to the true God—was often criticized by the Bible writers, especially when they detected a tendency of the people to substitute ritual for that which it symbolized:

> Hear the word of the Lord,
>   you rulers of Sodom!
> Give ear to the teaching of our God,
>   you people of Gomorrah!
> "What to me is the multitude of your sacrifices?
>   says the Lord;
> I have had enough of burnt offerings of rams
>   and the fat of fed beasts;
> I do not delight in the blood of bulls,
>   or of lambs, or of he-goats.
> When you come to appear before me,
>   who requires of you
>   this trampling of my courts?
> Bring no more vain offerings;
>   incense is an abomination to me.
> New moon and sabbath and the calling of assemblies—
>   I cannot endure iniquity and solemn assembly.
> Your new moons and your appointed feasts
>   my soul hates;
> they have become a burden to me,
>   I am weary of bearing them.
> When you spread forth your hands,
>   I will hide my eyes from you;
> even though you make many prayers,
>   I will not listen;
>   your hands are full of blood.
> Wash yourselves; make yourselves clean;
>   remove the evil of your doings
>   from before my eyes;
> cease to do evil,
>   learn to do good;
> seek justice,
>   correct oppression;
> defend the fatherless,
>   plead for the widow."

(Isaiah 1:10-17)

If even Temple ritual itself could be viewed so negatively, how much more so any ritual activity that smacked of paganism. Finally, we can note that we have evidence for exactly this kind of rejection of sport by the Jews of later times, the times of the Maccabees (second century B.C.E.), because of the close identification of sport with Greek culture; although we can at the same time note that this rejection was not entirely successful, as Greek cultural ways began to exert a strong influence on Jewish customs.[10]

We have seen, then, that the Bible has little to say about sport. But what it does have to say offers tantalizing hints of more. We can conclude with near certainty that wrestling and perhaps other combat-type sports were known, Jacob and Samson being our best examples. Sport running, racing, was clearly a part of ancient Israelite society, and perhaps also sport swimming and hunting, as well as archery and other contests of target-shooting. Possibly there was even ball playing, though the fact that the one ball-playing image is a negative one (see above, p. 225) should serve as a warning against exaggerated claims for the role of sport in ancient Israel.

Our examination of the possible reasons why the Bible writers minimized that role, however, suggests at least the possibility that the few references to sport in the Old Testament perhaps *can* be taken as indications of a greater role for sport in Israel. But that "perhaps" can only be a "perhaps"; we must avoid dogmatism, and remain modest and tentative in our conclusions, lest we incur the wrath of that Greatest Ballplayer of them all.[11]

---

[10]See Harris's work, note 3 above.

[11] The best warning against exaggerated claims on our subject is Lämmer's article mentioned above, note 2. Possibilities for future research seem to me to lie not in further literary or philological analysis of the biblical text itself, nor in the archaeology of Israel—though neither of these resources should be forsaken—but in comparative study of the neighboring contemporaneous cultures (Egyptians, Babylonians, etc.). Professor Uriel Simri of the Wingate Institute for Physical Education and Sport in Netanya, Israel, has been a leader in this area; see the various publications of the Institute.

25

Combat and Contest: Athletic Metaphors for Warfare in Greek Literature

Thomas F. Scanlon

BILL COSBY IN ONE OF HIS CLASSIC ROUTINES called "Toss of the Coin" hypothesizes on what might have happened if at the outset of the American Revolutionary War the conditions of warfare had been determined by a simple toss of the coin, just as the initial kicking and receiving teams are determined in football games. The Americans win the toss, of course, and are allowed to hide behind rocks and trees and wear dark clothes, while the British are made to stand in rigid lines and wear bright red jackets. War is made more familiar and comprehensible by analogy with a game; the element of chance is formalized and the scales are tipped from the start; fixed rules determine the parameters of the fighting. What may be the greatest oxymoron is that war is made humorous and whimsical; like a game, it lacks the deadly seriousness of real war.

Whatever the distortions of comedy, Cosby's joke reminds us of the analogy between combat and contest, war and game, which had been inherent in the literature of all nations and ages. The present study aims to examine the agonistic metaphor for warfare in Greek literature, not as a purely literary phenomenon, but as a real expression of a mode of thought in Greek society of the eighth to fourth centuries B.C. From the time of Homer to that of Plato, athletics emerged as a dominant form of popular culture, seen most clearly in the early centuries of the Olympics, and as a cultural medium it both affected and reflected popular modes of thought.[1] Specifically, the athletic metaphor for military combat provided a facile schema, somewhat accurate

---

[1] The periods covered in this survey are those traditionally called the Archaic and Classical Ages, i.e. from 776 B.C., the traditional date of the founding of the Olympics, until 323 B.C., the death of Alexander the Great. Dates for Homer vary, but generally mid to late eighth century is cited, and Plato's dates are c. 429-347 B.C. The period under discussion encompasses the time when athletics developed, spread, and more or less reached a mature form of presentation in festivals which endured until the late Roman empire.

but oversimplified, for the Greek way of thought about war. This is not insignificant since for the Greeks peace was an aberration and war was the normal state of affairs.

In his thought-provoking chapter of *Homo Ludens* entitled "War and Play," Huizinga speculates on how far war is an agonistic function of society, i.e. to what extent does it spring from the same human impulse to play and compete.[2] It is true that war has many non-agonistic aspects in its darker forms: surprise attacks, punitive expeditions, ambushes, raids, and wholesale extermination. Similarly, of course, the political objectives of war are extra-agonistic: conquest, subjugation, and domination of a people. Agonistic contests are played out for no direct, immediate political gain, despite the many indirect and long-term political motives for some sports. And a true contest, a good match, is held when both antagonists are relatively evenly matched and the rules are obeyed.

Yet, as Huizinga points out, in archaic thought war came to share many aspects of athletics. Both war and play became a test of the will of the gods since both were bound up with chance, fate, and divine volition. The "might" of superiority of the gods grants the "right" of justice to the victor in agonistic, political, legal, or religious dispute. As war became ennobled, the warrior became heroized. War was played out more or less in conformity with the ideal of it being a sacred duty and an honorable action. The warrior-hero adopted a chivalrous code, a set of rules whereby it became easy to envision war as a noble game in which enemies exchanged civilities. The Geneva Convention is the most obvious modern institutionalization of this chivalrous code, but it can be seen in Western society as early as Homer, where Glaukos and Diomedes cease fighting and exchange armor on the Trojan battlefield when they discover their ancestral ties of guest-friendship (Il. 6. 119-236). Not to mention conventions of truces to bury one's dead also customary since Homeric times.[3] The sense of rules derives from an unwritten, inherent sense

---

[2] J. Huizinga, *Homo Ludens: A Study of the Play-element in Culture* (Boston: Beacon Press, 1955) Chapter V, "War and Play," pp. 89-104.

[3] It is true that this "separate peace" between the Glaukos and Diomedes is a rare gesture in the midst of Homeric warfare, but it does illustrate the higher importance of certain Greek values, notably guest-friendship *philoxenia*, (cf. *xeinos philos*, "guest-friend," used to describe Diomedes in relation to Glaukos). That values such as this can override the normal battle ethic of fighting bitterly and to the death against the enemy is noteworthy in view of similarly strong, overriding values which can soften or even curtail the normally fierce competition in athletic contests in Homer. For burial truces among enemies, cf., for example, Achilles' permission for Priam and the Trojans to bury Hector (*Iliad* 24.659-804) and instances of burial truces in the Peloponnesian War of the fifth century [Thucydides 2.34-46, 4.99 and A.W. Gomme, *A Historical Commentary on Thucydides* Vols. 2 and 3 (Oxford: Clarendon Press, 1956) on the above passages]. It is uncertain whether such pauses in battle for burying fallen heroes have any historical relation to the "sacred truces" proclaimed for athletic festivals, but it is clear that such a relation existed in the realm of myth, as evidenced by the funeral games for Patroclus in *Iliad* 23 which take place during a lull in the battle, and by funeral games for other legendary figures. Cf. I. Weiler *Der Agon im Mythos* (Darmstadt Wissenschaftliche Buchgesellschaft, 1974) *passim*: see 'Leichenspiele' in index.

of honor which pervades both warfare and play in Western society. Certainly violations occur, but it is the overriding survival of codes of "the law of nations," "human rights," "chivalry," or whatever else it may be called, which distinguishes the ennobled and civilized form of warfare, which has supposedly evolved in our society, from a primitive, anarchistic war. Despicable as war is and has always been, it is controlled, not encouraged, by the formalization of rules. Huizinga would argue that the rules of war and the rules of play spring from essentially the same human well of our agonistic nature; or from our "selfish genes," as a social Darwinist might put it.

The Greek man has been called the agonal man, not because the Greeks were the only competitive race, but because they were the first and most obvious in Western culture.[4] Competition permeated all levels of Greek social activity: law courts, political elections, music contests of singing and playing, choral dance contests, dramatic competitions, and of course athletic contests. All of the above were developed by the Greeks in forms remarkably unchanged by later centuries of European peoples. The very Greek vision of life was polarized by strife, or *eris*, which Hesiod (*Works and Days* 11-26) tells us can be of the good sort, like wrestling with the soil or hunting wild animals, or the evil sort which greedily seeks to gain more wealth at another's expense. So wars and contests were a part of the fabric of Greek social interaction, but they were by nature neither good nor evil since their morality depended upon their context. Civil war was always a great evil; but interstate rivalries were justifiable as a necessarily destructive and violent means to an ultimately desirable end.[5] Most contests were welcome occasions, enforced relief in the form of religious festivals from the usual succession of toils (Thucydides 2.38.1, quoted below). But unfair competition, i.e. violation of set rules, was discouraged by strict penalties.

That games were separate from the normal course of events, that they occupied a special quality of time and place apart from the political and military regimen of society, and that they were therefore sacred activity associated by both spectators and participants with the patron gods, are all phenomena evident from the physical disassociation of Greek sports from ordinary society. This "disassociative aspect," as I will call it, or *Verfremdungsaffekt* as a German might call it, can be seen on a social level, a personal level, and on a religious level where the individual at the games is taken away from normal events. On a social level there are special costumes, or lack of them in most cases for participants, special venues (*stadion*, *hippodrome*, etc.), special prizes (valuable tripods or symbolic crowns), special rule-givers and rule- enforcers, special ranking of victors independent of birth

---

[4] I. Weiler, *Der Agon im Mythos: Zur Einstellung der Griechen zum Wettkampf*, Impulse der Forschung Band 16 (Darmstadt: Wissenschaftliche Buchgesellschaft, 1974) and ibid., *Der Sport bei den Volker der alten Welt* (Darmstadt: Wissenschaftliche Buchgesellschaft, 1981), has demonstrated with much cross-cultural, anthropological evidence that J. Burckhardt's charaterization of the Greeks as the "agonal race" is an inaccurate one. But history of the European peoples at least requires acknowledgement of the Greek's essential role in the genesis of our competitive Western society.

[5] Cf. G.E.M. de Ste Croix, *The Origins of the the Peloponnesian War* (London: Duckworth, 1972), 16.

or status in the external world, and the very special interaction between spectators as worshippers at a rite and athletes acting out a ritual.[6] On the religious level in early Greece, contests were set apart as part of a festival for gods and heroes. On the personal level participants sought renewal of their minds, bodies, and spirits through activity which produced both pleasure and pain, *ponos* and *terpsis.*

All of these qualities separate games from society, but more importantly there are a host of what I call *associative aspects* of contests which encourage our comparison of them with war. As one might expect, the martial and agonistic spheres have a vocabulary in common in Greek as they do in English. *Agon* and *Aethla*, the Greek terms for contest, can also, in certain contexts, mean war between states, between individuals, or any labor requiring physical or mental agony. Victory in games or war is *nike;* defeat is more often expressed as the passive form of the verb "to win," i.e. "to be beaten," but is the same for games and war. The actual form of Greek sports, especially the combat sports of boxing, wrestling, and pancration, strongly resemble primitive fighting and therefore share many descriptive terms. We may recall that the final contest of the ancient Olympics was the *hoplitodromos* or hoplite race, the "race in armour" in which runners wore a helmet and greaves and carried a hoplite warrior shield. Plutarch (*Moralia* 639e) informs us that "the race in armour is presented after all the rest of the athletic events, so testifying that military fitness is the aim of athletics and competition" (Loeb library translation). Cp. Philostratus, *Gymnastics.*[7]

A more direct and widely recognized associative tie which war shared with athletics was the fact that since about the sixth century B.C. Greek city states depended upon local gymnasia to furnish training for their native soldiers.[8] The efficacy of gymnastic exercise as preparation for warfare was

---

[6] The separative quality of athletics is seen in the etymology of the word "sport" from the Old French *desport* from Latin *deportare* meaning "to carry away," where the original sense of leisure activity is derived from the activity of removing oneself from daily chores. Cf. Erwin Mehl, "Sport kommt nicht von *dis-portare*, sondern von *de-portare,*" *Die Leibeserziehung* 15 (1967) 232-233. Separation from society in athletic contests may be related to the hypothesis held by some, that Greek athletics became allied to religious festivals through athletic "tests of strength" practiced as part of local initiation ceremonies for boys and girls. In such ceremonies, initiants were distinguished from others by certain practices such as separation from society, segregation of sexes, special diet and clothing, age groupings, and other activity which may have been formalized later in the training and competition of young athletes. Cf. A. Brelich *Le iniziazione, parte seconda* (Rome: Edizioni dell 'atena, 1962) 83-105; ibid. *Paides e Parthenoi,* Vol. I (Rome, 1969) 449-456; H. Jeanmaire *Couroi et Couretes* (Lille, 1939) 413-418.

[7] See my article, 'The Vocabulary of Competition: *Agon* and *Aethlos,* Greek Terms for Contest,' *Arete : The Journal of Sport Literature* 1.1 (1983): 147-162.

[8] H.W. Pleket 'Zur Soziologie des antiken Sports,' *Mededelingen van het Nederlands Instituut te Rome,* N.S.36 (1974) 62 on the importance of the institution of gymnasia as training centers for hoplites and as the beginnings of the democratization of sport in sixth century Greece. My debt to the careful collection of sources on the conduct of war by W.K. Pritchett, *The Greek State at War: Part II* (Berkeley and L.A.: University of California Press, 1974) and to the observation by A.J. Holladay, 'Hoplites and Heresies,' *Journal of Hellenic Studies* 102 (1982) 94-103 will be obvious throughout the following section of the paper. My use of their evidence in the present context is, to my knowledge, original. My thanks to Steven Lattimore for advice and encouragement on this and other sections of this study.

generally acknowledged by the Greeks of all periods. In a dialogue set in the sixth century B.C. but actually written in the second century A.D., Lucian puts the following words into the mouth of the Athenian statesman Solon: "That [athletics], Anacharsis, is the training we give our young men, expecting them to become stout guardians of our city and that we should live in freedom through them, conquering our foes if they attack us and keeping our neighbors in dread of us, so that most of them will cower at our feet and pay tribute" (*Anacharsis* 30; see other passages *passim*; Loeb tr.). Athenians had the *ephebeia* or youth organization which, prior to the mid-fourth century B.C., was probably a purely military training camp but later assumed the duties of physical and intellectual education, morals, and civic behavior. Athenian physical and military education in former times was largely a matter of individual responsiblity and not, as at Sparta, an obligation to the state from earliest youth (Cf. Thucydides 2.38-39). Spartan physical education, which made them renowned in war and athletics prior to 580 B.C., was built upon their insistance that coaches know all about military tactics since they considered the contests a preliminary training for war (Philostratus, *Gymnastics* 19). But when Spartan training ceased to be the best, they were defeated by the Boeotians in the disastrous battle of Leuctra in 371 B.C. The Boeotians, we are told by Xenophon (*Hellenica* 5.5.23), "delighted in the victory and all practiced athletics (*egymnazonto*) for military training." But what the fourth century Boeotians learned after the fact, the Thebans practiced in preparation for their great battle. When Alexander the Great attacked Thebes 335/4 B.C., the Macedonians were superior in numbers, "but the Thebans were superior in bodily strength and in their constant training in the gymnasium (*tois en tois gymnasiois synekhesin athlemasin*)" (Diodorus 17.11.4). It was also in the fourth century that Athens began to realize that her non-compulsory physical training of former days was proving ineffective; thus we observe the required training of the *ephebeia* and the warnings of Xenophon and others during this period: "Nor, because the city does not require warlike exercises publically, ought we, on that account, to neglect them privately, but rather to practice them the more; for be well assured that neither in any contest, nor in any affair whatever, will you come off the worse because your body is better trained" (Xenophon, *Memorabilia* 3.12.5, Pritchett, tr.). So Plato (*Republic* 3.404) recommends through Socrates: "Then, I said, a finer sort of training will be required for our warrior athletes who are to be like wakeful dogs, and to hear and see with utmost keenness. . . . I conceive that there is a gymnastic which, like our music, is simple and good; especially the military gymnastic . . ." (Jowett, tr.). This orientation to special exercises suited to military training is repeated in Plato *Laws* (832e) where it is recommended that: "The next step, then, is to remind ourselves with regard to gymnastic contests, that all such as afford training for war should be instituted, and should have prizes assigned them, but all that do not do so must be set aside" (R. G. Bury, tr.). Philopoemen of Megalopolis (ca. 253-182 B.C.) also realized the advantage of selective exercise for military training: "He aimed less at great strength than agility; for he thought the former was necessary for athletes, but the latter would be helpful in warfare. Accordingly he trained himself thoroughly in running and wrestling. . . ." (*Cornelius Nepos* 15.2.4-5, Dryden tr.). Boxers, we learn from Epeios of *Iliad* (23.665-670) and Boiskos of Xenophon's *Anabasis* (5.8.23), were typically poor soldiers, presumably because they lacked the agility necessary in front-line fighting. In Hellenistic times the Greeks acquired a sense that regular and even enforced athletic training was necessary to build a successful army, and that certain events were better preparation for combat than others.

Thus in the realm of training the assimilation of athletics and military affairs is total for the Greeks by the Hellenistic age although it has roots in Homeric or pre-Homeric times. The relationship is so complementary and the association so close in literary sources from Homer on that we cannot trace its origin, but we can observe the formal development of training systems for the warrior-athlete in historical times. There are other less obvious manifestations of the "associative aspect" of war and athletics in historical practice pertaining to the actual conduct of Greek warfare. Of the many topics which one might discuss, I will treat briefly the site of contest, the challenge to fight, discipline, the goal of the contest, victory monuments, and awards for bravery.

The typical Greek battle, like the athletic contest, was fought on a wide, open space despite the mountainous terrain which offered many chances for surprise attacks and ambuscades. The latter did occur, to be sure, but mostly after the late fifth century B.C.; hoplite battles from the late eighth century to mid-fifth century B.C. were usually conducted on an open space and by public challenge (see Pritchett [above note 8] vol. II, 156-189). The *locus classicus* for this practice is Herodotus (7.9) where the Persian Mardonius marvels at Greek military behavior: "And yet, I am told, these very Greeks are wont to wage wars against one another in the most foolish way, through sheer perversity and doltishness. For no sooner is war proclaimed than they search out the smoothest and fairest plain that is to be found in all the land, and there they assemble and fight; whence it comes to pass that even the conquerors depart with great loss; I say nothing of the conquered for they are destroyed altogether" (G. Rawlinson, tr.). Cf. also Polybius (13.3.2-7) on the absence of fraud and the custom of selecting a battle site among Greek peoples at war. In one remarkable instance the assimilation between battle site and contest site is total. Following the battle of Leuctra, Epaminondas, commander of the Theban forces, invades Sparta and on the third or fourth day of the invasion in 370 B.C. the cavalry advanced into the hippodrome by squadrons in order of state affiliation. The horsemen of the Spartans then arranged themselves against them, although inferior in number. The Spartans won the battle with the assistance of hoplites planted in ambush nearby. Xenophon's account in *Hellenica* (6.530-531), according to Pritchett (above note 8, vol. II, p. 150), "serves to illustrate the rules of the game which governed the marshalling of armies before ancient battle." It also illustrates how in warfare the odds can be overcome by breaking the rules by use of an ambush.

The arrangement of a site for battle also presumes a challenge to fight, just as entering an athletic contest presumed a challenge to competition. Similarly, a city's unwillingness to fight meant automatic victory to the challenger, just as the failure of opponents to meet the challenge of another athlete would give the victory to the challenger with the designation *akoniti* or "walkover." We may also note that taunts or insults to the enemy/athletic opponent were as common to the Greeks as they were to warriors and athletes of people throughout history: cp. the Persian insult to the Greeks, calling them "women," in Herodotus (9.20) (and Pritchett (above note 8) (vol. II, 153-5 for other examples) and Epeios' boast before boxing in *Iliad* (23.667-675).

"Good discipline" (*eutaxia*) was also an element common to both combat and contests among the Greeks. Xenophon *Anabasis* (3.1.38) reports that "good discipline seems to save men, but lack of discipline has already destroyed many." Victors in gymnastic contests were praised for their *eutaxia* in racing, boxing, etc. (e.g. *Inscriptiones Graecae* II².900) just as young soldiers were commended in inscriptions for their fighting with discipline (*eutaktōs*) while on patrol (*IG* II² 1011.15; C. Pelekidis, *Histoire de l'ephébie attique* (Paris, 1972) 38, 181, 272 and Pritchett above, note 8 Vol. II, 238). Punishment for laxity of discipline (*ataxia*) or insubordination included penalties of being cashiered, fined, or flogged by their commander (Xenophon, *Anabasis* 2.3.11); so athletes were punished by judges with fines, flogging or elimination from the contest (C.A. Forbes, "Crime and Punishment in Greek Athletics," *Classical Philology* 47 (1951-52) 169-173, 202).

Battles, like contests, were conducted with a single goal in mind among the Greeks: absolute victory. There were usually no second places in the games, certainly never at Olympia; rematches, terms of compromise, and ties were equally rare in games and war. Most battles and contests were quick and unambiguous in outcome.

The Homeric victor, athletic or military, sought the honor of victory for himself and, secondarily, for the reflected glory of kin and comrades. But with the advent of the *polis* (ca. 700 B.C.) the community shared the glory and joined in honoring its athletic sons with prizes, monuments, songs, and other privileges. The *polis* also honored military victors as a group and as individuals for their valor, sometimes even with material prizes (*athla*; cf. Polyainos 3.9.31). Plato *Laws* (12.943c) prescribes a wreath of olive leaves as a prize of merit for military assemblies and suggests that it be hung with an honorific inscription on the temple of a war-god of their choice. Plato *Republic* (5.468b) similarly recommends that someone who shows bravery in a campaign should be crowned by the boys and youths in turn.

The practice of awards for military valor shows influence from athletic practice. But the conduct of war according to discipline, by challenge, and on an open battle ground may resemble athletics more because of the similar nature of the two phenomena than direct influence of one upon the other. But all of the similarities, taken together, show that the "associative aspects" of war and games are united by the essentially agonal spirit of the Greeks throughout their history.

With regard to Greek literature, the most profitable source for examining the cross-fertilization between athletics and warfare is the metaphorical allusions to games in military contexts and to military concepts in agonistic descriptions. Homer is the natural place to begin our investigation of the metaphorical aspects. In the eighth century B.C. poet's world view the "heroic ethic" prevailed by which the individual hero sought imperishable fame by exercise of his virtue: in war or contest the value of his fame was directly tied to the real or symbolic value of his prizes and the rank of his opponents. The greater the stakes, the greater the potential fame. This ethic was thus common to the hero in peace or war. The extent of his fame depended on the quality of his existence, a fact which ultimately caused Achilles in the *Iliad* to choose a short and glorious life over a long and undistinguished one.

The most famous games in Homer are the Funeral Games of Patroclus, *Iliad* 23, and they include a chariot race, boxing match, wrestling, footrace, armed duel, throwing of the *solos* weight, archery, and javelin throwing. In the context of what is essentially an epic of war, it is remarkable that an entire book is devoted to the peaceful activity of funeral games. A partial explanation may lie in the fact that "Homer," or whoever was responsible for putting the epic in writing, probably lived in the mid-to-late eighth century, just after the reorganization of the Olympic games and during the period in which the athletic festival became popular throughout Greece. A panhellenic athletic festival would have been a popular topic, and what better place to enshrine the athletic tradition than within *the* Panhellenic epic, the *Iliad.* But this is only a social explanation.

Homer, first and foremost a poet, had poetic reasons for inclusion of the Funeral Games: the entire episode is a metaphor for the proper conduct of war. Homer exploits the "associative aspects" shared by games and war. Achilles, as the games' sponsor, plays the role of the fair and equitable prize-giver, analogous to the wise general, or perhaps even the overseer god, in a context of real war. The conduct of the competitors is also exemplary, especially with regard to the receiving of prizes. This is not incidental—or accidental—since you will recall the epic begins with Achilles' being deprived of his prize in battle by an imperious King Agamemnon. Unwritten codes of behavior in war and in games must be upheld. Note also that in the chariot race Antilochus, as junior participant, cedes his prize to the more deserving senior competitor, Menelaus, whom he had tripped in the race. Menelaus give the prize back out of a sense of generosity, however, and heroic magnaminity is preserved.[9] Likewise in boxing when Epeios helps his defeated

---

[9] In terms of Greek morality, Menelaus sought to restore the divine right or justice (*themis,* 581) of his claim to heroic excellence (*areten,* 571) since Antilochus admits the use of trickery (*dolo,* 585) in the race. *Themis* is a complex social term which includes custom, tradition, folkways, and *mores* whereby justice was determined between groups and individuals. Cf. M.I. Finley, *The World of Odysseus* (N.Y.: Viking, 1965) 83-84, 106-107, and esp. 114-120.

colleague Eurylaos off the ground after his defeat, there is again a sense of magnaminity.[10] The armed duel is cut short when the opponents come near to spilling blood. Games are to be violent and competitive, but they are to stop short of bloodshed, which is reserved for true warfare. The Greek verb *makhesthai*, "to battle," occurs 258 times in all of Homer, mostly in the context of warfare with 11 exceptions, two of which occur in the Funeral Games, once with reference to boxing, and once to the armed duel.[11] These two events are in essence closest to pure warfare, yet the game spirit is preserved even in the armed duel by avoiding bloodshed. Even though the armed duel may well be a later interpolation, like boxing and the chariot race, it shows that certain Greek values, at least in the idealized world of epic, override the desire for complete victory at any cost and without mitigation.

Is the avoidance of bloodshed and violence the dividing line between war and sport? Not really, if we can include blood-sports, such as the Roman gladiatorial games, in the category of real sport. They are unusual contests, true, and even loathsome to Judaeo-Christian society, but to the Romans, and to the Greeks, as the very existence of the armed duel suggests, not all human life was so sacred as to discourage *risking* one's life in certain contests. I would like to suggest that such sports, for the Greeks at least, were truly sporting since the challenge was not to actually kill others, but in noble fashion to stop short of killing and show mercy when the killing is not necessary.[12] The carnage of war provided bloodshed enough, at least in the context of the *Iliad*, and so the duel ends peacefully.

Just prior to the Funeral Games, Homer artfully prepares us for the game atmosphere and reminds us of the "disassociative aspect," of the sharp distinction between contests played for prizes and combat for one's life. The context is Achilles' chasing of Hector around the walls of Troy in the final pursuit before the Trojan is caught and slain:

> In front a good man fled, but a far better one pursued
> Swiftly; for it was not a sacrificial beast of bull's
> Hide, which are prizes for men's feet,
> But for the life of horse-taming Hector they ran.
> As when about the turnposts racing single-hoofed horses

---

[10] Epeios is called "great-hearted" or 'magnanimous' (*megathumos*, 694) just as Menelaus sought to show 'that the heart *thumos* is never arrogant nor stubborn within me' (611) in his treatment of Antilochus in the chariot race.

[11] Cf. *Il.* 23.670 where "battle" is applied to boxing and 23.814 where it is used for the armed duel. In general for a treatment of *makhesthai* and other battle terms in Homer see H. Trumpy *Kriegerische Fachausdrucke im griechischen Epos: Untersuchungen zum Wortschatze* (Basel: Publisher unknown, 1950).

[12] Another exceptional example which illustrates the normal Greek aversion to extreme violence and death in athletic competition is the story of Kreugas and Damoxenos in which the latter kills the former in a boxing match, yet the decision is given to Kreugas posthumously. The alleged grounds are that Damoxenos committed a technical foul (i.e. a straight-handed jab when only a punch was allowed), but the obvious sympathy here, as in the story of Arrachion's posthumous victory in pankration, is with the victim of excessive violence. Cf. Paus. 8 40.1-5, translated by S.G. Miller, *Arete* (Chicago: Ares, 1979) 27-28.

Run at full speed, when a great prize is laid up for their winning,
A tripod of a woman, in games for a man's funeral,
So these two swept whirling about the city of Priam
In the speed of their feet, while all the gods were looking upon them.

Il. 22.158-166

You will recall that the heroic ethic was to seek imperishable fame, and that the value of the fame was measured according to the value of the prize, in war or in contests. So Hector ran for his own soul and lost; Achilles for the prize of Hector, son of Trojan King Priam, and the mightiest of the Trojan warriors. His defeat of Hector was the symbolic defeat of Troy itself, although the actual sack of Troy takes place outside the purview of the epic. The audience undertands that Achilles has won his imperishable fame by his instrumental role, even though he did it at the cost of the length of his own life: Achilles dies before the end of the war and never sees old age in Thessaly. The immediate prize of a man's life, the ultimate prize of a city, and the unfortunate consequences for Achilles distinguish this duel from the ordinary contest. But the heroic excellence of Achilles essentially resembles that of the athletic hero. The magnitude of Achilles' valor is primarily a testimony to his own heroic prowess, as Homer tells that story. Achilles' heroism is that of an individual, prideful champion who sits out of battle for personal reasons and only joins it again for personal vengeance against the slayer of his best friend. His heroism is not altruistic and patriotic by any means. This also holds true for the conduct of the heroes in the Funeral Games: each primarily seeks individual glory, even though the incidental result is to give glory to the deceased hero and to the victor's family and colleagues.

The true measure of Achilles' heroism may be seen in the *Odyssey* where, in Book 24 set in the underworld, we witness a conversation of the recently dead Agamemnon with Achilles who has been in Hades for several years. In an earlier book (*Il.* 489-491) Achilles had told Odysseus that "It is better to break sod as a farm hand for some poor country man on iron rations than lord it over all the exhausted dead." Yet Achilles chose to die young, and Agamemnon, in the later passage, tells him of the festivities in his honor during his funeral games:

But your mother asked the gods and put out very beautiful prizes,
In the midst of the assembly for the best of Achaeans.
Already you have been present at the funeral games of many
Heroes, when at the death of a king,
The young men gird themselves and get ready for contests,
But if you would have seen those very beautiful prizes,
Which your mother, silver-footed Thetis, put out for you,
You would have indeed marvelled. For you were very dear to the gods.
Thus in dying you do not perish in name, but for you
There will be always among all men fair fame, Achilles

Il. 24.85-94.

The gods have ennobled the hero's death by giving him fame through games and prizes. The victors in the games also win prizes and get a share in heroic victory, albeit somewhat less than the battle hero's. The Homeric, heroic ethic is contractual and formulaic. It requires participation of the gods to endow the contest or combat with a sense of ultimate justice and sanctification. The reward is fame, the only share in immortality an ordinary mortal can hope to win. Yet the system, primitive as it may seem to us, preserved a sense of "law of the nations" which lifted Greek civilization to a higher plane than primitive anarchic violence with real aim.

Homeric contests were not all that grim and serious, since an essential ingredient was delight, Greek *terpsis*. Here is another clear difference between war and games. Pindar reminds the athlete that "for what hard works there was, the joy that follows is greater" (Nemean 7.74).[13] The levity accompanied the festival atmosphere of games, even funeral games, and shed over all the physical toil a liberating sense of holiday. The Homeric Hymn to Apollo (3.150) reports of the games of Delos: "Mindful they delight *terpousin* (in boxing and dancing) whenever they hold a contest." Odysseus (*Od.* 8.131) tells of the universal joy in competition by the island Phaiacians after their games in his honor: "But when they had all delighted in their hearts in the contest . . . " *(eterphthesan)*. And even the suitors at Odysseus' palace were in the habit of playing near the house. So Medon calls to the other suitors after they end their discus- and javelin-throwing in front of the palace:

> Youths, since you have all taken delight at heart in
> The contests, come to the house that we might prepare a feast.
>
> *Od.* 17. 174-175 (-4.625-627)

Little do they realize that this supper after the games will be their last. Penelope invites them to the contest of the bow, the winner to get her hand in marriage. But Odysseus turns the bow on the suitors and the contest becomes a combat. Blood is shed and the battle is joined in earnest as Odysseus is threatened by the suitors:

> Stranger, evilly do you shoot at men; never in other contests *(aethlon)*
> Shall you partake; now is certain your utter destruction *(olethros)*.

The contrast between games and a deadly fight is pointed by the word play in Greek at line ends, "contest" being *aethlon,* "destruction," *olethros.* The line is crossed between contest and combat, but not necessarily because men are killed, since we have seen that men can be deliberately killed in blood sport, but because the mood shifts from delight to deadly seriousness, and the aim of the game shifts from winning the bride by the rules to an extra-agonistic motive, a political goal of recapturing one's own palace and exterminating the interlopers.

During the archaic age following Homer (i.e. during the seventh to sixth centuries) Greek literature became more personal, and lyric or choral poetry on personal or local themes became the subject of songs composed for public

---

[13] Alicja Szastynska-Siemien, 'Le *ponos* du sportif dans l'epinice grec,' in *Acta Conventus XI 'Eirene,'* 21-25 Oct. 1968 (Warsaw, 1971) C. Kumaniscki, ed., pages 81-85, discussed the element of toil in Greek athletic victory hymns.

performance or for drinking parties. Comparisons of athletic and military excellence continue and, although there are changes in the heroic ethic, athletic heroism comes in second best, as it did in Homer.[14] One noteworthy figure relevant to our theme is the Spartan poet Tyrtaeus who lived during the second half of the seventh century B.C. Sparta was rising to the pinnacle of its military and cultural success. And its highly socialistic system of government required total devotion of oneself to the state—in body, mind, and spirit. So the heroic ethic shifted from the winning of fame for oneself to winning it for one's state of *polis*. The Spartan ideal of heroism was that man was not a single champion of his own fate, but fighting for the state, although, as the following poem tells us, one could putatively recognize other, lesser forms of honor:

> I would not say anything for a man nor take account of him
> For any excellence of his feet or wrestling he might have
> Not if he had the size of a Cyclops and strength to go with it,
> Not if he could outrun Boreas, the North wind of Thrace
> Not if he had all splendors except for a fighting spirit.
> For no man ever proves himself a good man in war
> Unless he can endure to face the blood and the slaughter
> Go close against the enemy and fight with his hands
> Here is courage, mankind's finest possession, here is
> The noblest prize that a young man can endeavour to win.
>
> *Tyrtaeus* 9.1-4, 9-14 (Diehl; Lattimore, tr.)

Nowhere in Greek literature are the ethics of the athletic and the military hero more directly contrasted. It is perhaps significant that during the period in which this poem was written Spartans were dominant as victors at the Olympic games, and remained so as long as they were at their acme of culture and their military might. For almost a century and a half, from 720 to 580 B.C., 43 of the 75 known Olympic victors were Spartans.[15] But with the advent of more specially trained athletes and fewer victors who had been trained primarily as soldiers, Sparta's prestige at the Olympic games declined in the late sixth and early fifth centuries.

That athletic prowess need not be an accurate indication of military might can be seen in the case of fifth century Athens who won but eight of the two hundred and one victors in the Olympics during that century, yet Athens in that same period came to rule an empire of unparalleled strength among Greeks prior to Alexander.[16] Nevertheless Athenian society often acknowledged

---

[14] Cf. most recently D.A. Campbell, *The Golden Lyre: The Themes of the Greek Lyric Poets* (London: Duckworth, 1983), chapter 3, 'Athletics,' pp. 54-83.

[15] L. Moretti, *Olympionikai, I Vincitori negli antichi Agoni Olympici* (Rome: Edizioni dell 'atena, 1957) pp. 62-69, nos. 17-19. See "Sparta" in Moretti's index for references to the 43 Spartan victors. See also Pritchett (above, note 8) vol. II, 209 and 218 n. 39 for alternate reasons for the dearth of Spartan victors.

[16] Cf. Moretti (above, note 15), nos. 242, 295, 247, 162, 275(?), 320, 345, and 357 for the names, contests, and source information regarding known Athenian Olympic victors from 496-400 B.C. Athens was at her political military acme from about 478 to 404 B.C. For further documentation see D. Kyle, *A Historical Study of Athletics in Ancient Athens* (Ph.D. diss., McMaster, 1981), DA 42.9, 4101-A.

the importance of athletic heroism, as is apparent from her art and literature. Athenians could follow the ideals of athletic excellence without real success in the panhellenic contests and apply those ideals to their unquestionably superior might. We can observe the natural association of warfare and athletics in the language and in the metaphors of classical Greek literature.

Early in the fifth century the meaning of the most common Greek word for contest, *agon*, wandered from its strict application to games to other related spheres of competition, including contests in war, contests in a court of law, other rhetorical contests, and metaphorical contests including struggles of the mind and the emotions. That there could be a confusion in ambiguous contexts regarding which kind of *agon* was meant is illustrated by a story from Herodotus (9.33) about a certain Tisamenus of Elis who, during the Persian War, consulted the Pythian oracle at Delphi and learned that he would win five *agonas*, which he took to mean athletic contests, specifically the pentathlon. So he trained rigorously and entered the Olympics, but lost the crown by a single fall in wrestling. The Spartans immediately reinterpreted the oracle to mean that he would win in five great military contests, and so sought to hire Tisamenus as a mercenary. He joined their ranks as honorary citizen and fought in five major, and successful, battles (cf. 8.142.2 where *agon* refers to the entire conflict between Persia and Greece).

The great Athenian historian of the Peloponnesian war, Thucydides, recounted the glories of the golden age of Athens in his famous Funeral Oration of the statesman Pericles. Among the Athenian achievements is their ability to relax from work well done: "We provide for the mind very many occasions for recreation from toils, since we customarily hold games and sacrifices year round, and we enjoy fine private luxuries, the daily delight *(terpsis)* in which drives away grief" (Thuc. 2.38.1). As in Homer's day, there is a recognition of the vital joy of competition which characterized the Greek spirit at its peaceful best. Yet Thucydides sees the inherent danger in mistaking contests without consequence from actual combat which decides the fate of states. Another statesman in his history, Cleon, denounces the deceptive, contest-like atmosphere in public debate on important issue (keep in mind that there were oratorical contests held for the sport of it in that time): "In such contests (of rhetoric) the state gives the rewards *(athla)* to others, and takes the dangers for herself. You who wrongly establish such contests *(kakos agonothetes)* are the guilty, you who are accustomed to become spectators of arguments, hearers of the facts examining future deeds and their feasibility from what is finely spoken, and looking at past deeds, and accepting as more trustworthy what you hear very cleverly argued than what you have seen happen with your own eyes" (3.38.3-4; cp. 3.40.4). In another debate, the Spartans are urged to take action against her foes and not merely to threaten them: "Offer an example to the Greeks that the contests to which you invite them are of deeds, not just words" (3.67.6, Thebans to Spartans revengeance on Plataeans). The distinction is to be made between ineffectual games, and real battle for high stakes.

Again in Pericles' famous speech on Athens, there is a comment on the seriousness of the present war since Athens itself, a city of high cultural distinction, is at stake in the games: "If I have dwelt at some length on the character of the city, it is to show that the contest is not for the same stakes *(peri isou)* for us as for those who have nothing to lose" (2.42.1). The metaphorical image of a war being for certain "stakes" is common in fifth century literature, historical and other, since it clearly illustrates in a simple image, the end price for the toil of the fight [cp. 1.73.3, Athenian to Spartan Assembly (re) Athens as formidable opponents in contest (Hdt. 8.3.2, 8.15.2. 8.108.4, 8.142.2; Thuc. 5.9.10, 6.34.4, 6.68.3, etc.)].[17] It reminds us of Homer's image of Achilles racing with Hector's soul at stake. Another clear example comes in Thucydides' report of the speech of the Athenian general Nicias before the climactic battle in Sicily when he tells his troops "Soldiers of the Athenians and of the allies, we have all an equal stake in the coming contest, in which salvation and the fatherland are at stake as much for us as for the enemy" (7.61.1). Most of these metaphorical references to war as contest concern battles in which the opponents are more or less evenly matched, and there is a fair chance for both antagonists. Pindar reminds us that the rewards for athletes and warriors are the same: "He who in contests or in war achieves the delicate glory is magnified to be given the supreme prize, splendor of speech from citizen and stranger" *(Isthmian* 1.51-53). But when there is not an even match, as often happens in war, there can be no real game. Like an unevenly matched sporting event, the victory is a walkover. So the Athenians warn a weak opponent: "You will not resist us, if you are well advised. Since the contest is not on equal terms for you with honor as the prize and shame the penalty, but it is a question of self-preservation, not to resist those who are much stronger" (5.101). "Might makes right" is a perhaps unfair reapplication of contest morality to war and politics by the Athenian since the restraint on the part of the stronger, traditional in war but alien to athletics, is ignored.

Perhaps a more positive metaphor for contest is seen in its application to life in the sense in which the apostle Paul said "I have fought the good fight, I have won the race." Thucydides' report of Pericles' oration alludes to the contest we face in life to live up to the reputation of those who have died heroically in battle (2.45.1). The metaphor occurs at the climactic end of the oration when Pericles puts the challenge to his fellow citizens that they rule the city during the present war with excellence equal to those war heroes metaphorically crowned by their death in battle:

> Those interred here have received part of their honors already; for the other part the city will rear their children at public expense up till manhood. This is a valuable crown *(stephanon)* which the state offers for those left behind in these contests *(agonon)*. For those whom the prizes *(athla)* of excellence *(aretes)* are greatest, the best men serve as citizens. (2.46.1)

---

[17] Cf. J.D. Ellsworth, *Agon: Studies in the Use of a Word* (Ph.D. diss., Univ. of Calif. Berkeley, 1971) p. 69, gives numerous references to the metaphorical use of "stakes" in a contest.

In a sense the whole Peloponnesian war between Athens and Sparta becomes framed in an agonistic metaphor for the historian Thucydides. These are two great antagonists, high stakes of honor and material prizes, and an equal match of power which makes for a good contest. Tragic violations for the heroic code of warfare and competition are deplored in the war when peoples are exterminated, and the innocent or poorly matched die. Yet it is the intrinsic excellence of the competitor, Athens, at her peak of power which merits the prizes of excellence because of the character of her free and democratic city. At this point in Greek literature the athletic metaphor for warfare which we first saw in Homer three hundred years earlier is so far abstracted from direct relation to real sporting competition as to suggest that the metaphor has become a mode of thought, more than a cliche, and agonistic vision of the life-and-death struggles of war deeply embedded in the Greek psyche. Plato some fifty years later takes the abstraction to its final step when he refers to the philosophers trained for his ideal state as "athletes of war," and "athletes for the greatest contest" (*Republic* 543.b 8-9, 403 e 8-9; cp. *Laws* 182 a 2-3, 830 a 2).

We may conclude that Plato, like Thucydides and Homer, was aware of the unique and valuable pragmatic contribution of athletics to recreation of the body and spirit. Athletics not only trained men for war and public service, it released them from their daily tedium by affording delightful diversions. Greek authors from Homer on were also aware that the popular athletic contests provided a powerful and easily accessible metaphor for the conduct and the stakes of warfare. Greek literature constantly reminded the people of the similarly high ideals and the rich rewards of athletic and military heroism. The danger in the athletic metaphor for warfare is that it provides easy analogies or slogans for popular politicians like Pericles, whereby the people seek victory as in a game at any cost and ignore the more complex causes, conduct, and outcome of real war which, as we know, does not often follow the rules. The Greek literary genius in the use of the metaphor is that individual authors were able to exploit the associative aspects of war and games, but they artfully contrasted the delight of contests with the the death of combat, excellence on the playing field with that on the battlefield, and the prizes of excellence when the stakes are a crown with those when the stakes are the fatherland itself. As the Greeks understood it, combat and contests were determined more by a combination of heroic excellence and divine favor rather than, as Cosby suggests, by a toss of the coin.

26

The Nature of Early
Greek Victor Statues

Steven Lattimore

One indication of the extraordinary esteem in which the Greeks held successful athletes was the practice, at least as old as the sixth century B.C., of commemorating their victories by erecting statues both in their native cities and at the sites of major athletic festivals, especially Olympia. Often they were fashioned by the leading sculptors of the day. A few, however, are of additional interest because they had strange histories, almost lives of their own.

Theagenes of Thasos was an Olympic victor in 480 and 476 whose total victories were recorded as at least 1200.[1] His bronze statue stood in the agora of Thasos, and, after the athlete's death, this image was flogged by an enemy until one night it toppled over and killed the man. The statue was convicted of homicide and consequently thrown into the sea. Famine ensued at Thasos, and the Thasians, on the advice of the Delphic oracle, restored the statue (conveniently recovered by fishermen) and worshipped Theagenes with divine honors. If the story of the vengeful statue is difficult to accept as a historical event,[2] neither does it belong to a common mythological pattern. The closest parallel is the story of Mitys, whose bronze statue in the agora of Argos fell on his murderer and killed him.[3] An athletic connection for Mitys is possible but uncertain; the story emphasizes his involvement in politics.[4]

---

[1] On Theagenes or Theogenes, cf. especially Paus. 6.6.5-6,11, Dio Chrys. 31 - 95-97, Hyde 364, Moretti 1953 51-56, Pouilloux 62-105, Amandry 65, 70, n. 31, Moretti 1957 88, Fontenrose 75-80, 83, 86, 88, 90, 91-92, Bohringer 6, 8-11, 15.

[2] Cf. Fontenrose 91, Pouilloux 101, Bohringer 9. The trial of the statue, however, reflects the impact of Athenian law on Thasos, cf. especially Pouilloux 101-103, also Bohringer n. 9.

[3] For Mitys or Bitys see Arist. *Poet.* 9.12, Plut., *Mor.* 553d, E. Rohde, *Psyche* (Tübingen: J. C. B. Mohr [Paul Siebeck] 1925) I, pp. 193-194, Fontenrose 90, 98, B. Frischer, *The Sculpted Word* (Berkeley: University of California Press, 1982) 115. Cf. also the avenging statue of Eros in Theoc., *Id.* 23.60.

[4] See A. Rostagni, *Aristotele Poetica* (Turin: Chiantore, 1945) 58-59, D.W. Lucas, *Aristotle's Poetics* (Oxford: Clarendon Press, 1968) 126-127 for the possible identification with the Mitys of [Dem.] 59.33.

Euthymos of Lokroi, an Olympic opponent of Theagenes in 480 won at Olympia in 484, 476, and 472.[5] We may well doubt that his statues at Olympia[6] and Lokroi were struck by lightning on the same day, but the tradition is appropriate to Euthymos' spectacular career outside the stadium, which culminated in his miraculous disappearance after he had enjoyed divine honors during his lifetime.

Still another statue recorded to have been damaged dramatically was that of Euthykles, another Lokrian.[7] The date of his pentathlon victory or victories is not known, but Moretti has good arguments for placing him towards the beginning of the fifth century.[8] Suspecting Euthykles of treachery, the Lokrians threw him into prison, where he died. They also mutilated his statue which stood in the agora. Like Thasos in the case of Theagenes, Lokroi suffered blight and famine. Again Apollo at Delphi advised compensation to both the man and the statue. An altar and cult of Euthykles were established at Lokroi, and his statue received honors like those the Lokrians accorded the statue of Zeus.

More brusquely dealt with was the statue of Astylos, whose career was probably more genuinely sordid than that of Euthykles and lacks the supernatural ending. As a citizen of Croton, Astylos won the *stade* and *diaulos* at Olympia in 488. To oblige Hieron according to a tradition,[9] but more likely for financial gain,[10] Astylos transferred his citizenship to Syracuse and as a Syracusan won the same Olympic races in 484 and 480, adding a *hoplite* victory in the latter Olympiad. Incensed at his defection, the people of Croton pulled down his statue there and transformed his house into a prison. No misfortune ensued for Croton, and no amends to the athlete or his statue are recorded.

Not long after these events, a statue and hero's honors were given to a much earlier athlete, Oibatos of Dyme.[11] The first Achaean victor at Olympia, he won the *stade* in 756. Angered at receiving no honor (γέρας) for this achievement, he prayed successfully (in the story, if not in fact) that the Achaeans win no subsequent victories at Olympia; athletic blight ended only after almost

---

[5]On Euthymos, cf. especially Plin., *HN* 7.47.152 (citing Callimachus), Paus. 6.6, Ael., *VH* 8.18, Dittenberger and Purgold 247-250, no. 144, Hyde 35, 38, 55, 62, 90,ʼ179, 183, 247, 342, 352, 364, Schweitzer 135, Amandry 64, n. 31, Moretti 1957 86, Fontenrose 79-82, 83, 91, Bohringer 5-6, 8, 9, 10, 11-12, 15, 16.

[6]By Pythagoras (Paus. 6.6.6.), cf. A. Linfert, "Pythagoras —einer oder zwei?" *AA* 1966 495-496.

[7]On Euthykles cf. Callimachus frs. 84-85 Pf., Moretti 1957 83-84, Fontenrose 74, 76, 77, 78, 79, 83, 87, 90, 91, 93, Bohringer 7, 9, 10, 11.

[8]Cf. also Bohringer 11. Fontenrose 87, 91, 93, however, is inclined to date Euthykles much earlier.

[9]Paus. 6.13.1. On Astylos cf. also Callimachus fr. 660 Pf., Hyde 33, 179, 363-364, Amandry 71, Moretti 1957 82-83, 84-85, 87, 90, no. 219, Bohringer 7, D. Young, "Professionalism in Archaic and Classical Greek Athletics," *Ancient World* 7 (1983) 49.

[10]While Amandry is skeptical about the story of Astylos overall, Young has convincingly placed him in a setting of large-scale subsidization of West Greek athletes; he argues that Croton was unable to outbid Syracuse for Astylos' services.

[11]Cf. Paus. 6.3.8, 7.17, 6-7, 13-14, Hyde 30, 32, 333, 343, Amandry 67-68, Moretti 1957 60, Fontenrose 74, 75, 77-78, 79, 83, 91, 93, Bohringer 7, 15.

three centuries, when the Achaeans set up a statue of Oibatos at Olympia after consulting the Delphic oracle.[12] The immediate result was the victory of the boy runner Sostratos of Pellene in 460.[13] Thereafter, Achaean athletes made sacrifices at the tomb of Oibatos before competing at Olympia, and the victors placed their wreaths on his statue there.

Regarding all these stories, what is important is not so much their historical credibility as what the Greeks believed, why, and when. Theagenes, by the early fourth century and perhaps in the late fifth century, was regarded as a god on Thasos, and his worship spread even outside Greece.[14] Euthymos was worshipped during his lifetime, apparently as a god. Posthumous heroic honors were accorded Euthykles and Oibatos. These cults appear to be no late development; Bohringer has shown convincingly that they were responses to momentous and threatening events confronting the athletes' cities in their own time.[15] We may say the same concerning the cult of another turbulent athlete: Kleomedes of Astypaleia, whose boxing prize at Olympia was withheld because of the brutality with which he had killed his opponent; after destroying sixty schoolchildren of his native city in a fit of madness, he escaped the wrath of the townspeople by a mysterious disappearance; Kleomedes, Apollo informed them, was no longer a mortal but a hero requiring sacrifice.[16] Perhaps also occurring in the early fifth century was the heroization of Orsippos of Megara, said to be an Olympic *stade* victor in 724 or 720.[17]

From subsequent history, we have little to compare with these fifth-century cults of fifth-century or earlier athletes except for the career of Polydamas of Skotussa, (Olympic victor in 408) who might be regarded as a late addition to the group previously discussed.[18] After a fabulous career and a colorful death, he became a hero whose statue at Olympia, by the fourth-century artist Lysippos, had healing powers.

---

[12]In actuality, there were several intervening Achaean victories, as Moretti 1957 60 and Bohringer 12 have pointed out. It is at the very least intriguing that, around the time of Oibatos' victory, Homer's *Iliad* celebrated the swift-footed "best of the Achaeans" who damned the cause of his compatriots after he was deprived of his γέραζ.

[13]See Moretti 1957 97, Ebert 85, 101.

[14]On the date of the cult see especially Pouilloux 103-105, 228, also Ebert 122, Bohringer 15.

[15]Bohringer 10-15.

[16]On Kleomedes cf. Paus. 6.9.6-8, Plut., *Rom.* 28, Moretti 1957 82, Fontenrose 73-74, 85, 90, 91, Bohringer 12.

[17]On Orsippos or Orrhippos, cf. *IG* VIII.52, Paus. 1.44.1, Moretti 1957 61-62, Fontenrose 92-93, Bohringer 8, 13-14, 15. Diognetos, of unknown date but perhaps *fl. ca.* 500 B.C., was honored as a hero on Crete, cf. Moretti 1957 84, Fontenrose 89, Bohringer 7, n. 28. Regarding Glaukos of Karystos, his historicity, date, and relation to a statue at Olympia are all extremely obscure, cf. Hyde 32, 122, 176, Amandry 65, 68, Moretti 1957 75-76, Gross 72, Fontenrose 89, 91, 99-103, Hermann 117, Hausmann 66, 132, Bohringer 9.

[18]On Polydamas or Pulydamas, cf. Paus. 6.5., Diod. 9.14-15, Lucian, *Hist. concr.* 35, *Deorum concilium* 12, Hyde 32, 45, 364, Amandry 65-66, Moretti 1957 110, Fontenrose 87-88, Cf. perhaps also Damarchos, see Paus. 6.8.2, Moretti 1957 112, Fontenrose 89-90, Bohringer 17.

Not every cult of a hero-athlete certainly involved a statue; none is recorded for Orsippos,[19] Kleomedes, or Diognetos.[20] Rather, two things should be stressed about the athletic statues so mentioned. First, the statues of Theagenes, Euthykles, Euthymos, Oibatos, and Polydamas are unique, as a group, for the extraordinary events that befell them and the worship they received. Equally suggestive is the high degree of identification between athlete and statue, eventually extending into Olympia with the offering of wreaths to Oibatos, and also pronounced in the story of the non-hero Astylos.

The identification of the statue with the athlete is consistent with Pausanias' statements that the statues of athletes at Olympia were among the honors awarded to the victor—not dedications to Zeus.[21] Although his testimony would seem the more credible in that it apparently does not reflect the practice of his own time,[22] it has often been questioned because of the presence of the word ἀυέθηκε ("he dedicated") in inscriptions on early bases of victor statues found at Olympia. Hyde concluded that "the truth must lie somewhere between the extremes [that all early victor statues were honorific, or that they were votive]. . . . Some athletic statues may have been votive, while others were not."[23] Recent scholarship has inclined sharply towards the view that, down to the late fifth century, statues of victors set up in the Altis at Olympia were regularly votive offerings.[24] Schweitzer has given the evolution of victor statues at Olympia from votive to personal monuments a decisive place in the development of Greek portraiture.

The evidence of the Olympia inscriptions, however, is neither so extensive nor so consistent as to encourage so absolute a rejection of Pausanias as "Il se trompait, au moins pour les statues du Ve siecle."[25] The inscriptions must be considered together with our other evidence concerning early victor statues.

The only inscription from Olympia earlier than 500 B.C. is that of Pantares of Gela; its relevance is doubtful, since, while clearly votive, it is not certainly associated with a statue.[26] Moreover, the victory was probably equestrian.

---

[19]Despite the mention of one by Moretti 1957 61.

[20]Cf. supra, n. 17.

[21]Paus. 5.21.1, 5.25.1

[22]See Hyde 39.

[23]*Ibid., loc. cit.*

[24]See especially Amandry 69-71, also Schweitzer 135-138, Gross 64, Ebert 16-22, Herrmann 114, Hausmann 131. For early discussion cf. Hyde 38-40. The votive-or-honorific distinction, which Herrmann considers anachronistic and E.N. Gardiner, review of Hyde in *JHS* 42 (1922) 123, a false one, is apparently not absolute but a matter of emphasis. Cf. Ebert 22.

[25]Amandry 69.

[26]Dittenberger and Purgold 242-244, no. 142, Schweitzer 135, Moretti 1957 151, Ebert 44-46, Herrmann 117. It is disputed whether the inscription—with ἀυέθηκε —of Milon's statue (cf. infra, n. 31) is preserved, cf. recently Moretti 1957 73 and Herrmann n. 446.

Equestrian monuments at Olympia were definitely votive in character[27]—and consequently will not be considered here. Regarding Olympia, we may probably accept Pausanias' designation, as the earliest statues of athletes, of those of Praxidamas and Rhexibios, victors in 544 and 536 respectively;[28] while Eutelidas may have won as early as 628, his statue was probably not set up before the fourth century B.C.[29] Oibatos has already been discussed. If Chionis, a seventh-century Olympic victor, had a statue, this was made in the fifth century.[30] Milon, an Olympic victor in 532, 528, 524, 520, and 516 after winning as a boy in 540, personally carried and set in place his statue, the work of the otherwise-unknown Dameas.[31] There is no good reason to doubt that this happened before *ca.* 500. Two late archaic bearded and helmeted heads found at Olympia may well belong to statues of victors.[32] Thus, if the statues of Anochos (victor in 520 and 516?) and Timaisthenes (victor in 516?) by Hageladas were made before 500, they were not necessarily as isolated as Amandry suggests.[33]

There were statues at Olympia commemorating a number of athletic victories from 500-480 B.C., the end of the archaic period, but several of these are likely to have been made after 480.[34] Possibilities from before 480 include the statues of Meneptolemos,[35] Agiadas,[36] Philon,[37] Agameter,[38] and Philles.[39] Meanwhile, there is evidence for athletic statues outside Olympia, usually in the agora of the athlete's home city. That these statues were honorific has hardly been in doubt. Amandry, addressing himself to the fifth century, regards such statues as posthumous, marking the athletes' heroization.[40] Xenophanes does not mention statues among the honors lavished on successful athletes by Greek cities; this may be because the honor was posthumous,[41]

---

[27]See Dittenberger and Purgold 239-240, Hyde 37, 40, Gross 71.

[28]See Paus. 6.18.7, Hyde 106, 333, 337, Amandry, 68, Moretti 1957 71, 72, Herrmann 115.

[29]Cf. *IG II² 2326*, Paus. 5.9.1, Hyde 106, 333, 337, 346, Amandry 68, Moretti 1957 67, Gross 64, Herrmann n. 441.

[30]Cf. Hyde 32, 333, 352, 362, Amandry 68, Moretti 1957 64, Herrmann n. 441. For Glaukos see supra, n. 17.

[31]On Milon cf. especially 6.14.5, Philostr. *VA* 4.28, Hyde 31, 106-107, Amandry 68, Moretti 1957 72-74, Gross 71-72, Fontenrose 88-89, Herrmann 116-117, Bohringer 7, 14. See also supra, n. 26.

[32]Cf. Hyde 162-163, Moretti 1957 77, nos. 142-144, 78, np. 151, Hausmann 62-65.

[33]Amandry 69.

[34]See ibid 70.

[35]See Moretti 1957 80.

[36]See Hyde 123, Moretti 1957 84.

[37]See Hyde 122, Moretti 1957 80, Amandry n. 31.

[38]See Moretti 1957 80, Amandry n. 30.

[39]See Hyde 344 (cited as Phillen or Philys), Moretti 1957 177-178, Amandry n. 30.

[40]Amandry 72.

[41]See Amandry n. 38 on Xenophanes *apud* Ath. 10.413-414.

or it may be because few such monuments existed in Xenophanes' lifetime. The earliest[42] seems to have been that of Arrhachion of Phigaleia[43] a pankratiast who died—apparently of a broken neck[44]—in the moment of winning his third Olympic victory in 564. His statue in the agora of his native city is described by Pausanias as archaic in appearance.

With the beginning of the fifth century, we return to the athletes already discussed. The story of Euthykles, who does not certainly belong to this period, indicates that his cult was posthumous—but that his statue at Lokroi was not. Whatever the precise date of Astylos' statue at Olympia,[45] his statue at Croton was apparently erected when he was in his prime.[46] A date ca. 476 for the statue of Theagenes at Olympia is plausible;[47] his statue at Thasos was probably considerably later, but not certainly posthumous.[48] Euthymos' statue at Lokroi can not be dated, except possibly by association with the one at Olympia by Pythagoras,[49] who also made the Olympian statue of Astylos and, perhaps considerably later, those of Protolaos,[50] Mnaseas,[51] and Leontiskos.[52] On the base of Euthymos' statue were recorded his three Olympic victories, so the inscription at least is later than 472. This inscription has survived[53]—perhaps the earliest for a non-equestrian Olympic victor—to become the object of a controversy which is central to the problem of fifth-century athletic statues. It reads:

Εὔθυμος Λοκρὸς ᾱστυκλέος τρὶς Ολύμπί ἐνίκων
    ἐικσνα ἔστησεν τήνδε βροτοῖς ἐσορᾶν
Εὔθυμος Λοκρὸς ἀπὸ Ζεφυρίο ἀνέθηκε
    Πυθαγόραζ Σάμιος ἐποίησεν.

Euthymos of Lokroi, son of Astykles, thrice Olympic victor,
    Set up this image for mortals to behold.
Euthymos of Epizephyrian Lokroi dedicated it.
    Pythagoras of Samos made it.

---

[42]The date and function of the statue, on the Athenian acropolis, of the seventh-century Olympic victor Kylon is problematic, cf. Hyde 362, Moretti 1957 365, Herrmann n. 442.

[43]Paus. 8.40.1-2, cf. Hyde 100, 326-328, 332-333, 335, 337, 363, Moretti 1957 70, Herrmann 115-116, R.H. Brophy III, "Deaths in the Pan-Hellenic Games," *AJP* 99 (1978) 363-382. On the variants of the name see now Brophy n. 6.

[44]See Brophy (supra, n. 43), especially 380-381.

[45]After 480? See Amandry 71.

[46]*Pace* Amandry 71, a date between 484 and 480 is almost certain; a statue in *Croton* after 484 makes no sense in the story's context.

[47]Cf. Pouilloux 360, Amandry 65.

[48]Pouilloux 75, 103-104 believes that the statue was posthumous but much earlier than the cult; see also 67, 228, cf. recently F.Chamoux, "Le monument 'de Théogénès': autel ou statue?" *BCH-Supp.* 5 (1979) 143-153.

[49]See supra, n. 6.

[50]Cf. Hyde 179, 353, Amandry n. 31, Moretti 1957 95.

[51]Cf. Hyde 161, 179, 181, Moretti 1957 87.

[52]Cf. Hyde 62, 179, 183, 249, Moretti 1957 98, Ebert 160.

[53]Dittenberger and Purgold 247-250, no. 144, Ebert 69-71.

The first two lines are metric, the third and fourth prose. The letters are neatly cut in *stoichedon* arrangement except for the last three of the second line ("for mortals to behold"), which in a *rasura*, and the word ἀνέθηκε at the end of the third line; these are cut much less carefully and regularly. Dittenberger and Purgold concur with previous scholars in believing that these words were carved later, the original inscription having recorded (in the present *rasura*) the city of Lokroi as dedicant; they suggest that the authorities at Olympia required the susbtitution of Euthymos as dedicant and the addition of ἀνέθηκε in accordance with established custom.[54] Thus the Eleans checked a premature expression of assertiveness which re-surfaced at Olympia when the inscription of Hellanikos, a winner in 424, recorded only the victor's name— so that Hellanikos, rather than playing the role of dedicant, seems to establish his presence by speaking out as the statue.[55] Amandry, however, believes that the entire inscription was carved in the second quarter of the fifth century; at a later time, the inscription was "refraîche," modernizing the letters somewhat, except for the word ἀνέθηκε—which had by then gone out of fashion— and the phrase ending the epigram.[56] Unlike the previous theory, however, this account of the inscription does not explain the *nichtssagende Phrase*[57] "for mortals to behold," nor the *rasura* in which it stands, nor is it easy to understand how the re-cut letters came to be in the *stoichedon* arrangement. Amandry perhaps places too much weight on the dating of letter-forms; a conservative stone-cutter could have been responsible for the words which Dittenberger and Purgold believe to have been added later—in an operation which certainly reflected conservatism in thought.[58]

The authorities at Olympia were less vigilant in the case of Kallias' inscription, which may be approximately contemporary with Euthymos' (since he won in 472).[59] Here we read:

Καλλιας Διδυμίο͂ ἀ̓ζηναῖος παγκράτιον
Μίκων ἐ̓ποιησεν ἀ̓θηναῖος.

Kallias the Athenian, son of Didymios, [won] the pankration.
Mikon the Athenian made [the statue].

---

[54]Dittenberger and Purgold rightly reject an earlier theory according to which Euthymos became the dedicant in fact, assuming an expense originally to be born by his father or his city. See also Hyde 38, Schweitzer 135, Moretti 1953 30-32, Moretti 1957 86.

[55]See especially Schweitzer 136, also Gross 75; for the inscription see Dittenberger and Purgold 267-272, no. 155.

[56]See Amandry n. 6.

[57]Schweitzer n. 68.

[58]Cf. A.G. Woodhead, *The Study of Greek Inscriptions* (Cambridge: Cambridge University Press, 1981) 62-63 Ebert 10, n. 2, also rejects Amandry's theory.

[59]Dittenberger and Purgold 249-252, no. 146. Moretti 1953 33-35 believes that the date may be considerably later, perhaps just after 450. Cf. also Hyde 45, 129, 251, 352, 365, Schweitzer 135, Amandry n. 29, Moretti 1957 91, Gross 62, 74, and—for the inscription of Philon— Ebert 56-57.

The inscription of the statue-base of Tellon, yet another victor in 472, does include ἀνέθηκε[60], and we should therefore regard this statue as votive,[61] like that of Kyniskos (victor in 460?).[62] The inscription of Agiadas (victor in 488?), containing ἀνέθηκε, may be preserved.[63] Another inscription with ἀνέθηκε appears on the base of a statue made by Pythagoras for an athlete whose identity is now lost;[64] there is uncertainty about the incomplete inscription of Diagoras and Damagetos.[65] The epigraphic evidence prior to 424 is, then, inconclusive. The inscriptions of Euthymos and Kallias are not decisively outnumbered in the fifth century and nothing from the sixth century can be compared), and, if they are regarded as Ionisms, they are no less significant for that.[66]

The complaints of Xenophanes, no less than the epinikian poetry of Pindar, Bacchylides, and Simonides, indicate that the late sixth century to the first half of the fifth century was the period of the most extreme adulation of athletes, especially among the West Greeks.[67] Bohringer has shown that the establishment of cults honoring athletes has its roots in this time. The inscriptions allow the possibility that after 480—but before 424—the "personality cults" (so as to include an athlete like Kallias, who was not heroized) extended even to some of the statues at Olympia. The honors accorded to Oibatos' statue there warn against drawing a firm distinction between statues at Olympia and statues elsewhere. As to statues at Olympia which were explicitly labeled as dedications, the very confusion of language mentioned by Amandry may have led, even immediately, to the perception of these monuments as "of" the athletes[68]—especially when the statues were athletic in form.

Much has been written concerning the appearance of early classical victor statues, which, certainly not actual portraits, represented athletes both in action and at rest.[69] Evidence for the archaic period is scant (especially since archaic

---

[60]Cf. Dittenberger and Purgod 253-256, nos. 147-148, Hyde 31, 240, 345, 352, Moretti 1957 92, Gross 74, Ebert 64-66.

[61]See Dittenberger and Purgold 240, Hyde 40.

[62]Cf. Dittenberger and Purgold 255-258, no. 149, Hyde 74, 117, 156-160, 239-240, Schweitzer 135, Moretti 1953 32-33, Amandry 75, 77, 84, Moretti 1957 97, Gross 74.

[63]Cf. Dittenberger and Purgold 257-260, no. 150, Hyde 123, Moretti 1957 84.

[64]Dittenberger and Purgold 249-250, no. 145.

[65]Cf. Dittenberger and Purgold 259-264, nos. 151, 152, Hyde 36, 46, 130, 342-343, 352, Schweitzer 135-136, Amandry 67, Moretti 1957 94-95, 100, 102.

[66]On the Ionian influence on the development of Greek portraiture see Schweitzer 126-138. On the possible Ionism of Euthymos' inscription see Schweitzer 135, n. 71; Kallias', Dittenberger and Purgold 252. Cf., however, the base with Pythagoras' signature and ἀνέθηκε, supra, n. 64.

[67]Cf. Amandry 70-71, Bohringer 10, H.M. Lee, "Athletic Arete in Pindar," Ancient World 7 (1983) 31-37.

[68]Amandry 69, cf. supra, n. 24.

[69]Cf. Gross 61-76.

statues were not copied in the Roman period),[70] but some of it has suggested the type most characteristic of archaic sculpture: the "kouros," a youthful male figure whose stance is a stiff, ambiguous stride, and whose nudity, sometimes called "athletic," probably pre-dates the practice of nude athletic competition among the Greeks.[71] In a recent review of the functions of the kouros, Ducat does not include victor statues; he does mention—as the only votive kouroi " 'représentants' sûrement des personnes réelles"—Kleobis and Biton.[72] The story of Kleobis and Biton, whose names are commonly given to a pair of early sixth-century kouroi found at Delphi,[73] is one of the most famous in Herodotos: prize-winning athletes of unusual strength, their piety towards their mother earned them "the best death" from the gods as well as the great honor of posthumous "likeness" (εἰκῶνες) at Delphi. These statues were, of course, hardly an athletic monument— at best, one of an unparalleled nature (unless a more mundane episode underlies the tradition in Herodotos). As for the Delphi kouroi, it has recently been argued very persuasively that they actually represent the divine twins Kastor and Polydeukes.[75] Anticipating, and sharing, dismay at this substitution of the more common Dioscuri for Kleobis and Biton, Vatin stresses the athletic character of Kastor and Polydeukes, and their role as patrons of athletics. He suggests that the Delphi kouroi may have been an *ex-voto* on the occasion of a victory; "mais quels qu'aient été les dédicants, je pense qu'ils voyient dans ces deux héros, avant toute chose, la parfaite incarnation des vertus athlétiques."[76]

A passage in Ridgway's recent book makes several points so succinctly that it is worth quoting: "We also know that at least two sixth-century winners chose to have their statues in wood. One may wonder whether this medium was preferred to marble because it allowed more active poses—therefore the apparent rejection of the kouros type as a victory monument may have

---

[70]Numerous archaic and early classical athletic statuettes have been found at Olympia and elsewhere, but their relation to major statuary is uncertain. Cf. Gross 62, Hausmann-61, 66, 131, 133, R. Thomas, *Athletenstatuetten der Spätarchaik und des strengen Stils* (Rome: Bretschneider, 1981) especially 20.

[71]On the use of the term "kouros" to describe these statues made in quantity by the Greeks from the later seventh century to *ca.* 480 see recently B.S. Ridgway, *The Archaic Style in Greek Sculpture* (Princeton: Princeton University Press, 1977) 45. For kouroi as early victor statues cf. Hyde 100-109, Hausmann 66, 132, Herrmann 115, 117; Gross 64 and Amandry 69 are skeptical, for Ridgway's opinion see infra.

[72]J. Ducat, "Fonctions de la statue dans la Grèce archaique: *kouros* et *kolossos*," *BCH* 100 (1976) 239-245, quotation from 243.

[73]For the statues see recently Ridgway (supra, n. 71) 26, 33, 36, 47, 58, 70, 81, 234, n. 16, 296, 301.

[74]Herodotos 1.31.

[75]See C. Vatin, "Monuments votifs de Delphes," *BCH* 106 (1982) 509-525, also *idem*, "Couroi argiens à Delphes," *BCH-Supp* 4 (1977) 13-22.

[76]*Ibid.* (1982) 525. The Delphi statues are in fact among the most powerfully athletic of kouroi, see Ridgway (supra, n. 71) 70; she does not regard them as canonical kouroi, see infra.

been due to its rather neutral appearance. On the other hand, the statue that the Olympic pankratiast Arrichion of Phigalia set up in his home town is described by Pausanias (8.40.1) as a typical kouros. But here it is perhaps significant that Arrichion's image stood in Phigalia and not at the site of victory."[77] The two wood statues mentioned were those of Praxidamas and Rhexibios.[78] Since, according to Pausanias, these were the earliest victor statues at Olympia, the use of wood is an appropriate link with the mysterious beginnings of Greek sculpture. What we know about early Greek wood sculpture—based partly on Pausanias' references to now-vanished *xoana*, partly on inference[79]— does not suggest any but the stiffest poses. Economy may rather have dictated the use of wood for these early victor statues.[80] If it was desired that archaic victor statues exhibit somewhat more action than the kouros, the type which held the hands forward rather than at the sides may have been a possibility, as Ridgway tentatively suggests.[81]

This brings us to the monument of Arrichion or Arrhachion.[82] His statue at Phigaleia, described by Pausanias as old-fashioned, with the feet close together and the arms hanging down at the sides, complies with the kouros format. The identification of the torso found at Phigaleia in 1890 as Arrhachion's statue has been championed especially by Hyde,[83] recently rejected by Gross and Herrmann.[84] For Ridgway, the Phigaleia torso probably represents Apollo; it does not conform to Pausanias' description because "he holds his arms flexed and his hands forward at different levels, presumably with attributes,"[85] while Pausanias very explicitly refers to the hands-down pose of the canonical kouros.[86] If, however, we are deprived of "the oldest date victor statue,"[87] we are left with Pausanias' evidence that the kouros was employed for one of the few recorded archaic statues of Olympic victors.

---

[77]Ridgway (supra, n. 71) 48; on the apparent rejection of "generic" kouroi as victory monuments cf. also 51, 53-54.

[78]Cf. supra, n. 28.

[79]On early Greek wood sculpture see recently Ridgway (supra, n. 71) 23-24.

[80]See Hyde 326, on the factor of cost also Gross 63. Cf. P.C. Bol, *OlForsch* 9 (1978) 9.

[81]Ridgway (supra, n. 71) 49, cf. the discussion of "related male figures," 73-74.

[82]Cf. supra, n. 43.

[83]Hyde 326-328, *idem*, "The Oldest Dated Victor Statue," *AJA* 18 (1914) 156-164.

[84]Gross 64, n. 3, Herrmann 115. Cf. also G.M.A. Richter. *Kouroi. Archaic Greek Youths* (London and New York: Phaidon, 1970) 67, no. 41, 77 ("There must have been many kouroi at Phigalei"—a dubious statement about this town which enters history with the story of Arrhachion) and the opinions cited in Brophy (supra, n. 43) n. 8.

[85]Ridgway (supra, n. 71) 47, see also 48, 61, 74. I am grateful to her for discussing with me the observations she made at the Olympia museum: the remains of the upper arms (*pace* Hyde, 328) indicate the pose she refers to, and there are no traces of attachment of the hands on the thighs.

[86]We should probably not suppose that the old-fashioned appearance of the statue led Pausanias into carelessness when he described the position of the arms.

[87]See supra, n. 83.

It is appropriate that this investigation, which began with Theagenes, conclude with the greatest of Olympic victors: Milon, who played an active role in the military, religious, and intellectual life of his city at a time when Croton was at the height of its power and driving towards unprecedented athletic supremacy.[88] After mentioning his statue at Olympia, Pausanias does not describe it but instead recounts peculiar feat of strength attributed to Milon: he could stand on a greased discus so that no one could push him off; grasp a pomegranate so firmly, yet without crushing it, that no one could wrest it from him; break a fillet around his forehead by swelling his veins. According to Philostratos, the statue stood with feet close together on a discus, wore a fillet, and held a pomegranate in the left hand; it has been supposed (following a lead by Philostratos) that the local stories mentioned by Pausanias, more briefly by Philostratos, developed as explanations of the statue's appearance. Scholars are often reluctant to rely on Philostratos as a source, and Frazer believed that his description of the statue is imaginary—embodying the athlete's legendary feats.[89] But it is impossibly fortuitous that such an endeavor by Philostratos should have resulted in a recognizable archaic kouros (or perhaps, to observe Ridgway's distinction, a "related figure").[90]

In summary, there is reason to conjecture that even the earliest victor statues were regarded as honorific representation of the athletes, that this signal honor soon contributed to the aura which surrounded both men and statues, and that the late archaic kouroi which are preserved approximate the appearance of at least some of these forerunners of the true Greek portrait.

---

[88]Young, *loc. cit.* (supra, n. 9). On Milon see supra, n. 31.

[89]J.G. Frazer, *Pausanias' Description of Greece* (London: Macmillan, 1898, reprinted New York: Biblo and Tannen, 1965) IV, p. 44.

[90]See especially Hyde 107, Moretti 1957 73.

Abbreviations

For abbreviations, I have followed the practice of the *American Journal of Archaeology* and *Oxford Classical Dictionary*, with the additions listed below:

Amandry. P. Amandry, "A propos de Polycléte: Statues d'Olympioniques et carriere de sculpteurs," *Charites* (Bonn: Athenaum-Verlag, 1957) 63-87.

Bohringer. F. Bohringer, "Cultes d'athletes en Grece classique: propos politiques, discours mythiques,"*REA* 81 (1979) 5-18.

Dittenberger and Purgold. Dittenberger and K. Purgold, *Die Inschriften von Olympia* (Berlin: A. Asher, 1896; reprint Amsterdam: A. M. Hakkert, 1966).

Ebert: J. Ebert, *Griechische Epigramme auf Sieger an Gymnischen und Hippischen Agonen*, Berlin Akad.-Verlag (Berlin, 1972). (I am indebted to T.F. Scanlon for this reference).

Fontenrose: J. Fontenrose, "The Hero as Athlete," *CSCA* 1 (1968) 73-104.

Gross: W. H. Gross, "Quas iconicas vocant. Zum Porträtcharakter der Statuen dreimaliger olympischer Sieger," *NAkG* 1969-1971, pt. 3, pp. 61-76.

Hausmann: U. Hausmann, *Der Tubinger Waffenlaufer* (Tübingen: Wasmuth, 1977).

Herrmann: H. V. Herrmann, *Olympia* (Munich: Hirmer, 1972).

Hyde: W. W. Hyde, *Olympic Victor Monuments and Greek Athletic Art* (Washington: Carnegie Institution of Washington, 1921).

Moretti 1953: L. Moretti, *Iscrizioni Agonistiche Greche* (Rome: Sigmorelli, 1953).

Moretti 1957: L. Moretti, "Olympionikai, i vincitori negli antichi agoni olimpici," *MemLinc* ser. 8, vol. 8 (1957-1959) 55-198.

Pouilloux: J. Pouilloux, *Recherches sur l'Histoire de les Cultes de Thasos* I (Paris: De Boccard, 1954).

Schweitzer: B. Schweitzer, "Studien zur Entstehung des Porträts bei Griechen," *Zur Kunst der Antike* (Tübingen: Wasmuth, 1963) I, pp. 115-167 (first published in 1940).

27

The Riddle of the Rings

David C. Young

I

The Canadians blew it into bubbles (Figure 1). The Russians built a Kremlin-like tower above it (Figure 2). ABC superimposes its circular initials over the top three rings (Figure 3). The Los Angeles Organizing Committee crowns them with a flying star (Figure 4). At Sarajevo the rings themselves were uppermost (Figure 5). But Hitler placed them down below, firmly gripped in the talons of the Nazi eagle (Figure 6). It is perhaps the best-known logo in the world.

Figure 1.

Figure 2.

Figure 3.

Figure 4.

Figure 5.

Figure 6.

Wherever one looks now, on the television screen, highway billboards, on a California supermarket bag—on candy bar wrappers—there are the five interlocked circles. Everyone knows what the circles represent: the Olympic Games. But beyond that, no one knows much about them at all. Every four years a new troop of experts comes out to tell the "Truth of the Rings." Even *Love Story* author Erich Segal once had a go at it. But now a rather new theory is the most widely accepted: the five interlocked Olympic circles *were an ancient Greek symbol for the Games.* "The interlocking circles," *The Official 1980 Olympic Guide* tells us, are "3,000 years old." The Modern Games, other Olympic authors claim, just "adopted" the ancient symbol as their own—"a link between ancient and modern Olympics," as yet another book now says. It is a wonderful notion, full of romance. Too bad it is nonsense, as well.

I must begin this comedy of errors with a photo from James Coote's popular *1980 Book of the Olympics* (Figure 7)[1] Coote thinks this altar is ancient. And he locates it at Delphi, site of ancient Greek athletic games ranked second only to the Olympics. But the altar was actually made in A.D. 1936 for the

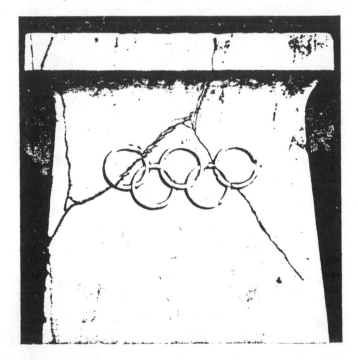

The altar at Delphi with the five rings later to be adopted as the symbol of the modern Olympics.

Figure 7. (*The caption is Coote's*).

---

[1]James Coote, *The 1980 Book of the Olympics* (London: Webb Publications, 1980), p. 8.

modern International Olympic Committee (IOC). It has never been at Delphi. For some time it stood near the entrance to the archaeological site at ancient Olympia, along with the stele which encases the heart of Baron Pierre de Coubertin, founder of the IOC. But in 1961 the IOC founded the International Olympic Academy a few kilometers northeast of the ancient Olympic site. It soon became an impressive group of buildings set amidst plush landscaping. At that time the marble altar (with five rings) and the stele (with one heart) were moved to the grounds of the Academy.[2] There they both sit today, available for viewing by any pilgrim who wanders up the modern road which leads east from the ancient stadium at Olympia (Figures 8 & 9).

The source of Mr. Coote's confusion? Another book. In their *History of the Ancient Olympic Games* (New York, 1963) Lynn and Gray Poole publish a photo of that same modern altar at Olympia (Coote's ancient "altar at Delphi"), duly labeled a "modern altar" and properly placed at Olympia.[3] But just a few pages before, the Pooles print *another* photo of a wholly *different* object, which they call an "altar at Delphi."[4] Coote just confused those two photos in the Pooles' book.

Figure 8. *(above)* Modern altar at Olympia.
Figure 9. *(right)* Stele with Coubertin's heart.
(Photos by author, Summer 1983)

---

[2]Alfred Mallwitz, director of the recent German excavations at Olympia, has confirmed for me the altar's 1936 origin (private conversation). The modern inhabitants of Olympia have always given an accurate account of the altar's date and history.

[3]Lynn Poole and Gray Poole, *History of the Ancient Olympic Games* (New York: I. Obolensky, 1963), pp. 129-130.

[4]Ibid, pp. 118-119.

That leaves the by-now-mysterious "altar at Delphi." The Pooles' photo, their heading caption is shown in Figure 10.
The Pooles elaborate:

In the stadium at Delphi, there is a stone altar on which is carved five rings symbolic of the quinquennial timing for the celebrated games. The design of five circles on the Delphi altar is today the symbol of the Olympic Games. The circles form a link between ancient and modern Olympics.

Altar in stadium at Delphi, with the five rings indicating the quidquennial spacing of the games. These five rings were adopted by modern Olympics as their official symbol.

Samivel Photo

Figure 10.

It is exciting to view the rings as an ancient symbol, bridging the millennia. And if they were in fact used in the ancient contests at Delphi, there would be a legitimate "link" between the modern games and antiquity. But no. The Pooles, too, are completely wrong.

The object in their photo did once rest in the stadium at Delphi, but it is not an altar, just a stone block. And it is not ancient at all. The Pooles may be the "experts" in General Grombach's claim:

> The interlocking circles found on the altar at Delphi and definitely connected with the ancient games, are considered by experts to be 3,000 years old (*Official 1980 Olympic Guide*).[5]

But the real experts, the French archaeologists who excavated the antiquities at Delphi, date those rings a little later—2,952 years later: The Delphi rings "date, in fact, from 1936."[6] The circles on the block at Delphi are no remembrance of ancient Greece; they are a memento of Adolf Hitler.

As propaganda to legitimize his Olympic Games—and his Nazi government—Hitler sought to associate the 1936 Berlin Olympics with the Olympics of ancient Greece. His Olympic organizer, Carl Diem, dreamed up the first Olympic torch relay from Olympia (the torches made by the Krupp Company, better known for its arms). The marble altar was built at Olympia for this occasion. To clothe this first Torch Relay all the more in antiquity (there was no ancient equivalent) Diem had the runners, on their way from Olympia to Berlin, detour to Delphi.[7] Then they circled the ancient stadium, the best preserved in Greece (and very photogenic). To enhance that Delphi detour, the 1936 Olympic Organizing Committee inscribed the stone block with the five modern circles and placed it in the Delphi stadium. When the Pooles visited Delphi about 1962, they were misled by the block's crude appearance, and mistook it for an ancient object. They published their mistake, which now misleads others, such as Grombach and Coote.

You will not find the Pooles' "altar" in the Delphi stadium today. In May 1972 the Greek minister of the archaeological site there, Mr. Petrarchou, had it removed far from the legitimate antiquities. The Greek Olympic Committee had requested permission for a night ceremony in the stadium—replete with burning torches. It was again, it seems, part of the hype for the upcoming German Olympics (Munich). Petrarchou, fearing that this modern intrusion might damage the hallowed ground, refused. But he allowed the night Olympic ceremony outside the boundaries of the site, near the fabled ancient spring of Kastalia.[8] That spring still bubbles beside the road to Athens, a little east

---

[5]John V. Grombach, *The Official 1980 Olympic Guide* (New York: Times Books, 1980), p. 280.

[6]Pierre Aupert and Olivier Callot, *Fouilles de Delphes* (École française d' Athènes) Vol. 2, Part 3, Fascicle 2: *Le Stade* (Paris, 1979), p. 6.

[7]Richard Mandell, *The Nazi Olympics* (New York: Macmillan, 1971), p. 132.

[8]I thank the excellent staff at the Archaeological Museum, Delphi (especially Mr. N. Foutzoutzoglou and Ms. S. Stylianou) for their help, finding and letting me see the pertinent records.

of the ancient sanctuary. The block inscribed in 1936 with the modern Olympic rings was moved to that spot at that time. It sits there now still—available for public examination—just a few steps off the pavement where the tour buses whiz by (Figures 11, 12, 13). It is an object of petty historical value; but only in Greece would it remain undisturbed. In America, land of vandals and fraternity capers, it would not last two nights.

Figure 11. *(top)* The 1936 Delphi block.
Figure 12. *(left)* From the north, toward the Athens Road.
Figure 13. *(right)* From the south, at the entrance to the spring.
(Photos by author, August 1983)

II

If not from ancient Greece, when and where *did* our interlocked rings first appear? The comedy of errors continues; so does the mischief of books. Grombach's *Official 1980 Olympic Guide* throws a new wrinkle in the riddle. Before spreading the error about the "altar at Delphi," General Grombach traces the modern use of the symbol back to another time, Modern Olympiad I—1896 at Athens.

> Another myth is that which surrounds the famous Olympic symbol, the five interlocking circles. . . . According to many, this is the property of the IOC, and its various applications on national emblems were developed by the various committees; . . . the superimposing of the five interlocking circles on the U.S. shield is reportedly a recent creation of the USOC (United States Olympic Committee). The symbol was allegedly first used at the 1924 games. But it is actually far from modern. The official guide and report of the *1896 games* . . . has, on page 63, the U.S. Olympic shield, down to the thirteen stripes *and the five interlocking rings.* And to go back even further . . . 3,000 years old (emphasis added).[9]

Sure enough, in the "guide and report" in question, right there on p. 63 (also on p. 3) looms the American Olympic shield—with the five interlocked circles boldly inset at its top. And, sure enough, the date on the title page reads "1896."

Poor General Grombach. The date is a fake. The book was published in 1941. In that year the American Olympic Committee (now USOC) reprinted some of the English portion of the original 1896 publication, which was printed by Greeks in Athens. For its own reprinting, the USOC scuttled some of the illustrations that appeared in the authentic 1896 Greek edition, replacing them with pictures of the 1941 U.S. Olympic shield (Figures 14 and 15). It boldly

ERST wenige Jahre sind vergangen, seit unsere Generation Zeuge der wunderbaren Aufdeckung des alten Olympia geworden. Hervorragende Werke griechischer Kunst wurden dadurch ans Licht gefördert, unsere archaeologischen und historischen Kenntnisse in hohem Grade bereichert. Das Altertum aber, das in so vielen Dingen unser Lehrmeister gewesen, soll uns Epigonen nicht nur durch die glänzenden literarischen und künstlerischen Schöpfungen, die es uns vererbt, in Staunen versetzen; wir sollen uns nicht auf das blosse Studium und die blosse Bewunderung der Meisterstücke der alten Literatur

BUT a short time has elapsed since the present age witnessed the wonderful discovery of ancient Olympia, through which were brought to light master-pieces of Hellenic art, which have greatly enriched our knowledge both of archeology and of history. It has not however sufficed for antiquity, which has been in so many respects our instructor, to astonish us by the great bequest of its splendid literary and artistic master-pieces. We are not limited to the study and admiration of the glorious remains of ancient intellect and art. With the same zeal we seek for information as to the life of the ancients, and advance rejoicing towards the imitation of all that antiquity can present to us of great and beautiful. We shall then before long enter on the twentieth century crowned with the fair flowers of ancient civilization. It is for this reason that the present generation, desiring to raise athletic exercises to their

BUT a short time has elapsed since the present age witnessed the wonderful discovery of ancient Olympia, through which were brought to light master-pieces of Hellenic art, which have greatly enriched our knowledge both of archeology and of history. It has not however sufficed for antiquity, which has been in so many respects our instructor, to astonish us by the great bequest of its splendid literary and artistic master-pieces. We are not limited to the study and admiration of the glorious remains of ancient intellect and art. With the same zeal we seek for information as to the life of the ancients, and advance rejoicing towards the imitation of all that antiquity can present to us of great and beautiful. We shall then before long enter on the twentieth century

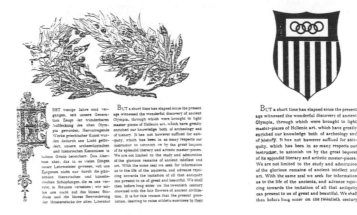

Figure 14. ***(left)*** **Beginning of authentic edition, published in Athens, 1896. A drawing of an olive wreath heads the text.**
Figure 15. ***(right)*** **Beginning of 1941 "1896" edition, published by American Olympic Committee. The anachronistic shield with five rings heads the text.**

---

[9]Grombach, *The Official*, p. 280.

placed its own name and address, "American Olympic Committee, 233 Broadway, New York," on the original title page (there was no such committee in 1896). But it left, quite misleadingly, the date "1896"—in old-fashioned 19th century lettering—on that same title page (Figures 16 and 17). The *National Union Catalogue* (vol. 430, p. 242) has the matter straight, and keeps the 1896 and 1941 editions quite distinct. So what Grombach saw is real, but not authentic—a hybrid book purporting to date from 1896, but with a glaring anachronism; namely, the five-ring Olympic symbol, which did not yet exist in 1896.

The five-ring symbol did not exist in ancient Greece, nor in 1896. We

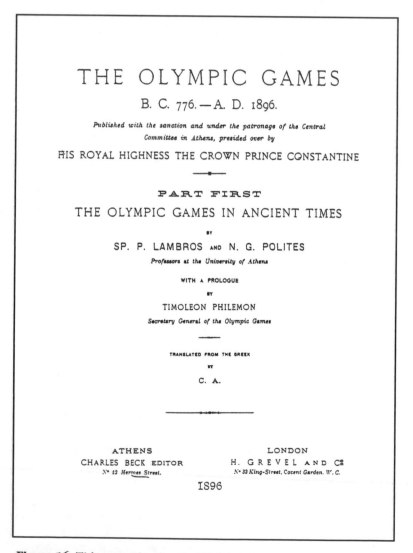

Figure 16. Title page of authentic 1896 Greek edition.

must look more recently, and elsewhere. The general motif of interlocked circles is common in the modern world. Six interlocked circles are the symbol of Olympic Airways, the national airline of Greece. We see four interlocked circles daily, on every Audi automobile. Three joined circles represent the fraternal organization, International Order of Odd Fellows; they also represent Ballantine's Beer. But the best-known three-circle version symbolized terror to many Europeans through two world wars, trademark of the Arms of Krupp. (Krupp's three circles originally stood for railroad car wheels, not three open cannon barrels as later generations had it.)

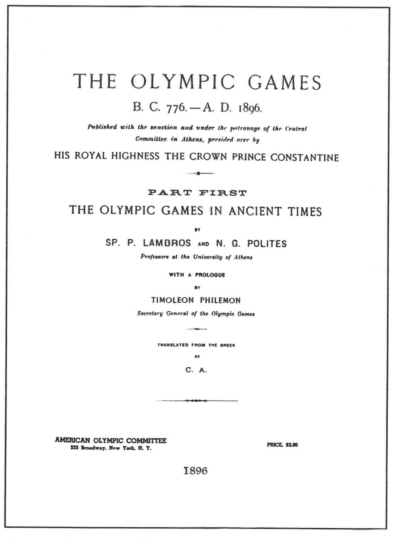

Figure 17. Title page of 1941 American Olympic Committee edition (note misleading date at bottom, and absence of actual date).

Yet the least familiar version is perhaps the most relevant: two interlocked circles symbolized Coubertin's own French athletic union, the *Union des sociétés françaises de sports athlétiques* (USFSA, comparable to our AAU or the British AAA). French athletes at Olympiad V in 1912 wore that emblem. The French runner Lermusieux wore the two-ring emblem at Athens in 1896. But it was much older. The two interlocked rings appeared on the jerseys of a USFSA rugby team which played a British Civil Service club in London, February 13, 1893 (Figure 18). That was three years *before* Olympiad I. And the same two rings appeared as a USFSA logo as late as 1924 (Figure 19).[10] The conjoining of two rings in the USFSA symbol apparently represented the friendly conjoining of the two specific French athletic organizations which merged to form the USFSA (namely, Georges St. Clair's "Union of French Foot-Racing Societies" and Coubertin's own "Committee for the Propagation

l'équipe de l'Union et le Civil Service F. C. à Richmond, le 13 février 1893
Bellencourt, L. Dedet, P. Gariel, F. Reichel, Sienkievicz, Thorndike, d'Este,
Niet, Arnaud, Ellemberger, de Palissaux, Geo Deschamps, Gaston Deschamps.

Figure 18. The USFSA Rugby team, 1893, two interlocked circles on jerseys.

[10]The USFSA itself disbanded into various sports federations in the 1920's. The history of the USFSA may be found in *Encyclopédie des sports* (Paris, 1924), vol. 1, Chapters "Aux XIXe siècle" and "Organisation du sport en France." The illustrations of the two-ring logo here come from pp. 145 and 165.

of Physical Exercise in Education"). Since he was the first Secretary-General of the USFSA, we may assume that Coubertin himself designed the symbol; a symbol where the choice of two interlocked rings made good historical sense.

Two, three, four—six. But the IOC uses precisely *five* interlocked circles. What is the meaning of the number five? And, still, where *did* our symbol originate? In 1950 the IOC issued a little booklet intended to answer such questions.

Figure 19. The USFSA logo (the banner woven between the two interlocked circles reads *Ludus pro patria*, "Sport for the fatherland"). Both photos taken from *Encyclopédie des sports*, vol. 1 (Paris, 1924).

It was in 1914 that on the proposal of Baron Pierre de Coubertin the IOC decided on the creation of the Olympic Rings. It was however only in 1920 that they appeared for the first time on a flag with a white ground. These rings represent the five continents, blue for Europe, yellow for Asia, black for Africa, green for Australia and red for America.[11]

Historical at last! *Definitive.* There is no nonsense here about antiquity or bogus editions.

The IOC's 1950 explanation generally agrees with an account of the rings published by the USOC in 1948, with Avery Brundage's *imprimatur.* But it does not wholly agree. The 1948 USOC says,

The colors of the rings are Blue for Europe, Yellow for Asia, Black for Africa, Green for America, and Red for Australasia.[12]

What color *does* represent America? "Green," as the USOC tells us, or "red," as the IOC has it? The correct answer is—neither. The comedy of errors marches on. Red doesn't represent America, but green doesn't represent it, either. In fact, scarcely a phrase in either the IOC or USOC account is fully accurate. Coubertin created the rings in 1913, not 1914—and just one year (we shall see) makes a world of difference. The flag in question first flew in 1914, not 1920. And *none of the colors represents any continent at all.* My information comes straight from the Baron's pen.

III

When Coubertin first designed the five interlocked circles, he never intended them as a general symbol of the Olympic games. He designed them instead as an *ad hoc* symbol for a specific Olympic conference; namely, the "World Congress" held in Paris in June, 1914. Almost a year before the congress met, Coubertin, as President of the IOC, wrote the following item in the August, 1913 *Revue Olympique* (official organ of the IOC).

The Emblem and the Flag of 1914

The emblem and the flag chosen to honor and to represent this 1914 World Congress, which will place the definitive seal on the Olympic revival, has started to appear on various preliminary documents: five rings regularly interlocked. Their diverse colorings—blue, yellow, black, green, and red—are set off against a background which is paper white. These five rings represent the five parts of the world from this point on won over to Olympism and given to accepting fruitful rivalry. Furthermore, the six colors thus combined reproduce the colors of all the nations, with no exception. The blue and yellow of Sweden, the blue and white of Greece, the tricolors of France,

---

[11](International Olympic Committee), *The International Olympic Committee* (Aigle, Switzerland, 1950), p. 18.

[12](United States Olympic Committee), *Report of the United States Olympic Committee: Games of the XIVth Olympiad, London, England, 1948* (n.p., n.d.), p. 14. In 1948 Brundage was strongly anti-communist: perhaps he could not accept "red for America" and just traded the unwanted "red" to Australasia for its "green."

England, and America, Germany, Belgium, Italy, Hungary, the yellow and red of Spain
next to the novelties of Brazil or Australia, with old Japan and the new China...[13]

No *color* represents any continent, certainly not any of the "five continents."
As the Baron (who viewed them as six, not five) explains the colors themselves,
he speaks of *countries*, not continents. He nowhere mentions Africa. Black
cannot stand for Africa. And yellow stands for Asia no more than black for
Africa. Those are apocryphal explanations, founded no doubt on racial
stereotypes. Black, if it represents anywhere, is Germany, the first nation in
Coubertin's list to display black in its flag. So much for the five *colors*, each
as an emblem of a specific continent. It is simply not true.

But Coubertin does say the five *rings* "represent the five parts of the
world." Europeans do not always divide "America" into its parts. For them
"The New World" is one, the continents are five—and geography is in the
eyes of the beholder. When the IOC and USOC say that the "five continents"
are the five items symbolized by the five *rings*, they are perhaps faithful to
what Coubertin wrote here. But was Coubertin himself candid? Did even
he divulge the full "Truth of the Rings"? There is strong reason to doubt
it. "Part" is an imprecise, flexible term.

When Coubertin lists the nations, and the colors to be found in their
respective flags, he does not select countries at random, in a random order.
Far from it. I repeat the list sequentially here:

1) Sweden, 2) Greece, 3) France, 4) England, 5) "America" (U.S.A.), 6) Germany,
7) Belgium, 8) Italy, 9) Hungary, 10) Spain, 11-14) Brazil, Australia, Japan, China.

This precise sequence, in fact, unfolds a relentless logic—which leads to a
frightening conclusion.

First comes Sweden, sponsor (as Coubertin wrote) of the most recent
Olympic Games, Olympiad V (Stockholm, 1912). Next comes Greece, site
of the first International Olympics, Olympiad I (Athens, 1896). The next three
countries, France, England, and America (USA), fill in the three Olympiads
in between (II: Paris, 1900; IV: London, 1908; III: St.Louis, 1904). Can it be
just chance that the first five countries in Coubertin's list just happen to be
the first five sites of his International Olympic Games? No; nor is it mere
coincidence that the sixth nation on the list, Germany, was still scheduled—
as the Baron wrote in 1913—to host the next edition, Olympiad VI (Berlin,
1916). Seventh on the list is Belgium. The Belgians indeed sponsored Olympiad
VII (Antwerp, 1920).

The *first seven countries* on Coubertin's list are the host countries *of
the first seven Olympiads*. Italy, listed eighth, did not host the Olympics until
1960. But Rome had been awarded the Olympic host contract for Olympiad

---

[13]Pierre de Coubertin, "L'emblème et Le Drapeau de 1914," *Revue Olympique*, August 1913, pp.
119-120 (translated from the French by the present author).

IV in 1908. An eruption of Vesuvius, among other things, had forced her to withdraw. Even at ninth, Hungary, the principle does not break down. Budapest had already bid, along with (successful) Antwerp, for the host contract for Olympiad VII. Coubertin obviously saw Hungarian games likely in the Olympic future, probably Olympiad VIII or IX. I know of no specific plans for Spanish Olympics (tenth); but by number ten the Baron seems to begin thinking in general, grandly global terms. Yet the first nine countries listed establish a perfect pattern: as he explained his own "Riddle of the Rings," Coubertin himself thought in specific *sequential* terms of the Olympic *host countries.*

Coubertin's own words suggest even more. Grombach and all other English speaking authors speak of the five Olympic "circles." Coubertin *never* calls them *circles* (French *cercles*). He always uses the French word *anneaux.* We may translate it properly as "rings." But *anneaux* also means, "links," as in the links of a chain. And that seems to be the imagery which the Baron uses in this article—*the links of a chain which must continue unbroken.* Coubertin himself says that the logo with "five links" was designed specifically for the 1914 World Congress—when there had been precisely five Olympiads. I draw the obvious conclusion: in late 1912 or early 1913, when the Baron first designed the 1914 Congressional symbol, the five links stood for the first *five Olympiads* and their respective countries, Greece, France, U.S.A., England, and Sweden—now linked in friendship by the Olympic movement. The symbolism would operate in exactly the same way as Coubertin's previous two-ring version, the logo that apparently represented the formal and historical linking of two specific French athletic entities through the single organization, the USFSA.

In all his "Congresses," "Jubilees," and other meetings, Coubertin was the Master of Symbolism as well as Ceremony. Once he conceived a theme for a specific occasion, he carried it out in meticulous detail.[14] His writing the two years before the 1914 Congress teems with the fat Roman numerals, "Olympiads III and IV," "*Olympiad V*"—"*Olympiad VI*"—with an almost subliminal effect. As Master of Staging, he planned many months before each production. "A large quantity of 1914 Olympic flags," he later reported, "was made ahead of time, to grace the walls and banquet tables of the Congress." At one climactic point during the 1914 Congress, he recalls for us: "A procession of young women, in ancient costume, came to *wreathe* the flags of the *host nations of the first five Olympiads: Greece, France, the United States, England, and Sweden*"[15] (emphasis added). I go even further—beyond suggesting each

---

[14]When produced by Coubertin, Richard Mandell writes, "A 'congress,' a 'jubilee,' . . . had to have a setting, a *theme, continuity*, intermissions, and a suitably prepared audience," *The First Modern Olympics* (Berkeley: University of California Press, 1976), p. 71 (emphasis added). Cf. pp. 76, 80 f., 86 f.; John J. MacAloon, *This Great Symbol* (Chicago: University of Chicago Press, 1981), pp. 154-194, etc.

[15]Pierre de Coubertin, *Memoires olympiques* (Lausanne: International Olympic Committee, 1931), p. 145. In 1935 Coubertin wrote that the very first appearance of the five-ring flag was on

ring was first designed to symbolize a specific Olympiad and country. I believe that Coubertin originally planned to add a new ring at each new Olympiad, expanding the five "links" of the "chain" until the Olympic flag was filled with happily interlaced circles—the nations of the world joyfully linked in Olympism.

It will again help us to understand if we go back a bit in time; namely, to the 1892 USFSA "Jubilee" meeting—the very genesis of Coubertin's Olympic movement. There the Baron made public for the first time his grand idea of an Olympic revival. These international athletic games could be, he claimed, "a strong ally" in "the *cause of peace*" (emphasis added).[16] To expect a sudden "elimination of war" was too utopian. But, Coubertin predicted, athletics could do "more for peace" than diplomacy. The expressed and realistic goal of his Olympic games was "the *progressive* lessening of the chances for war"[17] (emphasis added). Perhaps even the Baron occasionally forgot it; but his "Olympic movement" was openly and from the outset a movement in the cause of world peace ("universal peace," as he called it.)[18]

In July 1912 (just after Olympiad V and a year before his 1913 article on the rings) Coubertin's *Revue Olympique* published an article expressing the hope that the Olympics would, in fact, bring about world peace. It was entitled "Pax Olimpica" (i.e., "Olympic Peace") in bold (and misspelled) imitation of the renowned Pax Romana of the Roman Empire. The author[19] is quick to praise the success of the 1912 Stockholm Games: "the Fifth Olympiad has acquired much of the dignity which it was hoped from the first that the events would obtain." It was, we read in this 1912 "Pax" article,

> . . . an appropriate moment at which to allude to one of the noblest hopes concerning the influence that coming Olympiads may wield — the establishment . . . of a state of *universal peace* . . . . [I]f the current of popular opinion is given a proper direction, there is no knowing to what volume it will grow . . . it is unnecessary to attempt to trace the stages by which the expansion of the ideal will take place, until it becomes

---

June 13, 1914, just before the opening of the Congress, in the Bois de Boulogne, at a party given by the Count and Countess Bertier (unpublished document in IOC Archives, Lausanne); the flag then flew frequently during the Congress, both inside the buildings and out of doors (e.g., on a railroad train used on an excursion by the delegates). The IOC Archives contain numerous photos of the five-ring flag displayed at various functions of the 1914 Congress, and I thank Jean-Loup Chappelet and Karl Wendel of the IOC staff for access to the archives and for showing me these photos.

[16]Mandell, *The First Modern*, p. 81(with Coubertin. *Campagne de 21 ans* [Paris. 1908], p.90).

[17]Ibid. Coubertin's success lay in this extraordinary combination of visionary and realistic principles.

[18]Pierre de Coubertin, "Olympic Games of 1896," *Century Magazine* 53 (1896), p. 53.

[19]Like virtually all the items in the *Revue olympique*, this article is unsigned. Later, in *Memoires Olympiques*, p. 124, Coubertin attributed this article to his close friend and IOC colleague from England, Rev. Laffan (with some apologies for "Laffan's" idealistic naivety). But there is much in the phraseology of "Pax Olimpica" that reminds one of Coubertin's 1892 speech, his 1913 article on the rings, and other writing. The English may be Laffan's; the *Revue Olympique* did not print unsigned opinions unless they were Coubertin's.

a national, an international and a world-wide tenet . . .. Happily, war has ceased to
be a form of rather violent amusement. Nations only go to war nowadays when serious
issues are at stake . . . and so the establishment of a world-wide Pax Olimpica may
be a remote possibility" (emphasis added).[20]

Wouldn't a flagful of Olympic rings well symbolize that happy state, the Great
Olympic Pax—Universal World Peace?

But if all that is true, that each ring originally represented a specific Olympiad
and Coubertin expected to add a sixth and seventh ring, and so on, why
did he change his mind? Why in August 1913 did he *instead* say that the
five rings represented the vague "five parts of the world"—instead of those
five specific countries? Why, to be exact, did he *not* fly a flag with seven
interlocked rings at Olympiad VII in Antwerp?

IV

The answer is War, and is again found in Coubertin's own sentences,
this time not between the lines. A year after printing "Pax Olimpica,"
Coubertin—in his 1913 article on the Rings—becomes obsessed with war,
distracted. He digresses from his explanation about the Rings:

> These five links—are they solidly clinched the one to the other? Doesn't a war some
> day threaten to break our Olympic substructure? That is a question which has already
> been posed. Since the occasion is here, I welcome the chance to answer.

The founder of the IOC here proceeds to insist on his high ambitions
for the spreading Olympic movement—it intends to march on no matter what.
No one should underestimate its permanence nor its progressive momentum:

> Therefore a war could not stop nor thwart its progress. As the Preamble to the Rules
> of the [1914] Congress says, "An Olympiad might not be celebrated, but neither the
> order nor the intervals can be changed." If—*God forbid*—the VIIth or the VIIIth
> Olympiad cannot be celebrated, the *IXth will be celebrated* (emphases added).

But then Coubertin digresses further on War, even becoming a bit bellig-
erent. Yet he catches himself:

> So here we are, perhaps far from our subject. . . . Let me come back to it, reiterating
> that war would have no influence on the Olympic future and that, when peace does
> come, *the IOC will be at its desk* continuing its global work. That is why the new
> emblem (the five rings) in its eloquent language evokes *not only the territory conquered*
> but also the assurance of its permanence (emphases added).[21]

---

[20]"Pax Olimpica," *Revue Olympique* (July 1912), pp. 99-102.

[21]Coubertin, *"L'embleme et Le Drapeau,"* pp. 119-120. The French I have here translated as "territory
conquered" is *l'espace conquis.* How could the "five continents"—especially the vast
continents of Africa and Asia—be called "conquered territory," "won over to Olympism"
in 1913? Perhaps Coubertin switched to the continent-version after this article was already
in draft (the first five Olympic host nations suit his phraseology much better).

The final image there, "territory conquered," astonishes. It is an image taken from military conquest. Coubertin saw his "Olympism" as an army of Peace, waging war against War. Already five nations were "conquered by Olympism," their rings now fixed in friendship on the banner of the Olympic host. Germany was scheduled as the next to fall, the next nation to succumb to Peace, a victim of Olympic ring number six.

Yet by August, 1913 Coubertin could not help but already see the 1914 War around the corner ("when peace comes")—a crack in the next link, dark clouds over the Olympic movement. As the Berlin Olympic Committee prepared for Olympiad VI, the 1916 Games, the Berlin government prepared for Great War I, the 1914 edition. Coubertin speaks guardedly and theoretically only of "the VIIth or VIIIth Olympiad" as a possible war victim. But he knew. Like a superstitious man knocking on wood, he avoids direct mention of the imminent VIth Olympiad, Berlin.

In late June, 1914 the long ballyhooed 1914 World Olympic Congress assembled in Paris; but as it actually sat in session — in Sarajevo a gunshot felled Archduke Ferdinand. It was heard round the world, but loudest in Paris. Coubertin's First World Congress adjourned not under the auspices of spreading world peace, but under the spectre of universal mobilization. Within the month German armies marched against Paris. The nations of the world were locked in mortal combat, not linked in love and "universal peace." The once pacifist Coubertin tried to enlist in the French army, now wanting to fight with guns the same Germany he had hoped to conquer with long-jumping[22]. His own army rejected him. Too old. Embittered, he removed to Switzerland and took up his pen instead. *Olympiad VI would not take place.* Coubertin was no doubt relieved he had foreseen the probability, and given a contingency explanation of the rings. The Baron and his 1913 "1914 emblem" retrenched, solidified. There would be no sixth ring.

When the War ended, the IOC as Coubertin predicted was "at its desk." The Games survived. Olympiad VII took place as scheduled. There at Antwerp in 1920—Coubertin noted with pride—"One could see the five multi-colored rings everywhere."[23] But there could *never* be a sixth ring. No Frenchman, not one of Germany's enemies, would have brooked an Olympic symbol whose last Ring of Friendship stood for Germany and for a non-event. If no Olympiad could be skipped, as Coubertin had insisted, Olympiad VI, the

---

[22]In an undated letter (late 1914) addressed to members of the IOC Coubertin briefly resigned the presidency of the IOC, turning it over to his friend Baron Godefroy de Blonay of Lausanne. He explained that he wanted "to participate" in the war, and he thought it incorrect for "a soldier" to head the IOC. "Coubertin was not so much against war as for peace," as MacAloon correctly puts it (above, n. 14, p. 107), distinguishing the Baron's brand of pacifism from other types. Despite his work for peace, there was always a strain of militarism running through Coubertin's words and deeds. The letter in which he resigns to become "a soldier" is reproduced in Otto Mayer, *A Travers les Anneaux Olympiques* (Geneva: publisher unknown, 1960), facing p. 33.

[23]Coubertin, *Mémoires Olympiques*, p. 160.

first non-Olympiad, needed another treatment (silence). So did the Olympic logo—crystallized in its 1913 configuration—now permanently and vaguely representing the "five parts" of the world, not the "first five Olympiads". Olympiad VI was too awful to behold. Even now it is still shocking. (Figure 20).

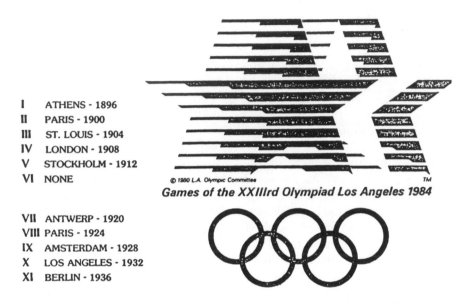

I	ATHENS - 1896
II	PARIS - 1900
III	ST. LOUIS - 1904
IV	LONDON - 1908
V	STOCKHOLM - 1912
VI	NONE

© 1980 L.A. Olympic Committee   TM

Games of the XXIIIrd Olympiad Los Angeles 1984

VII	ANTWERP - 1920
VIII	PARIS - 1924
IX	AMSTERDAM - 1928
X	LOS ANGELES - 1932
XI	BERLIN - 1936

Figure 20. From a placemat used in Santa Barbara restaurant, Spring 1984.

V

Since this paper was delivered at the Sport Literature Association meeting in San Diego, July 27, 1984—the eve of opening day, Olympiad XXIII in Los Angeles, the rings have continued to be a potent source for editorial comment. These comments closely relate to Coubertin's original perceptions of the meaning of the rings and to some of his comments (*e.g.*, "are they solidly clinched, the one to the other?" See the examples of national magazine covers from Spring 1984 (Figures 21, 22 and 23). Unfortunately, these magazines were not so concerned about the integrity of the rings in Spring 1980. A Conrad cartoon (Figure 24, the rings as peace sign) which was published in the *Los Angeles Times* as Olympiad XXIII headed for its Closing Ceremonies comes, I suspect, closest to Coubertin's original design.

VI

Our beloved Olympic flag is a specifically 1913 "1914" flag, a frozen fossil, with a crystallized logo from a very special time and place. That time and place is not idyllic ancient Greece, as the rash of recent Olympics books

Figure 21.

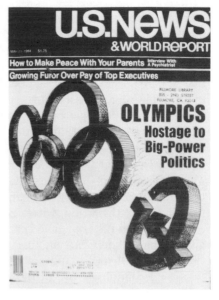

Figure 22.

Figure 23.

Figure 24.

would have us believe.[24] The five rings come directly from pre-World War I Europe, where naive visions and high hopes of universal peace ran rampant—only to be shattered and dashed in utter disillusion.

Perhaps it is good that our logo is frozen right there—the five Olympic rings a constant reminder of how the best laid plans of men and Barons may go awry. And even if Coubertin did not at first intend the five rings of the 1914 Congress as a permanent symbol, they became one. That is reality. Coubertin put his finger on one of the few authentic items that the modern Olympics have extracted from the ancient games, continuity. The Olympics are above—more permanent than—the coming and going of whole nations. They survived the First World War, outliving many of those one-time countries. They outlived Coubertin himself, a Second World War, and the three circles of the Arms of Krupp. Increasingly, the Olympics are the meeting place of the citizens of the world, where people from diverse governments meet to contend not on the battlefield but in the stadium. Contestants and spectators alike come to know one another as people instead of stereotyped enemies or allies. The Olympic Games of 1952-1976 probably did more to foster world-wide understanding than all the diplomacy, peace movements, and other cultural exchanges combined—precisely as Coubertin predicted in his first Olympic call of 1892.

Some governmental leaders in pursuit of national gain—or to emphasize the divisive character of world politics—have misused the Games. They did not understand that the Games belong to the citizens of the world, their own special weapons for peace. But in the long run nationalistic propaganda and "boycotts" probably cannot undo the athletes' own truly important work toward a Pax Olympica. War itself—even death—could not break the link of friendship (founded 1936) that joined the American Jesse Owens and the German athlete Luz Long. After Long himself fell in the War, his son continued as friend of his father's friend from America until Owens died in 1980.[25] Let's hope that the *people* of the world continue to meet under Coubertin's 1913 "1914" aegis, the five rings of the first five host countries—even under that phantom sixth ring. Let's hope that they may become friends in the long-jump pit instead of corpses in the trenches. That is the meaning of the Olympics, and the true symbolism of the Olympic logo—just five little links straining to make an infinite chain.

---

[24]See above, Section I. "The ancient Greeks," the historically inept Avery Brundage claimed, "used to stop fighting to stage the (Olympic) games. Now we stop the games to stage our wars" (Dick Schaap, *Illustrated History of the Olympics*, 3rd. ed. [New York: Knopf, 1975], p. 4). Actually, the Greeks neither stopped their wars to have Olympics nor stopped their Olympics to have wars. Somehow they always managed to do both.

[25]"Owens wanted 'Boycott' and Moscow Games, too," *Los Angeles Times*, April 1, 1980, Part III, pp. 1, 8.

Bibliography

Alexander, Charles C. *Ty Cobb: Baseball's Fierce Immortal.* New York: Oxford University Press, 1984.

Anderson, Douglas A. "Sports Coverage In Daily Newspapers." *Journalism Quarterly* 60 (1983): 497-500).

Anderson, William Gilbert. *Anderson's Physical Education.* Broadway, New York: A.D. Dana, 1897.

Angell, Roger. "Baseball—The Perfect Game." *New York Times,* 1 April 1984, 8-E.

————. *Late Innings: A Baseball Companion.* New York: Simon and Schuster, 1982.

————. *The Summer Game.* New York: Popular Library, 1972.

Ashe, Arthur with Neil Amdur. *Off The Court.* New York: New American Library, 1981.

Baden-Powell, Sir Roger. *Quick Training for War: A Few Practical Suggestions Illustrated by Diagrams.* London: Herbert Jenkins, 1914.

Baker, William J. *Sports in the Western World.* Totowa, N.J.: Rowan and Littlefield, 1982.

Baker, William J. and James A. Rog. *Sports and the Humanities: A Symposium.* Orono, Me.: University of Maine at Orono Press, 1983.

Barich, Bill. *Laughing in the Hills.* New York: Viking, 1980.

————. *Traveling Light.* New York: Viking, 1984.

Barth, Gunther. *City People.* New York: Oxford University Press, 1980.

Becker, Ernest. *The Denial of Death.* New York: The Free Press, 1973.

Beezley, William H. *Locker Rumors: Folklore and Football.* Chicago: Nelson-Hall, 1986.

Bergan, Ronald. *Sports in the Movies.* New York: Proteus Books, 1982.

Berman, Neil David. *Playful Fictions and Fictional Players: Game, Sport, and Survival in Contemporary American Fiction.* Port Washington, N.Y.: Kennikat, 1981.

Bernstein, B. *Class, Codes and Control.* London: Routledge and Kegan Paul, 1971.

Betts, John. *America's Sporting Heritage.* Reading, Mass.: Addison-Wesley, 1974.

————. "Mind and Body in Early American Thought." *The Journal of American History* 54 (1968): 787-805.

Birdwell, Cleo. *Amazons: An Intimate Memoir by the First Woman Ever to Play in the National Hockey League.* New York: Holt, Rinehart and Winston, 1980.

Blake, Kathleen. *Play, Games, and Sport: The Literary Works of Lewis Carroll.* Ithaca: Cornell University Press, 1974.

Blanchard, Kendall A. *Mississippi Choctaws at Play: The Serious Side of Leisure.* Champaign: University of Illinois Press, 1982.

Boorstin, Daniel. *The Image or What Happened to the American Dream.* New York: Atheneum, 1962.

Boswell, Thomas. *How Life Imitates The World Series: An Inquiry Into the Game.* Garden City, N.Y.: Doubleday, 1982.

————. *Why Time Begins on Opening Day.* Garden City, N.Y.: Doubleday, 1984.

Bouton, Jim. *Ball Four.* New York: World, 1970.

Bowen, William Edward. *Edward Bowen, A Memoir.* London: Longmans, 1902.

Bowra, Cecil Maurice. *Heroic Poetry.* London: Macmillan, 1966.

Boyle, Robert C. *At The Top Of Their Game.* Piscataway, N.J.: Winchester, 1983.

————. *Sport: Mirror of American Life.* Boston: Little, Brown, 1963.

Brashler, William. *The Bingo Long Traveling All-Stars and Motor Kings.* New York: Harper & Row, 1973.

Brelich, A. *Le iniziazioni, parte secunda.* Rome: Edizioni dell'atena, 1962.

————. *Paides e Parthenoi vol. 1,* Rome: Edizioni dell'atena, 1969.

————. Brode, H. *Günter Grass.* München: Beck, 1979.

Brodie, John with James D. Houston. *Open Field.* Boston: Houghton Mifflin, 1974.

Brosnan, Jim. *The Long Season.* New York: Harper, 1960.

Broun, Hob. *Odditorium.* New York: Harper & Row, 1983.

Brown, Rita Mae. *Sudden Death.* New York: Bantam, 1984.

Buckley, Vincent. *Poetry And Morality.* London: Chatto and Windus, 1959.

Burdick, Eugene. *The Ninth Wave.* Boston: Houghton Mifflin, 1956.

Cady, Edwin H. *The Big Game: College Sports and American Life.* Knoxville: University of Tennessee Press, 1978.

Campbell, D.A. *The Golden Lyre: The Themes of the Greek Lyric Poets.* London: Duckworth, 1983.

Campbell, Joseph. *The Hero With A Thousand Faces.* New York: Meridian, 1956.

Camus, Albert. *The Myth of Sisyphus and Other Essays.* New York: Vintage, 1960.

Carkeet, David. *The Greatest Slump of All Time.* New York: Harper & Row, 1984.

Carlyle, Thomas. *On Heroes, Hero-Worship and the Heroic in History.* New York: Crowell, 1841.

Carroll, John B. *Language, Thought and Reality: Selected Writings of Benjamin Lee Whorf.* New York: Wiley, 1959.

Cawelti, John G. *Adventure, Mystery, and Romance: Formula Stories as Art and Popular Culture.* Chicago: University of Chicago Press, 1976.

Chapman, Abraham, ed. *Jewish-American Literature*. New York: Signet, 1974.

Charyn, Jerome. *The Seventh Babe*. New York: Arbor House, 1979.

Checkley, Edwin. *A Natural Method of Physical Training*. Brooklyn, New York: Bryantland, 1894.

Choice, Harriet. "Life After Rocky." *Chicago Tribune Magazine*, May 1982, 12-15.

Coffin, Tristram Potter. *The Old Ball Game in Folklore and Fiction*. New York: Herder and Herder, 1971.

Cohen, Eliot, ed. *Commentary on the American Scene*. New York: Knopf, 1953.

Colegate, Isabel. *The Shooting Party*. New York: Viking, 1982.

Collins, Larry and Dominique Lapierre. *I'll Dress You in Mourning*. New York: Simon and Schuster, 1968.

Cooney, Ellen. *All The Way Home*. New York: Putnam's, 1984.

Coote, James. *The 1980 Book of the Olympics*. London: Webb Publications, 1980.

Coover, Robert. *The Universal Baseball Association, Inc., J. Henry Waugh, Prop*. New York: Random House, 1968.

Coubertin, Pierre de. *Mémoires Olympiques*. Lausanne: International Olympic Committee, 1931.

————. "Olympic Games of 1896." *Century Magazine* 53 (1896): 53.

Crabbe, John K. "On the Playing Fields of Devon." *English Journal* 52 (1963): 109-111.

Craig, John. *Chappie and Me: An Autobiographical Novel*. New York: Dodd, Mead, 1979.

Creamer, Robert W. *Babe: A Legend Comes to Life*. New York: Simon and Schuster, 1974.

————. *Stengel—His Life and Times*. New York: Simon and Schuster, 1984.

Crepeau, Richard C. *Baseball: America's Diamond Mind, 1919-1941*. Orlando: University Presses of Florida, 1980.

Crews, Harry. *Karate Is a Thing of the Spirit*. New York: Quill, 1983.

Croix, G.E.M. de Ste. *The Origins of the Peloponnesian War*. London: Duckworth, 1972.

Culler, Jonathan. *Structuralist Poetics*. Ithaca: Cornell University Press, 1975.

Daley, Robert. *Only a Game*. New York: New American Library, 1968.

Deford, Frank. *Everybody's All-American*. New York: Viking, 1981.

DeLillo, Don. *End Zone*. New York: Pocket Books, 1973.

Dewey, John. *Experience and Nature*. New York: Dover, 1958.

Dizikes, John. *Sportsmen and Gamesmen: From the Years that Shaped American Ideas about Winning and Losing and How to Play the Game*. Boston: Houghton Mifflin, 1981.

Dodge, Tom, ed. *A Literature of Sports*. Lexington, Mass.: D.C. Heath, 1980.

Dolson, Frank. *Beating The Bushes*. South Bend, Ind.: Icarus, 1982.

Dryden, Ken. *The Game: A Thoughtful and Provocative Look at a Life in Hockey*. New York: Times Books, 1983.

Duncan, David James. *The River Why.* New York: Sierra Club (Random House), 1982.

Duncan, Don. "Sports Cliches—The 'Real' Story From A Report That Came To Play." *APME News,* May 1978, 4-5.

Duncan, Hugh Dalziel. *Language and Literature in Our Society.* London: Bedminster Press, 1961.

————. *Symbols in Society.* New York: Oxford University Press, 1968.

Eisen, George. "Physical Activity, Physical Education and Sport in the Old Testament." *Canadian Journal of History of Sport and Physical Education* 6 (1975): 44-65.

Ellis, James. "A Separate Peace: The Fall from Innocence." *English Journal* 53 (1964): 313-318.

Ellsworth, J. D. "Agon: Studies in the Use of a Word." Ph.D. diss., University of California, Berkeley, 1971.

Evans, David Allan. *Real And False Alarms.* Kansas City: BKMK Press, University of Missouri-Kansas City, 1984.

Evans, G. Blakemore, ed. *The Riverside Shakespeare.* Boston: Houghton Mifflin, 1974.

Everett, Percival L. *Suder.* New York: Viking, 1983.

Faulkner, William. *Go Down, Moses.* New York: Curtis, 1942.

Fiedler, Leslie. *What Was Literature?* New York: Simon and Schuster, 1983.

Finley, M. I. *The World of Odysseus.* New York: Viking, 1965.

Fishwick, Marshall W. *American Heroes: Myth and Reality.* Washington: Public Affairs Press, 1954.

————. *The Hero American Style.* New York: D. McKay, 1969.

Fitzgerald, F. Scott. *The Great Gatsby.* New York: Scribner's, 1925.

Fleischer, Charles. "A Bit of Baseball Biography." *Baseball Magazine* 1 (1908): 34-35.

Fleming, G.H. *The Dizziest Season: The Gashouse Gang Chases the Pennant.* New York: William Morrow, 1984.

————. *The Unforgettable Season.* New York: Holt, Rinhart & Winston, 1981.

Folsom, James K. *The American Western Novel.* New Haven: College and University Press, 1966.

Frank, Lawrence. *Playing Hardball: The Dynamics of Baseball Folk Speech.* New York: Lang, 1983.

Frazer, J. G. *Pausanias' Description of Greece.* New York: Biblo and Tannen, 1965.

Frewin, L. *An Anthology of Cricket.* London: MacDonald, 1968.

Friedman, Melvin J., ed.. "Focus on Academics in Sports" *Journal of American Culture* 4 (1981).

Frischer, Bernard. *The Sculpted Word.* Berkeley: University of California Press, 1982.

Frye, Northrop. *Anatomy of Criticism: Four Essays.* Princeton, N.J.: Princeton University Press, 1957.

————. *The Stubborn Structure: Essays on Criticism and Society.* Ithaca, N.Y.: Cornell University Press, 1972.

Gale, Norman. *More Cricket Songs.* London: Alston Rivers, 1905.

Gallico, Paul. *Farewell to Sport.* New York: Knopf, 1938.

Gent, Peter. *The Franchise*. New York: Villard Books (Random House), 1983.

Gerber, Ellen and William Morgan, eds. *Sport and the Body*. 2nd ed. Philadelphia: Lee and Febiger, 1979.

Gerlach, Larry R. *The Men in Blue: Conversations with Umpires*. New York: Viking, 1980.

Giamatti, A. Bartlett. "The Green Fields of My Mind." *Yale Alumni Magazine*, November, 1977: 295-297.

Gifford, Barry. *The Neighborhood of Baseball: A Personal History of the Chicago Cubs*. San Francisco: Creative Arts, 1981.

Girouard, Mark. *The Return to Camelot: Chivalry and the English Gentleman*. New Haven: Yale University Press, 1981.

Glader, Eugene A. *Amateurism and Athletics*. West Point: Leisure Press, 1978.

Glicksberg, Charles I. *The Tragic Vision in Twentieth Century Literature*. Carbondale: Southern Illinois University Press, 1963.

Goldstein, Jeffrey H., ed. *Sports, Games, and Play: Social and Psychological Viewpoints*. New York: Halsted Press, 1979.

————. *Sports Violence*. New York: Springer-Verlag, 1983.

Goldstein, Richard. *Spartan Seasons: How Baseball Survived the Second World War*. New York: Macmillan, 1980.

Golenbock, Peter. *An Oral History of the Brooklyn Dodgers*. New York: Putnam's, 1984.

Gomme, A.W. *A Historical Commentary on Thucydides*. Oxford: Clarendon Press, 1956.

Goodhart, Philip M.P. and Christopher Chataway. *War Without Weapons*. London: W. H. Allen, 1968.

Grass, Günther. *Dog Years*. New York: Fawcett Crest, 1979.

————. *Katz und Maus*. Neuwied: Luchterhand, 1964.

————. "Sport ohne Stoppuhr." *Olympische Jugend* 11(1971): 8-10.

Gray, H.B. *Public Schools and the Empire*. London: Williams and Norgate, 1913.

Green, Gerald. *My Son the Jock*. New York: Praeger, 1975.

————. *The Last Angry Man*. Mattituck, N.Y.: American Reprint, 1980.

————. *To Brooklyn With Love*. New York: Pocket Books, 1969.

Greenberg, Eric Rolfe. *The Celebrant*. New York: Everest House, 1983.

Greiling, Franzeska Lynne. "The Theme of Freedom in *A Separate Peace*." *English Journal* 56 (1967): 1269-1272.

Greimas, A. J. and F. Rastier. "The Interaction of Semiotic Constructs." *Yale French Studies* 41 (1968): 86-105.

Greimas, J. Courtes. *Semiotics and Language: An Analytical Dictionary*. Translated by Larry Crist. Bloomington, Ind.: Indiana University Press, 1982.

Grella, George. "Baseball and the American Dream." *Massachusetts Review* 16 (1975): 560-565.

Grombach, John V. *The Official 1980 Olympic Guide*. New York: Times Books, 1980.

Gropman, Donald. *Say It Ain't So, Joe!: The Story of Shoeless Joe Jackson*. Boston: Little, Brown, 1979.

Grossinger, Richard. *The Temple of Baseball*. Berkeley, Ca.: North Atlantic Books, 1985.

Gruneau, Richard S. "Freedom and Constraint: The Paradoxes of Play, Games and Sports." *Journal of Sports History* 7 (1980): 68-86.

Gumperez, J. amd Dell Hymes, eds. *Directions in Socio-Linguistics*. New York: Holt, Rinehart & Winston, 1972.

Gunn, Giles B. *Literature and Religion*. London: SCM Press, 1971.

Guttmann, Allen. *From Ritual to Record: The Nature of Modern Sports*. New York: Columbia University Press, 1978.

————. "Le Plaisir du Sport." *Arete: The Journal of Sport Literature* 1(1983): 113-124.

————. *The Games Must Go On: Avery Brundage and the Olympic Movement*. New York: Columbia University Press, 1984.

Haig-Brown, Alan R. *The OTC and the Great War*. New York: Scribner's, 1915.

Halberstam, David. *The Amateurs: The Story of Four Young Men and Their Quest for an Olympic Gold Medal*. New York: Morrow, 1985.

————. *The Breaks of the Game*. New York: Knopf, 1981.

Halio, Jay L. "John Knowles's Short Novels." *Studies in Short Fiction* 1(1964): 107-113.

Hall, Donald. *Fathers Playing Catch With Sons: Essays on Sport*. San Francisco: North Point, 1985.

Hannah, Barry. *The Tennis Handsome*. New York: Knopf, 1983.

Hano, Arnold. *A Day in the Bleachers*. New York: DeCapo, 1982.

Harris, Harold Arthur. *Greek Athletics and the Jews*. Cardiff: University of Wales Press, 1976.

Harris, Mark. *Bang the Drum Slowly*. New York: Knopf, 1956.

————. *It Looked Like For Ever*. New York: McGraw-Hill, 1979.

————. *The Southpaw*. New York: Bobbs-Merrill, 1953.

Harrison, Don. *The Spartan*. Boston: Alyson Publications, Inc. 1982.

Harrison, Walter. "Six-Pointed Diamond: Baseball and American Jews." *Journal of Popular Culture* 15 (1981): 112-118.

Harvey, Stephen. "Is the Western Really Dead, Or Simply in Disguise?" *New York Times*, 15 July 1984, Sect. 2, p. 16.

Hawke, Terence. *Structuralism and Semiotics*. London: Methuen, 1977.

Hays, Donald. *The Dixie Association*. New York: Simon and Schuster, 1984.

Hemingway, Ernest. *A Farewell to Arms*. New York: Scribners's, 1929.

————. *The Dangerous Summer*. New York: Scribner's, 1985.

————. *The Short Stories of Ernest Hemingway*. New York: Scribner's, 1938.

————. *The Sun Also Rises*. New York: Scribner's, 1926.

Hemphill, Paul. *Long Gone*. New York: Viking, 1979.

Herrigel, Eugen. *Zen in the Art of Archery*. New York: Random House, Vintage Books, 1971.

Higginson, Thomas Wentworth. "Gymnastics." *Atlantic Monthly* 7 (1861): 283-302.

Higgs, Robert J. *Laurel and Thorn: The Athlete in American Literature*. Lexington, Kentucky: University Press of Kentucky, 1981.

————. *Sports: A Reference Guide.* Westport, Conn.: Greenwood, 1982.

Hill, I. William. "Negative Sports Reporting Irks Top Team Coaches." *Editor and Publisher* 14 June 14 1980, 17.

Hoberman, John M. *Sport and Political Ideology.* Austin: University of Texas Press, 1985.

Holladay, A.J. "Hoplites and Heresies." *Journal of Hellenic Studies 102* (1982): 94-103.

Holtzman, Jerome, ed. *No Cheering in the Press Box.* New York: Holt, Rinehart, and Winston, 1973.

Honig, Donald. *The Last Great Season.* New York: Simon and Schuster, 1979.

Horowitz, I.L., ed. *Power, Politics and People: The Collected Papers of C. Wright Mills.* Oxford: Oxford University Press, 1973.

Howarth, Patrick. *Play Up and Play the Game: The Heroes of Popular Fiction.* London: Eyre Methuen, 1973.

Howe, Irving. *World of Our Fathers.* New York: Harcourt Brace Jovanovich, 1976.

Huenergard, Celeste. "No More Cheerleading on the Sports Pages." *Editor and Publisher* 6 June 16 1979, 11.

Huizinga, Johan. *Homo Ludens: A Study of the Play-Element in Culture.* Boston: Beacon Press, 1955.

Inglis, Fred. "Good and Bad Habits: Bourdieu, Habermas and the Condition of England." *Sociological Review* 27 (1979): 353-369.

————. *Ideology and the Imagination.* Cambridge: Cambridge University Press, 1975.

————. *The Name of the Game: Sport and Society.* London: Heinemann, 1977.

Isaacs, Neil. *Jock Culture, USA.* New York: Norton, 1978.

Jacques, T.D. and G.R. Pavia, eds. *Sport in Australia: Selected Readings in Physical Activity.* Sydney: McGraw-Hill, 1976.

James, C. L. R. *Beyond a Boundary.* New York: Pantheon, 1983.

James, Z. "Sport: A Myth About Consciousness." *Quest* 30 (1978): 28-35.

Jameson, Fredric. *Marxism and Form.* Princeton: Princeton University Press, 1971.

————. *The Political Unconscious.* Ithaca, New York: Cornell University Press, 1981.

————. *The Prison House of Language.* Princeton: Princeton University Press, 1972.

Janes, Lewis. *Health Exercises: The Rationale and Practice of the Lifting Cure or Health Lift.* 7th ed. New York: Lewis G. Janes, 1873.

Jenkins, Dan. *Dead Solid Perfect.* New York: Atheneum, 1974.

Jenkyns, Richard. *The Victorians and Ancient Greece.* Cambridge: Harvard University Press, 1980.

Johnson, Don. *The Importance of Visible Scars.* Green Harbor, Mass.: Wampeter Press, 1984.

Johnson, W. Stacey. *The Voices of Matthew Arnold.* New Haven: Yale University Press, 1961.

Jones, David A. and Leverett T. Smith, Jr. "Sports in America." *Journal of Popular Culture* 16 (1983).

Jones, James. *From Here to Eternity.* New York: Scribner's, 1951.

Jones, Robert F. *Blood Sport: A Journey Up the Hassayampa.* New York: Simon and Schuster, 1974.

Kahn, Roger. *The Boys of Summer.* New York: Harper & Row, 1972.

———. *Good Enough to Dream.* New York: Playboy Press, 1985.

———. *Seventh Game.* New York: New American Library, 1982.

Kaplan, Jim. *Pine-Tarred and Feathered: A Year on the Baseball Beat.* Chapel Hill, N.C.: Algonquin Books, 1984.

Kazin, Alfred. *A Walker in the City.* New York: Harcourt Brace, 1951.

Kennedy, Ian. "Dual Perspective Narrative and the Character of Phineas in 'A Separate Peace'. " *Studies in Short Fiction* 12(1970): 353-359.

Kennedy, William. *Ironweed.* New York: Viking, 1983.

Kerrane, Kevin and Richard Grossinger, eds. *Baseball Diamonds: Traces, Visions, and Voodoo from a Native American Rite.* New York: Anchor Press/Doubleday, 1980.

Kerrane, Kevin. *Dollar Sign on the Muscle, The World of Baseball Scouting.* New York: Beufort Books, 1984.

Kiesling, Stephen. *The Shell Game: Reflections on Rowing and the Pursuit of Excellence.* New York: Morrow, 1983.

Kinsella, W. B. *The Iowa Baseball Confederation.* New York: Penguin, 1985.

———. *Shoeless Joe.* Boston: Houghton Mifflin, 1982.

———. *The Thrill of the Grass.* New York: Penguin, 1984.

Klapp, Orrin E. *Heroes, Villains, and Fools: The Changing American Character.* Englewood Cliffs, N.J.: Prentice Hall, 1962.

Klein, Dave. *The Pro Football Mystique.* New York: New American Library, 1978.

Kluger, Steve. *Changing Pitches.* New York: St. Martin's, 1984.

Knowles, John. *A Separate Peace.* New York: Bantam, 1969.

Koppett, Leonard. *Sports Illusion, Sports Reality: A Reporter's View of Sports, Journalism, and Society.* Boston: Houghton Mifflin, 1981.

Kramer, Jerry, with Dick Schaap. *Distant Replay.* New York: Putnam's, 1985.

Kyle, D. "A Historical Study of Athletics in Ancient Athens." Ph.D. diss., MacMaster University, 1981.

Lachtman, Howard, ed. *Sporting Blood: Selections from Jack London's Greatest Sports Writing.* Novato, Calif., Presidio Press, 1981.

Lapchick, Richard. *Broken Promises: Racism in American Sports.* New York: St. Martin's/ Marek, 1984.

Lasch, Christopher. *The Culture of Narcissism: American Life in an Age of Diminishing Expectations.* New York: Norton, 1979.

Laurenson, Diane and Alan Swingewood. *The Sociology of Literature.* London: MacGibbon and Kee, 1972.

Ladyard, W. Sargent, ed. *Dudley Allen Sargent: An Autobiography.* Philadelphia: Lea and Febiger, 1927.

Lee, H.M. "Athletic Arete in Pindar." *Ancient World* 7 (1983): 31-37.

Leonard, Fred Eugene and George B. Affleck. *A Guide to the History of Physical Education.* 3rd ed. Philadelphia: Lea and Febiger, 1947.

Levin, Jenifer. *Water Dancer.* New York: Poseidon, 1982.

Levine, Peter. "The Promise of Sport in Antebellum America." *Journal of American Culture* 2 (1980): 623-634.

————. *A. G. Spalding and the Rise of Baseball: The Promise of American Sport.* New York: Oxford University Press, 1985.

Lewis, Dio. "Dumb Bell Exercises." *Lewis' Gymnastic Monthly and Journal of Physical Culture* 2 (1862): 121-168.

————. "Physical Culture." *The Massachusetts Teacher* 8 (1860): 375-377.

————. *The New Gymnastics for Men, Women, and Children.* Boston: Ticknor and Fields, 1861.

Lipman, Samuel. "Bartok at the Piano." *Commentary,* May 1984, 56-61.

Lipsky, Richard. *How We Play the Game: Why Sports Dominate American Life.* Boston: Beacon, 1981.

Lipsyte, Robert. *SportsWorld: An American Dreamland.* New York: Quadrangle, 1976.

Llosa, Mario Vargas. *The Cubs and Other Stories.* New York: Harper & Row, 1979.

Lorenz, Tom. *Guys Like Us.* New York: Viking, 1983.

Lowenfish, Lee, with Tony Lupien. *The Imperfect Diamond: The Story of Baseball's Reserve System and the Men Who Fought to Change It.* New York: Stein and Day, 1980.

Lubin, Harold, ed. *Heroes and Anti-Heroes: A Reader in Depth.* San Francisco: Chandler, 1968.

Lucas, D. W. *Aristotle's Poetics.* Oxford: Clarendon, 1968.

Lucas, John. *The Modern Olympic Games.* New York: A.S. Barnes and Co., 1980.

MacAloon, John J. *This Great Symbol: Pierre de Coubertin and the Origins of the Modern Olympic Games.* Chicago: University of Chicago Press, 1982.

McClanahan, Ed. *The Natural Man.* New York: Farrar, Straus and Giroux, 1983.

McClusky Jr., John. *Mr. America's Last Season Blues: A Novel.* Baton Rouge: Louisiana State University Press, 1983.

MacDonagh, Michael. *In London During the Great War: The Diary of a Journalist.* London: Eyre and Spottiswoode, 1935.

McGuane, Thomas. *An Outside Chance: Essays on Sport.* New York: Farrar, Straus and Giroux, 1980.

McIntosh, Peter. *Fair Play: Ethics in Sport and Education.* London: Heinemann, 1978.

Mack, E.C. *Public Schools and British Opinion 1780-1860.* New York: Columbia University Press, 1941.

MacLean, Norman, *A River Runs Through It.* Chicago: The University of Chicago Press 1982.

McPhee, John. *A Sense of Where You Are.* New York: Farrar, Straus and Giroux, 1965.

————. *Giving Good Weight.* New York: Farrar, Straus and Giroux, 1979.

————. *Levels of the Game.* London: Macdonald and Company, 1969.

————. *Table of Contests.* New York: Farrar, Straus and Giroux, 1985.

Magill, Frank M. *Contemporary Literary Scene II.* Englewood Cliffs, New Jersey: Salem Press, 1979.

Malamud, Bernard. *The Natural.* New York: Dell, 1970.

Mandell, Richard. *Sport: A Cultural History.* New York: Columbia University Press, 1984.

————. *The First Modern Olympics.* Berkeley: University of California Press, 1976.

————. *The Nazi Olympics.* New York: Macmillan, 1971.

Mangan, J.A. *Athleticism in the Victorian and Edwardian Public School.* Cambridge University Press, 1981.

————. "Philathlete Extraordinary: A Portrait of the Victorian Moralist, Edward Bowen." *Journal of Sports History* 9 (1982): 23-40.

————. *The Game is Played by Decent Chaps. The Games-Ethic and Imperialism—Aspects of the Diffusion of an Ideal*: Allen Lane/Penguin, 1985.

Mason, Tony. *Association Football and English Society 1863-1915.* Sussex, England: The Harvester Press, 1980.

Mayer, Robert. *The Grace of Shortstops.* Garden City, N.Y.: Doubleday, 1984.

————. *Midge & Decker.* New York: A.& W. Publishers, 1982.

Mehl, E. "Sport kommt nicht von dis-portare, soncern von de-portare," *Die Leibesuebungen* 15 (1967): 232-233.

Meltzer, Milton. *Taking Root.* New York: Dell, 1977.

Messenger, Christian K. "The Dynamics of Ritual and Play: Kesey's One Flew Over the Cuckoo's Nest." *Arete: The Journal of Sport Literature* 1 (1983): 99-107.

————. *Sport and the Spirit of Play in American Fiction: Hawthorne to Faulkner.* New York: Columbia University Press, 1981.

Mewshaw, Michael. *Short Circuit.* New York: Atheneum, 1983.

Mihalich, Joseph C. *Sports and Athletics: Philosophy in Action.* Totowa, New Jersey: Rowman and Littlefield, 1982.

Miller, Jason. *That Championship Season.* New York: Atheneum, 1972.

Miller, S. G. *Arete: Ancient Writers, Papyri, and Inscriptions on the History and Ideals of Greek Athletics and Games.* Chicago: Ares, 1979.

Mitchell, R. "A Conceptual Analysis of Art as Experience and Its Implications for Sport and Physical Education." Ph.D. diss., University of Northern Colorado, 1974.

Moretti, L. *Olympionikai, I Vincitori Negli Antichi Agoni Olympici.* Rome: Edizioni dell'atena, 1957.

Morgenstein, Gary. *The Man Who Wanted to Play Center Field for the New York Yankees.* New York: Atheneum, 1983.

Morris, Willie. *Always Stand in Against the Curve and Other Sports Stories.* Oxford, Miss.: Yoknapatawpha Press, 1983.

————. *The Courting of Marcus Dupree.* Garden City, NY: Doubleday, 1983.

Morris, Wright. *The Hugh Season.* New York: Viking, 1954.

Mrozek, Donald J. *Sport: And American Mentality, 1880-1910.* Knoxville: University of Tennessee Press, 1983.

Mungo, Raymond. *Confessions from Left Field: A Baseball Pilgrimage.* New York: Atheneum, 1981.

Murdock, Eugene C. *Ban Johnson: Czar of Baseball.* Westport, Conn.: Greenwood, 1982.

_____. *Mighty Casey: All-American.* Westport, Conn.: Greenwood, 1984.

Nachbar, Jack, ed. *Focus on the Western.* Englewood Cliffs, N.J.: Prentice-Hall, Inc., 1974.

Neuhaus, V. *Günter Grass.* Stuttgart: Metzler, 1979.

Nieman, Fraser. *Matthew Arnold.* New York: Twayne, 1968.

Nietzsche, Friedrich. *Thus Spoke Zarathustra: A Book for All and None.* Translated by Walter Kaufmann. New York: Viking, 1954.

Novak, Michael. "The Game's the Thing: A Defense of Sports as Ritual." *Columbia Journalism Review* 15 (May/June 1976): 33-38.

_____. *The Joy of Sports.* New York: Basic Books, 1976.

Nunn, Ken. *Tapping the Source.* New York: Delacorte, 1984.

Nygaard, Gary. *Law and Sport.* New Brighton, Minn.: Brighton, 1981.

O'Connor, Philip F. *Stealing Home.* New York: Knopf, 1979.

O'Faolain, Sean. *The Vanishing Hero: Studies in Novelists of the Twenties.* London: Eyre and Spottiswoode, 1956.

Olsen, Lyle and Alfred F. Boe, eds. *Arete: The Journal of Sport Literature* 1 (1983).

Oriard, Michael. *Dreaming of Heroes: American Sports Fiction, 1868-1980.* Chicago: Nelson-Hall, 1982.

_____. "On the Current Status of Sports Fiction." *Arete: The Journal of Sport Literature* 1 (1983): 7-20.

_____. *The End of Autumn.* Garden City: Doubleday, 1982.

Osborne, John. *The Voluntary Recruiting Movement in Britain 1914-1916.* Palo Alto: Stanford University Press, 1979.

Paul, Joan. "The Health Reformers: George Barker Winship and Boston's Strength Seekers." *The Journal of Sport History* 10 (1983): 41-57.

"Pax Olimpica." *Revue Olympique* (July, 1912): pp. 99-102.

Peterson, Robert. *Only the Ball Was White.* Englewood Cliffs, N.J.: Prentice-Hall, 1970.

Pino, John C. *Cliff Walk.* El Dorado Hills, Calif.: Moveable Feast Press, 1985.

Pleket, H.W. "Zur Soziologie des antiken Sports." *Mededelingen van het Nederlands Institut te Rome* n.s. 36 (1974): 57-87.

Plimpton, George. *One More July: A Football Dialogue With Bill Curry.* New York: Harper & Row, 1977.

Pomeranz, Gary. *Out at Home.* Boston: Houghton Mifflin, 1985.

Poole, Lynn and Gray Poole. *History of the Ancient Olympic Games.* New York: I. Obolensky, 1963.

Pound, Reginald. *The Lost Generation.* London: Constable, 1964.

Pritchett, W.K. *The Greek State of War: Part II.* Berkely: University of California Press, 1974.

Quarrington, Paul. *Home Game.* Garden City, N.Y.: Doubleday, 1984.

Quigley, Martin. *The Crooked Pitch: The Curveball in American Baseball History.* Chapel Hill, N.C.: Algonquin Books, 1984.

Rader, Benjamin G. *American Sports: From the Age of Folk Games to the Age of Spectators.* Englewood Cliffs, N.J.: Prentice-Hall, 1983.

_____. *In Its Own Image: How Television Has Transformed Sports.* New York: The Free Press, 1984.

Raglan, Lord. *The Hero: A Study in Tradition, Myth and Drama.* New York: Vintage Books, 1956.

Rank, Otto. *The Birth of the Hero and Other Essays.* New York: Vintage Books, 1964.

Rice, Grantland. *The Tumult and the Shouting.* New York: A.S. Barnes, 1954.

Richter, G. M. A. *Kouroi, Archaic Greek Youths.* New York: Phaidon, 1970.

Ridgway, B. S. *The Archaic Style in Greek Sculpture.* Princeton: Princeton University Press, 1977.

Riess, Steven. *Touching Base: Professional Baseball and American Culture in the Progressive Era.* Westport, Conn.: Greenwood, 1980.

Ritz, David. *The Man Who Brought the Dodgers Back to Brooklyn.* New York: Simon and Schuster, 1981.

Roberts, Randy. *Papa Jack: Jack Johnson and the Era of White Hopes.* New York: The Free Press, 1983.

Rogosin, Donn. *Invisible Men: Life in Baseball's Negro Leagues.* New York: Atheneum, 1984.

Rohde, E. *Psyche.* Tübingen: J.C.B. Mohr, 1925.

Ross, Murray. "Football Red and Baseball Green: The Heroics and Bucolics of American Sport." *Chicago Review* 1 (1971): 30-59.

Rostagni, A. *Aritolel Poetica.* Turin: Chiantore, 1945.

Roth, Philip. *Goodbye, Columbus.* Boston: Houghton Mifflin, 1959.

Russell, Bill. *Go Up for Glory.* New York: Coward-McCann, 1966.

Russell, Bill and Taylor Branch. *Second Wind: The Memoirs of an Opinionated Man.* New York: Random House, 1979.

"Saints and their Bodies." *Atlantic Monthly, March 1858, 582-595.*

Samuel, Raphael and Gareth Stedman Jones, eds. *Culture, Ideology and Politics.* London: Routledge and Kegan Paul, 1982.

Sargent, Ledyard W., ed. *Dudley Allen Sargent: An Autobiography.* Philadelphia: Lea & Febiger, 1927.

Satterthwaite, Frank. *The Three-Wall Nick and Other Angles: A Squash Autobiography.* New York: Holt, Rinehart, and Winston, 1979.

Scanlon, Thomas F. *Greek And Roman Athletics: A Bibliography.* Chicago: Ares, 1984.

_____. "The Vocabulary of Competition: *Agon* and *Aethlos,* Greek Terms for Contest." *Arete: Journal of Sport Literature* 1 (1983): 147-162.

Schaap, Dick. *Illustrated History of the Olympics.* 3rd ed. New York: Knopf, 1975.

Schacht, Al. *Clowning through Baseball.* New York: Bantam, 1949.

Schiffer, Michael. *Ballpark.* New York: Simon and Schuster, 1982.

Scholes, Robert. *Structuralism in Literature.* New Haven, Conn.: Yale University Press, 1974.

Schultheis, Rob. *Bone Games: One Man's Search for the Ultimate Athletic High.* New York: Random House, 1984.

Schwed, Peter and Herbert Warren Wind eds. *Great Stories from the World of Sport.* 3 vols. New York: Simon and Schuster, 1958.

Shaw, Irwin. "The Eighty-Yard Run." *In his Mixed Company,* 13-28. New York: Random House, 1950.

―――――. *The Top of The Hill.* New York: Delacorte, 1979.

Shryock, Richard H. "Sylvester Graham and the Popular Health Movement, 1830-1870." *Mississippi Valley Historical Review* 18 (September 1931): 172-183.

Simon, Brian and Ian Bradley. *The Victorian Public School: Studies in the Development of an Educational Institution; Symposium.* Dublin: Gill and Macmillan, 1975.

Simpson, Peter L. *Stealing Home.* Kansas City: BkMk Press, University of Missouri-K.C., 1985.

Simri, Uriel, ed. *Physical Education and Sports in the Jewish History and Culture: Proceedings of an International Seminar.* Netanya, Israel: Wingate Institute, 1973.

―――――. *Play in Physical Education and Sport: Proceedings of an International Seminar.* Netanya, Israel: Wingate Institute, 1975.

Siner, Howard (ed.). *Sports Classics.* New York: Coward McCann, 1983.

Shields, David. *Heroes.* New York: Simon and Schuster, 1984.

Slack, Enid. "Skating Dances into Art Form." *USA Today,* 23 July, 1984.

Slusher, Howard S. *Man, Sport and Existence.* Philadelphia: Lea and Febiger, 1967.

Smith, David L. "A Half-Dozen Steps to the Sports Section of Tomorrow." *ASNE Bulletin,* April 1983, 8-9.

Smith, Leverett T. *The American Dream and the National Game.* Bowling Green, Ohio: Popular Press, 1975.

Smith, Red. *To Absent Friends.* New York: Atheneum, 1982.

―――――. *Views of Sport.* New York: Knopf, 1954.

Smith, Ronald A. "A Centennial Moses Coit Tyler's *The Brawnville Papers.*" *Journal of Health, Physical Education and Recreation* 41 (1970): 71.

Solomon, Stanley J. *Beyond Formula: American Film Genres.* New York: Harcourt Brace Jovanovich, Inc., 1976.

Ste. Croix, G.E.M. de. *The Origins of the Peloponnesian War.* London: Duckworth, 1972.

Stein, Harry. *Hoopla.* New York: Knopf, 1983.

Stonecipher, Harry W., Edward C. Nicholls, and Douglas A. Anderson. *Electronic Age News Editing.* Chicago: Nelson-Hall, 1981.

Storey, David. *The Sporting Life.* London: Longman, 1960.

Tennebaum, Silvia. *Rachel, The Rabbi's Wife.* New York: William Morrow, 1978.

Terraine, John. "Christmas 1914 and After." *History Today* 29 (1979): 781-789.

―――――. *The Smoke and the Fire: Myths and Anti-Myths of War 1861-1945.* London: Sidgwick and Jackson, 1980.

Tevis, Walter. *The Queen's Gambit.* New York: Random House, 1983.

Thorn, John (editor). *The Armchair Book of Baseball.* New York: Scribner's, 1985.

Thrall, William Flint, Addison Hibbard, and C. High Holman. *A Handbook to Literature.* New York: Odyssey Press, 1960.

Toomay, Pat. *On Any Given Sunday.* New York: Donald I, Fine, 1984.

Tuchman, Barbara W. *The Proud Tower: A Portrait of the World Before the War, 1890-1914.* New York: Macmillan, 1965.

Tyler, Moses Coit. *The Brawnville Papers: Being Memorials of the Brawnville Athletic Club.* Boston: Fields, Osgood, 1869.

Tygiel, Jules. *Baseball's Great Experiment: Jackie Robinson and His Legacy.* New York: Oxford University Press, 1983.

Umphlett, Wiley Lee, ed. *American Sport Culture: The Humanistic Dimensions.* Lewisburg, Pa.: Bucknell University Press, 1985.

————. "The Dynamics of Fiction on the Aesthetics of the Sport Film." *Arete: The Journal of Sport Literature* 2 (1986): 113-121.

————. *The Sporting Myth and the American Experience.* Lewisburg, Pa.: Bucknell University Press, 1975.

Underwood, John. *Death of an American Game: The Crisis in Football.* Boston: Little, Brown, 1979.

————. *Spoiled Sport: A Fan's Notes on the Troubles of Spectator Sports.* Boston: Little, Brown, 1984.

Updike, John. *Rabbit is Rich.* New York: Knopf, 1960.

————. *Rabbit Redux.* New York: Knopf, 1971.

————. *Rabbit Run.* New York: Fawcett Crest, 1960.

Vachell, Horace Annesley. *The Hill.* London: J. Murray, 1905.

Van Dalen, Deobold B. and Bruce L. Bennett. *A World History of Physical Education.* 7th ed. Englewood Cliffs, N.J.: Prentice-Hall, 1971.

Vanderwerken, David and Spencer K. Wertz, (eds.). *Sport Inside Out: Readings in Literature and Philosophy.* Fort Worth: Texas Christian University Press, 1985.

Vincent, Ted. *Mudville's Revenge: The Rise and Fall of American Sport.* New York: Seaview Books, 1981.

Voigt, David Q. *America through Baseball.* Chicago: Nelson-Hall, 1976.

Walvin, James. *The People's Game: A Social History of British Football.* London: Allen Lane, 1975.

Watson, Emmett. *Digressions of a Native Son.* Seattle: The Pacific Institute, 1982.

Weber, Ronald. "Narrative Method in *A Separate Peace*." *Studies in Short Fiction* 3 (Fall 1965): 63-72.

Wecter, Dixon. *The Hero in America, A Chronicle of Hero Worship.* Ann Arbor: University of Michigan Press, 1963.

Weiler, I. *Der Agon im Mythos: Zur Einstellung der Griechen zum Wettkampf.* Darmstadt: Wissenschaftliche Buchgesellschaft, 1974.

————. *Der Sport bei: den Völker der alten Welt.* Darmstadt: Wissenschaftliche Buchgesellschaft, 1981.

Wellek, Rene. *A History of Modern Criticism 1750-1950.* New Haven: Yale University Press, 1965.

Westlake, Donald E. *Kahawa.* New York: Viking, 1981.

West, Paul. *Out of My Depths: A Swimmer in the Universe.* Garden City, NY: Anchor Press/Doubleday, 1983.

Whedon, Julia. *A Good Sport.* Garden City, N.Y.: Doubleday, Inc., 1981.

Wheeler, Paul. *Bodyline.* New York: Atheneum, 1984.

Willard, Nancy. *Things Invisible to See.* New York: Knopf, 1984.

Wilson, Monica. *Religion and the Transformation of a Society.* Cambridge: University Press, 1971.

Wind, Herbert Warren. *Following Through.* New York: Tichnor & Fields, 1985.

————. *Game, Set, and Match: The Tennis Boom of the 1960's and 70's.* New York: Dutton, 1979.

Windship, G.B. "Autobiographical Sketches of a Strength Seeker." *Atlantic Monthly,* January 1862, 102-115.

Winter, D. "Time Off from Conflict: Christmas 1914." *Royal United Services Institute Journal* 115 (1970): 41-46.

Witherington, Paul. "*A Separate Peace:* A Study in Structural Ambiguity." *English Journal* 54 (1965): 795-800.

Wolfe, Peter. "The Impact of Knowles's *A Separate Peace.*" *The University of Kansas City Review* 36 (1970): 189-198.

Wolfe, Thomas. *Look Homeward Angel.* New York: Modern Library, 1929.

Woodhead, A.G. *The Study of Greek Inscriptions.* Cambridge: Cambridge University Press, 1981.

Woodward, Stanley. *Sports Page.* New York: Simon and Schuster, 1949.

Yadin, Yigael. "Let the Young Men Arise." *Journal of Palestine Oriental Studies* 21 (1948): 110-116.

Young, Al. *Ask Me Now.* New York: McGraw-Hill, 1980.

Young, D. "Professionalism in Archaic and Classical Greek Athletics." *Ancient World* 7 (1983): 49.

Young, David C. *The Olympic Myth of Greek Amateur Athletics.* Chicago: Ares, 1984.

Young, Michael, ed. *Knowledge and Control.* London: Collier and Macmillan, 1971.

Young, Philip. *Ernest Hemingway: A Reconsideration.* University Park: Pennsylvania State University Press, 1966.

Zuckerman, George. *Farewell, Frank Merriwell.* New York: Dutton, 1973.

Notes on Contributors

DOUGLAS A. ANDERSON is professor of journalism and director of graduate studies in the Walter Cronkite School of Journalism and Telecommunication at Arizona State University. He is the author or co-author of four books and numerous articles.

FRED BOE teaches English and Comparative Literature at San Diego State University and has recently "burned out" from ten years of coaching Little League baseball and Boys' Club soccer and basketball.

ELIZABETH S. BRESSAN is Associate Professor in the Department of Physical Education and Human Movement Studies at the University of Oregon. Her area of scholarly focus is on the significance and meaning of the sport, dance and exercise experience both on a social and a personal level. She coordinated the 1986 *Arete* International Issue which published original works from scholars outside the United States. She is also the President of the Northwest District Association for Health, Physical Education, Recreation and Dance.

KENT CARTWRIGHT is assistant provost and assistant professor of English at the University of Maryland, and he was formerly assistant dean of Arts and Sciences at Kansas State University. Dr. Cartwright was educated at the University of Michigan and at Case Western Reserve University, where he studied Renaissance literature with Robert Ornstein. He has published articles on Shakespeare, the Renaissance stage, and the modern American novel, and with Mary McElroy, he has co-authored several studies of sport and literature.

TOM DODGE is Professor of English at Mountain View College in Dallas, Texas. Dodge is the author of the widely used anthology, *The Literature of Sports*. Along with writing his own poetry, Dodge is noted for translating ancient Greek poetry. He is also an accomplished speaker appearing before numerous college audiences. Dodge has overcome the effects of starring on a Texas high school golf team and his son Lyndon says "he plays the hell out of a guitar."

NANDA FISCHER is a faculty member at the Zentralinstitut für Sportwissenschaften of the Technische Universität München. Before she taught German literature at Loyola University in Chicago. She is the author of numerous articles on Sport Pedagogy and

20th century German literature, and having been a tennis player and a coach for years, she is also the author of a book on junior tennis, which has been translated into different languages.

WALTER HARRISON is a public relations consultant with Gehrung Associates University Relations Counselors in Keene, New Hampshire. He wrote his doctoral dissertation on baseball fiction at the University of California, Davis, and has published articles on baseball fiction in *The Journal of Popular Culture*. He has served as president of the Midwest Popular Culture Association and as sports area chair of the Popular Culture Association. Given to pontificating occasionally in the popular press under the title Dr. Baseball, he is a lifelong Pittsburgh Pirates fan.

SEYMOUR KLEINMAN is Professor in the Movement Arts Section, School of Health, Physical Education and Recreation at Ohio State University. He also serves as Director of the Institute for the Advancement of the Arts in Education, an organization which initiates and sports encounters between artists and their arts with educators. His interests are in the area of sport and movement theory and philosophical conceptions of the body.

STEVEN LATTIMORE is associate professor of Classics and Classical Archaeology at UCLA, where he has recently been teaching a course in Greek and Roman athletics. As a result, he has come to realize what should have been obvious to him all along: virtually every aspect of Greek culture—including his specialty, Greek sculpture— has some connection with athletics. Some time ago, Lattimore gave up mountaineering in favor of the more arduous sport of keeping up with his children.

J. A. MANGAN read social anthropology at the University of Durham, later studied the sociology of education at the University of Oxford and obtained his doctorate in social history and education from Glasgow University. He is a Fellow of the Royal Historical Society and a Fellow of the Royal Anthropological Institute. He is also a founder member and Inaugural Chairman of the British Society of Sports History, the founder and Senior Editor of the *British Journal of Sports History*, and a member of the International Editorial Boards of several academic journals. He is an authority on the nineteenth century public school system and has published many articles on the subject. His research interests embrace anthropological, sociological, and historical issues and he is currently researching the games-ethic within the context of liberal education at the universities of Oxford and Cambridge in the late nineteenth century. Publications include *Athleticism in the Victorian and Edwardian Public School: The Emergence and Consideration of an Educational Ideology* (C.U.P., 1981) and *The Games Ethic and Imperialism: Aspects of the Diffusion of an Ideal* (Allen Lane/Penguin, 1985). Forthcoming publications will include *Morality, Metaphysics and Manliness: Images of the Male in the Old and New Worlds* (with James Walvin); *From 'Fair Sex' to Feminism: Sport and the Socialization of Women in the Industrial and Post-Industrial Eras* (with Roberta J. Park) and *Pleasure Profit and Proselytism: British Culture and Sport at Home and Abroad 1750-1914*.

MARY McELROY is Associate Professor of Physical Education at Kansas State University in Manhattan, Kansas. Dr. McElroy has authored numerous articles focusing on social class and sport involvement, and is presently interested in the sporting behaviors among the English commoners in sixteenth century England. Together, with Kent Cartwright she published *Expectation, True Play, and the Duel in Hamlet* in the first issue of *Arete: the Journal of Sport Literature*.

CHRISTIAN K. MESSENGER is Associate Professor of English at the University of Illinois at Chicago. He is finishing the sequel to his *Sport and the Spirit of Play in American Fiction: Hawthorne to Faulkner* (1981). His contribution to this volume is an adaptation of an introductory chapter in that sequel.

STEPHEN MOSHER misspent his youth preparing for a centerfield career with the Boston Red Sox. Since realizing his folly, he merely observes and writes about sport, especially as it is represented in motion pictures and fiction. Currently, he and his family live in Amherst, Massachusetts where he coaches several youth sports teams and has shifted his athletic aspirations to maintaining his .750 batting average in the local slow pitch softball league, reducing his golfing handicap to a single digit, and touching the basketball rim at least once each season.

LYLE I. OLSEN is a professor of Physical Education at San Diego State University having retreated to the position from the baseball coaching world. Olsen's proudest achievement, outside of coaching, is being one of the founders of the Sport Literature Association and it's publication *Arete: The Journal of Sport Literature*. Currently Olsen is working and studying in preparation for an examination of the codes of conduct found in the games recounted in the Islandic Sagas. None of the above activities, however, are allowed precedence over his mad quest to play in the Senior's division at Wimbledon.

MICHAEL ORIARD is Associate Professor of English at Oregon State University and the author of two books: *Dreaming of Heroes: American Sports Fiction, 1868-1980,* and *The End of Autumn: Reflections on My Life in Football.* He has also written on sport and sports literature in the *Journal of American Culture* and *Arete: the Journal of Sport Literature,* as well as *Sports Illustrated* and the *New York Times;* and on American literature in *Modern Fiction Studies,* the *Southern Literary Journal, Studies in American Fiction,* and *Critique,* among others.

JOAN PAUL is Professor and Chairperson of the Department of Physical Education at University of Tennessee at Knoxville. Special interest is sport history. Hobbies are dichotomous—sitting in University archives and playing tennis, badminton or what have you.

PROFESSOR TOM SCANLON is an Assistant Professor of Classics at the University of California, Riverside. His major publications have been *Greek and Roman Athletics: A Bibliography* (Chicago: Ares, 1984), and *The Influence of Thucydides on Sallust* (Heidelberg: Carl Winter, 1980), as well as numerous articles and reviews on ancient sports and Greek and Roman historical writing. The highpoint of Tom's own athletic career was rowing in the "gentlemen's boat" of Corpus Christi College, Cambridge, in 1976-77.

ERIC SOLOMON is Professor of English at San Francisco State University. A specialist in Nineteenth-Century British and American fiction, he has written or edited four books and many articles. He also published pieces on American sport and culture and is currently working on a book, *Jews, Baseball, and the American Novel.* Dr. Solomon no longer dreams about playing left field for the Boston Red Sox.

DAVID L. VANDERWERKEN directs the Graduate Program in English at TCU while suffering the slings and arrows of Horned Frog athletics. He was President of the Sport Literature Association and senior editor of *Sport Inside Out: Readings in Literature and Philosophy* (1985).

DAVID C. YOUNG is Professor of Classics at the University of California, Santa Barbara. Best known for his research on the Greek poet, Pindar [author of the *Victory Odes* for ancient athletes], Young has now turned to athletic history, both ancient and modern. His most recent book is *The Olympic Myth of Greek Amateur Athletics* (Ares Publishers, Chicago, 1984).

Index